W9-AFE-211
DISCARDED

LIFTING OUR VOICES

Lifting Our Voices

The Journeys into Family Caregiving of Professional Social Workers

Joyce O. Beckett

COLUMBIA UNIVERSITY PRESS  New York

Columbia University Press
Publishers Since 1893
New York   Chichester, West Sussex

Library of Congress Cataloging-in-Publication Data
Lifting our voices : the journeys into family caregiving of professional social workers /
[edited by] Joyce O. Beckett.
p. cm.
Includes bibliographical references and index.
ISBN 978-0-231-14060-7 (cloth : alk. paper)—ISBN 978-0-231-14061-4 (pbk. : alk. paper)—
ISBN 978-0-231-51195-7 (electronic)
1. Social workers—United States—Biography. 2. Social workers—United States—
Case studies. 3. Caregivers—Family relationships—United States. I. Beckett, Joyce
Octavia, 1945– II. Title.
HV40.3.L49 2008
361.3092'273—dc22
2008020306

∞
Columbia University Press books are printed on permanent and durable acid-free paper.
Printed in the United States of America

c 10 9 8 7 6 5 4 3 2 1
p 10 9 8 7 6 5 4 3 2 1

This book is dedicated to the caregivers and care receivers described in this book and to all past, current, and future caregivers and care receivers.

When we cast our bread (words) upon the waters,
We can presume that someone downstream
Whose face we may never know
Will benefit from our action.

—Maya Angelou

Contents

Foreword

PETER B. VAUGHAN

Almost forty years ago, when I was an Army social worker, a social work technician who worked for me often raised a rhetorical question after a particularly difficult day of hearing the sad and true situations of soldiers engaged in combat and combat support operations: "Who treats the treaters?" More simply put, the questions was, "We take care of and confront the emotional pain of everyone who comes into this clinic; who helps us?" There are no easy answers as to who treats the treaters, but this book will go a long way in moving professional helpers closer to understanding the dynamics of caregiving and ways to achieve the best caregiving results. In their own voices, professional social workers and social work educators tell poignant stories of the responsibility of caregiving to their loved ones. The caregiving role knows neither gender nor race. Each caregiver voice tells a story of preparation by the loved one for this service. The now-vulnerable loved ones taught them lessons of sensitivity and caring during the socialization process and in the building of those relationships. In these relationships, as care was given and received, old difficulties between the caregiver and the cared-for relative were resolved, and new connections between them were made as the caregivers strove valiantly to acknowledge and respect old roles and the meaning of these roles to each of them while having to address changes in their respective roles. It is of note that these caregivers worked to make sure that their loved ones maintained as much autonomy as possible and that their loved ones were actively engaged in decision making about their care. All caregivers were aggressive in their advocacy efforts to ensure the ongoing respect by healthcare and service providers to their loved ones. In a straightforward way, the authors acknowledge the costs incurred to themselves and significant others in having to provide the kind of care that was needed. Each social worker and caregiver highlights the importance of a network of friends and family, creative caregiver coaches, and professional healthcare providers.

Race, ethnicity, and familial relationships notwithstanding, each of these social workers recounts the physical and emotional fatigue and social isolation brought about by the caregiver role. Yet each speaks about the joy and triumph he or she experienced in the caretaker role. Among those joys and triumphs were the strength they derived from their loved ones as those cared for tried to ease the burden through humor, expressions of reciprocal care, and genuine love and gratitude for the efforts being made so that they might live their lives in dignity and as adults.

Through the life stories, the book does a remarkable job of pointing out the value of educating professional social workers to assume and use the roles of broker, mediator, manager, and advocate to improve systems of care. These professionals played all these roles in providing care to their loved ones. They describe how they were strengthened through contacts with their individual family members and friends and with the friends and caring networks of their afflicted relatives. The authors recount the strategies they used for successful caregiving and the various ways they maintained a sense of personal integrity and inner peace as they strove to make the lives of their loved ones less chaotic, more manageable, and as fulfilling as possible.

It becomes apparent as one reads each of these stories that by recording their stories, the tellers impart valuable solace to those of us who are now or have been caregivers. Although turmoil and toil were essential elements of each author's experiences, they remained tenacious and courageous in their struggles to make sense of senseless service systems, incongruous insurance arrangements, unresponsive and poorly situated systems of care, and sometimes unresponsive family members. Each author portrays the caregiving experience as having made them more sensitive and more caring people and perhaps better social workers. Who treats the treaters? In some way the answer is different for each of these social workers, but support resided in the knowledge they had acquired as professionals about systems and system change, in the networks of care that existed for them or that they helped to create, in friends and family, and in the loved ones receiving care. Clearly, treatment inheres in the quality of relationships the caregiver has and is developing. The reading of these stories gives new meaning to the reality that weeping lasts for the night, but joy comes in the morning. Although the morning for each caregiver was different, it came when the pieces to the puzzle of caring for their loved ones eventually came together.

This book is a must-read for any helping professional who assists clients who are caring for a loved one. It is also a must-read for anyone who values the lessons learned from others who have faced caregiving responsibilities for elderly and infirm relatives and friends and the opportunities they present for living a fuller life by helping a debilitated loved one live a fuller life.

Acknowledgments

Many people have been intimately involved in the completion of this project. Thanks to all caregivers and care receivers who have made caregiving a topic of increased importance. I sincerely appreciate the contributors. In order to help others better understand the complexities of caregiving, they shared private caregiving experiences, whether joyful, challenging, or painful. They moved beyond the deep, sometimes painful, reawakened emotions accompanying their descriptions to apply theoretical understanding to their narratives. They graciously accepted tight deadlines and requests for changes. I am particularly grateful to Michelle Bayley, M.S.W., and Anne Jordan, M.S.W., who were phenomenal, supportive, and dedicated research and editorial assistants. Professors Albert Roberts and Gerry Schamess gave generous and enlightening comments and guidance on various iterations of the manuscripts. Lauren Dockett, executive editor at Columbia University Press, provided insightful suggestions and continuous understanding and support.

I am especially thankful to family and friends who demonstrated patience, understanding, and support during this project. Most importantly, without the enduring and generous love, guidance, advice, and support from John Purnell, my husband, through several of my personal challenges, I would not have completed this project. John helped me to better understand and appreciate my dual roles of caregiver and care receiver.

List of Contributors

Joyce O. Beckett received her A.B. from Temple University and her M.S.S. and Ph.D. from Bryn Mawr College. She completed postdoctoral studies in gerontology at the Center for the Study of Aging and the Department of Psychiatry at Duke University in Durham, North Carolina. Dr. Beckett's professional career, spanning more than thirty-five years, includes clinical work in: medical and mental health facilities, nursing homes, halfway houses for previously incarcerated and substance-abusing women, a college counseling center, and private practice. She taught courses in master's and doctoral programs on social justice, mental health, family therapy, clinical practice, interventions with people of color, and human behavior at schools of social work at Bryn Mawr College, the University of Michigan in Ann Arbor, and Virginia Commonwealth University in Richmond. Dr. Beckett has done research and published on several topics, with emphases on social supports that people of color and women use to buffer the deleterious effects of racism, sexism, oppression, and poor physical and mental health. She has served on the editorial boards of several academic journals and currently is a reviewer for many professional journals. She is a professor emerita of Virginia Commonwealth University.

Shirley Bryant is an associate professor in the School of Social Work at Virginia Commonwealth University's northern Virginia campus in Alexandria. She received her D.S.W. from Howard University, her M.S.W. from Fordham University, and her B.A. from Hanover College. Dr. Bryant served as director of the VCU northern Virginia campus from 1995 to 2004. She teaches macro practice and policy, administration, and planning courses, and her research interests include child welfare, impact of violence on children, and African American women. She currently serves as a member of the Council on Social Work Education's Council on Racial, Ethnic and Cultural Diversity and the Commission on Diversity and Social and Economic Justice. She is a member of the Metro D.C. Chapter of the National Association of Social Workers, where she recently completed a term of office on the board of directors. Dr. Bryant is also a member of the editorial board of the journal *Affilia*.

King E. Davis is executive director of the Hogg Foundation for Mental Health and holds the Robert Lee Sutherland Chair in Mental Health and Social Policy at the University of Texas at Austin School of Social Work. Dr. Davis earned his Ph.D. from the Florence G. Heller School for Social Policy and Management at Brandeis University in 1971 and his master's and bachelor's degrees in social work (concentration in mental health) from California State University in Fresno. Dr. Davis was a professor of public mental health policy and planning at the Virginia Commonwealth University, Richmond, from 1984 to 2000. From 1998 to 1999, he held the William and Camille Cosby Chair at Howard University, Washington, D.C. Dr. Davis is a former commissioner of the Virginia Department of Mental Health, Mental Retardation and Substance Abuse Services, and he is co-author of *The Color of Social Policy.*

Erica Edwards is the executive director of LINC, Incorporated, a center for independent living for people with disabilities in Belleville, Illinois. She is a licensed clinical social worker with an M.S.W. from Virginia Commonwealth University and a concentration in nonprofit planning and administration. She has also earned a bachelor of arts in Spanish and a bachelor of business administration from the University of Texas at Austin. She has worked recently as a geriatric care manager and professional education coordinator for the Alzheimer's Association, St. Louis Chapter. As the founder of the Missouri Coalition Celebrating Care Continuum Change, Ms. Edwards is very active with advocacy activities, especially relating to long-term care and resident choice and empowerment. She has spoken at national and statewide conferences on dis-

academia, he practiced full time in various clinical settings and currently has a part-time clinical practice with groups. He is a social work professor emeritus.

Peter B. Vaughan received a B.A. in sociology from Temple University, an M.S.W. in group work from Wayne State University, and an M.A. in psychology and a Ph.D. in social work and psychology from the University of Michigan. Dr. Vaughan is currently the dean and professor of Fordham University Graduate School of Social Service. He has also served as the associate dean for academic programs and associate professor at the University of Pennsylvania School of Social Work, as an associate professor of social work at Wayne State University, and as director of the Life Stress Center at University Health Center/Detroit Receiving Hospital, Detroit, Michigan. His teaching has been primarily in the areas of social work practice and human behavior. He has demonstrated a lifelong commitment to working for equality and constructive social change for all people, especially those of color. His recent research concerns enhancing the health, social health, and life chances of African American boys. He is a board member of several community agencies and national advisory organizations.

LIFTING OUR VOICES

Caregiving

ONE

JOYCE O. BECKETT

SALLY: Good morning. How was your weekend?

JOAN: Really busy. I had to fly to Ohio to handle a crisis with my mother, who's in assisted living. The facility wanted to move her because her kitchen smoke detector has gone off too often. Several times, she forgot she was cooking. The facility only allows a certain number of alarms before people are moved. Fortunately, I persuaded Mom to take all her meals in the dining room and removed her pots and pans. Joan, my cousin in Ohio, will visit Mom more often, and I will call each morning to check on Mom.

BARBARA: Sorry I am late for this meeting. Today is my day to take my mother for dialysis. I scheduled the appointment so that I would have enough time to get to our meeting, but her treatment was delayed for an hour.

JOAN: No problem. We started and will provide a review for you. I'm sorry about your having to wait for dialysis. I guess that was frustrating.

SALLY: Are you okay? You look a little tired.

CARMEN: I'm okay. No, I'm not okay. One of my best friends was diagnosed with cancer, and I'm in shock. We've known each other since elementary school; I can't believe she—we—are facing this. She lives in Charlottesville but has no family there. I spent the weekend with her. I want to visit again this weekend, but I have a proposal due the next Monday. I'm so torn. How can I help her and get the proposal written? It's impossible to do both.

SALLY: I'm so sorry about your friend's diagnosis and the dilemmas you're facing. It has to be difficult to be pulled in two separate directions. I would be happy for us to think about this coming weekend to find a way that you can do both or some other acceptable plan. I wonder if your friend is well enough to come here or if you could visit her for an evening instead of staying for the entire weekend.

Discussions like these are one impetus for this book. Increasingly, the editor has heard workplace conversations like these. Many of my colleagues and I were providing caregiving for family, friends, and loved ones. We shared our experiences and discovered common challenges and rewards. This book captures and vividly describes these rich and informative caregiving experiences, analyzes them, and draws implications for various societal levels. Some readers will view the book as a collection of first-person stories, but, as will be discussed later, they are also the results of a narrative, qualitative research study.

INTRODUCTION

An increasing number of social work practitioners and academicians are caregivers. These experiences along with their professional training are a rich, often untapped knowledge source. This book begins with an overview and history of family caregiving and includes a discussion of the information gathering techniques and results. Ten chapters follow, each written by a professional social worker. Each describes the author's caregiving roles with family members, some with debilitating illnesses. Topics such as long-distance caregiving, lifelong caregiving, negotiating human service agencies, and the importance of quantitative and qualitative research methods in knowledge and theory building are discussed. Unlike most books on caregiving, this volume addresses how the workplace can support and hinder the professional's personal caregiver role. The effectiveness of various other resources is also addressed.

THE ISSUE

A surge in literature that describes, explains, and develops implications for interventions in all areas of family caregiving has emerged (e.g., American Association of Retired Persons [AARP] Travelers Foundation 1988; Barresi and Stull 1993; Burton and Dilworth-Anderson 1991; George and Gwyther 1996; Greene et al. 1982; Hernandez 1991; John et al. 2001; Kosloski et al. 1999; Marcell 2001; National Alliance for Caregiving 1997; San Antonio et al. 2006; Shibusawa et al. 2005; Shifren 2001; Skaff et al. 1996; Whittier et al. 2005). The death of President Ronald Reagan and the media have drawn the public eye to the issue of family caregiving ("Alzheimer's disease" 2004). Family caregiving in other families dealing with Alzheimer's has also attracted media attention ("Alzheimer's Association" 2004; "Companion Web site" 2004). This issue has become relevant to so many families that books and articles addressing caregiving have been promoted on various television programs ("Harvard Medical School" 2004; "New Merck guide" 2004) and been promoted by various television and movie personalities and celebrities, such as Maria Shriver, Anjelica Huston, and Leeza Gibbons ("Correcting and replacing" 2004; "New book" 2004). Further public awareness of the issue of caregiving has been evident in the proliferation of programs around the country that teach caregiving skills ("Extending a helping hand" 2004; "Metropolitan Family Services" 2003).

Most scholarly and popular media attention has been given to lay rather than professional caregivers ("Companion Web site" 2004; Patchett 2003). Even when human service professionals are family caregivers, we usually get a limited glimpse of their personal experiences as family caregivers ("Caregiving crisis" 2004; Finke 2004; Levine et al. 2000; Swenson 2004; Ward-Griffin 2004; Young and Holley 2005). Social work is the profession that delivers services to caregivers and their families. Much can be learned from professional social workers who provide such services to their own family members. This book focuses on the caregiving experiences of ten professional social workers. All were employed full time, most as academicians or practitioners. The remainder of this chapter discusses some critical issues in family caregiving and describes the book.

DEFINITIONS OF CAREGIVER

The National Family Caregiver Support Program provides one of the most comprehensive definitions of a caregiver: "anyone who provides assistance to another in need" (National Family Caregiver Support Program [NFCSP] 2004). They define care as "a broad and highly variable range of rehabilitative, restorative and health maintenance services that assist people with ADLs [activities of daily living], IADLs [instrumental activities of daily living], and the emotional aspects of coping with illness or disability" (NFCSP 2004).

In academic literature, the concepts of caregiving and care are both more specific and more abstract. For example, for Moroney (1998:50), "Caregiving is a human service transaction that is built on a relationship between caregivers and care recipients. There is a process of communication through which resources are transferred and through which the emotional process of caring develops." Also, Moroney states that caring "entails a caring and a cared-for person enhancing each other's human development, in effect, helping each other to grow, to become capable of meeting life's challenges in an ethical and meaningful manner" (1998:10). A strong point of this definition is its discussion of the mutuality and reciprocity of the caregiving process. However, it says little about the caregiver and the care receiver and focuses more on the process and outcome of caregiving.

Historically, the definitions of *caregiver* and *care recipient* have omitted important populations, such as young children (Kahana and Young 1990). For example, in an article in the *Encyclopedia of Social Work* (Hooyman and Gonyea 1995:951), the goal was to discuss families who care for members who are disabled: "frail elderly individuals, adults with developmental disabilities, and adults with serious and persistent mental illness." The article mentioned but gave little attention to children. This may be because parents are expected to provide care to their children. Currently, more attention is given to children as both caregivers and care recipients, especially those with special healthcare needs (Glass 2004; Guzell-Roe and Landry-Meyer 2005; Lee et al. 2005; Leiter et al. 2004; Williams and Cohen-Cooper 2004; Winston 2003; Yoon 2005; Young and Holley 2005).

The literature provides various distinctions in concepts related to caregiving. It discusses differences between formal and informal caregivers, primary and nonprimary caregivers, and care tasks. *Formal caregivers* are helping professionals; *informal caregivers* are nonprofessionals who provide care services, including family, friends, neighbors, and volunteers (Aneshensel et al. 1995; Briggs 1998; Caston 1997; Lefley 1996; Lo Sasso and Johnson 2002; NFCSP 2004). Primary caregivers provide a majority of the care or coordinate the care (Aneshensel et al. 1995; Briggs 1998; Caston 1997; Lefley 1996; NFCSP 2004). Nonprimary caregivers are all other people who provide care (Briggs 1998; Geiger 1996). Care tasks are the specific activities caregivers perform, including transportation, and personal and emotional support (Aneshensel et al. 1995; Briggs 1998; Caston 1997; Lockery 1992; Moroney 1998; NFCSP 2004).

SOCIETAL TRENDS AND CAREGIVING

There is a huge dilemma in healthcare: As the number of people who need medical care has grown rapidly, inpatient medical services have decreased. This was one of the most important and intriguing phenomena of the late 20th century. Simultaneously, economic, demographic, social, medical, and technological trends have culminated in increased accessibility of medical care. The availability of private health insurance, Medicare, Medicaid, and medical advances have all but eradicated some illnesses such as infantile paralysis and smallpox, prevalent in the early 20th century. These paradoxical events have generated an increase in lay and academic interests in caregiving, as family members have had to replace traditional inpatient medical providers with in-home care (Hokenstad et al. 2005; Leiter et al. 2004).

The movement of healthcare policy and treatment toward a wellness model has reduced morbidity from other diseases such as influenza, measles, and staphylococcal and streptococcal infections. Survival rates for once deadly conditions such as cancer and severe brain injuries have increased dramatically. Lifesaving techniques for premature infants have increased their survival at younger gestational ages, but many develop disabilities and chronic health conditions, resulting in increased caregiving and parenting tasks. These changes have increased the need for outpatient medical services and for care by family members and friends (AARP 2000). Concomitantly, the Internet has made it possible for people to become more knowledgeable about health issues and health maintenance. Access to more information has led to more self-assessments, motivating people to seek medical treatment sooner. In turn, earlier medical intervention has increased longevity.

These trends all contribute to a longer life expectancy, resulting in a larger population of seniors. The number of people over sixty-five increased tenfold in the 20th century, with people eighty and older the fastest-growing segment of the population. The number of seniors is increasing as baby boomers reach retirement age. It is predicted that by the middle of the 21st century, a majority of the U.S. population will be over the age of sixty-five (www.msnbc.com/modules/ps/010524_Aging in America/ intro.asp?b = lo, January 17, 2002), and many may need family and institutional care.

Family Structure

These demographic changes, along with other factors, have hastened significant social changes that affect family structure and family caregiving. The increase in life expectancy and the smaller size of families has created the "verticalized," or "beanpole," family, composed of multiple generations but fewer members in each generation (Bengtson et al. 1990). Young adults in these four- and five-generation families face the possibility of caring for a greater number of frail elders while having fewer relatives with whom to share these tasks. Accordingly, women spend more years caring for aging parents and grandparents than for children. In the 1980s, for the first time in history, couples had more parents than children to care for (Bengtson et al., 1990, 2003). Women have also added employment outside their homes to their in-home responsibilities. Moreover, as the number of higher-wage occupations has increased, fewer women have been selecting traditionally female careers such as education and social work. Employment outside the home has reduced the number of women available for full-time, in-home caregiving. Even when women have time for family caregiving, they may live too far from relatives needing help. This geographic barrier often causes tension, anxiety, and guilt (Sherrell et al. 2001).

Family changes have resulted in new and creative approaches, including long-distance and male caregiving (Choi et al. 2007; Laditka and Laditka 2001; Marcell 2001). Even with these changes, women continue to be the primary care providers (Briggs 1998; Choi and Bohman 2007; Family Caregiver Alliance [FCA] 2003; Johnson and Lo Sasso 2006; Moroney 1998; Navaie et al. 2002; Wakabayashi and Donato 2005). In order to fulfill the family caregiver role, women may go to extraordinary lengths. To continue to integrate family caregiving, women use strategies ranging from taking leaves of absence from work to remodeling their homes to accommodate the family member who needs care (Bengtson et al. 2003; "Carers" 2004; FCA 2003; Wakabayashi and Donato 2005). Few societal supports, such as paid family care leave and reliable, affordable in-home care, exist for women who work outside the home and care for family members (Williams and Cohen-Cooper 2004).

Caregiving and Older Adults

Although some existing work–family policies have a negative impact on women's career advancement (Glass 2004; Kosloski et al. 1999), families provide primary, full-time care of 95% of frail older adults (AARP 2001; Crowley 2001; Kramer and Kipnis 1995). Fewer than 5% of older adults in the United States live in institutions (AARP 2000). The literature on dementia and Alzheimer's, the most prevalent type of dementia, provides much of our knowledge about caregiving (Kramer 1997). Testimony at congressional hearings in 2001 indicated that Alzheimer's disease had reached epidemic proportions (NBC News 2001). This was of great concern to baby boomers, who were very interested in degenerative diseases that both they and their elderly family members might face. Alzheimer's and other debilitating diseases among older adults affect families throughout the life span financially, emotionally, and in other ways (Laditka and Laditka 2001). Dementia has also become a concern of social institutions, such as the Veterans Administration and the penal system, as they cope with issues related to an aging population.

Caregiving Across the Life Span

Recently, family caregiving literature has extended to include people throughout the entire life cycle. Some literature (Bauman 2000; Dearden and Becker 1998; Gates and Lackey 1998; Lackey and Gates 1997, 2001; Shifren 2001) reports research on children and adolescents as caregivers and care recipients. Advances in medical technology have increased the life span of neonatal patients and patients with brain trauma. This has led to a redefinition of the parenting years as some disabled adults need parenting throughout their lives. Anxious parents, expecting to predecease their disabled children, must identify substitute parents.

Increasing need for surrogate parents contributes to emerging patterns in which people give and receive family care across the life span of both the caregiver and the care recipient. Mental illness, substance abuse, AIDS, and premature death among young parents have resulted in many relatives, some approaching or at retirement age, becoming care providers. For example, the mother of Bill Johnson, an Olympic gold medalist, has been caring for him since his horrific skiing accident in 2002. Thus, many adults are reintroduced to or continue caregiving roles for their children, grandchildren, or great-grandchildren.

Research and literature addressing unique caregiver and care receiver populations are limited. Male family caregivers have received little attention despite their significant contributions to caregiving (Briggs 1998; Geiger 1996; Hossain and Roopnarine 1994; Lieberman 2004; Navaie et al. 2002). School-age children care for parents with mental illness, physical disabilities, and debilitating illnesses, but their contributions have been difficult to measure and receive little attention in the literature (Aldridge and Becker 2003; Lackey and Gates 2001; Shifren 2001; Shifren and Kachorek 2003; Turner 2004). Siblings are another overlooked group. Of all caregivers, siblings provide the longest period of care (Lefley 1996).

Fictive kin (Hill 1972), people who are treated as family but are not biologically related, as well as godparents and "othermothers," have received scant attention (DeFiore 2002; Mikler and Roe 1993; Morycz 1993). Some literature has explored the idea of homecare workers becoming fictive kin in the eyes of the care receiver and his or her family (Barker 2002; Karner 1998). Othermothers are nonrelatives involved in direct child rearing, and sometimes they exert more authority over children than the biological parents. Furthermore, these fictive relationships exist for a variety of reasons, including a way for the community to respond to the biological parents' need for childcare and support (Beckett and Lee 2004).

Literature on grandparents as caregivers for grandchildren and great grandchildren (Bullock 2004; Caputo 2000; DeFiore 2002; Dowdell and Sherwin 1998; Hayslip and Golberg-Glen 2000; Guzell-Roe et al. 2005; Kelley et al. 1997; Nasser 1999; Pebley and Rudkin 1999; Pruchno 1999; Winston 2003; Yoon 2005) is growing. In some cases, the grandparent simultaneously provides care for several generations, including adult children, grandchildren, and great-grandchildren (Mikler and Roe 1993; Miltiades and Pruchno 2002). Because of longer life expectancy and an earlier age of procreation, people are increasingly in the grandparenting role for as long as three or four decades.

No matter where they are in the life span, family caregivers provide a valuable social service and significantly affect our economy ("At a time" 2004; Denes 2004; "Family caregivers" 2004; Langa et al. 2004). In 1999, family caregivers provided an estimated $196 billion in uncompensated care (Arno et al. 1999). By 2004, this figure had increased to an estimated $257 billion (NFCSP n.d.). Businesses also experience a financial impact from family caregiving, with annual productivity losses estimated at $11 billion to $29 billion (Denes 2004).

COMPLEXITY OF FAMILY CAREGIVING

Literature continues to indicate that family caregiving is a complex phenomenon. This section discusses some of the central issues in conceptualizing caregiving. For example, caregiver burden and caregiver rewards are essential to understanding caregiving, yet we know little about these multidimensional concepts (Foley et al. 2002; John et al. 2001).

Diversity in Caregiving

Caregiving means different things to different people. As far back as 1989, Lawton and associates called for additional research across different subgroups of caregivers to further our understanding of this important topic. To date, few scholars have studied the multidimensionality of caregiving across subgroups. As late as 2001, in a report of research on a tribe of American Indians, John and associates sanctioned Lawton's suggestion, adding, "There is every reason to believe [that caregiving] will vary between groups based on differences in cultural values and the existence of resources" (2001:218). The literature further supports this view (Daly et al. 1995; Dilworth-Anderson et al. 2002; Lefley 1996; Lockery 1992; Mercer 1996; Morycz 1993; Navaie-Waliser et al. 2001). Research on international populations also supports the influence of cultural values and availability of resources on variations in family caregiving (Hokenstad and Johansson 1990; Ikels 1990; Lefley 1996; Rhee and Lee, 2001; Zhan 2004).

Literature and research demonstrate that people of color see caregiving differently than European Americans (Aranda and Knight 1997; Beckett and Dungee-Anderson 2000; Fredman et al. 1995; Haley et al. 1995; Hinrichsen and Ramirez 1992; Lawton et al. 1992; Navaie-Waliser et al. 2001; Reinhard and Horwitz 1995). These groups report positive benefits and satisfaction from caregiving. Furthermore, the caregiving experience is quite different. Despite reporting providing more care for family members, people of color also experience greater caregiving satisfaction and less caregiving stress and burdens than European Americans (Choi and Bohman 2007; Cuellar 2002; Dilworth-Anderson et al. 2002; Lefley 1996; Lockery 1992; Martin 2000; Morycz 1993). Therefore people of color, especially older adults, are more likely to be cared for by family members rather than in institutions and live alone less often than European Americans (Beckett and Dungee-Anderson 2000; Knight et al. 2000; Owen et al. 2001; Peek et al. 2000). Nevertheless, families of color are changing in response to demographic and environmental influences. For example, family members have been dispersed throughout the United States rather than living in close physical proximity. These changes directly reduce their ability to provide in-person family care (John et al. 2001). Caregiving within families of color has also changed with variations in the level of socialization to the European value of individualism, level of acculturation, and adherence to cultural values of familism (Knight et al. 2002; Lefley 1996; Lockery 1992; Morycz 1993).

This book is a step in the direction of clarifying and supplementing previous findings. It gleans information from the experiences of professionally trained social workers who have served as family caregivers. It asks contributors to review their caregiving experiences using their professional and theoretical knowledge and to identify the positives and negatives of family caregiving. The sample of contributors varies by age, gender, ethnicity, race, and region of the country. Thus the book accepts Lawton's challenge to address diversity in caregiving. What could be a more potent source for informed data on this topic than a diverse group of professional social workers?

Consequences of Caregiving

Whether we use a disability, gerontological, or health perspective, social work and other human service professions must be concerned about family caregiving and its consequences for the caregiver and receiver. The problems that threaten the ability to provide both good services and necessary supports are also important. However, there is a need for more understanding of the interactions between the family caregiver, the care recipient, and other family members and how these factors influence the caregiving career (Braithwaite 1996; George 1994; Kosloski et al. 1999; Marcell 2001). Understanding and elucidating the personal consequences for the care provider and care receiver are also important. For example, caregivers aged faster than non-caregivers, but the effects vary with gender and other factors (Rivera et al. 2006; Wallstein 2000; White et al. 2000; Zhang et al. 2006). Most publications concentrate on negative effects of family caregiving (e.g., Baillie et al. 1988; Burns et al. 1993; Lawton et al. 1991; McFall and Miller 1992; Skaff and Pearlin 1992; Thompson et al. 1993). However, some report positive consequences such as intrinsic rewards, feelings of gratification, renewed sense of purpose, closer kinship ties, and increased self-efficacy (e.g., Foley et al. 2002; Kramer 1997; Lee Roff et al. 2004; Schwartz 2003; Young and Kahana 1995). Seltzer and Greenberg (1999:363) contend that "positive consequences exist side by side with the more negative outcomes that predominate."

Caregiver Burden and Rewards

Emphasis on the negative effects of family caregiving is an unfortunate trend ("Burden of dealing with dementia" 2004; "Caregivers at risk" 2004; "Caregiving" 2004; Dolliver 2004; "Emotional issues" 2004; "Enhanced counseling" 2004; Treasure 2004; Williams et al. 2003). Unfortunately, the positive consequences for both the caregivers and care receivers often are overlooked or trivialized (Chumbler et al. 2004; Crowley 2001; Martire and Stephens 2003; Wolff and Agree 2004).

One aspect of family caregiving research that led to the predominance of a negative perspective is the significant representation of care recipients with dementia or other long-term, degenerative illnesses in academic literature (de la Cuesta 2005; Depp et al. 2005; Li et al. 2004; Shurgot and Knight 2004; Sleath et al. 2005; Sorenson and Pinquart 2005). In these cases, outcomes for care receivers typically are bleak, and the amount of care needed is extensive. These situations have overshadowed important groups including child and teen, male, gay, lesbian, and transgendered caregivers, grandparents, and care receivers with temporary and nonterminal illnesses (Greenberg et al. 2004; Leiter et al. 2004; "New report" 2004).

OVERVIEW OF THE BOOK

In the next ten chapters, contributors describe their personal journeys and experiences in providing family care. Their challenges, frustrations, anxieties, burdens, joys, and victories are discussed. Each depicts negotiations between various agencies and institutions to obtain needed services and give vivid examples of lack of needed resources, such as reliable home healthcare. Discussions of startling implications for social work practice, policy, research, and education are included. Needed changes in the larger environment such as flexible work schedules are discussed. The authors' analyses indicate that no amount of professional education, training, or practice sufficiently prepared them for care provider roles. Academic preparation was no substitute for experiential learning.

Clarifying and supplementing previous findings, these diverse and personal stories provide valuable insights and expand caregiving, social work, and human service knowledge. Diversity among caregivers and recipients adds nuances that are often omitted from the current caregiving literature. For example, a man caring for his mother, who had dementia, discusses the lack of literature about this situation. A daughter of an African American minister is not sure how to handle the institutional staff referring to him by his first name. Contributors' personal poignant knowledge and experiences, along with the integration of literature included in this volume, support research findings that caregiving is a complex phenomenon with many independent and moderating variables. They underscore that a comprehensive understanding of family caregiving requires a multidisciplinary, multitheoretical approach (Braithwaite 1996; George and Gwyther 1996; Hennessy et al. 2001; Pearlin et al. 1990; Luborsky and Sankar 1993; John et al. 2001; Skaff et al. 1996; Treas 1997). These unique caregiving situations exemplify the complexity of family caregiving and provide understanding of a neglected but essential area of investigation: professionals providing family caregiving.

Although the specific family situations are unique, the joys and challenges of caregiving are remarkably similar. For example, whether attempting to obtain financial assistance or mental health services for siblings or moving an eighty-year-old mother from a skilled nursing home to a private ethnic group home, the authors met unanticipated obstacles they unrealistically expected to overcome because of their professional training. Their response was disappointment and guilt. Most experienced the "I am ordinary" revelation, realizing that their professional training and experiences had not equipped them to overcome some interpersonal and bureaucratic hurdles. Usually, the community resources viewed the contributors' professional training as a problem rather than a strength and dismissed their concerns. Most distressing, their thoughtful suggestions for policy and procedural changes often were rejected, producing frustration, anger, depression, and motivation. Current literature and the contributors' analyses of their experiences indicate that positive outcomes for care recipients depend largely on caregivers' acceptance that they are resources who must exercise self-care skills. Contributors' examinations of the literature and their experiences clearly demonstrate that knowledge and accessibility of community resources, along with the energy to respond creatively when needed resources are unavailable, are significant predictors of successful outcomes for caregivers and the family system.

INFORMATION COLLECTION

I made several information collection decisions involving collection methods, providers, what to collect, analyses, and reporting.

Collection Methods

The state of the knowledge about the topic, the research purpose, and the literature informed the choice of collection strategies. The purpose was to get information about family caregiving experiences and the personal and professional meanings the contributors attached. I used the best strategy for exploring a new topic and population: a qualitative, discovery-oriented, descriptive investigation (Mahoney and Daniel 2006; Maxwell 1996; Miles and Huberman 1994; Morris et al. 2006). This approach focuses on people's experiences and is "fundamentally well suited for locating the meanings people place on events, processes and structures of their lives . . . and for connecting the meaning to the social world around them" (Miles and Huberman 1994:10). The qualitative design provided a more holistic picture by the contributors and prevented me from imposing my worldview, possibly overlooking valuable data. The premise of qualitative information gathering is multiple realities, each determined by subjective experiences and meanings.

There are several qualitative frameworks. This book used the phenomenological approach and narrative methods, also called narrative analysis or life-story writing; both supported my decision to gather detailed accounts from a few contributors. Consistent with phenomenological tradition, the contributors' information was the sole source. One drawback was the reliance on one person to recount events from the past. However, the groundbreaking knowledge this method provided outweighed this disadvantage. Moreover, this information gathering challenge is shared with most research methods. The final narrative product can contain only a first-person or a second-hand description (Chan and Horrocks 2006). This project used both. The focus of the narrative content could also vary: spanning lifetimes, explaining only a particular experience, or representing only answers to specific questions (Petersen et al. 2005; Reissman 2007; Reissman and Quinney 2005; Välimäki et al. 2007).

The contributors reported caregiving experiences by responding to questions from the editor and added other helpful information Reissman (2004:706) says, "narratives are a particularly significant genre for representing and analyzing . . . [an experience] in its multiple guises in different contexts." Narratives help in understanding personal and professional experiences and their political, social, and cultural contexts (Reissman 2006, 2007). For example, one study indicates that practitioners emphasize instrumental roles, whereas family relationships are more important to caregivers and receivers (Guberman et al. 2006). Analyzing the group of narratives gives insight into the impact of political and social movements such as managed healthcare.

Providers of Information

To understand a behavior, one turns to the people who have performed it. Therefore, I invited social workers to participate in this project, a purposive convenience sample. I supplemented the caregiving literature by recruiting people who represented groups of special interest, including African Americans, men, granddaughters, and child caregivers. Using a life span perspective, I strove for an age range among caregivers and recipients. Ten social workers, including me, constituted the sample. My role as editor and contributor gave me a unique understanding of the chapter writing process.

Collection Process

In all formats, the narratives are subjective and meaningful representations of experiences rather than objective measurable, externally validated reports. I was not a distant objective observer or recorder. Instead, through guided questions I co-constructed with the participant opportunities to expand descriptions through interactional discourses, which refine and distill meanings (Mishler 1986). This process differs from one in which a set of questions are intended to yield predetermined or categorized answers. Narrative approaches offer material and data unobtainable through quantitative, more standardized methods. Mishler (1986) argues that in traditional interview studies, researchers attempt to standardize the meanings of responses. Ignoring context, possible cultural assumptions, and the opportunity for dialogue, the traditional methods fail to produce meaningful results. Although narrative approaches are less standardized, the examination of full narratives yields better information (Mahoney and Daniel 2006).

I began with a specific list of questions for the contributors (Table 1.1). Rather than just a list of topics for discussion, data gathering was an interactive process. Contributors' feedback informed changes in topics. For example, questions initially solicited information about *a* caregiving experience, reflecting my assumption that the contributor had only one caregiving experience. This was interesting because I had provided care to multiple family members. My questions reflected the literature and indicated that I viewed my personal caregiving experiences as atypical. In discussions with the contributors, I learned that some had provided sequential and simultaneous care that sometimes began in the caregiver's childhood. As additional knowledge emerged, I revised questions and added topics, providing greater understanding of the contributors' unique and shared experiences. From the dialogues emerged a more comprehensive and appropriate guideline and a template for an implication table.

Discussions were important for other reasons. For example, I noticed that most contributors experienced similar reactions as they worked on the chapter. Initially, authors approached the opportunity to share their stories with excitement and enthusiasm. Writing about the caregiving resulted in experiencing the original emotions we had faced during the actual caregiving experiences, surprising all. The writers knew intellectually that narrative strategies are used in clinical social work to elicit, revisit, and rework emotions. Nevertheless, none was prepared for these intense reactions and the concomitant writer's block. Somehow, we thought we were immune. As I began to acknowledge with the contributors these shared reactions, each was able to explore and discuss the process and

Table 1.1 Guidelines for Contributors

There are three priorities for each chapter:

1. A graphic description of your caregiving experience.

2. Integration of appropriate literature. This includes literature that relates to the general focus of the book and to the author's unique caregiving experiences (e.g., human service professionals providing care for family members, sons caring for mothers, long-distance caregiving).

3. Implications for social work and individuals and families who are caregivers for family members.

Below, I discuss these three priorities in more detail. Remember, however, that this is your chapter, and you need to decide exactly what is included and the most effective methods.

I. Description of the author's sociodemographics.

A. Include such things as your age, life cycle stage, marital status, geographic region, occupation, and any other important factors that are pertinent to preparation for caregiving and general experiences with the care recipients.

B. Your previous caregiving experiences and general experiences with the care recipient(s) before you began providing care for your family member(s).

II. Description of family member(s) for whom you provided care.

A. Biological and social relationship to you.

B. Sociodemographics of care recipient(s).

C. Care recipient's physical or emotional problems and levels of functioning.

III. Description of caregiving experience.

A. Reasons for accepting role of caregiver.

B. Date caregiving began and overview of your tasks and behaviors as well as those from other informal and formal resources.

C. Your and significant others' (e.g., patient, other family members, professionals, institutions) initial reactions to the care recipient's illness and the caregiving experiences and how they changed over time.

D. Description of caregiving experiences and process.

E. Factors influencing the caregiving successes and challenges, including ethical dilemmas.

IV. Analyses of caregiving experience.

Considering your knowledge base at the beginning of the caregiving experience, prior caregiving experiences, and their outcomes, address the following:

(continued)

Table 1.1 (continued)

A. Description of author's theoretical and service-oriented perspectives that helped you to understand and act in this situation.

B. Discuss how particular conceptual frameworks, strengths, individual or family life cycle, ecological, biological, economic, etc., factors were particularly helpful or problematic in your understanding and explaining your caregiving experiences.

V. Implications.

A. Based on your experience, the literature, and research, discuss suggestions for change for self, care recipient(s), other family members, friends and others in your immediate social support network, families facing similar situations, professionals, practice, policy change and development, institutions, education for human service professionals, research, etc.

B. How do your caregiving experiences and observations, current literature, and research relate to the suggestions you discuss for providing care to a family member?

VI. Reflections.

A. Your reactions to being asked to write about your caregiving experiences for a book that many may read.

1. What were your reactions?

2. How did you handle these reactions?

3. Did you have to overcome any reactions that might have prevented you from writing the chapter? Describe this process.

B. What process did you use to write your chapter? For example, did you write the description of your experiences first, gather the literature first, etc.?

1. What were the easiest things about writing the chapter? Please give examples.

2. What were the most challenging things about writing the chapter? Please give examples.

3. How did writing the chapter influence you?

4. Your perceptions of your caregiving experience.

5. Your perceptions of your self as a caregiver.

6. How much did the literature help you to understand your experiences?

C. Were there things that could have helped you to inform your readers that you did not put in the chapter? Give some examples and describe how they might have helped.

D. From your experiences of writing the chapter, what are your personal and professional reactions and suggestions about using narratives about caregiving to better understand your experiences and to develop implications for other caregivers and professionals?

feelings with me, close friends, and family members and then commence writing. Because of these events, I added another topic: description of the process of writing the chapter and its influences. The interactions, sharing, and additional materials produced richer descriptions and enhanced understanding of caregiving. Ironically, the catharsis allowed the contributors to have a more objective, realistic, humanistic self-view. We were able to forgive ourselves for our inability to perform every needed action. Accepting that we were human allowed us to see more strengths in ourselves and the care receivers. At the end of the writing experience, all experienced the impact of the narrative intervention model (Chan and Horrocks 2006; Mahoney and Daniel 2006; Morris 2006; Gillen and Peterson 2005). This book moves beyond traditional phenomenological methods by including the contributors in many phases of the process: formulation of the questions, description of their experiences, interpretation of the findings, and identification of solutions and resources to effect social change.

ANALYSIS

A clinical social worker and I read each chapter and independently identified themes. Next, we collaborated and developed a final list for each chapter. Finally, we reviewed the composite list of themes from all chapters and identified those occurring in multiple chapters. A description of the contributors, the themes, and their implications are discussed in the following section.

WHAT WE LEARNED

The Contributors

Some contributors had little formal knowledge or experience in healthcare; formal caregiving; age-related social, health, and mental health challenges; or other formal caregiving areas, whereas others were experts. Of the ten contributors, two were retired social work professors, six were full-time social work professors, and two were full-time social work practitioners (one a clinician and the other an administrator). Two contributors lived in the Midwest, two in south central states, one in the Northeast, and the remainder in the Mid-Atlantic. Their ages ranged from the late twenties to the seventies. The authors' ages of initiation in caregiving roles ranged from age three to the seventh decade of life. Two were male, seven African American, and three European American. Six were married. Four had children, most of whom had reached adulthood by the time their parents began caregiving. Some had grandchildren. Care recipients also varied. Most were elderly, but they ranged from preteen to over ninety years. The reasons for care included severe physical and mental illness and parental neglect. The recipients struggled with problems of employment, healthcare, housing, relocation, substance abuse, and grief and loss. Most were satisfied with their care, yet some were reluctant recipients. All retained some ambivalent feelings toward the loss of independence.

Caregiving situations were diverse, including care to parents, grandparents, siblings, other relatives, and fictive kin. Many contributors engaged in multiple caregiving, either simultaneous or sequential. For instance, one author cared for her brother for years, then for her terminally ill sister, before becoming the primary caregiver to her aging mother. Another caregiver provided simultaneous care to her mother, aunt, and cousin. Some were sole caregivers and provided care in the recipient's home; other recipients resided in their own homes or long-term care facilities. Some shared the caregiving tasks with family members, close friends, or professionals in an in-home, local, or long-distance capacity. Most performed caregiving in more than one of these arrangements at different times, depending on the changing needs and circumstances of the care recipient. Importantly, each caregiver provided help to loved ones in institutions—hospitals, mental hospitals, rehabilitation centers, or nursing homes—for a few weeks to several years.

Themes

The analyses of the chapters found eighteen shared themes, including caregiver burden, significance of changing residence, influence of cultural traditions related to caregiving, and financial issues. Despite diversity among caregivers and recipients, many contributors faced similar situations. For instance, most experienced caregiver stress. Many also emphasized positive personal and interactional outcomes and identified creative solutions and coping mechanisms such as spirituality, strong support systems, exercise, and respite care. These findings are consistent with the literature (Levkoff et al. 1999; Mausback et al. 2003; Miltiades and Pruchno 2002; Nightingale 2003; Poindexter et al. 1999). Most caregivers acknowledged stress, which is mediated by the co-presence of other factors. Several chapters focus on women who had full-time careers while simultaneously caring for their mothers. They struggled to balance the responsibilities of often competing roles and expectations. One daughter changed her mother's dialysis appointments to early mornings to accommodate her work schedule after a taxi service proved unreliable. On weekends, another cooked a week's supply of meals for her mother. One daughter, exhausted by the regular long-distance travel to care for her mother who lived several states away, clustered her mother's appointments to minimize time lost from work and developed mechanisms for managing her mother's finances and home repairs from a distance.

All contributors developed personal emotional support mechanisms and self-care strategies. Several discuss how spiritual beliefs supported the assumption of the caregiving role and offered the comforting expectation of a rewarding afterlife. Others found emotional and practical support from their and the recipients' faith communities. One contributor discusses the use of periodic spiritual retreats at a local monastery to renew her emotional energy. All contributors described their consumer roles in larger health and social service systems. Most recognized how their professional training helped them navigate these systems, simultaneously gaining a new appreciation for obstacles consumers typically encounter. For instance, one contributor was familiar with the process for obtaining Medicaid benefits but appalled by the time consumers waited in line, sometimes outdoors in extreme temperatures. A common unexpected discovery among authors was their emotional reactions. In one chapter, a man providing care for an aging mother with dementia struggled with feelings of guilt and inadequacy because he could not afford the level of care that family members expected. Although he successfully used his social work knowledge to secure appropriate medical care and services, he wanted to do and felt he should have done more. Another contributor, who parented her previously abused and neglected nieces and was an expert in intervening in similar situations, openly discusses how emotionally unprepared she felt for parenting. While becoming a successful surrogate parent, she was periodically angry, sad, and frustrated, and several interactions with social service agencies led to fear, hostility, and tears. All caregivers gained new appreciation for and understanding of care recipients' attributes, fortitude, and experiences.

Despite similarities, each author's experiences were unique. For example, many reported that caregiving experiences strengthened existing family relationships. One author noted that caregiving resulted in the close mother–daughter relationship she had longed for. Caring for her mother allowed another contributor to develop helping and closer relationships with other aging family members, whose children became secondary caregivers for her mother. Caregiving also exacerbated family tension, yet each experienced these conflicts differently. One author resolved residual pain and grief over a recent unexpected divorce when her ex-husband became an important secondary caregiver. For another, marital strain escalated when he began caring for his mother.

Some themes related to issues of gender and race. Whereas the female authors expected to someday become caregivers, the men were less prepared to assume this role. This observation was consistent with quantitative findings that most family caregivers are women. The European American authors never mentioned issues of race; racial issues did not seem to consciously affect these caregivers or their caregiving. Conversely, each African American contributor noted potential or definitive racial influences. One author described the painful loss of her mother after an ambulance never came, a common occurrence in her community. Instead, friends transported the mother to the hospital, and she died en route. Another faced locked public school doors, necessitating her secret attendance in another county. Race-related issues emerged in many ways, including disparities in the healthcare system, educational and professional opportunities, and cultural justifications for caregiving. Considerations of race, class, age, and gender added important understanding of caregiving experiences, yet none of these variables is singularly responsible for outcomes. Their intersectional influences provide the best illumination.

In every chapter, communication within caregiving families and between them and the healthcare system was a primary theme. The latter was always problematic. Chapters describe the diverse consequences of these problems. All findings graphically demonstrate the complexities of family caregiving, revealing how narratives using longitudinal lenses provide rich, new, and useful information.

Implications

Each chapter presents a set of implications, based on the specific caregiving processes. Some apply to unique caregiving dilemmas, whereas others address more recommendations for larger system changes.

Communication

Frequently implications included the need for improved planning and communication about current and anticipated caregiving. Caring for her beloved aunt, a niece carefully arranged for Auntie to move to a continuing care retirement community (CCRC) and then developed meticulous, effective processes for moves between facilities within the CCRC. Although this niece acknowledges that not all contingencies can be anticipated, an open and continual communication path and the maintenance of mutuality throughout the processes help ensure the best care with the least stress. Caregiving was unplanned for some.

One author was planning for retirement, not caregiving, when his wife had a stroke during their vacation. Far from home, he struggled to find services to meet their needs while feeling unsure about how to involve their adult children in decision making and care tasks. In another chapter, a traffic accident and absence of advance directives left family members unable to collectively decide between medical options for the care recipient. Even with such unexpected events, proactive planning—advance directives, designation of power of attorneys for all family members, and execution of wills—is essential. In addition, regular communication with the care recipient and significant others can help ensure the best decisions and meet the various needs. In one chapter, an aging spouse was placed in charge of caring for his wife, yet he was physically and mentally unable to assume this role. Had the family known more, they could have earlier identified needed supports, preventing the emerging problems.

Self-care

All contributors also recognized the need for self-care, including respite care, information, support groups, relaxation, and travel. Most were surprised by the encompassing nature of caregiving and need for personal supports. It is imperative that these supports be relevant to the varied and unique needs of our caregiving population. They must be culturally sensitive and include services for male caregivers, children, gay men and lesbians, long-distance caregivers, ill caregivers, and those employed full time. One contributor, who began caregiving as a young child, felt community supports to recognize and address her unique situation were absent. With the number of child caregivers increasing, it is crucial that services recognize their developmental needs. Some regions of the country have funding from the National Caregiver Support Program, which offers myriad services for caregivers. More information about recognizing and treating dementia is helpful; one author realized, only after she significantly declined, that his mother demonstrated symptoms of this illness for years. With greater knowledge, he might have been intervened sooner. One contributor noted the need to remove gender biases in caregiving literature and the suggestions he received in a caregiver support group.

Technology

Though not discussed by contributors, technology provides helpful tools, especially for nonresident caregivers (Finkel et al. 2007). In addition to video monitoring, caregivers can design voice or Internet prompts for recipients, reminding them to take medications, lock doors, eat a meal, or turn off appliances. These prompts can appear through daily personal or automated reminders, both appearing on a television or computer screen. Inexpensive in-home sensors, when triggered, can give directions to the recipient in the familiar and calm voice of a relative. For instance, an older adult with dementia who wanders the home at night would receive a voice message from an adult child instructing him to go back to bed if he triggered a motion sensor in the home. One emerging system alerts a distant family member each time a care recipient attempts to prepare a meal. Using speakers, microphones, and cameras, family members can connect at mealtime, providing opportunities for social connection and monitoring for safety and nutrition. Available programs allow people to remotely turn on computers and leave video, audio, and written messages. All these options may help recipients remain in their own homes longer and offer emotional and physical relief to caregivers. There are attendant financial and ethical considerations, of course. Many people cannot afford computers and other technological equipment, and some who have computers cannot afford Internet services. The digital divide, an ever-widening chasm, and universal Internet access are additional issues for action. Professionals must give consumers and caregivers information about literacy programs that provide free computers to low-income people.

New technology even addresses medical needs, including devices that monitor vital signs, such as blood pressure, heart, and blood sugar, and transmit these data via phone or the Internet. These monitoring systems can be worn or subdermally implanted and data transmitted automatically to the healthcare professional, allowing quicker and more effective medical intervention, especially for those with cognitive disorders, and help prevent hospitalization or medical crises. Some of this technology is used successfully in remote and rural areas. It does not require the care recipient to consciously activate the system or learn new technological skills. Once installed, the technology responds automatically to the recipient's situation, movements, and specific medical needs.

Healthcare

All authors made suggestions based on their personal experiences, yet each strongly emphasized flaws and gaps in the current healthcare system. The context of our current healthcare system informs many implications and points to the need for a paradigm shift. Millions of uninsured and underinsured Americans face insurmountable difficulties obtaining services, unable to afford even minimal care. As the chapters show, some have difficulty accessing adequate healthcare, even when insured. When one contributor attempted to secure psychiatric care for her sister, she was denied access, leading to a toxic level of psychiatric medication, decline in physical and emotional functioning, and months of hospitalization and rehabilitation. One author describes her experiences with medical professionals when her mother, a Medicare recipient, had an undiagnosed malignant breast tumor for years while under the care of a physician. The time and resources devoted to discharge planning are limited for monetary reasons, and nurses staff these positions, which social workers once occupied, and are expected to perform their traditional duties concurrently. One author who cared for her terminally ill grandmother was distressed when the discharge planner did not ensure that the primary caregiver, an ill spouse, had needed information and resources. In this same chapter, the author was frustrated by the delayed offering of essential hospice services.

The U.S. healthcare system is characterized by overworked and often underpaid providers. These professionals must operate under the mandates of profit-motivated insurance companies that make decisions that result in hospital stays and physician appointments too short for appropriate and effective care. This situation is stressful for healthcare providers and recipients. Healthcare providers' medical decisions are undermined by insurance and pharmaceutical companies. For instance, pharmaceutical companies dictate care by offering free continuing education units to doctors who attend industry-sponsored events that promote certain medications. Research shows that this sponsored training is the most significant factor in the subsequent selection of medications to prescribe. Medicare, not medical providers, decides how often a patient has a physical. Provisions for and encouragement of self-care are essential in these stressful work environments.

Lifelong Learning

In part because of knowledge explosion, the swift movement to more effective intervention strategies requires lifelong learning. Accessible training for all medical providers in areas where few receive formal training—gerontology, death and dying, culturally sensitive practice, and emerging fields—is necessary for effective care. One author describes how her own dementia training helped her soothe and interact effectively with her ill grandmother. She is angered when she observes the nurses on her grandmother's unit behave in opposition to these practices, probably because they have no formal training instructing otherwise. Another describes the methods she used, and shared with nurses, to comfort her hospitalized blind father.

Support for Caregiver Role

As these narratives and the literature suggest, informal family caregivers perform roles that are integral to the health of the recipient, family, community, and larger society. For this reason and because so many care recipients rely on informal care, the role of the family caregiver must be recognized and supported. Provision of respite care and significant financial reimbursement to family caregivers are examples of ways to officially acknowledge their valuable services. In addition, effective communication between the informal caregiver, the care recipient, and formal healthcare and other service providers is essential for the family to receive the best possible care.

As each chapter indicates, formal providers often give families insufficient support and information, resulting in uninformed and problematic decisions. Conversely, the information family members provide to these formal care providers can maximize care that family members receive. For instance, one author notes how sharing information about the recipient's personality and personal history helps medical staff holistically view that person and thus develop the most effective interventions. Researchers have examined the ways in which home healthcare clinicians from a variety of professional disciplines were able to interact with and meet the needs of informal family caregivers (Hokenstad et al. 2005). Through focus groups with clinicians, several areas for improved relationships between these formal and informal caregivers emerged. Findings indicate that increased training and support for family caregivers would help them perform their roles more effectively. They suggest that home health clinicians should dedicate at least one visit to train and educate the family caregiver. Currently, home health professionals are trained to focus on the patient; a more family-centered approach may be more helpful. Professional caregivers can effectively explain the limits of the home healthcare and train the family to advocate for more services. Healthcare professionals need to improve their advocacy strategies and better inform politicians and planners of needed changes that can result in first-rate healthcare.

Comprehensive Healthcare

In order to address current flaws in the healthcare systems, I advocate universal and accessible, comprehensive, effective, integrated healthcare for all Americans. No longer would physical health and emotional health services be separated. Instead, all healthcare consumers would be assessed and cared for according to the bio–psychosocial–spiritual model (Beckett and Johnson 1995). Implementation of this model is consistent with a preventive, early intervention, life span perspective. Universal, accessible, high-quality healthcare and prevention avert major illnesses and cost less than treatment. Employees' illness-related expenses and lost work time decrease as well. Complementary health currently uses this model and addresses the total patient. Many insurance companies provide no coverage for effective modalities such as acupuncture, massage, and yoga. Fortunately, some include prevention activities such as exercise and annual physicals because the carriers realize the positive financial benefits. Universal, integrated healthcare will help to protect our future—our children. Lack of insurance is a primary contributor to the childhood obesity and diabetes epidemics producing the first generation of children with a shorter life expectancy than their parents. We must overcome the barriers that permit the world's richest country to be the only industrialized nation without universal healthcare.

Summary

The suggestions made in this section entail reassessing our priorities, values, and worldview. Social work's belief in the dignity and worth of every person and success with advocacy, policy development, and coalition building can foster the achievement of these goals.

ORGANIZATION OF BOOK

The life span approach guides the organization of this book. In general, the chapters follow the age at which the contributor began caregiving, ranging from age four through young and middle adulthood into retirement. An exception is the last chapter. Although I began a caregiving career as a preschooler, the complexities and number of caregiving experiences I describe provide excellent closure to the volume. Each chapter includes a description of the contributor; a description of the caregiving experiences; analyses of the caregiving events; and implications for caregivers, social workers, and other helping professions. For the reader's convenience, the implications are summarized in a chart. Some chapters include copies of correspondence to formal caregivers. These can be useful guides for family caregivers.

Although the book is intended for a wide audience, professionals probably will find the discussion of theory and literature, especially in the analyses, of more interest. Both the narrative and more objective materials are essential but probably will spark different reactions from the reader. The rich, honest, and inspiring descriptions, like a novel, facilitate the reader's identification with the author's challenging and rewarding experiences, adventures, and emotional responses and are excellent learning tools. The analyses and implications are one way to discuss and learn from the narratives. However, the reader probably will feel an abrupt shift in attitude and feelings as she or he moves to less subjective discussion of theory and implications.

Because it includes two types of information—the more subjective narrative and the more objective research and theoretical and professional literature—the book may be used in several ways. The family caregiver may read the descriptions and find helpful strategies and resources. Professors may find diverse ways to use this text. For example, they may ask students to read only the descriptive sections, write their own analyses and implications, and later compare their findings with the author's. This type of assignment will help students understand that professionals can view things differently, partly because of their training and varying life experiences. The professor might select chapters particularly relevant to themes such as gender or ethnic differences in caregiving. The book lends itself to creative informational and educational uses for any reader. Short descriptions of the chapters follow.

Chapter 2, "Once, Twice, Always a Caregiver: Career Caregiving for Parents Who Abused Alcohol," by Cynthia Jones

An African American social work educator, only child, wife, and mother of two poignantly describes her lifetime journey of caregiving that began at age four. At times she provided local, long-distance, and in-home care for her parents and in-laws, who struggled with various physical and emotional concerns. Her struggle to achieve and simultaneously negotiate several often conflicting roles and the toll of the caregiving experiences on her physical and mental health are shared sensitively. She forthrightly discusses the current consequences of her decision to continue providing in-home care for her recently widowed and remarkably physically healthy mother. Role conflict and flexibility, personal and family struggles, strengths, and resilience are salient features of this chapter.

Chapter 3, "Responding to My Sister's Addiction: Fostering Resilience in My Nieces," by Darlene Grant

While completing her doctoral studies, this single African American clinical social worker (currently an educator and administrator) assumed responsibility for her twin sister's two latency-age daughters. Finding the nieces in drug-infested housing receiving minimal care, she and other family members creatively devised a means to get "custody," without state sanction. Persevering with clinical knowledge, family and colleague support, self-discipline, and the help of social workers' stereotypes of African American single mothers, the author empowers her nieces to overcome the challenges of their early deprivations. Family team caregiving journeys are followed through the launching process: One niece goes off to college, and the other returns to her rehabilitated mother.

Chapter 4, "Caring for My Grandmother: The Birth of a Gerontological Social Worker," by Erica Edwards

A recently married European American woman simultaneously began a graduate social work program and sharing long-distance care for her grandmother. She was a Hartford Gerontological Scholar, and her academic and practical experience interfaced. Unfortunately, her academic preparation and best family practices were dwarfed by the challenges and service gaps the family faced in securing adequate, humane care for the terminally ill grandmother and ill step-grandfather, the primary caregiver. The support of husband, family, friends, and professors helped the author to persevere. With help of a sister, a cancer survivor, this intergenerational caregiving family established needed communication with each other and healthcare providers. The author does a masterful job of integrating her academic, practical, and emotional educations, providing excellent implications for interventions with older adults.

Chapter 5, "Not an Option but a Duty: Caring for My Mother," by Yvonne Haynes

Born in Trinidad, this African American mother, grandmother, clinical social worker, and part-time educator journeyed into long-distance and in-home caregiving for her single mother, a healthcare provider who faced progressively deteriorating health. The caregiving role, her Christian duty, began as the contributor was adjusting to divorce after thirty-five years of marriage. Her story depicts how her cultural island heritage prepared her to accept this new and sometimes awkward journey. Relying on social supports—a strong extended family, including her former husband, neighbors, spirituality, her church family, and several effective self-care strategies—the author demonstrates how to successfully integrate several competing roles and cope with ongoing healthcare nightmares.

Chapter 6, "'My Last Born Shall Care for Me and Mine': Caring for Siblings and Mother," by Joyce E. Everett

When the author, a single African American woman and currently a social work educator and researcher, was eleven, her mother spoke the words in the title of this chapter. Now in middle adulthood, the author describes her caregiving journeys, which began in the 1980s, for an older brother who suffered serious brain damage in a vehicle accident, a sister terminally ill with cancer, and more recently her mother, who is close to ninety years of age. Each of these relatives has resided at least six hours from the author. The descriptions of these multiple and interrelated experiences are graphic and intertwined with discussions of teachable moments. The personal, family, community, and systemic concerns are highlighted along with helpful interventions. The importance of fictive kin is underscored.

Chapter 7, "Caring for My Mother: Four Phases of Caregiving," by Shirley Bryant

In middle adulthood, the author faced for the first time the responsibility of caring for another human being: her mother. In this chapter, a single African American social work educator describes the progression, struggles, challenges, opportunities, and spiritual journeys that caregiving provided. She chronicles unique concerns of various types of care, beginning with long distance—ten hours away in the mother's home—followed by care in the author's home, in the mother's nearby apartment, and finally in a nursing home. The positive influences of spirituality, extended family interdependence, and hope provided some solace as the mother faced major illnesses: heart failure, breast cancer, dialysis, and renal failure. The various formal systems and racial healthcare disparities are poignant reminders of current social injustices.

Chapter 8, "Aunt Doris's Moves," by F. Ellen Netting

This chapter describes the journey of a European American social work educator with her aunt, now age ninety, from the author's school years to the aunt's recent and current health and relocation concerns. The sincere bond between the women provides a loving backdrop for this discussion. The author—a married gerontologist in her late fifties—caringly and meticulously describes twenty years of long-distance care for her widowed, organized, and articulate aunt who lives eight hours away. After her years of caring for a wheelchair-bound spouse and working outside the home, Aunt Doris's saga concentrates on the unique issues of living in several continuing care-retirement community settings and a skilled nursing home. The author aptly demonstrates that gerontological expertise, coupled with intergenerational, observational learning, was helpful but not sufficient to orchestrate Aunt Doris's complex relocations.

Chapter 9, "Closing Muriel's House: Caring for My Mother," by King E. Davis

While sending a daughter off to college and facing marital problems, this African American social work professor and former state commissioner of mental health suddenly faces the challenge of providing a major portion of long-distance care for his widowed mother. As Muriel's functioning, safety, and health become increasingly compromised by vascular dementia, the author describes the difficult decisions he and his older brother make and their effects on the families, neighbors, and communities. The importance of informal and professional networks and changes in social policies in the care of the mother are emphasized. Throughout the chapter, there are delightful episodes of humor, spirituality, tenderness, love, and self-awareness along with events that underscore unique issues for men's caregiving journeys.

Chapter 10, "Social Worker Husband as Caregiver of Social Worker Wife," by Samuel Peterson

This chapter candidly and perceptively explicates how the author, a husband, father, and retired European American social work educator and active clinician, battles to smoothly integrate his ongoing scholarly, clinical, and leisure experiences with an unexpected caregiving journey. The chapter was written a few years after his wife, a retired medical social worker who worked with stroke survivors, suffered a stroke at age sixty-eight. It chronicles her significant but incomplete recovery. The author describes several aspects of coping: anxieties about his wife's health, sadness over the loss of their very active lifestyle, new responsibilities such as cooking and household management, guilt about attempts to balance his needs, and frustration with her continuing speech difficulties. The complex, irrational healthcare system hurdles and physical barriers to wheelchairs are considered carefully.

Chapter 11, "What Goes Around Comes Around: Career Caregiving in the Caring Village," by Joyce O. Beckett

This African American wife, mother, and retired educator and private practitioner was taught as a preschooler to provide care to ill neighbors. She cogently and meticulously describes her career caregiving journeys. The mutuality and reciprocity of caregiving experiences are highlighted. Membership in a close, intergenerational family provides her numerous opportunities for caregiving and care receiving. She focuses on sharing caregiving responsibilities for her grandmothers, mother, father, and older sister. The importance of a nurturing African American community in buffering the deleterious influences of the larger, often explicitly hostile environment on family members is remarkably portrayed. With tenacity, enduring social supports, and a strong spiritual core, she performs admirable feats in getting needed care from disorganized, distant, and incoherent physical and mental health systems. She shares several coping skills for handling disappointments, grief, and her own health challenges. Resiliently, she faces odds and continues her caregiving while being a care receiver.

REFERENCES

Alzheimer's Association applauds legislation that authorizes increased funding for Alzheimer research and caregiver support. 2004, June 16. *PR Newswire*, n.p.

Alzheimer's disease: Experts explain the impact of caregiving on the former First Lady and others. 2004, June 14. *M2 Presswire*, n.p.

American Association of Retired Persons. 2000. *A Profile of Older Americans*. Washington, D.C.: Author.

American Association of Retired Persons. 2001. *The Costs of Long-Term Care: Public Perceptions Versus Reality*. Washington, D.C.: Author.

American Association of Retired Persons Travelers Foundation. 1988. *National Survey of Caregivers: Final Report*. Washington, D.C.: AARP.

Aneshensel, C. S., Pearlin, L. I., Mullan, J. T., Zarit, S. H., and Whitlatch, C. J. 1995. *Profiles in Caregiving: The Unexpected Career*. San Diego: Academic Press.

Aranda, M. P. and Knight, B. G. 1997. The influence of ethnicity and culture on the caregiver stress and coping process: A sociocultural review and analysis. *Gerontologist* 37 (3): 342–354.

Arno, P. S., Levine, C., and Memmott, M. M. 1999. The economic value of informal caregiving. *Health Affairs* 18: 182–188.

At a time when nearly one quarter of American households provide care to relatives or friends over 50, a new report by the Family Caregiver Alliance has studied the economic impact on caregivers who leave the work force to assist. 2004, March 19. *National Catholic Reporter* 40 (20): 6.

Baillie, V., Norbeck, J. S., and Barnes, L. E. A. 1988. Stress, social support, and psychological distress of family caregivers of the elderly. *Nursing Research* 37: 217–222.

Barker, J. C. 2002. Neighbors, friends, and other nonkin caregivers of community-living dependent elders. *Journals of Gerontology Series B: Psychological Sciences and Social Sciences* 57 (3): S158–S167.

Barresi, C. and Stull, D. (Eds.). 1993. *Ethnic Elderly and Long-Term Care.* New York: Springer.

Bauman, L. 2000. A patient-centered approach to adherence: Risks for non-adherence. In D. Drotar (Ed.), *Promoting Adherence to Medical Treatment in Chronic Childhood Illness: Concepts, Methods, and Interventions,* 71–93. Mahwah, N.J.: Erlbaum.

Beckett, J. and Dungee-Anderson, E. 2000. Older persons of color: Asian/Pacific Islander Americans, African Americans, Hispanic Americans, and American Indians. In R. Schneider, N. Kropf, and N. Kisor (Eds.), *Gerontological Social Work: Fundamentals, Service Settings, and Special Populations,* 2d ed., 257–301. Pacific Grove, Cal.: Brooks, Cole & Wadsworth.

Beckett, J. and Johnson, H. 1995. Human development: Biological, psychological and sociocultural perspectives. In R. Edwards (Ed.), *Encyclopedia of Social Work,* 1385–1405. Washington, D.C.: NASW.

Beckett, J. and Lee, N. 2004. Informing the future of child welfare practices with African American families. In J. Everett, S. Chipungu, and B. Leashore (Eds.), *Child Welfare Revisited: An Africentric Perspective,* 93–123. New Brunswick, N.J.: Rutgers University Press.

Bengtson, V. L., Lowenstein, A., Putney, N., and Gans, D. 2003. Global aging and the challenge to families. In V. L. Bengtson and A. Lowenstein (Eds.), *Global Aging and the Challenges to Families,* 1–26. New York: Aldine.

Bengtson, V. L., Rosenthal, C. J., and Burton, L. M. 1990. Families and aging: Diversity and heterogeneity. In R. Binstock and L. George (Eds.), *Handbook of Aging and the Social Sciences,* 3d ed., 263–287. New York: Academic Press.

Braithwaite, V. 1996. Between stressors and outcomes: Can we simplify caregiving process variables? *The Gerontologist* 36: 42–53.

Briggs, R. 1998. *Caregiving Daughters: Accepting the Role of Caregiver for Elderly Parents.* New York: Garland.

Bullock, K. 2004. The changing role of grandparents in rural families: The results of an exploratory study in southeastern North Carolina. *Families in Society: The Journal of Contemporary Human Services* 85 (1): 45–55.

Burden of dealing with dementia prompts caregivers to misjudge patient happiness. 2004, June 2. *Biotech Week,* p. 704.

Burns, C., Archbold, P., Stewart, B., and Shelton, K. 1993. New diagnosis: Caregiver role strain. *Nursing Diagnosis* 4: 70–74.

Burton, L. and Dilworth-Anderson, P. 1991. The intergenerational family roles of aged black Americans. *Marriage & Family Review* 16: 311–330.

Caputo, R. 2000. Trends and correlates of coresidency among black and white grandmothers and their grandchildren: A panel study, 1967–1992. In B. Hayslip and R. Goldberg-Glen (Eds.), *Grandparents Raising Grandchildren: Theoretical, Empirical, and Clinical Perspectives,* 351–367. New York: Springer.

Caregivers at risk for deteriorating health. 2004, June 21. *Health & Medicine Week,* p. 763.

The caregiving crisis: New survey shows lack of planning for eldercare. 2004, Jan. 20. *PR Newswire,* n.p.

Caregiving may take a physical toll. 2004, Jan. *Clinician Reviews* 14 (1): 42.

Carers: Family duties force many out of jobs. 2004, March 18. *Community Care,* p. 15.

Caston, C. 1997. *Burnout in African American Family Caregivers: Nursing Interventions.* New York: Garland.

Chan, K. and Horrocks, S. 2006. Lived experiences of family caregivers of mentally ill relatives. *Journal of Advanced Nursing* 53 (4): 435–443.

Choi, N. and Bohman, T. 2007. Predicting the changes in depressive symptomatology in later life. *Journal of Aging and Health* 19 (1): 152–177.

Choi, N., Burr, J., Mutchler, J., and Caro, F. 2007. Formal and informal volunteer activity and spousal caregiving among older adults. *Research on Aging* 29 (2): 99–124.

Chumbler, N. R., Pienta, A. M., and Dwyer, J. W. 2004. The depressive symptomatology of parent care among the near elderly: The influence of multiple role commitments. *Research on Aging* 26 (3): 330–352.

Companion Web site to PBS series *The Forgetting:* A portrait of Alzheimer's offers unique, innovative resource for patients, families, and caregivers. 2004, Jan. 13. *Internet Wire,* n.p.

Correcting and replacing: When Alzheimer's hits home: TV personality/activist Leeza Gibbons available to comment on family dynamics, importance of caregivers. 2004, June 6. *Business Wire,* p. 5048.

Crowley, S. 2001. A daughter's ordeal sheds light on caring. *AARP Bulletin* 42. Washington, D.C.: AARP.

Cuellar, N. G. 2002. Comparison of African American and Caucasian American female caregivers of rural, post-stroke, bedbound older adults. *Journal of Gerontological Nursing* 28 (1): 36–45.

Daly, A., Jennings, J., Beckett, J. O., and Leashore, B. R. 1995. Effective coping strategies of African-Americans. *Social Work* 40 (2): 240–248.

Dearden, C. and Becker, S. 1998. *Sheffield Young Caregivers Projects: An Evaluation. (Interim Report April* 1997–*September* 1998*)*. Loughborough, England: Loughborough University, Young Careers Research Group.

DeFiore, J. 2002. Las madres en el barrio: Godmothers, othermothers, and women's power in a community of caregiving. In F. M. Cancian, D. Kurz, A. S. London, R. Reviere, and M. C. Tuominen (Eds.), *Child Care and Inequality: Rethinking Carework for Children and Youth*, 37–50. New York: Routledge.

De la Cuesta, C. 2005. The craft of care: Family care of relatives with advanced dementia. *Qualitative Health Research* 15 (7): 881–896.

Denes, S. 2004, May–June. Employees and elder care. *Rural Telecommunications* 23 (3): 8.

Depp, C., Sorocco, K., Kasi-Godley, J., Thompson, L., Rabinowitz, Y., and Gallagher-Thompson, D. 2005. Caregiver self-efficacy, ethnicity, and kinship differences in dementia caregivers. *American Journal of Geriatric Psychiatry* 13 (9): 787–794.

Dilworth-Anderson, P., Williams, I. C., and Gibson, B. E. 2002. Issues of race, ethnicity, and culture in caregiving research: A 20-year review. *Gerontologist* 42 (2): 237–272.

Dolliver, M. 2004, April 26. Whether willingly or otherwise, we've become a nation of caregivers: Stress is part of the deal. *Adweek* 45 (17): 39.

Dowdell, E. and Sherwin, L. 1998. Grandmothers who raise grandchildren: A cross-generational challenge to caregivers. *Journal of Gerontological Nursing* 24 (5): 8–13.

Emotional issues are number one cause of stress in caregivers for elderly, according to survey by ComPsych: Despite "care load" and crunch for time, almost half of working caregivers report emotional issues—not tasks—are the main cause of stress. 2004, June 1. *PR Newswire*, n.p.

Enhanced counseling eases depression among Alzheimer caregivers. 2004, May 29. *Obesity, Fitness & Wellness Week*, p. 298.

Extending a helping hand, American Red Cross offers training to millions of family caregivers. 2004, April 26. *The America's Intelligence Wire*, n.p.

Family Caregiver Alliance, National Center on Caregiving. 2003. *Fact Sheet: Women and Caregiving: Facts and Figures*. Retrieved June 22, 2004, from www.caregiver.org/.

Family caregivers called "cornerstone of national healthcare system": Provide $257 billion annually in services. 2004, Feb. 26. *Ascribe Business & Economics News Service*, n.p.

Finke, L. 2004. Families: The forgotten resource for individuals with mental illness. *Journal of Child and Adolescent Psychiatric Nursing* 17 (1): 3–5.

Finkel, S., Czaja, S., Schulz, R., Martinovich, Z., Harris, C., and Pezzuto, D. 2007. E-care: A telecommunications technology intervention for family caregivers of dementia patients. *American Journal of Geriatric Psychiatry* 15 (5): 443–448.

Foley, K., Tung, H., and Mutran, E. 2002. Self-gain and self-loss among African American and white caregivers. *Journal of Gerontology* 57B: S14–S22.

Fredman, L., Daly, M., and Lazur, A. 1995. Burden among white and black caregivers to elderly adults. *Journal of Gerontology: Social Sciences* 50B: S110–S118.

Gates, M. and Lackey, N. 1998. Youngsters caring for adults with cancer. *Image: Journal of Nursing Scholarship* 30: 11–15.

Geiger, B. 1996. *Fathers as Primary Caregivers*. Westport, Conn.: Greenwood.

George, L. 1994. Caregiver burden and well-being: An elusive distinction. *The Gerontologist* 34: 6–7.

George, L. and Gwyther, L. 1996. Caregiving well-being: A multidimensional examination of family caregivers and demented adults. *The Gerontologist* 26: 253–259.

Gillen, J. and Peterson, A. 2005. Analysis discourse. In B. Somekh and C. Lewin (Eds.), *Research Methods in the Social Sciences*, 146–154. London: Sage.

Glass, J. 2004. Blessing or curse? Work–family policies and mother's wage growth over time. *Work and Occupations* 31 (3): 367–394.

Greenberg, J. S., Seltzer, M. M., Chou, R. J., Hong, J., and Krauss, M. W. 2004. The effect of quality of the relationship between mothers and adult children with schizophrenia, autism, or Down's syndrome on maternal well-being: The mediating role of optimism. *American Journal of Orthopsychiatry* 74 (1): 14–26.

Greene, J., Smith, R., Gardiner, M., and Timbury, G. 1982. Measuring behavioral disturbance of elderly demented patients in the community and its effect on relatives: A factor analytic study. *Age & Ageing* 11: 121–126.

Guberman, N., Lavoie, J., Pepin, J., Lauzon, S., and Montejo, M. 2006. Formal service practitioners' views of family caregivers' responsibilities and difficulties. *Canadian Journal of Aging* 25 (1): 43–53.

Guzell-Roe, J. R., Gerard, J. M., and Landry-Meyer, L. 2005. Custodial grandparents' perceived control over caregiving outcomes: Raising children the second time around. *Journal of Intergenerational Relationships* 3: 43–61.

Haley, W., West, C., Wadley, V., Ford, G., White, F., Barrett, J., Harrell, L., and Roth, D. 1995. Psychological, social, and health impact of caregiving: A comparison of white and black dementia family caregivers and noncaregivers. *Psychology and Aging* 10: 540–552.

Harvard Medical School provides useful information to caregivers about caring for the ill, elderly, and disabled. 2004, April 28. *PR Newswire*, n.p.

Hayslip, B., and Goldberg-Glen, R. 2000. *Grandparents Raising Grandchildren: Theoretical, Empirical, and Clinical Perspectives*. New York: Springer.

Hennessy, J., Dyeson, C., and Garrett, T. 2001. Toward the conceptualization and measurement of caregiver burden among Pueblo Indian family caregivers. *The Gerontologist* 41: 210–219.

Hernandez, G. 1991. Not so benign neglect: Researchers ignore ethnicity in defining family caregiver burden and recommending services. *The Gerontologist* 32: 271–272.

Hill, R. 1972. *The Strength of Black Families.* Washington, D.C.: National Urban League, Research Department.

Hinrichsen, G. and Ramirez, M. 1992. Black and white caregivers: A comparison of their adaptation, adjustment, and service utilization. *The Gerontologist* 32: 379–381.

Hokenstad, A., Hart, A., Gould, D., Halper, D., and Levine, C. 2005. Closing the home care case: Clinicians' perspectives of family caregiving. *Home Health Care Management and Practices* 17 (5): 388–397.

Hokenstad, M.C. and Johansson, L. 1990. Caregiving for the elderly in Sweden: Program challenges and policy initiatives. In D.E. Biegel and A. Blum (Eds.), *Aging and Caregiving: Theory, Research, and Policy,* 254–269. Newbury Park, Cal.: Sage.

Hooyman, N. R. & Gonyea, J. G. 1995. Family caregiving. In R. L. Edwards (Ed.), *Encyclopedia of Social Work,* 19th ed., 951–959. Washington, D.C.: National Association of Social Workers.

Hossain, Z. and Roopnarine, J.L. 1994. African-American fathers' involvement with infants: Relationships to their functioning style, support, education, and income. *Infant Behavior and Development* 17 (2): 175–184.

Ikels, C. 1990. Family caregivers and the elderly in China. In D.E. Biegel and A. Blum (Eds.), *Aging and Caregiving: Theory, Research, and Policy,* 270–284. Newbury Park, Cal.: Sage.

John, R., Hennessy, C., Dyeson, T., and Garrett, M. 2001. Toward the conceptualization and measurement of caregiver burden among Pueblo Indian family caregivers. *The Gerontologist* 41: 210–219.

Johnson, R. W. and Lo Sasso, A. T. 2006. The impact of elder care on women's labor supply at midlife. *Inquiry* 43 (3): 195–210.

Kahana, E. and Young, R. 1990. Clarifying the caregiving paradigm: Challenges for the future. In D.E. Biegel and A. Blum (Eds.), *Aging and Caregiving: Theory, Research, and Policy,* 77–97. Newbury Park, Cal.: Sage.

Karner, T.X. 1998. Professional caring: Homecare workers as fictive kin. *Journal of Aging Studies* 12 (1): 68–82.

Kelley, S., Yorker, B., and Whitley, D. 1997. To grandmother's house we go . . . and stay: Children raised in intergenerational families. *Journal of Gerontological Nursing* 23 (9): 12–20.

Knight, B.G., Robinson, G.S., Longmire-Crystal, V.F., Chun, M., Nakao, K., and Kim, J.H. 2002. *Ageing International* 27 (3): 70–94.

Knight, B.G., Silverstein, M., McCallum, T.J., and Fox, L.S. 2000. Sociocultural stress and coping model for mental health outcomes among African American caregivers in southern California. *Journals of Gerontology Series B: Psychological Sciences and Social Sciences* 55B (3): P142–P150.

Kosloski, K., Young, R., and Montgomery, R. 1999. A new direction for intervention with depressed caregivers to Alzheimer's patients. *Family Relations* 48: 373–379.

Kramer, B. 1997. Gain in the caregiving experience: Where are we? What next? *The Gerontologist* 37: 218–232.

Kramer, B. J. and Kipnis, S. 1995. Eldercare and work-role conflict: Toward an understanding of gender differences in caregiver burden. *Gerontologist* 35 (3): 340–348.

Lackey, N. R. and Gates, M. F. 1997. Combing the analyses of three qualitative data sets in studying young caregivers. *Journal of Advanced Nursing* 26 (4): 664–671.

Lackey, N. R. and Gates, M. F. 2001. Adults' recollections of their experiences as young caregivers of family members with chronic physical illnesses. *Journal of Advanced Nursing* 34 (3): 320–328.

Laditka, J. N. and Laditka, S. B. 2001. Adult children helping older parents: Variations in likelihood and hours by gender, race, and family role. *Research on Aging* 23 (4): 429–456.

Langa, K. M., Valenstein, M. A., Fendrick, A. M., Kabeto, M. U., and Vijan, S. 2004. Extent and cost of informal caregiving for older Americans with symptoms of depression. *American Journal of Psychiatry* 161 (5): 857–864.

Lawton, M., Kleban, M., Moss, M., Rovine, M., and Glicksman, A. 1989. Measuring caregiving appraisal. *Journal of Gerontology: Psychological Sciences* 44 (3): 61–71.

Lawton, M. P., Moss, M., Kleban, M., Glicksman, A., and Rovine, M. 1991. A two-factor model of caregiving appraisal and psychological well-being. *Journal of Gerontology: Psychological Sciences* 46: P181–P189.

Lawton, M. P., Rajagopal, D., Brody, E., and Kleban, M. 1992. The dynamics of caregiving for demented elder among black and white families. *Journal of Gerontology: Social Sciences* 47B: S156–S164.

Lee, R., Ensminger, M., and Laveist, T. 2005. The responsibility continuum: Never primary, coresident and caregiver—Heterogeneity in the African-American grandmother experience. *International Journal of Aging and Human Development* 60 (4): 295–304.

Lee Roff, L., Burgio, L., Gitlin, L., Nichols, L., Chaplin, W., and Hardin, M. 2004. Positive aspects of Alzheimer's caregiving: The role of race. *Journal of Gerontology* 59B (4): P185–P190.

Lefley, H. P. 1996. *Family Caregiving in Mental Illness.* Thousand Oaks, Cal.: Sage.

Leiter, V., Krauss, M. W., Anderson, B., and Wells, N. 2004. The consequences of caring: Effects of mothering a child with special needs. *Journal of Family Issues* 25 (3): 379–404.

Levine, C., Kuerbis, A., Gould, D., Navaie-Waliser, M., Feldman, P. H., and Donelan, K. 2000. *Family Caregivers in New York City: Implications for the Health Care System.* New York: The United Hospital Fund.

Levkoff, S., Levy, B., and Weitzman, P. F. 1999. Role of religion and ethnicity in the help seeking of family caregivers of elders with Alzheimer's disease and related disorder. *Journal of Cross Cultural Gerontology* 14 (4): 335–356.

Li, H., Edwards, D., and Morrow-Howell, N. 2004. Informal caregiving networks and use of formal services by inner-city African American elderly with dementia. *Families in Society: The Journal of Contemporary Social Services* 85 (1): 55–62.

Lieberman, L. 2004. More male caregivers break long term care gender barrier. *Contemporary Long Term Care* 27 (1): 10.

Lockery, S. A. 1992. Caregiving among racial and ethnic minority elders: Family and social supports. In E. P. Stanford and F. M. Torres-Gil (Eds.), *Diversity: New Approaches to Ethnic Minority Aging,* 113–122. Amityville, N.Y.: Baywood.

Lo Sasso, A. T. and Johnson, R. W. 2002. Does informal care from adult children reduce nursing home admissions for the elderly? *Inquiry* 39 (3): 279–297.

Luborsky, M. and Sankar, W. 1993. Extending the critical gerontology perspective: Cultural dimensions. *The Gerontologist* 33: 440–444.

Mahoney, A. and Daniel, C. 2006. Bridging the power gap: Narrative therapy with incarcerated women. *The Prison Journal* 86 (1): 75–88.

Marcell, J. 2001. *Elder Rage or Take My Father Please: How to Survive Caring for Aging Parents.* Irvine, Cal.: Impressive Press.

Martin, C. D. 2000. More than the work: Race and gender differences in caregiving burden. *Journal of Family Issues* 21 (8): 986–1005.

Martire, L. and Stephens, M. P. 2003. Juggling parent care and employment responsibilities: The dilemmas of adult daughter caregivers in the workforce. *Sex Roles* 48 (3/4): 167–173.

Mausback, B. T., Coon, D. W., Cardenas, V., and Thompson, L. W. 2003. Religious coping among Caucasian and Latina dementia caregivers. *Journal of Mental Health and Aging* 9 (2): 97–110.

Maxwell, J. A. 1996. *Qualitative Research Design: An Interactive Approach,* Vol. 41. London: Sage.

McFall, S. and Miller, B. 1992. Caregiver burden and nursing home admissions of frail elderly persons. *Journal of Gerontology: Social Sciences* 47: S73–S79.

Mercer, S. O. 1996. Navajo elderly people in a reservation nursing home: Admission predictors and culture care practices. *Social Work* 41 (2): 181–189.

Metropolitan Family Services provides support and respite to family caregivers. 2003, Dec. 18. *PR Newswire,* n.p.

Mikler, M. and Roe, K.M. 1993. *Grandmothers as Caregivers: Raising Children of the Crack Cocaine Epidemic*. Newbury Park, Cal.: Sage.

Miles, M. and Huberman, M. 1994. *Qualitative Data Analysis: An Expanded Sourcebook,* 2d ed. Thousand Oaks, Cal.: Sage.

Miltiades, H.B. and Pruchno, R. 2002. Effect of religious coping appraisals of mothers of adults with developmental disabilities. *Gerontologist* 42 (1): 82–91.

Mishler, E. 1986. *Research Interview: Context and Narrative.* Cambridge, Mass.: Harvard University Press.

Moroney, R.M. (General ed.). 1998. *Caring and Competent Caregivers.* Athens: University of Georgia Press.

Morris, L., Linkemann, A., and Kroner-Herwig, B. 2006. Writing your way to health? The effects of disclosure of past stressful events in German students. In M. E. Abelian (Ed.), *Trends in Psychotherapy Research,* 161–181. New York: Nova Science Publishers.

Morris, T. 2006. *Social Work Research Methods: Four Alternative Paradigms.* Thousand Oaks, Cal.: Sage.

Morycz, R. 1993. Caregiving families and cross-cultural perspectives. In S.H. Zarit, L.I. Pearlin, and K.W. Schaie (Eds.), *Caregiving Systems: Informal and Formal Helpers,* 67–73. Hillsdale, N.J.: Erlbaum.

Nasser, H. 1999, July 1. Raising grandkids: No day at the beach. *USA Today,* pp. D1–D2.

National Alliance for Caregiving. 1997. *Family Caregiving in the United States: Findings from a National Survey.* Washington, D.C.: Author.

National Family Caregiver Support Program. 2004. *Common Caregiving Terms.* Retrieved June 22, 2004, from www.aoa.gov/prof/aoaprog/caregiver/careprof/progguidance/resources/caregiving_terms.asp.

National Family Caregiver Support Program. n.d. *Fact Sheet: Family Caregiving.* Retrieved June 22, 2004, from www.aoa.gov/press/oam/May_2003/media/fact_sheets/National%20Family%20Caregiver%20Support%20Program.pdf.

Navaie, W.M., Spriggs, A., and Feldman, P.H. 2002. Informal caregiving: Differential experiences by gender. *Medical Care* 40 (12): 1249–1259.

Navaie-Waliser, M., Feldman, P., Gould, D., Levine, C., Kuerbis, A., and Donelan, K. 2001. The experiences and challenges of informal caregivers: Common themes and differences among whites, blacks, and Hispanics. *The Gerontologist* 41: 733–741.

NBC News. 2001, April 3. *Aging Boomers with Alzheimer's Could Overwhelm Medicare.* Retrieved April 3, 2001, from www.msnbc.com/news/554054.

New book meets growing need for information about aging and caregiving for older adults. 2004, June 9. *PR Newswire,* n.p.

New Merck guide for seniors, caregivers. 2004, June 12. *Obesity, Fitness & Wellness Week,* p. 483.

New report sheds light on caregiving in gay community. 2004, June 17. *US Newswire*, n.p.

Nightingale, M.C. 2003. Religion, spirituality, and ethnicity: What it means for caregivers of persons with Alzheimer's disease and related disorders. *Dementia* 2 (3): 379–391.

Owen, J.E., Goode, K.T., and Haley, W.E. 2001. End of life care and reactions to death in African-American and white family caregivers of relatives with Alzheimer's disease. *Omega: Journal of Death and Dying* 43 (4): 349–361.

Patchett, A. 2003, Dec. Caregiving: A love story. *O, The Oprah Magazine* 4 (12): 101–103.

Pearlin, L., Mullan, J., Semple, S., and Skaff, M. 1990. Caregiving and the stress process: An overview of concepts and their measures. *The Gerontologist* 30: 583–591.

Pebley, A.R. and Rudkin, L.L. 1999. Grandparents caring for grandchildren. *Journal of Family Issues* 20 (2): 218–242.

Peek, M.K., Coward, R.T., and Peek, C.W. 2000. Race, aging, and care. *Research on Aging* 22 (2): 117–142.

Petersen, S., Bull, C., Propst, O., Dettinger, S., and Detwiler, L. 2005. Narrative therapy to prevent illness-related stress disorder. *Journal of Counseling and Development* 83 (1): 41–47.

Poindexter, C.C., Linsk, N.L., and Warner, R.S. 1999. "He listens . . . and never gossips": Spiritual coping without church support among older, predominantly African-American caregivers of persons with HIV. *Review of Religious Research* 40 (3): 230–243.

Pruchno, R. 1999. Raising grandchildren: The experiences of black and white grandmothers. *Gerontologist* 39 (2): 209–221.

Reinhard, S.C. and Horwitz, A.V. 1995. Caregiver burden: Differentiating the content and consequences of family caregiving. *Journal of Marriage and the Family* 57 (3): 741–750.

Reissman, C. K. 2004. Narrative analysis. In M. S. Lewis-Beck, A. Bryman, and T. Futing Liao (Eds.), *Encyclopedia of Social Science Research Methods*, 705–709. Newbury Park, Cal.: Sage.

Reissman, C. 2006. Narrative in social work: A critical review. *Qualitative Social Work* 4 (4): 391–412.

Reissman, C. 2007. *Narrative Methods for the Human Services*. Newbury Park, Cal.: Sage.

Reissman, C. and Quinney, L. 2005. Narrative in social work: A critical review. *Qualitative Social Work Research and Practice* 4 (4): 391–412.

Rhee, K.O. and Lee, M.J. 2001. Comparison of caregiving burden among Korean and Japanese caregivers. *Hallym International Journal of Aging* 3 (2): 191–210.

Rivera, P. A., Elliott, T. R., Berry, J. W., Shewchuk, R. M., Oswald, K. D., and Grant, J. 2006. Family caregivers of women with physical disabilities. *Journal of Clinical Psychology in Medical Settings* 13 (4): 425–434.

San Antonio, P. M., Eckert, J. K., and Simon-Rusinowitz, L. 2006. The importance of relationship: Elders and their paid family caregivers in the Arkansas cash and counseling qualitative study. *The Journal of Applied Gerontology* 25 (1): 31–48.

Schwartz, C. 2003. Parents of mentally ill adult children living at home. *Health and Social Work* 27 (2): 145–154.

Seltzer, M. and Greenberg, J. 1999. The caregiving context: The intersection of social and individual influences in the experiences of family caregiving. In C. Ryff and V. Marshall (Eds.), *The Self and Society in Aging Processes*, 362–397. New York: Springer.

Sherrell, K., Buckwalter, K., and Morhardt, D. 2001. Negotiating family relationships: Dementia care as a midlife developmental task. *Families in Society* 82: 383–392.

Shibusawa, T., Kodaka, M., Shinji, I., and Kaizu, K. 2005. Intervention for elder abuse and neglect with frail elders in Japan. *Brief Treatment and Crisis Intervention* 5 (2): 203–211.

Shifren, K. 2001. Early caregiving and adult depression: Good news for young caregivers. *The Gerontologist* 41: 188–190.

Shifren, K. and Kachorek, L. V. 2003. Does early caregiving matter? The effects on young caregivers' adult mental health. *International Journal of Behavioral Development* 27 (4): 338–346.

Shurgot, G. and Knight, B. 2004. Preliminary study investigating acculturation, cultural values, and psychological distress in Latino caregivers of dementia patients. *Journal of Mental Health and Aging* 10 (3): 183–194.

Skaff, M. and Pearlin, L. 1992. Caregiving: Role engulfment and the loss of self. *The Gerontologist* 32: 656–664.

Skaff, M., Pearlin, L., and Mullen, J. 1996. Transitions in caregiving: Effects of a sense of mastery. *Psychology of Aging* 11 (2): 247–257.

Sleath, B., Thorpe, J., Landerman, L., Doyle, M., and Clipp, E. 2005. African-American and white caregivers of older adults with dementia: Differences in depressive symptomatology and psychotropic drug use. *Americans Geriatrics Society* 53: 397–404.

Sorenson, S. and Pinquart, M. 2005. Racial and ethnic differences in the relationship of caregiving stressors, resources, and sociodemographic variables to caregiver depression and perceived physical health. *Aging and Mental Health* 9 (5): 482–495.

Swenson, C. 2004. Dementia diary: A personal and professional journal. *Social Work* 49 (3): 451–460.

Thompson, E. H., Futterman, A. M., Gallagher-Thompson, D., Rose, J. M., and Lovett, S. B. 1993. Social support and caregiving burden in family caregivers of frail elders. *Journal of Gerontology* 48 (5): S245–S254.

Treas, J. 1997. Older immigrants and United States welfare reform. *International Journal of Sociology and Social Policy* 17: 8–33.

Treasure, J. 2004. Review: Exploration of psychological and physical health differences between caregivers and non-caregivers. *Evidence-Based Mental Health* 7 (1): 28.

Turner, T. 2004, Feb. 25. Young and free: New measures to support young carers of people with mental health problems could have wider implications. *Nursing Standard* 18 (24): 25.

Välimäki, T., Vehviläinen-Julkunen, K., and Pietilä, A. 2007. Diaries as research data in a study on family caregivers of people with Alzheimer's disease: Methodological issues. *Journal of Advanced Nursing* 59 (1): 68–76.

Wakabayashi, C. and Donato, K. 2005. The consequences of caregiving: Effects on women's employment and earnings. *Population Research and Policy Review* 24: 467–488.

Wallstein, S. S. 2000. Effects of caregiving, gender, and race on the health, mutuality, and social supports of older couples. *Journal of Aging and Health* 12 (1): 90–111.

Ward-Griffin, C. 2004. Nurses as caregivers of elderly relatives: Negotiating personal and professional boundaries. *Canadian Journal of Nursing Research* 36 (1): 92–114.

White, T. M., Townsend, A. L., and Stephens, M. P. 2000. Comparisons of African American and white women in the parent care role. *Gerontologist* 40 (6): 718–728.

Whittier, S., Scharlach, A., and Dal Santo, T. 2005. Availability of caregiver support services: Implications for implementation of the national family caregiver support program. *Journal of Aging and Social Policy* 17 (1): 45–62.

Williams, J. and Cohen-Cooper, H. 2004. The public policy of motherhood. *Journal of Social Issues* 60 (4): 849–865.

Williams, S. W., Dilworth-Anderson, P., and Goodwin, P. Y. 2003. Caregiver role strain: The contribution of multiple roles and available resources in African-American women. *Aging and Mental Health* 7 (2): 103–112.

Winston, C. 2003. African-American grandmothers parenting grandchildren orphaned by AIDS: Grieving and coping with loss. *Illness, Crisis & Loss* 11 (4): 350–361.

Wolff, J. L. and Agree, E. M. 2004. Depression among recipients of informal care: The effects of reciprocity, respect, and adequacy of support. *The Journals of Gerontology, Series B* 59 (3): S173–181.

Yoon, S. M. 2005. The characteristics and needs of Asian-American grandparent caregivers: A study of Chinese-American and Korean-American grandparents in New York City. *Journal of Gerontological Social Work* 44 (3/4): 75–93.

Young, D. and Holley, L. 2005. Combining caregiving and career: Experiences of social work faculty. *Affilia* 20 (2): 136–152.

Young, R. F. and Kahana, E. 1995. The context of caregiving and well-being outcomes among African and Caucasian Americans. *Gerontologist* 35 (2): 225–232.

Zhan, H. J. 2004. Willingness and expectations: Intergenerational differences in attitudes toward filial responsibility in China. *Marriage & Family Review* 365 (1–2): 175–201.

Zhang, J., Vitaliano, P. and Lin, H. 2006. Relations of caregiving stress and health depend on the health indicators used and gender. *International Journal of Behavioral Medicine* 13 (2): 173–181.

Once, Twice, Always a Caregiver

TWO

Career Caregiving for Parents Who Abused Alcohol

CYNTHIA JONES

On a cold day when I was eight years old, I tried to ignite a fire in a coal stove by pouring some rubbing alcohol on hot coal, and the stove exploded in my face, landing me across the room on the floor. I was taken to the hospital for damage to my eyes and skin.

One night my stepfather came home with groceries and became angry because my mother was intoxicated. He opened every can and package and dumped the food in the middle of the carpeted living room floor as I screamed and cried for him to stop. He told me he was sorry, but he had to do this.

DESCRIPTION OF CAREGIVER

I am a fifty-year-old African American woman, the only child of two alcoholic parents. My mother and stepfather married when I was very young. I never knew my biological father, who died when I was eight or nine. I grew up on the outskirts of a small rural town in a segregated southeastern state. An area with beautiful rolling hills, it was located about two hours from major cities. The unequal treatment of African Americans influenced much of my life. When I began first grade, for example, the county closed schools to prevent integration, and I had to be smuggled across school district boundaries every day.

There was never any question of my career plans: I would pursue a career in a helping profession. I always knew I would attend college; I just did not know how. One day my mother took me to a neighboring large city for an interview. She told me that because I had been ill (epilepsy) during high school, the interviewer might secure funds for college. I later realized I was at the state Vocational Rehabilitation Department. Years later, I learned the correct diagnoses were posttraumatic stress disorder (PTSD), depression, and panic disorder. Indeed, I was eligible, and off to college I went, to a small African American, state-supported college located a couple of hours from my hometown. I changed my major from special education to social work after only one semester. In my senior year, I married Paul, my high school sweetheart and only real boyfriend. When I was head majorette in high school, he was a four-lettered sports star (football, basketball, baseball, and track), handsome, popular, respectful, muscular, and athletic. Unlike me, he was able to view options and easily make decisions for himself, and in some ways he became my parent. Not fully comprehending the meaning of marriage, I knew this was the only way to escape my home, an ongoing stress factor in my life. Looking back, I think my three "c"s—compassionate, compliant, and complacent—were important explanations for his attraction to me. I lacked the fourth "c," the capacity to see that I had other avenues. I made these important decisions before the advent of the womanist movement (Banks-Wallace 2000; Brewer 1993; Collins 1990; Hill-Collins 2000; hooks 1993, 2000) and never considered moving to another city or getting an apartment in our small town because young women of my town did not fathom such alternatives. Over our thirty years of marriage, we have grown to be true soulmates although friends and family expected us to separate because of differences in our educational achievements. Now, at age fifty-three, Paul is the owner and operator of a small business. It has not always been easy, but we have worked together to build a good relationship and have concentrated on the high points of the years we have shared together.

Paul and I have two daughters, our first daughter born three years after we married. I knew I could be a good mother if I did the opposite of what my parents had done. Although my college growth and development courses were helpful, the most important factor was a parenting program at the medical center where our daughters were born. After each visit to the pediatrician, the program staff told us what to expect from our daughters during the period before our next visit. In addition, they helped us understand the girls' behaviors and develop strategies to respond appropriately. Later, counselors and I wondered whether parenting my daughters was an opportunity to vicariously parent myself. I am sure it was not by chance that I first taught each child to say, "I love you," words my mother never said to me. Seeing our daughters happily thriving was one of the most important and rewarding experiences of my adult life. The pediatrician's constant praise of our parenting was an enormous reward and great motivator. Our two daughters are adults now: The older is a teacher and master's student, and the younger is a law student. Each has brought joy into our lives, confirming our efforts to make parenting one of our top priorities. Although we tried to provide not only what our children needed but also most of what they wanted, they have grown to be independent.

I have worked in diverse settings. As a teenager, I worked in housekeeping, shoe making, short-order cooking, and retail sales to earn money for clothing and to assist my parents financially. My first professional position was as a social worker in a rural department of social services, where I worked with individuals, groups, and the community for ten years. Then I spent five years as a human service administrator in a private agency. For the last fifteen years, I have been a college administrator and faculty member in the social work program of a medium-sized southeastern state university. I earned a master of science in education while our children were young. Juggling my multiple roles as mother, wife, daughter, full-time employee, counselor, and motivational speaker, I learned I could not be everything to everyone. Despite many years of therapy and medications, I still struggled with PTSD, depression, and panic disorder. Some days I had to fight to get out of bed or to concentrate on tasks. I learned that my hypertension and diabetes were exacerbated by my emotional conditions.

More recently, I earned a doctorate in social work from a nationally recognized institution. The process was stressful. It required a three-hour commute for classes while I was teaching full time, preparing for tenure and promotion, and caring for my family and my terminally ill father. At times it looked as if my doctoral committee would implode, delaying the completion of my degree. Simultaneously, two recently hired administrators, hoping to raise the institution's teaching standards by increasing the number of faculty with doctorates, threatened me with dismissal and pay cuts. I reapplied for my position and was rehired. When I was introduced as a new faculty member, even my colleagues were puzzled. Although I received an Outstanding Teacher award and consistently high evaluations from my students, I hold the record for the length of time it took to receive tenure: a total of twelve years.

DESCRIPTION OF FAMILY MEMBERS CARED FOR

My maternal grandmother died in a vehicle accident when my mother was ten years old, leaving three young children, of whom my mother was the oldest. Because my grandfather was unable to care for three young children, they were sent to live with relatives in Pennsylvania, Maryland, and Virginia, but they were never separated. My mother and her sisters moved from family member to family member; most treated the girls poorly. In the pictures I have seen of them as youngsters, the sisters were nicely and appropriately dressed. This suggested they were physically well cared for. Probably because of my own childhood, I wonder whether they were emotionally abused. I recall my mother saying that their various caregivers often called them "out of their names." Other than these details, I know very little about my mother's early life and how it influenced her to drink. Because she did not like to talk about her childhood, I never delved into her early experiences. My mother completed high school and worked in a number of different service-oriented roles. She cleaned houses, provided care to a number of people, worked in a factory, cooked in a restaurant, and worked in a pharmacy. My stepfather was a vital part of my life from childhood through adulthood. He was the youngest of his family of four children and was the first to further his education beyond high school and the only one of his siblings to earn a graduate degree. When he married my mother, he had retired as an army captain but remained in the army reserve and taught school in a neighboring county. He spent forty years, many of them as a master teacher, in the public schools. He drank alcohol primarily on weekends and during the summer, and he was hospitalized for use and abuse at least twice.

The apple of my eye, though, was my maternal grandfather. Although he lived in another state, frequent family visits allowed us to spend a great deal of time together. Both he and my step-grandmother were in service-oriented jobs, he as a butler and doorman in a hotel and she as a maid or housekeeper. My grandfather seemed to be closer to my mother and me than to his other two children and five grandchildren. I am basing this on the fact that he spent nights in our home but not in theirs, and he sent me gifts of money and clothing on a regular basis. Both he and my step-grandmother were very heavy alcohol drinkers. When they spent time with us, usually during the summer or on special holidays, they drank with my parents. Often their drinking led to arguments and fights.

DESCRIPTION OF CAREGIVING EXPERIENCE

Caregiving in Early Childhood

I began to assume a caregiving role around the age of four. My mother and I moved to Virginia from Pennsylvania to allow my mother to provide around-the-clock care for a bedridden aunt who had suffered a stroke. As I slept in a twin bed next to the aunt, I first observed caregiving for a family member by a family member. My mother taught me at that young age that caregiving was a part of our family and ethnic cultures (Hill 1972, 1997). Within a short period, her aunt died, but the two of us remained in Virginia. Soon thereafter, my mother married a man who would be my stepfather for more than forty years.

For me, the inclusion of my stepfather in our family was difficult because I felt he and his family never accepted me. Although he taught in the county where I attended school through the second grade, he would not allow me to ride with him. Every day, my mother arranged for me to get a ride with whomever she could find. Although racial inequality was the reason that no school was available in my county, my stepfather was the reason it was so difficult for my mother to find dependable transportation for me. His taking me to school was not an option. Then, as in most of my life, I remained separate from my stepfather's family and professional world. Although my mother accompanied him, I did not attend his family gatherings, and his family called me "her" daughter, meaning Mother's daughter, rather than "his stepdaughter." People knew my stepfather was married to my mother, but his coworkers did not know I was a part of his family. Furthermore, Mother and I never attended any of his professional events. His colleagues' first knowledge of me occurred after he retired. Although I must have wanted a family in which to belong, as I grew older I was pleased I was not biologically related to such a hurtful person. As I write this, it seems strange that my stepfather kept Mother and me from his colleagues; but as a child I gave it little conscious thought. Like other things in my family, it was just the way things were.

About age seven, I began to accept more and more responsibility for the care of my mother and stepfather, both of whom were alcoholics. These responsibilities included locking the doors to secure the house, covering my mother and stepfather on cold evenings when the coal stove cooled, trying to make a fire to keep us warm, and steering the vehicle into the yard when my stepfather was too intoxicated to make the turn. My parents drank most weekends but not usually during the week. Thus for five days a week my mother took care of the family, cooking breakfast and dinner. I recall these as hot, nutritious, well-balanced, tasty meals. On weekends, beginning when I was quite young, I would look around the house for food. Later, as I watched her cook, I observed the skills I would try on the weekends. For example, I learned that adding baking soda to eggs resulted in beautifully fluffy scrambled eggs. Even now, I use her recipe for making yeast rolls.

I was a quick learner. From observing my parents, I knew how to light a lantern when a storm caused a loss of electricity. When I wanted something cold to drink, I made iced coffee and learned that mayonnaise sandwiches were filling. Often, on the weekends, I would prepare healthful meals, including a nourishing mixture of milk and raw eggs, the morning-after remedy to help my stepfather absorb the remaining alcohol and enhance his recovery. I think it was this schedule of taking over things on the weekend that later allowed me to go off to college but return home each weekend. Because I had no siblings or childhood friends close by, I spent a lot of time observing my parents' behavior and guessing at what was normal.

As a child, I was upset, frustrated, and frightened just thinking about weekends because I took care of not only myself but also my parents. Weekends were when my parents frequented the local beer joints, drank too much, and often began to fight—each other and drinking buddies. I have seen my father hit my mother with the back of his fist. As her teeth seemed to fly everywhere, I wondered, sometimes silently sometimes screaming, why she would not at least try to act right. In his relationship with my mother, my stepfather was possessive, jealous, and abusive. I recall that sometimes riding back from outings, he would hit my mother for having spoken to a man. Blood might fly everywhere, and often Mother had a black eye or swollen mouth the next day. When I screamed and yelled, demanding that he stop, my mother told me to be quiet. This was frustrating, of course, although I am not sure I felt it at the time. However, I did wonder why Mother refused to let me protect her. I thought only about the effect of my mother's behavior on the outcomes—if she did not drink, then there would be no fights—not realizing the importance of their interaction. On weekends I tried to keep them from drinking and helped after they drank too much. My weekend vigilance robbed me of sleep. Inevitably, I was physically and emotionally tired by Monday. It was almost as if my mother took care of me during the week so that I could care for her and my stepfather over the weekend. In general, I recall being a good child who did what I was told. In my entire life, I received only two spankings. Throughout my life, quiet and peace were my goals. When my parents fell asleep after drinking, I sometimes turned all the lights off, put the television on the floor, and covered it with a blanket. In the quiet dark I could watch the television. From the outside, their friends would think no one was home. I was afraid that if the friends saw lights, they would come, wake up my parents, and resume drinking. Even at a young age, in addition to the household responsibilities I assumed, I had to conduct myself in a mature manner and to be extremely responsible as though an adult. I felt a need to protect my parents, and I always thought that if something awful happened to my parents or the house, it would be my fault.

Moreover, I knew that I must keep secrets. No one else could know what was occurring in our home because my parents taught me that what went on inside the home and within the family was to remain there. Therefore, the few times I was left in the care of someone else for any period, I had to hide my tears of worry for my parents. I worried about what my parents would do without me to provide for them, but I couldn't explain my behavior to anyone else.

On the rare occasions when I visited and spent the night with the children of my parents' drinking partners, I cried because I never knew how things would be when I returned home. I think I cried whenever I parted from my parents, usually for the same reason: fear of what they would do to themselves, the house, and their friends in my absence. For quite some time I thought my parents' and their drinking partners' behavior was normal because I did not know families who lived differently. Furthermore, the stress from caregiving and separation from my parents caused me to be a regular bed wetter until age twelve and to have the first of many anxiety attacks. Neither my parents nor I gave any significant attention to these childhood behaviors. My parents simply called me a nervous child. Many who observed this behavior thought that I was a child who could not tolerate separating from my parents.

Later, my summer visits with my aunt, who lived a couple of hours north, provided a brief glimpse into normality. My aunt cared for me as she did her own children, and I was not responsible for any adult. My aunt questioned me about how things were at home. She seemed to understand my situation and inquired, "What have they [my parents] done now?" Knowing that I would not permanently leave my parents to live with her, she often advised me, "Just try to make it."

Although I took care of my parents and handled many of the adult responsibilities in the family, our roles sometimes were confusing to me. For example, I arranged to attend a church in my community, which became a significant, positive influence in my life. In addition to providing a social outlet and increasing my recitation skills, the church provided spiritual support and an opportunity to release pain and feelings. I was always grateful when various neighbors or distant relatives picked me up to go to church. My parents, though, attended only funerals and did not take me to church activities. In church, the moving choir selections and the stirring preaching helped me to forget about worldly concerns. Just as they had done during slavery (Hines and Boyd-Franklin 1996), the highly emotional services provided an escape and outlets for expressing my pain, humiliation, and anger. For a few hours, I had peace and camaraderie with others who shared my views about a supreme being and about the need to be a good and giving person and believed that we would be rewarded for our good behavior. Sometimes, after church, especially in the summer, there were wonderful dinners on the church lawn where we had fun in addition to continued fellowship. Despite the positive impact the church began to have in my life, my mother was livid when I decided to become a member of the church. She reprimanded me and said that I should not have joined church without consulting her and having her present with me. This was confusing to me because my mother did not attend church except to attend funerals. Because I was the one who was taking care of her, why should I seek permission?

Caregiving in Middle School and High School

My caregiving responsibilities increased as I grew older. When I was twelve years old and in the sixth grade, my grandfather suffered a stroke, which severely limited his mobility and eventually led to his confinement to a wheelchair. He continued to visit us every summer, giving his wife a much-needed break from taking care of him. I quickly learned how to provide his personal care when my mother wasn't available to do so. I shaved him, shampooed his hair, and washed all parts of his body except his private areas. Furthermore, I prepared nourishing meals and dispensed medication when needed. In school, I progressed to the best of my ability while continuing to take care of my grandfather and parents, especially during the weekends and summer vacations.

At church and school, I interacted with my peers but did not develop any enduring or deep friendships. I thought that friends would want to visit me, and I did not want anyone to know about my home life. Church gave me time to interact with others as I sang in the choir and participated in other activities. The church members saw me as a sweet little girl who never did anything bad. Although I seldom got into trouble, I did not think of myself as sweet and wondered what the church folks would think if they really knew my family and me. Many times, I felt like an impostor, a feeling that has remained with me. I had few outlets for my real emotions. By middle school I knew that my life was different from my peers'. They were not parenting their parents. They had parents to protect and care for them, whereas I often felt as if I had no one. By high school I interacted more, attending dances and sports events. Nevertheless, during most of my time living at home my social life was limited. I was busy caring for my family. During the week, I dreaded the upcoming weekend, fearing that they would drink and begin fighting one another or one of their drinking pals. I formed a close relationship only with Paul, my future husband, and his family. They unconditionally accepted me.

When I became a teenager, my caregiving experience took new forms, requiring even more from me and causing me greater pain. The year I graduated from junior high school, my stepfather, in an intoxicated state, had a severe vehicle accident a mile from our house. It was by the grace of God that my mother and I were not in the vehicle. He sustained multiple internal injuries, and he was admitted to the same hospital in which he died thirty-two years later. For a short time, my mother and I resided in the city where the hospital was located in order to be close to him. We moved from one extended family member's house to another while there. After I was out of school for the maximum number of days before I would fail a grade in school, my mother sent me back to our hometown to return to school. I lived with my stepfather's relatives until he returned from the hospital. Mother and I helped him to regain his strength and heal from his accident.

When I was sixteen, my mother was sent to a sanatorium for treatment of tuberculosis. I wasn't sure that I would survive her confinement. At least every other weekend, my stepfather and I drove three hours to visit her. At home, I took care of my stepfather, attended school, held a part-time job, and tried to withstand the taunting and teasing from people who did not know and could not know what had occurred in my home. I could not disclose the reason for my mother's absence because people who had tuberculosis and their family members were ostracized due to the stigma attached to having the disease. Without this knowledge, people in the community speculated about the reason my mother was not in the home. For example, some believed my stepfather and I were emotionally involved and that Mother left us when she learned. This was far from the truth and caused me additional hurt and stress.

One day during my mother's hospitalization, I found my stepfather scratching the paint off the walls in his bedroom as he tried to climb them. He had taken alcohol and prescription "nerve pills," and his body could not tolerate this lethal combination. The interaction was almost deadly for him, and he was hospitalized one a half hours away from our house. Therefore, while I was relieved for a month from cooking, cleaning, and ironing, I was left alone with no immediate family in the state where we resided. I had to find a place to stay at night after school. This was usually with my stepfather's brother's or sister's family. I also traveled one and a half hours to visit my stepfather. Together we would telephone my mother, who was still confined in the sanatorium. All this time, I had to hide from my mother the fact that my stepfather was a patient himself and that I was living alone. During their simultaneous hospitalizations, I felt inadequate, lost, and a bit guilty that I was not able to care for my parents.

As a child, I looked in the Sears catalogue and wished for things. Once I saw a tent and immediately thought it was perfect. From that day forward, the tent symbolized my dream house, a peaceful place in the yard where I would be away from my home. Interestingly, I visually pitched the tent in the yard, maybe so that I could still see and hear what was going on in my home. When the tent became a reality, I was not sure how to handle it. With both my parents hospitalized in separate facilities, my home was peaceful, serene, predictable, and clean. Initially, I enjoyed my peaceful tent. I was relieved that my parents were safe and had someone to care for them. My parents could not get into trouble. One might think I would have felt abandoned. I did not. To feel abandoned, one must first feel she had someone who loved and cared for her. I had no one to abandon me. In their absence, I cared for myself during the entire week instead of only on weekends.

Peace did not last long. Maybe my tasks and responsibilities actually took more of a toll than my usual routine when my parents were home. Determining which relative's home I would spend the night in, how I would get there and to school, and how I would get to visit my stepfather so we could telephone my mother and prevent her from knowing about his hospitalization probably took some new skills. I successfully accomplished these tasks and never thought of getting into trouble. However, I began to experience strange sensations. My heart beat so swiftly I thought it would run out of my chest, perspiration flowed profusely, a deep sense of dread reared its head, and my eyes wouldn't focus. As I think about it now, I wonder whether these symptoms somehow symbolized my conflict about expressing emotions. No one was there to hear my cries and screams and say, "Be quiet." Maybe unable to verbalize my feelings, my body acted them out and almost immediately became ill.

On one occasion after these physical symptoms occurred, I fell to the floor in my high school class and seemed to lose consciousness. The rescue squad transported me to the hospital, where they diagnosed me with seizures and prescribed antiseizure medication. Although neither parent accompanied me, the medical staff did not ask about my living situation or where my parents were. Nor did they address the possibility of emotional abuse. Racism, stereotypes about African American families, and lack of laws requiring investigation of child neglect probably contributed to the medical staff's lack of concern. I must have felt that professionals did not care about my plight. I had to wait until I completed college before doctors correctly diagnosed my symptoms as panic attacks and PTSD and prescribed the appropriate medication. Eventually, when both my parents were released from the hospital, I returned to my familiar duties of running the household and providing the support that helped my stepfather maintain his employment.

Caregiving in College

The expected relief of being away from home did not materialize. My weeks at school were similar. During the day, I attended classes; in the evenings, I sat at my dorm window, looked at other students scurrying around campus, and later did my homework. I constantly worried about what I would find when I returned home, and return I did, each weekend. Paul, my future husband, often brought me home on Fridays and back on Sundays. When he was not available, I secured a ride with someone else going in my direction.

Once when my mother needed money that I did not have, I became overwhelmed enough to confide in one of my social work professors. I vividly recall my sharing with her my family situation as she drove us around campus and the small college town, giving me time to vent. I cried endlessly, it seemed, as I wondered what I could do to help my mother. For the first time in my life, someone framed my usual interactions with my family as one of a number of ways I might respond. For example, the professor wondered aloud whether she or I could help my mother get a job, paving a way for her to provide income for herself. The consideration of options, even knowing that options existed, was new for me and started me thinking about alternatives. Nevertheless, my behavior remained the same, including weekend visits home to make sure all was well. One thing changed, however: I had a confidante, my professor, in addition to my aunt. The professor remained available to hear my concerns, offer support, and help me identify alternatives.

Caregiving in Adulthood

Over time, my parents drank less. I am not sure of all the reasons, but I can recall two events that resulted in reduced drinking. At some point when after I became an adult, my mother had my stepfather involuntarily committed to a private psychiatric hospital because of his drinking. I do not remember what led to her decision, but I ended up mediating between my mother and my stepfather's family, who were furious over my mother's actions. The second incident occurred about ten years after I married. After several occasions on which Paul and I took our daughters to see my parents, only to find them drunk, I told my parents they could not see the children unless they were sober. Thereafter, we called first and visited only when they were sober. Not seeing the children became an incentive for them to remain sober, at least on the days they expected us to visit.

Near the time of his retirement, my stepfather was still a very cautious drinker. As with other work-related festivities, he did not include my mother and me in his retirement celebration at school. Therefore I planned a surprise retirement party for him at my home. It was ironic that this was the first time his colleagues met my mother, my family, and me. Because I thought the surprise might be too much, I told him the day before the party about the party plans and that I had invited many of his colleagues. He told me he would not come, but he reluctantly came. I witnessed the surprise on many of his colleagues' faces when they realized he had a stepdaughter and that she had achieved much academically, financially, and professionally. Though not planned that way, the retirement party was much like the birthday party that famous therapist Murray Bowen describes (Anonymous 1972). Like the party for Bowen's aunt, the event dislodged family secrets, although that was not the original goal. My stepfather was the only father figure I had for much of my life, and I genuinely cared about him. The occasion of his retirement was an opportunity for me to show it.

As drinking became less of a problem, my stepfather's health began to decline. The result was that I faced additional caregiving tasks at a time when I was already overcommitted trying to balance family, professional, and educational responsibilities. While I was working on my doctorate, my stepfather learned that an earlier malignancy had flared up. He decided, without discussion with any family member, on a course of treatment that was available in another city, about an hour and a half away. When he told me about his illness, he praised me for the first time ever, saying that he was proud of my educational accomplishments. He told me that I had gone above and beyond his expectations for me and that I should always remember how proud he was of my accomplishments. Finally, he stated that he was not telling me this because of his illness; he just wanted me to know. Because neither of my parents had ever acknowledged any of my achievements, I was very pleased with my stepfather's affirmation. His acknowledgment was also significant because I felt it showed he had finally accepted me. However, this one positive interaction was the last time I had an intimate conversation with him. During the three months he received outpatient chemotherapy and radiation, my parents lived in housing for out-of-town patients. My family and I helped my parents with transportation and grocery shopping, even though they lived an hour and a half away, in the city where the medical center was. This type of long-distance caregiving can be very difficult for the family, causing both emotional stress and physical and financial strains associated with travel (Koerin and Harrigan 2002; Wagner 1997). Things got worse a few months later, however, and my stepfather was moved to the intensive care unit (ICU) of the same veteran's hospital where he had been confined twice before in his life. For the first five days of his confinement in the ICU, my mother and I slept on the sofas in the waiting room just a few feet away from him. He was unconscious during this time, but finally I was able to tell him that I loved him. I felt that it was impossible to leave him or my mother because of my continued perceived responsibility to care for them. Therefore, my husband and children had to live without me and meet their own needs, which they did.

Fortunately, these events occurred during the summer when I had no classroom teaching responsibilities, but I continued my administrative and supervisory duties for social work interns. Finally, when the fall term began, I knew I had to return to work and family. I devised methods to communicate with medical staff, arranged for support systems for my mother, and managed things by phone. From the time I returned to work after my stepfather's admittance to the ICU until his death, I did not discuss my personal life with any of my colleagues. Although I perceived that I had supported them emotionally over the years, I didn't know whether they would reciprocate. However, I am not sure that I encouraged reciprocity because I hid behind my work and did not freely discuss my situation with anyone. Therefore, they did not know what my needs were. I separated myself from them and generally left my office only to teach my classes. I felt that I did not need to burden others with my problems. Although I was a part of a human service program that constantly encouraged our students to self-evaluate and to confront and share various problems, I felt that no one could understand what I was experiencing. I thought I was protecting my emotional status by leaving my problems outside the university door and proving to myself that I was a master teacher. Despite my failures to confide in my teaching colleagues or administrators, however, they seemed to respect me professionally and voted to give me tenure and promotion. This was a wonderful source of validation for me.

As my stepfather's hospitalization continued, I began to suffer physical and emotional ailments that prevented me from traveling to see him on a daily basis. As a diabetic, I suffered a hemorrhage in one of my eyes, resulting in its blindness for several months. The retinal specialist suggested that stress could have played a part in the hemorrhage. In addition, my primary care physician prescribed additional medication to address the anxiety and depression I suffered. Scholars have found that caregivers experiencing physical health problems were more likely to become emotionally distressed while performing caregiving duties (Chang and Horrocks 2006; Dilworth-Anderson et al. 2002, 2004). Knowing that my stepfather would not recover, I dealt with my anxiety by starting to make long-range plans for my mother's care, while she, characteristically, denied the seriousness of his illness and lashed out at me for being so fatalistic.

My stepfather died after several months of treatment and hospitalization. In consultation with my mother, I planned the funeral. His family demonstrated their characteristic feelings and behaviors toward me even on this sad occasion. Immediately after the services, his only surviving sibling, a sister, said to me, "Why are you doing this alone? He has people." This meant she did not view me as one of his family. I stayed in Mother's home for a week immediately after my stepfather's death. Within a month, I arranged to move Mother into our home. I thought that this was the only way I could survive without constantly worrying about her well-being and splitting my time between her house and ours.

Four years after my stepfather's death, my mother continues to live with my family and to be a source of stress for us. She is physically and emotionally needy but rarely listens to suggestions that might improve her situation. She does not leave the house often and has few interactions with people other than my husband, our children, and me. She was especially upset when my mother-in-law came to live with us for several months when other family members could not care for her. My mother resented having another person in the house and made life very difficult for everyone. She acted differently in front of my husband, but when no one else could hear, she badgered me about my mother-in-law residing with us. In addition, she told the few people with whom she interacted that we were using her to care for my mother-in-law. When we hired people to care for my mother-in-law, my mother had only negatives to say about the two people, and she actually ran one away from the house and was verbally abusive, screaming at the second one. Having two mothers in our home meant that my husband and I had little privacy and little time for each other. Someone always needed us to do something. We had to continue to do the best we could despite the stresses. We cared for my mother-in-law until she was no longer mobile and then placed her in a facility where she could receive around-the-clock care. Thereafter, we visited her daily, and our daughters took turns visiting the nursing home to feed her at least once a day. Three months after the death of my mother-in-law, my husband awoke one morning with stomach pains, and by the end of the day he had a major portion of his intestines removed. He was diagnosed with a rare form of cancer. We do not know what will occur in the future, but I anticipate that my daughters and I will become his caregivers in the years to come.

Positive Role Model

Through all these years of caregiving, my maternal aunt has been the major role model and the person who helped me to gain sufficient strength to overcome obstacles and become successful. She and her husband had two children, one of whom was close to me in age. My aunt, a high school graduate, spent a career with the federal government. Despite working full time and caring for her family, she always helped her extended family when needed and when she had the ability. In caring for her family, she insisted on good grooming, well-balanced meals, and a clean and organized house. She demanded quality in everything that affected her family, whether it was in their behavior, educational endeavors, or purchasing practices. She served as my role model and treated me as an equal to her children and the rest of the world. I learned from her about the primacy of family and how to fulfill multiple roles. As an adult, I recognize that I have patterned many of my behaviors after hers. Although she is now more than seventy years old, she continues to assist me and to serve as a role model. If I have problems, I make a telephone call to her even today.

ANALYSES

I know that my lifelong pattern of taking care of others has figured into the manner in which I have conducted my life, including my choice of social work as a career. What I haven't always understood is that other people had similar experiences or that there were intellectual frameworks for making sense of them. Through many years of therapy and doctoral study, however, I have learned to name these experiences and to find a larger framework within which to place my narrative. However, I couldn't have known that intellectual world when I was living through my own personal nightmare. Sometimes naming something helps one to embrace it. In this section I provide a brief summary of the concepts from the professional literature that I found to be especially helpful. My discussion includes definitions of caregiving, rewards and perils of caregiving, cultural and gender differences in caregiving, issues specific to the experiences of child caregivers, behaviors of adult children of alcoholics, somatic and emotional expressions of depression, and social work as a career choice for caregivers. In addition, I explain why I reject the pathology and deficit models for understanding African American families in favor of the more positive ones such as the strengths, systems, and ecological models. Because the concepts and numbers found in quantitative research do not always capture the essence of an experience, I instead rely on portions of my personal narrative in the discussion where they appear to be relevant.

One definition of caregiver is "one who provides for the physical, emotional, and social needs of another person, who often is dependent and cannot provide for his or her own needs" (Barker 1999:61). Furthermore, caregivers are sometimes called trained adults, whether lay or professional. These definitions are not appropriate for my early caregiving of my parents. In some ways, my parents could provide for themselves and me; they succeeded with my physical care five days each week. On the weekends, however, they turned to alcohol, and I became the caregiver. During my childhood, my active caregiving was part time, on the weekends. The definition that appears appropriate in this narrative is "informal care [giving] is help provided by a non paid person" (Bullock et al. 2003:155). Levine (2003–2004) reports that family caregivers are expanding in categories. They can be people of all ages, from teenagers and young adults to middle-aged or older adults. The culture, and its attendant norms, helps to shape who gives informal care and determines whether families use formal support and intervention (Dilworth-Anderson and Gibson 1999). Traditionally, African Americans have used less formal caregiving support. "African Americans have a legacy of reinforcement in providing for their family members through natural support. Certain exchange networks exist when there are social rewards such as belonging, self worth, dignity, and validation of family traditions" (Bullock et al. 2003:155). I became a caregiver because I felt there was no alternative. African American traditions such as refraining from discussing family business with outsiders supported my actions. The view that many African Americans have of "we care for our own" underlay many of my caregiving choices. The fact that I was an only child and had no extended family in close proximity meant that, except for medical care, I have been a sole caregiver to my parents.

Being female has meant that people expected me to be the primary caregiver, just as I was with my mother-in-law. Although my lifetime caregiving has caused anxiety because of the need to balance so many roles, it also provided feelings of achievement and belonging. On some level, I suppose that caring for my parents has provided vicarious satisfaction. In caring for others, I provide the care I need myself. Although the number of men in caregiving roles is increasing (Chesler and Parry 2001), the primary caregivers of chronically ill family members are women, especially adult daughters (McInnis-Dittrich 2002). Often adult daughters, the most frequent providers of parental caregiving, have sympathy for their parents' losses and are eager to do anything to help (Cunningham 1994). Greater numbers of women are entering the workforce despite the need for additional informal caregiving. Many women, especially women of color, work outside the home full time and have other major household responsibilities (Conway-Giustra et al. 2002). Caregiving caused me anxiety but also provided feelings of achievement and belonging.

Gratification can be one of the rewards of serving in various roles. One study indicates that a mutual sense of obligation and responsibility provides the impetus for caregiving. Most of the participants in this study said caregiving provided a mutual interchange of different resources. However, it is possible that the caregiver receives nothing in return (Tarlow 1996). In many instances, especially when I was small and sometimes currently, I think my relationship with my parents was not reciprocal. At these times, my view is that I received nothing in return. Additional consideration suggested that my early caregiving helped to ensure I would continue to have the physical presence of my parents. Their presence, usually providing little or no emotional support and guidance, was better and more predictable than the unknown. Perseverance in caregiving often relates to the meaning the family member ascribes to caregiving. Many family members continue in the caregiving role because they feel a moral responsibility and want to repay past kindnesses (Noonan 1996; Noonan et al. 1996).

A spiritual gift of caregiving is the meaning it provides to life. Furthermore, "the value of transcending self, or sacrificing for another, is at the center of much religious tradition" (Doka 2003–2004:46). My caregiving has related more to the religious admonition to honor and care for parents. My religious teaching requires that I help others and indicates that my major rewards may wait until I reach Heaven. After reading the popular best-seller *The Purpose-Driven Life* (Warren 2002), I concluded that caregiving is an important purpose in my life for which God has ordained me. The many blessings I have already received are my earthly rewards. Throughout my life spirituality, religion, and my church family have provided comfort, strength, and support for my caregiving roles.

Even though I am now able to make sense of my early caregiving experience in a way that is positive and meaningful, it is important to understand the ways in which being a child caregiver can pose an emotional and developmental risk (Hunt et al. 2005). Although not all children who provide care for family members experience negative consequences, child caregivers are more likely to experience depression in adulthood (Shifren and Kachorek 2003). Child caregivers are also more likely to experience anxiety, feel as if no one loves them, or feel as if they are worthless and inferior at least some of the time (Hunt et al. 2005). These negative feelings, particularly depression, tend to be more likely to occur when the child caregiver and the care recipient live in the same household. I experienced each of these symptoms at some point throughout my caregiving experience, and I continue to struggle with anxiety today. Scholars report that children in households of people of color are particularly at risk for developing depression and anxiety, and they are less likely to feel as if it is worthwhile to share negative feelings with others (Hunt et al. 2005). Therefore, children in these households are more likely to need emotional support but less likely to seek it or demonstrate a need for it. If service providers are aware of this information, they can develop assessments and interventions that are culturally sensitive.

Although many child caregivers share common experiences, caring for a parent who abuses drugs or alcohol can amplify or present additional challenges. One of the profound characteristics of adult children of alcoholics (ACOAs) is that they have to guess at what is normal (Woititz 1983:24). Although some ACOA families are dysfunctional, some are not. Although I would not label my nuclear family dysfunctional, I clearly saw some deleterious effects that caring for my parents had. Because of caring for my parents, I was less available to my husband and children. Currently, my children visit less often because of my mother's attitude toward them and problematic interactions with me. When they were young, I had to protect my children from my parents. For example, at one point I told my parents that my family would have to curtail our usual Sunday afternoon visits until they stopped drinking. They responded by postponing drinking until after our visits. Paul and I could not allow my daughters to see my mother and stepfather drunk.

In a study of college students, the results indicate not only that "parental alcoholism contribute[s] significantly to stress but that adult children of alcoholics are a unique population regarding their likelihood of having grown up in a dysfunctional family" (Fischer et al. 2000:154). Some children of alcoholics find it difficult to share their feelings, needs, and concerns with others. As described earlier, I have some of the classic symptoms—difficulty in expressing needs and feelings and in trusting others—of an ACOA.

Some adult children of alcoholics choose to go into social work or other helping professions. This does not appear to be an unusual decision. One study examined six social workers who are ACOAs (Coombes and Anderson 2000).

Whether they had one or both alcoholic parents, the social workers had cared for the physical and emotional needs of their parents. In addition, they described themselves as possessing characteristics germane to experienced helpers. For example, they reported empathy, courage, and perseverance. This study also found evidence of the social workers "often pushing themselves to the limit but they were able to utilize strategies to modify and balance the stress caused by this behavior" (Coombes and Anderson 2000:296). I certainly display empathy, courage and perseverance. The latter two allowed me to complete my doctoral studies and reapply for the academic position I already held. All have helped me to juggle multiple roles.

Research and projections indicate that it is likely that a professional social worker will serve in a family caregiver role because of the dramatic increase the number of people sixty-five years of age and older (McInnis-Dittrich 2002). "The aging of the population will exacerbate an existing crisis of informal caregiving in the United States" (Conway-Giustra et al. 2002:307). It is expected that the cohorts of baby boomers will be caregivers through their retirement age (Cunningham 1994). I hope the candid discussion of my experiences will help them and other family caregivers. Caregiving for elderly relatives should be a shared experience, especially among siblings, because it can be overwhelming for one caregiver.

For those without siblings, formal and informal systems can provide support. Too often caregivers are unable to use support systems because of the demands of caregiving; this can lead to self-care of the caregiver being compromised (McInnis-Dittrich 2002). Locating the necessary formal supports and overcoming barriers to using them often are a challenge. It took years for me to find an understanding, comprehensive primary care physician. Many times, the closest treatment facility for me and other member of the family was in a city an hour and a half away; the round-trip travel time was three hours, a hefty chunk of time. This distance barrier was daunting. For example, when I could not drive for several months, Paul or a daughter had to take me to my follow-up appointments with my eye surgeon. My husband's and much of my stepfather and mother's healthcare was also in that city. Because of my work schedule, it was often difficult to coordinate my schedule with the medial providers. Fortunately, more recently, some providers have added Saturday appointments. It has been impossible for me to secure stable counseling services. Again, distance was a barrier. Insurance company changes in provider coverage have meant several abrupt terminations of helpful counseling relationships. Locating new medical providers because of changes in insurance coverage is a wearisome process.

Caregivers may suffer from depression, which results from the their sense of burden, social isolation, and self-blame that they are not doing all they could be for the care receiver, combined with physical and emotional exhaustion (McInnis-Dittrich 2002:317). Caregivers of color are more likely to express depression somatically than emotionally by developing health problems not seen as directly related to the demands of caregiving (Cox 1995). This finding may help to describe the panic attacks I experience. The literature on long-distance caregiving suggests that it is more difficult than contemporaneous caregiving (Koerin and Harrigan 2002; Longo 1995) and is similar to case management services (Franklin 2000). According to Franklin (2000), the caregiver often isolates herself.

In reviewing my past and current caregiving experiences, I believe that there is a relationship between the hardships of growing up in an alcoholic household, my caregiving experiences, my professional training as a social worker, and my educational experiences. The theoretical concept of resilience helps to explain these relationships. With help from God, my church family, my aunt, and my counselors, I was able to move through the developmental stages of my life and soar over the barriers placed before me. The result was my ability to serve in diverse roles, including successfully running for political offices. I was more of a parent to my parents than a daughter to them, but there were times when they attempted to place me in my proper child role. In addition, for a portion of my childhood I was a student, an occasional friend, or an employee while providing care to my parents and grandfather. I learned to successfully multitask at an early age. I am quite organized and some say meticulous. Only with organization can I carry out my various roles.

The caregiving experiences I had as a child had an impact on my life both physically and socially. For example, I was a bed wetter until the age of twelve. In addition, I was very emotional, had an extreme attachment to my parents, and worried about them when we were apart. Socially and emotionally, I was not able to interact with my peers and therefore did not form lasting and significant relationships. I was able to talk to only one family member, my aunt, in whom I continue to confide. Although I am socially active at work, at church, and in social organizations such as the Alpha Kappa Alpha sorority, I continue to isolate myself. Developing close friendship takes time and trust, and I continue to have little of either. Fighting recurring depression and physical problems, such as diabetes and chronic back pain, takes energy as well. Some of the methods, such as daily walks with Paul, to cope with my illnesses also take effort and time but are effective. "Resilience implies that potential subjects are able to negotiate significant challenges to development yet consistently 'snap back' in order to complete the important developmental tasks that confront them as they grow" (Driscoll 1994:1). In addition, resilience can be seen as one's ability to revise and adapt one's coping strategies and competencies (Coombes and Anderson 2000). In their small study of ACOAs, Coombes and Anderson found that participants changed their coping skills as they aged. During the early stages of development, escaping cognitively and emotionally helped the participants move through the developmental stages. As I read, I felt that I was a respondent in this study because I use some of the same words to identify my childhood feelings, such as "shame, embarrassment, guilt, confusion, or helplessness" (Coombes and Anderson 2000:291).

Furthermore, even after stressful and neglectful lives, resilience is possible and probable. In college, I entered counseling and have continued, though sporadically, to this day. Using resilience models, each counselor successfully helped me address several issues. It is wonderful to now feel more worthy and have fewer symptoms of panic disorder. Because scholars often study African American families in the context of a deficit model as opposed to a strengths perspective, they often overlook resilience. Many times when researchers compare African American and European American families (Carter-Black 2001), they pay little attention to the impact of culture or gender on developmental stages of life (Devore and Schlesinger 1999) or resilience. In a review of studies examining family caregiving stressors, Pinquart and Sorensen (2006) found no comprehensive theory on ethnic differences in caregiving

Middle- and lower-class African American families use similar resilience strategies and child-rearing practices to promote the development of their children. Both groups use achievement-oriented trajectories as they socialize their children to become successful adults (Carter-Black 2001). For example, middle-class and lower-class African American families teach their children many of the same values and lessons. These include knowing when one has achieved success in contemporary America, the importance of acquiring an education, selective exposure to activities and events, the importance of the family and kinship, responsibility and respect for self and others, importance of religion, protection of children, racial socialization, and gender-specific socialization. Although they share similar strategies and goals, it is logical to think that lower-class families spend a significant amount of time simply trying to provide for the basic needs of their children. The primary difference between class groups is that middle-class families have richer resources than lower-class families (Carter-Black 2001). Although they were alcoholics, my parents emphasized my need to achieve. As mentioned, my mother was ingenious in locating funds for my college education. My aunt had high standards for me and supported my reaching goals. In addition to ongoing support and motivation, she gave me an expensive piece of jewelry to celebrate each degree.

The ecological model of human behavior emphasizes that people are in constant interaction with their physical and social environments and that they develop and adapt through these transactions (Zastrow 2004). The model also guides intervention by identifying dysfunctional transactions (Zastrow 2004). My interaction with diverse systems was limited. I interacted primarily with my family and educational, religious, health, and mental health systems. I received minimal support from the traditional educational system and less support than was available from the religious system because I did not discuss my home life with others. As previously mentioned, my college experience was life changing. It was the first time I discussed my family with an outsider, my professor. Our relationship helped me to begin to understand that I had options in several interactions with my parents and others.

IMPLICATIONS

Although my caregiving experiences are unique—they occurred across my life span and were coupled with other social problems—they can be beneficial to those interested in caregiving. Primarily, we need to reevaluate the commonly held view that child abuse and neglect inevitably leads to pathological behaviors. A more helpful perspective is to see problematic behavior as a necessary and normal response to a pathological situation. Intervention concentrates on helping the person identify normal situations and develop appropriate behaviors. Use of a strengths perspective rather than a medical model is more helpful in explaining and changing behaviors. In this way, we can concentrate on the positives and not the shortcomings and dysfunctions of individuals and groups (Zastrow 2004). Relatives, professionals, and my own recognition and identification of my strengths and my efforts to build on them have contributed to my healing and to my successes.

Second, professionals should view the informal caregiver and the care receiver as systems in an environment that includes multiple systems. Understanding the relationship and transactions between the individual and his or her environment is a necessary precursor to identifying where support systems are functioning or what systems are available or absent. The ecomap is a helpful tool for describing these situations. It can graphically delineate the systems in the environments of the caregiver and care receiver, helpful systems that are missing from the environments, the relationship between the caregiver and care receiver, the types of interactions between the individuals and the environmental systems, and the transactions between the systems in the environment. The ecomap can help the practitioner order an often overwhelming amount of data, including biological, physical, psychological, social, and spiritual variables, about the client in his or her life space.

For example, during my childhood I was plagued with many physical health problems, probably related to stressors in my life. If a healthcare provider had inquired about my family interactions and completed an ecomap, she would have noticed the absence of many healthy systems in my and my family's environment. In addition, she would have seen that most of the interactions between my parents and their environments were with alcohol and medical-related systems. Currently, medical providers have an ethical duty to report instances of child abuse and neglect. However, child abuse and neglect laws and the healthcare system do not specifically address child caregiving and may be insufficient to reveal detrimental child caregiving situations. Other countries, such as England, Australia, and New Zealand, have made more progress in recognizing and supporting child caregivers and in developing effective family interventions that protect their emotional and physical needs (Hunt et al. 2005). Ongoing support from professional organizations, healthcare providers, and researchers can help ensure the enactment of similar beneficial plans in the United States.

Third, research and policy must give more attention to explicating cultural, gender, and workplace influences on informal caregiving. For example, specific cultures, especially the African American culture, emphasize that caregiving to elderly relatives is a responsibility and an expectation. In addition, many women, especially African Americans, work outside the home to supplement or provide the entire household income. For instance, policymakers must revisit and support the provision of adequate financial support and respite care for family caregivers. Fourth, communities need to invest in enhancing current resources and in identifying and developing additional resources and nontraditional programs, including intergenerational day care and collaboration between public and private institutions such as the church. The church continues to be a strong institution for the African American communities and thus provides accessibility, but churches may not be able to afford to operate diverse programs.

Last, it is imperative that professionals incorporate culturally specific questions in assessment to uncover hidden problems such as alcohol and drug abuse. During my formative years, forty or so years ago, I had little knowledge about alcoholism or drug abuse; however, if asked about weekend activities, I would have divulged some interesting information. With 1.3 to 1.4 million children currently providing some level of care to older family members, child caregivers deserve professional recognition and support (Hunt et al. 2005). See table 2.1 for a summary of these implications.

Table 2.1 Implications

	Issues and Problems	Strategies for Change
Individuals	Some cultures are more willing to provide caregiving to their elderly family members.	Must learn how to overcome obstacles and take care of self. Must identify or develop resources and use them.
Families	Families should be aware of the transactions and systems involved in the caregiver experience.	Must be willing to support the caregiver socially, physically, and emotionally.
Communities	Communities should be aware of the diversity in culture, ethnicity, and minority status.	Must be willing to explore creative resources and develop support services.
Practitioners	Caregiving needs will increase throughout the 21st century.	Increase level of sensitivity to issues pertaining to caregiver needs.
Social work educators	Knowledge of informal caregiving in the context of diversity must be imparted.	Disseminate information about older adults and caregiving.
Researchers	Negative experiences can lead to positive outcomes through the process of resilience.	Encourage scholars to conduct research in this area using both qualitative and quantitative methods. Replicate some of the current studies.

REFLECTIONS AND CONCLUSIONS

In looking back over my own experiences of giving and receiving care over a period of fifty years, I believe that I have been a good daughter, granddaughter, wife, mother, social worker, and teacher. Although I believe that I was cheated out of my own childhood, I worked very hard to provide a safe and nurturing childhood environment for my two daughters. At times, in fact, I tried to do too much for them instead of empowering them to do for themselves. Over the years, my therapist has helped me focus on how special a person I was to have come away from my childhood with scars, but scars that did not keep me from accomplishing some of my life's goals. Many of my positive attributes were not always apparent to me, or at least I did not give them a lot of thought. For example, I have the ability to multitask, and I learned that many people do not possess that skill. I also have known how to think and process information as an adult for a very long time, because I had to make major decisions and take care of business transactions throughout my life. As a result, I find that I have to be careful not to do too much for other people or to get impatient in responding to young people who have had limited life experiences.

Compiling my personal narrative has been a painful but therapeutic project for me. Part of my healing has been in knowing that my narrative could take on more meaning when connected to the larger world of ideas in the professional literature of social work and caregiving. I began this journey by writing my experiences as they related to caregiving across my life span. I found that I could relate to some of the literature pertaining to African American families, caregiving, and ACOAs. However, it was not until I reviewed the literature on resilience that I became overwhelmed with how significant and relevant the information was to my life and to my experiences. I gained a certain validation that indicates to me that my life is worth living and that there is a purpose to my life. It is obvious that I am where I am today because I had many negative experiences, which I turned into positive outcomes. I believe that I am living evidence that some abused and neglected children can be positive contributors to society. I have explored both qualitative and quantitative approaches in my search to understand more about caregiving. Although much information was available to me in the professional literature, I felt that caregiving was a topic that needed a narrative. In constructing my narrative, I have been able to come to terms with my beliefs and behaviors. By adding the perspectives of my professional self, I have helped my personal self to grow.

> And then the day came when the risk to remain tight in a bud was more painful than the risk it took to blossom.
>
> —Anaïs Nin

It is only now that I reflect and realize that I was and am resilient. The more I consider that I survived, and in some ways thrived, the more I am empowered to accept challenges in my life. I was, and still am, an active church member. Even now, it is difficult for me to decline when asked to do some tasks. Therefore, I hold several offices in the church that take much time. I have been active in the larger community as well and was the first woman to be appointed and elected to the Board of Supervisors for the county in which I live. Additionally, I served as a member of a local mental health board, a board member of a community theater organization, and chair of the County Department of Social Services Board. I have also received several awards recognizing my work and community contributions, including multiple awards for distinguished and meritorious service to the sorority to which I belong and the Woman of the Year Award from my town's Business and Professional Woman's Club.

My current position as a college professor is one for which I have worked hard. I spend a great deal of time at the office, sometimes, I think, to keep from going home. It is easier to be in a space in which one has been successful than to share a home with a mother whose actions often result in frustration and anger. Although I always wanted to share my perceptions of my childhood and its attendant feelings with my parents, they were never mature enough for such a discussion. When I discuss other topics with my mother, like many alcoholics she has the uncanny ability to turn it around and say it is my fault. I bring up my parents here because I think my experiences with them have influenced my actions in my current position. Being a caregiver as a child destined me to be a leader at the university and in other places. I doubt it was only luck that made me the director of my department. My inability to demonstrate my feelings as a child has carried over to the work environment as well. Like a child, I am often silent until I cannot take more. Then, instead of screaming as I did as a child, I decide the best way to handle the situation and then act. Sometimes my actions include returning to my childhood tent, that is, removing myself from the situation.

Recently, for example, I finally spoke up about a work problem. After requesting and not receiving needed support for several months, I was angry and frustrated. I felt used; the more I did, the more the administration expected from me and the less support I received. I met with the dean and said, "I cannot effectively complete my teaching and administrative tasks without sufficient clerical help. I am going home and will be back to work when there is the needed support in place so that I can perform the job you hired me to do. And by the way, I know how to file bankruptcy." This latter comment indicated that I had no worries about the loss of my salary should she fire me. I went home, turned on the television in my bedroom, and calmly watched Oprah. In a few days, the administration hired a secretary, and back to the office I happily went.

When a friend questioned how I could take such appropriate, effective, and self-supportive measures at school and not with my mother, I said that work was the place I received my gratifications and rewards; there, I was respected for my time commitment, my products, and the person I have become. I was not going to let the university jeopardize what I do well.

Over the age of fifty, I cannot go back and get what I have lost in the relationship with my mother. I do not see confrontations with my mother or moving her out of my home as options. As adults, my daughters have visited my home less often because they hated to see how Mother interacted with me. They suggested I move her out. Paul thinks I should overlook my mother's demanding and problematic behavior, especially because he benefits from her presence. With Paul, as with my stepfather, Mother caters to him, asking whether he is hungry or thirsty or has other needs and either meets those needs or screams for me to do so. Maybe I have been stuck in some interactions with my mother, but I refuse to be mired in other situations and relationships. The clerical situation at school, though tangential to my relationship with my mother, stirred many of the same feelings I had about my earlier family life. It may be that with additional age and wisdom, the length of the tangent will shorten and I will be able to choose to react more appropriately to my mother.

REFERENCES

Anonymous. 1972. Differentiation of self in one's family. In J. L. Framo (Ed.), *Family Interaction*. New York: Springer.

Banks-Wallace, J. 2000. Womanist ways of knowing: Theoretical considerations for research with African American women. *Advances in Nursing Science* 22: 33–45.

Barker, R. L. 1999. *The Social Work Dictionary*. Washington, D.C.: National Association of Social Workers.

Brewer, R. 1993. Theorizing race, class, and gender: The new scholarship of black feminist intellectuals and black women's labor. In S. James and A. Busia (Eds.), *Theorizing Black Feminisms: The Visionary Pragmatism of Black Women*, 13–30. New York: Routledge.

Bullock, K., Crawford, S., and Tennstedt, S. 2003. Employment and caregiving: Exploration of African American caregivers. *Social Work* 48 (2): 150–163.

Carter-Black, J. 2001. The myth of "the tangle of pathology": Resilience strategies employed by middle-class African American families. *Journal of Family Social Work* 39: 75–100.

Chang, K. H. and Horrocks, S. 2006. Lived experiences of family caregivers of mentally ill relatives. *Journal of Advanced Nursing* 53 (4): 435–443.

Chesler, M. A. and Parry, C. 2001. An integrative analysis of the experiences of fathers of offspring with cancer. *Qualitative Health Research* 11: 307–312, 363–384.

Collins, P. H. 1990. *Black Feminist Thought.* Boston: Unwin Hyman.

Conway-Giustra, F., Crowley, A., and Gorin, S. H. 2002. Crisis in caregiving: A call to action. *Health and Social Work* 27 (4): 307–312.

Coombes, K. and Anderson, R. 2000. The impact of family of origin on social workers from alcoholic families. *Clinical Social Work Journal* 28 (3): 281–302.

Cox, C. Meeting the mental health needs of the caregiver: The impact of Alzheimer's disease on Hispanic and African American families. In D. K. Padgett (Ed.), *Handbook on Ethnicity, Aging, and Mental Health,* 265–283. Westport, Conn.: Greenwood.

Cunningham, G. 1994. Caregivers: How do you find the strength to carry on? *U.S. Catholic* 59: 27–33.

Devore, W. and Schlesinger, E. 1999. *Ethnic Sensitive Social Work Practice,* 3d ed. Boston: Allyn & Bacon.

Dilworth-Anderson, P. and Gibson, B. E. 1999. Ethnic minority perspectives on dementia, family caregiving, and interventions. *Generations* 23 (3): 40–45.

Dilworth-Anderson, P., Goodwin, P. Y., and Williams, S. W. 2004. Can culture help explain the physical health effects of caregiving over time among African American caregivers? *The Journals of Gerontology Series B: Psychological Sciences and Social Sciences* 59: S138–S145.

Dilworth-Anderson, P., Williams, I., and Gibson, B. 2002. Issues of race, ethnicity, and culture in caregiving research: A 20-year review (1980–2000). *The Gerontologist* 42 (2): 237–272.

Doka, K. 2003–2004. The spiritual gifts and burdens of family caregiving. *Generations* 27 (4): 45–48.

Driscoll, E. H. 1994. *Alzheimer's: A Handbook for the Caregiver.* Boston: Branden Books.

Fischer, K., Kittleson, M., Ogletree, R., Welshimer, K., Woehlke, P., and Benshoff, J. 2000. The relationship of parental alcoholism and family dysfunction to stress among college students. *Journal of American College Health* 48 (4): 151–156.

Franklin, M. B. 2000. Caring across the miles. *Kiplinger's Personal Finance Magazine* 54 (11).

Gordon, S., Benner, P., and Noddings, N. (Eds.). 1996. *Caregiving: Readings in Knowledge, Practice, Ethics, and Politics.* Philadelphia: University of Pennsylvania Press.

Hill, R. 1972. *The Strengths of Black Families.* New York: Emerson Hall.

Hill, R. 1997. *The Strengths of Black Families: Twenty-five Years Later*, Rev. ed. Washington, D.C.: R & B Publishers.

Hill-Collins, P. 2000. Core themes in black feminist thought. In *Black Feminist Thought: Knowledge, Consciousness, and the Politics of Empowerment*, 2d ed., 45–201. New York: Routledge.

Hines, P. and Boyd-Franklin, N. 1996. African American families. In M. McGoldrick, J. Giordano, and J. Pearce (Eds.), *Ethnicity and Family Therapy*, 66–84. New York: Guilford.

hooks, b. 1993. *Sisters of the Yam: Black Women and Self-recovery.* Boston: South End Press.

hooks, b. 2000. *Feminist Theory: From Margin to Center.* Cambridge, Mass.: South End Press.

Hunt, G., Levine, C., and Naiditch, L. 2005. *Young Caregivers in the U.S.: Findings from a National Survey.* Bethesda, Md.: National Alliance for Caregiving & the United Hospital Fund.

Koerin, B. and Harrigan, M. 2002. P.S. I love you: Long-distance caregiving. *Journal of Gerontological Social Work* 40 (1/2): 63–81.

Levine, C. 2003–2004. Introduction: Family caregiving—Current challenges for a time-honored practice. *Generations (San Francisco, Calif.)* 27 (4): 5–8.

Longo, T. 1995. When distant parents need your help. *Kiplinger's Personal Finance Magazine* 49: 91–92.

McInnis-Dittrich, K. 2002. *Social Work with Elders: A Biopsychosocial Approach to Assessment and Intervention.* Boston: Allyn & Bacon.

Noonan, A. 1996. Meaning in caregiving for frail elders and caregiver well-being. *Dissertation Abstracts International* 57 (3B): 2180.

Noonan, A., Tennstedt, S., and Rebelsky, F. 1996. Making the best of it: Themes of meaning among informal caregivers to the elderly. *Journal of Aging Studies* 10 (4): 313.

Pinquart, M. and Sorensen, S. 2006. Ethnic differences in stressors, resources, and psychological outcomes of family caregiving: A meta-analysis. *The Gerontologist* 45 (1): 90–106.

Shifren, K. and Kachorek. L. V. 2003. Does early caregiving matter? The effects on young caregivers' adult mental health. *International Journal of Behavioral Development* 27 (4): 338–346.

Tarlow, B. 1996. Caring: A negotiated process that varies. In S. Gordon, P. E. Benner, and N. Noddings (Eds.), *Caregiving: Readings in Knowledge, Practice, Ethics, and Politics*, 56–82. Philadelphia: University of Pennsylvania Press.

Wagner, D. 1997. *Comparative Analysis of Caregiver Data for Caregivers to the Elderly.* Bethesda, Md.: National Alliance for Caregiving.

Warren, R. 2002. *The Purpose-Driven Life: What on Earth Am I Here For?* Grand Rapids, Mich.: Zondervan.

Woititz, J. G. 1983. *Adult Children of Alcoholics.* Hollywood, Fla.: Health Communications, Inc. Enterprise Center.

Zastrow, C. 2004. *Introduction to Social Work and Social Welfare: Empowering People.* New York: Brooks/Cole.

THREE

Responding to My Sister's Addiction

Fostering Resilience in My Nieces

DARLENE GRANT

DESCRIPTION OF CAREGIVER

A child of the 1960s, born and raised in Cleveland, Ohio, I was influenced by inner-city poverty, yearly summer vacations to family in Alabama, the civil rights movement, and a religious upbringing. All my life, my mother, my two sisters, and I were affected by my father's severe alcoholism and chronic unemployment. I believe the model my mother provided—long suffering, compassion, spiritual grounding, and unflinching commitment to children and family—was in part why I am a social worker. I stumbled into social work; a sociology professor, observing my work on his child abuse research project, suggested it. Never having had any family or personal problems adequately addressed by social workers, I initially had little respect for the profession. But with no employment options, I applied to the master's program in Cleveland. My first social work job was as a night shift counselor in a battered women's shelter. As a shoulder to cry on, a connection to resources, and an avid listener, I began to respect the profession.

Using school financial aid and shelter earnings, I financially helped my mother and sisters, providing immense self-satisfaction. My only niece at that time, four-year-old Tamika, often stayed overnight with me on campus and accompanied me to class and the library. After graduation I started in child psychotherapy and moved into substance abuse treatment and family therapy upon moving to Knoxville, Tennessee, four years later. Finding substance abuse my professional niche, I honed my craft, understood myself as an adult child of an alcoholic and my roles, and used this understanding to strengthen my practice. After years of being the only degreed African American practitioner in my work settings and having my clinical judgments countermanded by European American colleagues and supervisors, I entered a doctoral program to earn credentials to enable others to respect my professional judgments. As a never-married thirty-year-old full-time doctoral student, I decided to include training helping professionals to understand the importance of race, gender, and culture.

In my second year, Carlene, my fraternal twin sister, and her two daughters became homeless because of her crack use. The family's descent into crack addiction, violence, and homelessness was not a unique story in the large urban African American community, nor was our family's informally placing my nieces in the care of their aunties. I grew up among families who helped kin survive the challenges of impoverished Cleveland neighborhoods. Becoming family caregivers was our only option as we engaged our own informal child protective services (CPS) system. That's how two aunties came to provide caregiving for two little girls from 1990 to 1997. After years of worry and concern about the safety of our nieces and unsuccessful attempts to secure CPS involvement, my newly married younger sister Regina (Jean), age twenty-eight, and I drove cross-country and took their care into our own hands. At that time I had no money and terrible credit, and I was completing the doctoral program at the University of Tennessee. In 1994 I took a position as a new assistant professor of social work at the University of Texas at Austin. My life revolved around securing university tenure, an arduous and time-consuming process, and caring for my nieces.

With my family's permission and encouragement, this chapter highlights the impact of my twin sister's drug addiction on her two daughters, the family intervention to remove these two girls, and the challenges Jean and I faced, living in different cities and jointly caring for our nieces. It explores how Carlene's struggles influenced everyone's life. While a full-time student, I cared for eleven-year-old Tamika and seven-year-old Ebony in the summers. During these three years, the girls spent the school year with Jean in Birmingham.

I describe issues we encountered with social services: seeking financial assistance, immunizations, legal aid, medical and dental care without insurance, mental health services, and school enrollment. I also discuss the culturally grounded mandate to pay attention to the girls' religious and moral development. Although my younger sister and I were inextricably connected during the years we co-parented our nieces, this chapter is written from my perspective as a caregiver and social worker. In the initial sections of this chapter, the context of parenting between my sister and me is highlighted, setting the stage for my experience as the primary caregiver from 1995 through 1997.

My Nieces' Early Years

My twin sister, Carlene, had her first child at seventeen, her second child three and a half years later, and her third daughter one year after the December 1990 family intervention to remove her two older children. Tamika had been severely abused from infancy. My brief and sporadic interventions during breaks from school, while I was experiencing my own developmental struggles, were futile at best. By graduate school, I often took Tamika on campus. Throughout the next three years, I focused on learning how to be an effective psychotherapist. My clinical work was in the area of sexually abused children and adult survivors of childhood abuse. Carlene continued to be physically and emotionally abusive toward Tamika, but no one suspected that she was addicted to drugs at that time. I viewed my time with Tamika as respite from her mother and their unrelenting cycle of anger, frustration, and pain. The presence of Ebony's father forestalled her experience of physical and verbal abuse.

During my field placement in CPS, I made a lasting friendship with Lenward Brown, investigator extraordinaire who supported my numerous nonanonymous reports to CPS. Several times, CPS investigators visited Carlene; only an initial investigation was completed. Given the daily cases those investigators saw, they never deemed circumstances to warrant removal. In addition, they never required Carlene to seek help. I relocated to Knoxville, Tennessee, in 1986 and secured a job as a family therapist on the addiction treatment unit of a small psychiatric hospital. With a new perspective and critique of family functioning, when I subsequently visited my hometown, I defined Carlene's problems more objectively.

Thanksgiving of 1990, I called home to talk to everyone traditionally gathered at my maternal Auntie Lalee and Uncle Willie's house. Auntie Lalee reported that Tamika's long, pretty hair was falling out from ringworm and that Ebony had demonstrated some strange behavior: She kept washing her hands over and over. After years of working with abused children and their families who manifested washing behaviors, I had additional concerns and felt spurred into action.

Deciding to Become a Caregiver

I began an informal family assessment. I learned that my twin sister had been using crack to the point of prostituting herself in exchange for drugs. Why hadn't anybody told me before then? Enough was enough! I called Jean in Birmingham to share my worst fears about our nieces. I was determined to rescue the girls, which required my being in Ohio. Before leaving for Ohio, I made a few phone calls. My concerns were confirmed after I talked with CPS and the Cleveland police. The girls had been going to school and earning average grades. After responding to several reports alleging neglect and abuse, CPS had uncovered no evidence that warranted intervention on the girls' behalf. I learned that Carlene would be evicted in two weeks. I reacted with a familiar dilemma: Do I use the money I had saved from working two jobs and my school financial aid to help her and the girls? How would I survive? I can't let the girls go homeless. I felt I had no option but to pawn more of my belongings to make ends meet.

Carlene wasn't working. Clearly, her Aid to Families with Dependent Children (AFDC) money was not going toward upkeep of the girls or the monthly rent. She received no child support. Furthermore, the entire family suspected she was abusing drugs. She frequently appeared high and incoherent, begged for money, or stole from family members' homes. By November 1990, she had been unable to adequately care for the girls for more than a year. Frantic with worry, I called the police for assistance; I didn't really know what kind of assistance I needed. I just hoped to create a situation that would force my sister to get treatment or change her behavior. The police reported that Carlene's home was a known crack addict hang-out and was being watched. They wouldn't give any more information to me, a distraught woman trying to piece together her sister's situation via long-distance phone calls from Knoxville, Tennessee.

Assuming the Caregiver Role

One week after Thanksgiving, Jean and her new husband, Derek, drove to Knoxville to pick me up; we left immediately for Cleveland with the goal of removing Tamika and Ebony from their home. We planned to raise them ourselves for a year or two until Carlene could get her life together enough to raise them herself. We arrived in Cleveland around 6 A.M. I dropped Jean off at mom's house and alone went to pick up the girls. I didn't want Jean's tearfulness and conciliatory stance to break down my resolve about what needed to be done.

Snow was piled high on the side of the roads the morning I arrived to remove my nieces from their most recent home. Carlene let me into the downstairs apartment from which they were scheduled to be evicted in a few days. The stink of old garbage and the outlines of clothed dirty bodies of drunks and drug addicts sleeping on the floors in the dark were surreal. I could barely contain my anger and fear for what my nieces had been exposed to. My plan was to assure my sister that I would treat the girls to breakfast then drive them to school.

I found the girls huddled together under a thin, dirty sheet in a twin bed. Excited about the surprise visit, Tamika found clothes among a dirty pile at the bottom of their small closet. Roaches crawled everywhere. As a social worker, I had witnessed similar scenes before, but its inclusion of my own family was like a strong kick in the stomach. Unaware of Jean and my real intentions, the girls washed their faces, packed their backpacks, and hugged and said goodbye to their mother. At breakfast, the girls talked freely about how they were living. We headed straight to my mother's apartment, where she and Jean waited, and we explained our plan to convince their mother to enter drug rehab. The plan included our hope that the girls wouldn't mind living with Jean and me as co-guardians until their mother got back on track. Not surprisingly, the girls thought this was a good plan.

When my family and I visited Carlene the next afternoon, there was some yelling and hurt feelings, but overall it went much smoother than I'd ever hoped. In hindsight, I think Carlene was relieved: Our plan offered her an alternative to placing the girls into the foster care system. Carlene gave Jean the birth certificates, shot records, and other papers that we hoped would enable us to enroll the girls in school in Birmingham, our next destination.

Reasons for Accepting the Role of Caregiver

Kinship care of children is a long tradition in the African American community, dating to slavery, when adults cared for children displaced from sold parents. During the great migration of the 1920s and 1930s, children were left with grandmothers and other kin as parents sought their fortune in the North. In more recent times, grandmothers and other kin have cared for children of incarcerated, drug-addicted, and otherwise absent parents (Gibson 1999; Waldrop and Weber 2001; Young and Smith 2000). There were several reasons why my little sister and I became caregivers instead of my mother. We wanted to spare our mother from Carlene's harassment and manipulation. Cleveland was a place where whispered stories and more blatant newspaper reports of callous neglect and abuse of African American children in the foster care system kept us fearful of what would happen if we didn't take on that responsibility. We knew that formal kinship care arrangements were possible through CPS, but we feared that some unforeseen glitch or rule would result in the girls being taken away from the family. Moreover, we grew up mistrusting, even fearing the government system of social services, especially CPS. What if CPS assessed us ineligible to be kinship caregivers, imposed the caregiver burden on our mother without sufficient support, or did not protect the girls from further abuse?

Taking the girls out of state was an extended family decision including our mother, aunts, and uncles. Stories from my maternal grandmother about her grandmother's life in slavery and about postslavery conditions made it clear that many African American families adapted and survived using a patchwork approach to family arrangements. That we established an interstate tag-team arrangement for raising the girls is consistent with our understanding of an adaptive and flexible family structure. We also learned, from our religious upbringing and flexible family structure, to hope and expect Carlene's return to parenting whenever she demonstrated the ability and stability.

The family knew that the impact of this new caregiving responsibility would be formidable. A built-in support system for parenting seemed a logical and healthy arrangement. I knew this much from my perusal of the writings (Garbarino and Associates 1982; Garbarino and Gilliam 1980; Garbarino et al. 1986) I had begun reading for my dissertation research on the functioning of adult children of alcoholics. We hoped that we could provide a positive and stabilizing influence in the girls' lives that would mediate the dysfunction they had experienced. We expected that keeping their care in the family, with aunties they knew and loved, would help them overcome the maternal and paternal abandonment they would emotionally wrestle with later in life. Our entire family prayed that the girls would withstand and rebound from early adversity, the crux of the concept of resilience (Walsh 2002).

DESCRIPTION OF FAMILY MEMBERS CARED FOR

The impact of their mother's drug addiction and related lifestyle, and the absence of Ebony's father since she was four years old, was physically and emotionally evident by the time the girls moved to Birmingham with Jean. Considering Erikson's eight stages of development (Schriver 2001), at seven years of age Ebony seemed to be resolving the initiative versus guilt psychosocial conflict in favor of guilt and shame. Tamika's feelings about her mother's situation were less clear because she seemed to adjust easily to the change. Ebony's confusion, anger, and frustration were tangible. Her early clinging indicated that Jean, Derek, and I were important to her. It was similarly clear to me that she was angry and held me responsible for her separation from her mother, whom she loved. It took me years to realize that to remain loyal to her mother, Ebony had to work hard to dislike me. The dissonance that this double bind created for her must have been horrible to manage. Withstanding Ebony's anger and lashing out at me during the long school years in Austin became one of my greatest caregiver challenges. Years later I realized that I had missed a lot of the signals and symptoms of Tamika's responses to problems in her life. Her responses to her childhood trauma were hidden behind our concern about what to do with Ebony.

The first school year the girls were in my care, I cautiously talked to an agency about becoming their foster parent so I could get financial assistance for the mental health and medical care they needed. Learning that I would have to sign their custody over to CPS and risk being evaluated for appropriateness as a foster caregiver, I gave up. Instead, I kept searching for community support without divulging my lack of legal status for the girls. It was easy to keep up the façade, often stating that I was a social worker and encouraging the girls to do the same, so that we would call little attention to the fact that a professor at a prestigious state university was seeking care for her children in a community clinic serving low-income families.

I entered into parenting my nieces out of love and with significant naivety. I have a newfound respect for parents of children with behavioral and mental health problems. Some social work scholars (Beckett and Dungee-Anderson 1998; Dungee-Anderson and Beckett 1995; Walsh 2002) discuss how clinicians and researchers bring their own assumptions and worldviews into every evaluation and intervention, along with their cultural norms, professional orientations, and personal experience. I hope that this chapter helps students and other practitioners acknowledge their naivety wherever it lies, encourages them to suspend judgment based on stereotypes and their own assumptive maps, and helps them persist in finding the strengths families can build on when in distress.

Positive that I had grown into a really good clinical practitioner, I was never quite sure I was up to the test of parenting my nieces. The change in environment was generally positive for Tamika, who was easily engaged in conversation, eager to please, and helpful around the house. Ebony was morose, did not engage in conversation, and made no effort to develop relationships with her aunties or anyone else. Even as late as 1995 through 1997, Ebony needed reminding that "in this family, when we do something like cook pancakes on Saturday morning, we ask whether anyone else would like pancakes also." Ebony did not demonstrate the common courtesies usually practiced in our family without constant reminding.

Kinship caregivers often question their competence in the role of parent, and they worry about the impact of early trauma on the abilities of children to learn and establish healthy relationships. Although Jean and I felt that we had no choice in becoming parents, because we wanted our nieces to avoid further damage and trauma, we were also angry about the impact this role had on our own life plans. I've grown to believe that some of this anger was normative to becoming a kinship caregiver. If this anger is not addressed, it festers into depression and other illness. Without the support of a co-caregiver, a good family therapist, and colleagues who cared, I have no doubt that I would have had a much harder time as a caregiver. In our case, the outcome was mostly positive. Tamika graduated from an Austin high school in May 1997 and began her freshman year at Texas Southern University. That same year, Ebony returned to Cleveland and completed her two remaining years of high school while living with her mother, who had successfully recovered and had established a somewhat stable home.

DESCRIPTION OF CAREGIVING EXPERIENCE

Beginning of Caregiving Tasks and Behaviors

While the girls spent their summers with me, the impact on my life plan was minimal. Though filled with challenges, giving up summers seemed less like real parenting than when the girls came to live with me full time in Texas during the 1994 school year. My more intensive caregiving responsibilities began in preparation for their arrival. The consequences of my nebulous position as an informal, nonlegal guardian became more real. Because I had never successfully secured a letter from their mother granting me guardianship responsibilities, I was scared. I had to depend on no one asking too many questions when I registered the girls in school and took them to a local community center for their immunization shots and basic healthcare. Faced with these challenges along with the need for dental care and emergency room visits to manage Ebony's chronic asthma, I had a newfound respect and admiration for all the informal kinship caregivers facing similar dilemmas with little or no social service assistance. Our greatest assets included having the same last name and my having a good-paying job with a well-respected entity.

Initial Reactions to the Care Recipients and Caregiving Experiences

After moving the girls, I worried about how to raise girls with some sense of self-esteem and ability for healthy functioning in school and relationships (Turnage 2004). The unspoken hope was that family togetherness and love would serve the bulk of their psychological needs. The family depended on my being a social worker, assuming I would be smart about the girls' emotional health. I knew that we had evidence of their resilience on our side (Walsh 2002). After sorting through anger at their mother, I also recognized their mother's history of overcoming adversity. She was a survivor. I held dear these characteristics of all the women in our extended maternal family in my attempt to interject some hope in our collective futures. Given their history of neglect and exposure to maternal addiction, the main message I wanted the girls to have was to maintain strength and courage and focus on overcoming adversity.

Social Service Agencies

One of my most vivid memories of my co-parenting adventure is sitting unserved for eight hours in a Birmingham AFDC (now Temporary Assistance for Needy Families [TANF]) office with Jean, her newborn son, Tamika, and Ebony as we sought formal assistance for taking on their care and upbringing. As the only one in my family with an advanced degree, I remember the rage and shame I felt as I used my professional demeanor to convince the people behind the glass-enclosed front desk that I was a social worker, knew how the system worked, and would appreciate the courtesy of collegial treatment, only to be rebuffed and turned away to continue to wait. I remember saying, "Could you just call Mrs. X, and tell her that I'm a social worker from Tennessee, and that I would really like her assistance in getting my nieces some help after we had to rescue them from their drug-addicted mother in Cleveland, Ohio?" All I got in return was, "We've let Mrs. X know you are here. She will come and get you when she can. You're not the only one she's scheduled to see today."

Today, I have grown from the idea of demanding collegial courtesy to demanding universal courtesy to all clients. Everyone seeking financial and mental health services deserves the courtesy of being seen within one hour of their scheduled appointment. Everyone seeking financial and mental health services deserves an explanation for significant delays. When Jean heard me say, "What did you say to me?!" from across the waiting room, she knew I was winding up to hurl a few expletives. She rushed over and convinced me not to jeopardize any help we could receive by cursing at the staff. I remember saying, "I'm a professional. I know how cussing doesn't get things done any faster, if at all, but these people are wrong to treat us like this. I'm surprised I haven't heard more cussing here today."

We hadn't anticipated so long a wait. How many clients in crisis do? I'm sure the other women with children left waiting for hours on end hadn't anticipated so long a wait, either. I overheard some of the waiting clients calling the people who had driven them to their appointments, begging them to wait just a little longer before giving up on them and leaving them stranded at the welfare office. I felt personally and professionally incompetent, helpless, and furious, and at one point I broke into tears. Having scheduled an 8:30 A.M. appointment, we were finally seen at 4:30 P.M. No apology for the wait was made, and we were coldly informed that we didn't have the paperwork necessary to proceed with getting services for Tamika and Ebony. We would have to set another appointment, something we could have been told in five minutes earlier in the day.

I took on the care of Tamika and Ebony against their mother's wishes, knowing that I would be ineligible for financial and other social services that formal kinship caregivers receive. Jean was able to get a letter from Carlene giving her temporary guardianship of the girls and subsequently was able to secure a Medicaid card and some food stamp assistance, but Carlene refused to provide a letter or other notarized document authorizing me to provide guardianship that would have helped me obtain similar services. I remember drilling Tamika and Ebony before dentist visits or school registration, "Remember, while we're in there, don't call me Auntie, and for goodness' sake, don't tell anyone I'm a professor at U.T. They'll think we have money." Because I lacked even the most informal permission for guardianship, I could not access Medicaid for the girls' healthcare, nor could I put them on my own insurance plan. I had to pay cash for all medical and dental services. Both girls had significant dental needs. I found a children's dentist who allowed me to set up a cash payment schedule. I imposed on colleagues who lent me money, setting up similar payment schedules. Consistent with my image of struggling single parents the world over, I made many financial deals and often was late on other bills to cover school and the healthcare needs of the girls.

Emergency Room Visit

Late one evening, Tamika ran into my room reporting that Ebony couldn't breathe. When I checked, Ebony was wheezing severely, unable to take in much air. Tamika was crying and anxious. We rushed Ebony in my car to the emergency room. I prayed aloud the entire drive. I was scared for Ebony and afraid of being discovered an illegal guardian, ineligible to sign for medical care. I was armed with the girls' birth certificates, Social Security cards, immunization records, report cards, and everything else that I carried around as proof that I was taking care of them. Up to that point I had been able to get away with taking the girls to a community clinic on the east side for their immunization shots without too many questions. But this was an emergency, and they would find out quickly that I didn't have Ebony on my insurance. I cursed the situation. Once the nurse on duty saw Ebony's distress, she rushed her to the back, instructing me to stay out front to complete the registration. When we hit the "No she is not on my insurance, and no we do not have a Medicaid card," I was crying. After questioning I shared all the paperwork I carried and resorted to begging for help. I promised to apply for Medicaid the next morning. With the acuity of Ebony's distress we did get the help she needed, and I signed a promissory note for the bill. Afraid of dire consequences, I never pursued a Medicaid application.

The First Year

Throughout their first year with me, I remember finding sandwiches and snacks hidden under the bed and other places around the apartment. Scholars (Garbarino and Associates 1982) discuss the hoarding response to child abuse. As Ebony worked to ensure security and access to food whenever she was hungry, I worried about these behaviors manifesting so long after the initial family intervention that removed her from homelessness and hunger. Showing little initiative or creativity in her daily interactions, Ebony evidenced few peer group skills, preferring to sit near adults or hang around the fringes of groups (family and peer groups) rather than play or join in. In what little play she participated in, she would quickly disengage when the other children did not follow her wishes.

Ebony's strength was in her academic performance. She loved to read. She performed in the top percentile for her age group on all state and national reading and comprehension tests.

Tamika, on the other hand, was quite social but quickly anxious when conflict arose and easily defeated when challenged or discouraged. Demonstrating greater social skills than her little sister, Tamika related well with peers. In interactions involving peer pressure, she seemed easily confused about what was right and wrong. She seemed desperately to want to fit in. Like Ebony, Tamika was similarly rigid about food but did not seem to hide it.

Both girls initially were rigid around food and clothing: Matching food and matching clothing were important. I had a hard time discerning whether this rigidity was normative for their ages or their response to early childhood trauma. I could understand their fashion sense, the need to have colors and patterns of clothes that matched. I'm the same way. But when the girls started criticizing my cooking ("Auntie those don't go together," and "Auntie, I can't eat this"), I just about threw up my hands and feet. I found it interesting that kids who had gone hungry, not knowing where or when they'd get their next meal from day to day, would be so picky about food. During one of our late night calls, I explained to Jean, who had just found a bowl of moldy macaroni and cheese that had been hidden during the girls' last visit to Birmingham, that children who have spent time homeless or neglected to the point of hunger sometimes save scraps to ensure that they will have something to eat later. I explained that that was what I thought Ebony was doing. I told my little sister that we would just have to be patient. We just had to reassure Ebony and Tamika of our constancy and remind Ebony that she didn't have to hide food, for she had access to the refrigerator any time she was hungry. It was more than a year before we stopped finding hidden food in our respective apartments.

After struggling to cook foods they would eat together in one meal, I realized I was working too hard at something they could and needed to learn for themselves. I was surprised when they quickly agreed that they would be responsible for developing the menu and cooking dinner two nights a week. After I talked them out of frying everything, Ebony became an expert on cooking baked pork chops and macaroni and cheese, and Tamika loved to find magazine recipes to try out. I taught the girls to shop for bargains and was proud of the time they began going to the grocery store by themselves after developing the grocery list with me at home. They loved walking the two blocks to the grocery store, spending lots of time looking for bargains and reading labels, and coming home to share their adventures in grocery shopping.

Religious Training and Parenting

We attended church almost every Sunday while the girls were in Tennessee and Texas. I always had a church home, consistent with my own upbringing and family tradition. I counted on the African American Baptist church and church family relationships to help in the development of the girls' moral and spiritual compasses. I sang in the senior choir in Knoxville, and the girls sat proudly in the congregation waiting for me to sing my occasional solo. Armed with their own Bibles, the girls mimicked me as they highlighted passages and later made comments on the sermon in the car on the way home or when we later went out to eat. I often found myself hoping that I had enough good habits for them to mimic to counteract the destructive habits they had witnessed in their life with their mother. Whereas Carlene had mostly abusive men in and out of her life, I had very few and made it a point to talk about the importance of selectivity in friendships. Jean and I grounded our lives in our religious value system as best we could. We also worked with the girls on understanding their own value as women, how they deserved to be treated well by boys and men who were respectful, honest, and hard working. The reader might imagine at this point that I got a lot of eye rolling and heavy sighs from the girls during these discussions. "I'm talking about your empowerment, ladies! Your empowerment," I would comment. Yes, they would roll their eyes in horror at my commentary. After a while that was our little family joke, but I think some of it made an impression.

One "First Sunday," Communion was being distributed. In the Baptist tradition, communion is a monthly sacrament of wine (or grape juice) and unleavened bread. After years of going to church with the girls and letting them take communion, I suddenly recalled that our belief system did not condone Communion if a person has not been baptized (full immersion in a pool of water) by an ordained minister (Billingsley 1992; Frazier 1966). I leaned over and asked both Tamika and Ebony whether they'd been baptized and got the whispered response, "No." The weight of the responsibility for the girls' baptisms overwhelmed me. Tears ran down my face as I explained that they couldn't take Communion because the rules of our faith said they had to be baptized first. A whispered argument ensued, of course. "Well, we've been taking it all this time." "Auntie Jean let us take communion." "Granny let us take communion." Of course, being the bad guy is a part of parenting that strikes me as the most salient part of the job. Discussing their baptism with the girls was also a great source of pride for me. I also wrestled with some sadness for Carlene, who would miss this once-in-a-lifetime religious developmental milestone.

Several Sundays later we had a conversation with our deacon about the girls formally joining the church, baptism, and Communion. We left the choice, time, and place up to the girls. It's traditional in the African American Baptist church to leave the choice about membership and baptism up to the child who has been educated in the faith and practices of the church. A few months passed, and one Sunday during the last part of church service, when the minister offered the right hand of fellowship (i.e., asked whether anyone would like to join the church through Christian experience or baptism), Tamika boldly stood up and walked to the front of that small country church. I started crying quietly. I wished my mother and Jean could have been there to see it. I wished their mother could have been there to see it, too. Ebony, not one to be in the spotlight without support, pulled me with her as she decided to join Tamika and make it a family affair. When asked to declare her faith, Tamika, an actress at heart, spoke clearly into the microphone about her life and faith that God would watch over her and her little sister and how important her aunties were to them in that process. When asked to declare her faith, Ebony wouldn't speak up. So the minister asked her a few questions and she quietly responded "Yes" to each question. Their baptism was set for a month or so later, and we called Cleveland and Birmingham with the good news. Everyone was so happy. My mother wanted to fly right to Austin to be with the girls on that day. Jean did, too. But practicalities intervened, and John and Bettye McNeil, colleagues who became pseudo-grandparents to the girls, were the only other family present during the early morning baptismal service. I had a nice clean hankie for the occasion, and Bettye and I cried and cried and laughed and laughed as Tamika walked into the baptismal pool smiling at the congregation like the model superstar she fancied herself becoming someday. Ebony was rigid and looked frightened but followed through like a champ. We all went out to dinner after church and celebrated.

Special Caregiving Challenges and Dilemmas

No social worker was available to meet with us during our emergency room visit for Ebony's asthma attack. Looking back, I wonder whether, if I had been able to talk to a social worker, I would have been able to tap a social service resource that would have helped me with the medical bills for the girls. We had two subsequent asthma-related emergency room visits, with the bills totaling a few thousand dollars. I was always aware of other families in the emergency room—families a lot worse off than we were. Having an advanced degree and a good job, and listening to these families, I felt petty and guilty for wanting relief from total responsibility for those medical bills. I stopped seeking help and resolved to make small monthly payments until I paid every medical bill owed.

Caregiving challenges were always more emotional than financial. After entering into this kinship care arrangement, I always remembered my sense of helplessness when I considered keeping the girls from seeing their mother when we visited Cleveland, Ohio. We feared she would disappear into the bowels of the city with the girls on that first visit, a year after we took the girls away; we allowed visits only when we were present the entire time. She got into a drug rehabilitation program later that first year. Jean and I were able to drive north to attend a family therapy session with Carlene and the girls while she was in treatment. I think it did us all some good. Carlene didn't complete the full treatment regimen. That hurt. Years later, Jean and I loosened our grip on the girls (mainly from exhaustion and resignation that either the girls had learned self-care skills while with us or they hadn't), and the girls spent a night or two with their mother during our visits north. I was afraid Carlene would disappear with the girls every time we left them with her. But somehow, even as she struggled to get her life together, still in and out of abusive relationships, struggling to get sober, and in and out of battered women's and other shelters, she knew that the best thing for them was to stay with us.

Building Support Networks

Throughout my years as a caregiver, I relied on both formal and informal forms of social support to help me address the challenges of caregiving. When my little sister and I decided to co-parent our nieces, we realized that we would need to help each other as much as we could. A five-and-a-half-hour drive from each other, we became each other's primary emotional and financial resource and support. There were nightly long-distance phone consultations that usually began with, "G-I-R-L! Let me tell you what your nieces did today!" Almost every night my little sister called with some harrowing story. I heard Derek filling in the gaps in the story in the background. Even as a new member of our family, he was a 100% participant. We constantly questioned our ability to competently raise the girls. "What would you do? You're the social worker," was the question and accusation I frequently heard from Jean. Feeling hypocritical and ineffectual, I tried to explain away my fly-by-the-seat-of-my-pants parenting strategies. I hid behind the "surgeons cannot do surgery on loved ones because of lack of objectivity" metaphor. My sister and brother-in-law never bought it.

Once the girls moved to Austin, the faculty at U.T.'s School of Social Work became their extended family and my primary support system. Having raised two foster sons, Clay Shorkey, a faculty colleague, took me to the school district office to register the girls. Clay had taken on such a committed role in supporting me and the girls that he was the one to anxiously call out their names when the woman behind the counter asked the names of the children to be enrolled in school. Laughing, I leaned over and whispered to my faculty colleague, "Thanks, but I think I can handle it from here on in." When Ebony had her asthma attack, Clay told us where to take her, even offering to meet us at the hospital at 1:00 A.M.

Other faculty supporters included John McNeil and his wife, Bettye, who kept the girls whenever I needed a weekend respite and when I had out-of-state conferences. While I ate bologna sandwich lunches and prayed for a free meal here and there at a conference, John and Bettye served the girls lamb chops and rice, which quickly became Ebony's favorite meal. Faculty members such as Cynthia Franklin, Kate Wambach, Clay Shorkey, and Diana DiNitto had the girls over to their homes for lunch, swimming, and holiday celebrations, sharing their culture with them. Marian Aguilar rented videos and served the girls authentic Mexican food, sharing her culture with them. I mention these names purposefully because they are social work authors. A reader across the country encountering their work can now warmly recall their roles in raising Tamika and Ebony.

Family Therapy

In addition to family and friends, I sought formal sources of support, such as family therapy, in 1995. At times I was locking myself out of the house, pacing and cussing, trying to manage my own anger and frustration. Ebony was still breaking things, Tamika was ditching school and sneaking around with boys, and each experienced emotional tailspins after receiving letters from Carlene. I eventually asked, "You wouldn't happen to have gotten a letter from your mom in the last couple of days, would you?" I invariably heard, "How'd you know?" My intellectual understanding of family dynamics did little to help manage the girls' behaviors. I provided each with a supply of envelopes and postage stamps and encouraged them to write her letters and call her on Sunday nights. The girls sent her a copy of their yearly school pictures. None of it seemed enough. I often feared that these efforts inflamed Carlene's anger rather than offered her comfort that the girls were doing okay.

Family therapy with Joanna Labow, a licensed clinical social worker in Austin, saved me and my relationship with adolescent Tamika and Ebony and helped me better understand the challenges of parenting. I always feared how the impact of their separation from their mother and the circumstances around it would manifest in the girls' adolescence. We learned to listen to each other and to count five seconds before responding to give us time to consider what was said and what was intended and to make our intentions clearer when we did speak. From a minimally demonstrative family in terms of hugging and showing affection, I learned to hug with words, increase the physical hugs, and focus on their strengths and skills, so that we had more things to applaud and celebrate between dealing with rule infractions. There were sessions when magically, the girls shared what they missed or what they were angry about. During one session, Tamika tearfully said that she didn't want her mother to be angry with her for liking Auntie Darlene, and she had to assure her mother of her continued love and loyalty. Ebony intently watched Tamika during these times, then wordlessly assessed my reactions. With our therapist's help, I realized how tough it was for them to be unable to see or feel that I loved the person that they never stopped loving, and consequently I verbalized my lifelong struggle with understanding Carlene and promised to work on loving my twin. Importantly, we began discussing a reunification plan, later including Jean and, later still, Carlene. Until that time, Tamika and Ebony had not felt safe to verbally express the desire to return to Carlene.

ANALYSES

Helpful Theoretical and Service-Oriented Perspectives

The ecological system perspective, social constructionism, risk and resilience theory, and family therapy theory are the perspectives that inform my understanding of the challenges of kinship care over time (Johnson and Grant 2005). The girls and I in Austin, Texas, their mother and my mother in Cleveland, Ohio, and my little sister and her husband in Birmingham all formed the micro-level system. Our interactions with mezzo-level community institutions including schools, community clinics, and emergency rooms were always in the context of lacking permission from the girls' mother and filled with my own fear of being discovered as ineligible to authorize needed healthcare and other care. Many people we encountered in the social service industry assumed I was their single mother. I found it ironic that the stereotype of the single African American mother struggling to raise children alone helped. This image of what's ordinary in the African American community kept people from looking below the surface, and it possibly contributed to my inability to get real kinship care assistance.

If you get little else from this chapter, please note the importance of developing ways to financially and emotionally assist families providing kincare. This is not to say we should forgo thorough assessment and investigation. I want practitioners to support only kin intervention that is in the best interest of the children. You will note that this story included input from numerous family members and the children regarding their mother's functioning before the intervention to remove the children took place. Furthermore, there was never a desire to dissolve all parental rights or adopt the girls. We've always believed that Carlene would get better. Her children grew up with this hope. We've always framed their life with their aunties as an intervention that would offer their mother a chance to improve her life enough to raise them. Despite our family's decisions and course of action, I appreciated the macro-level laws and policies that make it difficult for someone to abscond with someone else's children and set up a family in another state just because they define it as in the best interest of the children. This systems perspective "emphasizes the connectedness between people and their problems to the complex interrelationships that exist in the client's world (Johnson and Grant 2005:4).

Risk and resilience theory suggests that the life trajectory of all children from circumstances involving absent parents or parents who cannot parent (e.g., because of HIV and AIDS complications, substance abuse, mental illness) may not be significantly impaired given the mediating effects of the love of a caring adult: a grandmother, auntie, or teacher (Bogenschneider 1996). After just one year of living between Birmingham and Knoxville, the lights came on in Tamika's eyes. With encouragement, her vocabulary doubled from one easily considered developmentally delayed due to a lack of exposure. We'd be running an errand across campus, and she'd be talking up a storm and use a big word. Then she would look up at me and ask, "Auntie, did I use that word correctly?" Over the years it became a point of pride for both of us, and I'd stop in my tracks: "Bravo for you! You go, girl!" And she absolutely sparkled. Her hair grew back in, covering the bald spots she had had from the effects of a ringworm infection. There was some evidence that the roles Jean and I took as caregivers for our nieces was having a positive impact on them. Although Ebony's behavior at home remained challenging, she blossomed in school. She very quickly began and continued blowing the top off standardized tests. Academics were where we could connect with little friction, and I lavished praise in front of all our academic friends and my students at the university. She was never one to sparkle in response to praise like Tamika, but it was still evident that the praise helped Ebony: She walked around the school quietly showing different members of the faculty and staff her report cards. It is still up to social work and other helping professions to put into place the resources necessary to make the trajectory of risk change to one of resilience.

Tamika and Ebony spent their early formative years in a family with poverty, drug addiction and abuse, parental violence, and criminally involved parents, in a gang-infested community. Family intervention that resulted in two aunts co-parenting had the goal of helping the girls overcome the odds they faced. Family members viewed their lives with a college professor auntie as more hopeful, manifesting more resilience than risk. Tamika's transformation into a child with a larger vocabulary and increased social skills demonstrated the family's belief in developmental and social achievement despite risk and adversity. Ebony's scholastic achievements were an example of the type of transformation possible for children exposed to early adversity. It is up to our and other helping professions to provide resources necessary to make this trajectory change from only risks to include great possibilities. Positive socialization, love, role modeling, consistency, boundaries, religious education, extended family and friendship network support, guardian involvement, and therapy are all presented in this chapter as antidotes (resilience factors) to the risk factors related to maternal drug addiction and mother–child separation. Many resilience factors are purposeful coping strategies traditionally used in African American families and communities that European American professionals overlook because of misinterpretation or lack of knowledge. The story of Tamika, Ebony, Auntie Jean, and Auntie Darlene displays the capacity for resilience, by which children and adults are able to develop and sustain caring relationships that help them develop social competence, problem-solving skills, critical thinking, spiritual consciousness, autonomy, and a sense of purpose in life. Empowering these girls to find their strength and integrity boosted their confidence and transformed their aunties and Uncle Derek to influence their respective work, church, and school communities, particularly on behalf of children.

I was slow to realize that Carlene's influence overcame distance (Turnage 2004). The girls' moods would swing into depression, sadness, anger, and belligerence. When Ebony broke items she knew to be important to me, such as a small green antique lamp that was my maternal grandmother's, I purposefully locked myself out of the apartment and spent some time stomping around the parking lot cussing to myself and thinking about how Carlene was a hitter. I feared losing control and becoming a parent who hit her kids. I came close to hitting Ebony on many occasions and actually slapped her on a few; this is an important confession for a social worker. As a trained social worker and a darn good family therapist, I knew it was time to get some professional help. I spent a lot of time riddled with anger, fear, and shame after hitting Ebony. At some point, I tied their deteriorating behaviors to letters from Carlene. Given permission by Tamika, I read one letter filled with declarations of love and commitment to improving her life and anger at my insensitivity to her need for a relationship with her children. Concurrently, family reported that Carlene's life remained transient, filled with violent relationships and chronic unemployment.

My expertise in substance abuse and family dynamics did little to help me manage the impact of Carlene's messages on the girls' feelings and behaviors. Social constructionism helped me understand that "people's behavior does not depend on the objective existence of something, but on their subjective interpretation of it" (Johnson and Grant 2005:9). With family therapy, I understood my nieces' perceptions of being away from their mother. I couldn't focus just on the objective reality of their mother's continued instability as a rationale for keeping them apart. I had to find ways to let them share their feelings and desires in order to reduce the likelihood that they would feel misunderstood and act out accordingly.

IMPLICATIONS

The availability of gender- and parent-sensitive substance abuse treatment and alternatives to the incarceration of nonviolent offenders would significantly reduce the number of children entering the foster and kinship care systems in our country. Family education and support programs in substance abuse treatment would strengthen the ability of children and family members to care for themselves and each other. Enhanced sensitivity to various adaptive and flexible family forms when assessing for formal kinship care systems is my primary suggestion for addressing the needs of these children. Flexibility and shared care could decrease the sense of being a burden to others that kinship foster children might feel. Co-parenting family members would likewise feel less burdened and more amenable to asking for help from other family members and formal social service systems. Social service providers would be called on to educate the adult caregivers about the available services and strategies to obtain them. This might mean assigning a primary caregiver who will maintain health, school, and other records and share copies with other caregivers when necessary. At the policy level, a system of interstate Medicaid agreements in the case of kinship foster children may be useful to these families. Where needed services and resources are unavailable, professionals will successfully advocate.

Caregiving Experiences and Current Literature and Research

Current kinship care literature and research suggest that the formal system of foster care in the United States is based on an idealized nuclear family substitute that does not work in an age of increasing need for foster parents and culturally competent placements for children (Brown et al. 2002; Testa, and Slack 2002). It is perhaps this idealized two-parent foster care model that has kept many prospective kinship caregivers from offering their homes to the formal care system. Furthermore, the adaptability and flexibility of African American extended families lack the look and feel of the idealized two-parent model on which the current foster care system is based (Brown et al. 2002). Unfortunately, shared care of children across several family settings would not be viewed as a strength in the traditional nuclear family model. However, reliance on kin who take on multiple roles is one of the primary characteristics of African American family survival (Billingsley 1992; Brown et al. 2002; Gibson 2002). Role flexibility within extended family networks protects children from the disruption caused by employment, marital, and housing instability. In such families, members "pool resources and build community while coping with long-term poverty and growing unemployment rates among men"; family members may "absorb others into the household, or may assist with child rearing and social regulation" (Brown et al. 2002:55–56). There are significant protective factors inherent in nonconformist African American family structures, including flexibility, built-in respite care, intergenerational connections, sharing of economic burdens, and sharing of resources (Brown et al. 2002; Testa and Slack 2002). Scholars (Testa and Slack 2002) suggest that future research should focus on kinship care outcomes among children placed in one relative's home or in multiple homes of kin caregivers before replacement. It is hypothesized that the children in the latter group would not likely be replaced into nonrelated foster care.

The social work practice implications are myriad. First, there is an important need to support the guardians providing formal and informal kinship care. Policies that require the state to have formal custody while grandparents, aunts, and uncles take care of children in their families result in many families avoiding the system for real fear of losing their children to bureaucratic snafus. Second, experience as a social worker does not directly translate into skill as a guardian or parent. This may seem obvious, but it bears repeating. We are less effective if we enter kinship care as the all-knowing social worker versus the learner. Third, we must do something about the treatment people receive in AFDC and TANF, Medicaid, and other social welfare offices around the country. Insensitive professionals stereotype families in need and treat them like undeserving animals. Our experiences in the AFDC offices inspired an entrepreneurial idea: getting corporations to underwrite small business loans so that some of these parents can set up coffee stands in the waiting rooms of some of the larger of these social welfare offices. A hot cup of coffee and a smile could have gone a long way to soothing my upset on that long day of waiting. But coffee cannot replace workers treating clients, no matter how far they are from the worker's own values and beliefs, with dignity and respect.

Another idea is to start a grassroots education and empowerment movement within these waiting rooms—rooms that are filled with women and children, just waiting and waiting and waiting. If people are going to be inconvenienced in the way described in this chapter, arranging to buy cab vouchers at a discount for distribution to families who miss their rides by waiting hours after their scheduled appointments is the least we can do in this so-called service industry. Support systems can spring up through the neighborhood, workplace, and church. The school of social work, where I found significant unexplored and untapped support, is a natural setting for supporting student, staff, and faculty parents struggling financially and emotionally. An important question to ask is, "What can we do to make our schools of social work into models for the rest of society to follow, including assisting students with child care and establishing relationships with corporations to develop systems of care?" Table 3.1 describes these implications.

REFLECTIONS AND CONCLUSIONS

The following is a series of disconnected but pertinent reflections on my writing about and the actual kinship care experiences. The editor of this book recalled my sharing a little about my adventures in kinship care years after meeting me as I interviewed for a junior faculty position at her institution. Thus, I initially saw being asked to write about my caregiving experiences as a

Table 3.1 Implications

	Issues and Problems	Strategies for Change
Individuals	Maternal substance abuse and criminal justice involvement compromise ability to parent.	Increase availability of gender- and parent-sensitive substance abuse treatment and alternatives to incarceration of nonviolent offenders. Provide kinship care and access to child care to reduce exposure to instability typical in the foster care system.
Families	Family history of substance abuse may mean children are at high risk of substance abuse themselves (possibly never addressed). Communication is lacking about the status of the children's care and the need for earlier family intervention that may reduce the need to remove children.	Address the predisposition of children to seek relief from their problems by using drugs and the related genetic predisposition to become addicted. Educate all kin caregivers about the signs and symptoms of substance abuse and different types of intervention and support available.
Communities	Availability of affordable and safe housing, child care, and job training and support for single mothers with dependent children is limited.	Provide sensitive media exposure of the issues to enhance understanding of the complex dynamics and empathy with the mother as well as the children. Establish an advisory committee to the city council and state government that focuses on bridging foster care, substance abuse providers, and the criminal justice system to address the problems listed here to develop a solution with accountability indexes.

(*continued*)

Table 3.1 (continued)

	Issues and Problems	Strategies for Change
Practitioners and educators	School teachers and administrators are overwhelmed by social service needs of greater numbers of children in their classrooms. Overburdened child protective systems lack funding for adequate levels of staff for home evaluations and intervention or cultural diversity training for all staff. Law enforcement lacks prevention programming and alternatives to incarceration of nonviolent offenders.	Increase numbers, training, visibility, and involvement of school social workers with all children. Develop child protective service response teams and training to help parents in trouble before the trouble escalates to child removal. Increase community outreach programs that contribute to job opportunities and child care for single mothers in high-risk neighborhoods.
Institutions	Child protective systems require relinquishment of custody to the state before credible family members who do not meet all foster care provider criteria can receive training and financial and other help raising the children.	Improve child protective service response time and quality of response to noncrisis negligence cases. Expand and enhance options for certifying kinship care. Recognize, understand, and sensitively respond to cultural concerns about the plight of African American children in foster care systems.
Researchers	Outcomes of formal and informal kinship care situations are understudied and unknown to practitioners and policymakers.	Study life trajectories of children exposed to early intervention in cases of neglect. Foster care system can fund dissertation research on kinship care outcomes across various related disciplines including social work, child development, family therapy, substance abuse treatment, and criminal justice. Fund and require mandatory longitudinal studies on formal and informal kinship care placements.

great compliment. However, this writing task has been a bit nerve racking as I have attempted, through numerous rewrites, to tell a good story while being professionally informative. Furthermore, this writing process has enabled me to join the ranks of social workers willing to tell their stories as a tool for teaching (Grobman 1999; LeCroy 2002).

Use of the narrative to pass along problem-solving tips for living to the next generation is consistent with my rearing in the African American community. That this story will leave the confines of my family causes some anxiety. Were my nieces, my mother, or my little sister to read this chapter, would they be embarrassed or angry? When they proffered their approval to tell their story, Tamika and Ebony did so in the hope that this would help other children who find themselves in kinship care situations and the social workers and other service providers they encounter. I was surprised at how readily Tamika, Ebony, Jean, and my brother-in-law Derek agreed to my writing about the often painful aspects of the girls' lives and our adventures in parenting. In retrospect, a part of this response is quite culturally grounded. "If another family can learn from our experience, that would make me very happy" was Tamika's heartfelt response. It is these moments of depth of insight and courage that fill my heart and make me nostalgic, wishing these two young women had less to overcome as they negotiate adulthood and their own roles as young adult parents today. In conversation with Tamika, Ebony, and my little sister, we agree that the benefit to readers far outweighs any discomfort we may feel in airing our family saga.

The easiest thing about writing the chapter was recalling the stories of child rearing. We have dozens and dozens, some funny, some not so funny. The reader is encouraged to imagine the forty-two-page first draft of the description of the caregiving experiences, just one section of the chapter. It follows that the biggest challenge I faced in writing this chapter was brevity and focus. Life doesn't happen linearly for me. One step forward and two steps back is a classic description of my experiences with Tamika, Ebony, and my sisters. I have worked hard for linearity, brevity, and honoring family members and others who contributed to this real-life adventure in kinship co-parenting. Our lives did not proceed as smoothly as presented here, and my memory of parenting does not come back as sequentially as presented.

Although my perceptions of myself as a caregiver were mixed, I wouldn't trade the experience for all the money in the world. Looking back, my fear of being discovered and having the children taken away drove a lot of how I negotiated parenting. I will always wonder whether the experience would have been better for the girls had I taken a chance and accessed the more formal kinship care system.

Today, I am forty-five, and thus far Tamika and Ebony are the only children I have had the privilege to parent. The experience was a gift. We remain quite close. Ebony finished her last years of high school back in Cleveland, living with her mother, who had two years of clean time under her belt. It has been rocky, but they are doing well. Tamika remained in Texas, attended a historically black college for a year, and married. I visit her family, including my two great-nephews in Dallas, at least once a month. Those boys are like grandsons to me, and they are the joy of my life. I have not delved to any great length into the intersecting issues of race, gender, and class in this chapter. Many service providers we encountered assumed I was the single mother of Tamika and Ebony. I found it ironic that the stereotype of the single African American mother struggling to raise children alone helped me get help while all the time I feared discovery as a fraud.

In closing, the subtext of this story is that of coming full circle. Today, as a social work academic, I teach at the University of Texas at Austin School of Social Work. So I am indeed training the new generation of the profession to understand "The Foundations of Social Justice: Values, Diversity, Power and Oppression," a course I helped design and have taught for nine years. As a social work researcher, I evaluate a program providing services for incarcerated women and their noncustodial daughters; most are living in kinship care situations.

As I introduce these issues to social work students, I am adamant that culturally sensitive practice is about suspending judgment and stereotypes in the face of what may be absolutely abhorrent and foreign to your experience. Culturally sensitive practice involves the difficult task of advocating for the mother of the precious child sitting in front of you with clumps of her hair missing due to ringworm and inattention to her hygiene—not judging that mother out of hand. It's taken me a long time to note my sister's strengths as a survivor. As I wrestled with the challenges of family, it would have been a blessing to have a social service system that could have helped us both—twin survivors of life with an alcoholic father, each finding a way to save herself and the subsequent generation. Well, she's been clean for a few years now, no longer hooked on drugs, and is working hard every day to make up to her now adult daughters for her inability to parent them through their childhood and adolescence. Family and our cultural grounding enabled her to reach out to her children when she could, all the while offering them an all-important safety net all the way.

REFERENCES

Beckett, J. and Dungee-Anderson, D. 1998. Multicultural communication in human service organizations. In A. Daly (Ed.), *Diversity in the Workplace: Issues and Perspectives,* 191–214. Washington, D.C.: National Association of Social Workers.

Billingsley, A. 1992. *Climbing Jacob's Ladder: The Enduring Legacy of African-American Families.* New York: Simon & Schuster.

Bogenschneider, K. 1996. An ecological risk/protective theory for building prevention programs, policies, and community capacity to support youth. *Family Relations* 45: 127–138.

Brown, S., Cohon, D., and Wheeler, R. 2002. African American extended families and kinship care: How relevant is the foster care model for kinship care? *Children and Youth Services Review* 24 (1/2): 53–77.

Dungee-Anderson, D. and Beckett, J. 1995. A process model for multicultural social work practice. *Families in Society: The Journal of Contemporary Human Services* 76: 459–466.

Frazier, E. F. 1966. *The Negro Family in the United States.* Chicago: University of Chicago Press.

Garbarino, J. and Associates. 1982. *Children and Families in the Social Environment.* New York: Aldine.

Garbarino, J. and Gilliam, G. 1980. *Understanding Abusive Families.* Lexington, Mass.: Lexington Books.

Garbarino, J., Guttmann, E., and Seeley, J. W. 1986. *The Psychologically Battered Child.* San Francisco: Jossey-Bass.

Gibson, P. A. 1999. African American grandmothers: New mothers again. *Affilia* 14: 329–343.

Gibson, P. A. 2002. African American grandmothers as caregivers: Answering the call to help their grandchildren. *Families in Society* 83 (1): 35–43.

Grobman, L. M. 1999. *Days in the Lives of Social Workers: 50 Professionals Tell "Real-Life" Stories from Social Work Practice.* Harrisburg, Pa.: White Hat Communications.

Johnson, J. L. and Grant, G. Jr. 2005. *Foster Care.* Boston: Allyn & Bacon.

LeCroy, C. W. 2002. *The Call to Social Work: Life Stories.* Thousand Oaks, Cal.: Sage.

Schriver, J. M. 2001. *Human Behaviour and the Social Environment: Shifting Paradigms in Essential Knowledge for Social Work Practice.* Boston: Allyn & Bacon.

Testa, M. F. and Slack, K. S. 2002. The gift of kinship foster care. *Children and Youth Services Review* 24 (1/2): 79–108.

Turnage, B. F. 2004. African American mother–daughter relationships mediating daughter's self-esteem. *Child and Adolescent Social Work Journal* 21 (2): 155–173.

Waldrop, D.P. and Weber, J.A. 2001. From grandparent to caregiver: The stress and satisfaction of raising grandchildren. *Families in Society* 82 (5): 461–472.

Walsh, F. 2002. A family resilience framework for intervention and prevention. In A.R. Roberts and G.J. Greene (Eds.), *Social Workers' Desk Reference*, 246–251. New York: Oxford University Press.

Young, D.S. and Smith, C.J. 2000. When moms are incarcerated: The needs of children, mothers, and caregivers. *Families in Society* 81 (2): 130–140.

Caring for My Grandmother

FOUR

The Birth of a Gerontological Social Worker

ERICA EDWARDS

In the fall of 1999 through the spring of 2001, I attended school in Richmond, Virginia, to become a social worker. This was a very difficult time for me because not only was I dealing with the life stressors of being newly married and recently relocated, I was also learning about new social work theories that I thought I would never use. In addition, I entered school with heightened stress because my grandmother became ill the summer before I started graduate school. For more than a year I fulfilled multiple roles until her death on Thanksgiving Day, 2000: new wife, caregiver for my grandmother, emotional outlet for my mother, and student. I was not only learning about social work practice from textbooks, I was also living it. Lack of information, unreliable personnel, and a fragmented medical system plagued my family as we cared for my grandmother. The troubles I encountered as a caregiver provided me with information that was valuable to me as a student, professional geriatric care manager, and social worker in an aging society.

This chapter describes my experiences as a caregiver and student and how those experiences have shaped me as a professional gerontological social worker. This chapter also includes social work theories and literature that will help guide implications from a macro and micro perspective to improve practice in hospitals and community-based settings so that caregiver stress and anxiety may be minimized.

DESCRIPTION OF CAREGIVERS

My father has one daughter and my mother two from previous marriages. My sisters were fifteen, fourteen, and twelve years older. I was quite close to all of my sisters, although they had left home by the time I was school age. My birth was an accident; my parents, father age forty-five and mother age thirty-six, did not plan to have more children. I was born in Florida. Often away for up to six months, my father was a captain for a container ship company, and my mother was a homemaker and former elementary school teacher. In Florida, my maternal grandmother and great-grandmother lived near us and were very involved in my early life. My great-grandmother noticed that my right limbs differed from the left. Initially, my pediatrician thought there were no problems. Because of my great-grandmother's persistence, my parents began a long journey of consultations with specialists. After two years of exhaustive medical testing and evaluations, I was diagnosed with cerebral palsy. Thus began my ongoing and frequent contact with medical providers.

Fortunately, my family did not accept the dire prognosis, teaching me that the human spirit is stronger than medical prognoses. Today, I have mostly invisible residuals of cerebral palsy: no fine motor control in my right hand, immobile right foot, and mild scoliosis. A special shoe remedies the two-inch leg differential. I run two miles a few times every week; and to give my right hand exercise, I purchase only cars with stick shifts. When asked how cerebral palsy affects me, I reply, "I don't know" because I have known no other life. I use my physical challenges and life experiences in my profession; for example, I used being different to connect with teens.

I attended public schools in Florida and Texas. Texas allowed Dad to be closer to his mother, who resided in the Southwest, and to hold a job that ensured noninvolvement in the 1980s Iran–Iraq controversy. I graduated from the University of Texas at Austin in 1996.

After my maternal grandfather's 1992 death from cancer and my father's retirement, my parents settled in a Florida ocean town about forty-five minutes from her mother. After their move, I returned home for a year, 1996 to 1997, after graduating with a degree in business. Unable to land a challenging position, I had the best year of my life getting to know my father. Father developed hypertension and had a severe allergic reaction to a prescription, laser surgery for cataracts, and skin surgery to remove a cancerous tumor. Building our adult relationship was his pleasant distraction.

In 1997, my oldest paternal sister invited me to visit her and search for employment in Iowa, where I found employment, a husband, and the need for graduate school. I worked with children in a residential psychiatric facility where my sister was a board member. The work was educational and emotionally and physically draining. Without the use of my right side, I found restraining a child impossible and had to learn verbal negotiation skills. Quickly, I burned out and realized the need for graduate education. At a Jaycee meeting, I met Rodney (Rod), my future husband.

In 1998, soon after I met Rod, Dad died of a sudden heart attack. After tennis and dinner at his favorite steak restaurant, he died while starting the car. His body was found a day later, and the family was notified two days later. The situation, devastating and shocking, increased my gratitude for my postcollege time at home. That my father liked Rod helped me to make the decision to marry him. For the convenience of our friends and families, we wed in Iowa and Florida, in June and July 1999, respectively.

First, I invited Rod, a person who had lived only in Iowa, to vacate his secure state construction inspector position to accompany me to Richmond, Virginia, home of Virginia Commonwealth University (VCU), where I attended social work graduate school. School ranking, cost, and location informed my decision. To Richmond we went with my promise of an Iowa wedding. Fortunately, Rod secured a parallel position in Virginia, and I worked in a homeless shelter and volunteered at a nursing home. I knew I wanted to be an advocate for the disenfranchised. My work and health challenges, the healthcare experiences of my grandmother since her 1985 diagnosis of colon cancer, and my pragmatism identified older adults as the group. I thought that work with older adults would ensure employment in social work. At that time, few were spearheading the necessary changes in services for older adults. A bonus was VCU's selecting me to participate in a funded gerontology training program. Everything was set until I learned that my maternal grandmother was seriously ill.

My grandmother, age eighty-one, and I had a very close relationship, although we lived miles apart. She was with me when I ran my first race at age nine and when I got my ears pierced when I was twelve years old (behind my mother's back), and she helped me get my first job at age sixteen. She sent me letters and care packages in college, and she made me her famous fudge when I came home for Christmas. Family was very important to her, and she never failed to demonstrate this, especially when someone needed help. When she became ill, the roles were reversed, and she was the one who needed help.

Although everyone loved her, it became a challenge to help her because of distance.

My grandmother and step-grandfather, Paul, lived in Florida, hours away from my other sister, Marie, in Georgia, and me. Paul, the primary caregiver, was seventy-eight and frail. Marie was a cancer survivor whom doctors misdiagnosed twice before finding the disease in her lymph nodes. She had also taken care of her paternal grandmother, who died of Alzheimer's in a substandard nursing home and had vast experiences with the healthcare system and caregiving. Because she had two small children, Marie could not help often, producing role conflict. My mother and I had no experience. Furthermore, my mother suffered from gallstones and lived 45 miles away from Grandmother.

Marie, Mother, and I were among the more than seven million long-distance caregivers (National Institute on Aging 2006) who supported in-home caregivers (Miles Away 2004). Unfortunately, like many long-distance caregivers, my family believed that Paul could care for Grandmother, especially because he was living with her. He did as well as he could. For five years Paul had cared for his previous wife, helping her battle cancer. Facing Grandmother's cancer along with his chronic pain from esophageal ulcers and multiple medications produced growing stress, confusion, and depression. Paul consequently occupied the dual family caregiver–care recipient roles. In addition, the entire family was frustrated because inadequate, incorrect medical information sabotaged our efforts.

DESCRIPTION OF FAMILY MEMBER CARED FOR

Grandmother, Elizabeth Wilson, born in 1918 to a German family, grew up on an Ohio farm with two sisters and two brothers. At eighteen she married her neighbor and high school sweetheart. They had one girl, my mother, Lois Carter. During an era when women's work outside the home was frowned upon, she worked to pay her husband's way through college. After becoming a bookkeeper, she became the first female general manager for a federal credit union and revitalized the failing financial institution, creating a legacy many read about today. At retirement, she earned more than her college-educated husband. After retirement she did many things: walking and biking every day, running and winning a 2-mile race at sixty-five, and hiking through mountains. Well into her seventies, she enjoyed walking miles each day and riding her bicycle. These activities provided physical fitness and increased her immunity and resilience. For example, she conquered colon cancer twice, surprising doctors with her determination to survive despite her low odds. Unfortunately, my physically active grandfather was less fortunate and died of a sudden heart attack in the summer of 1992.

In 1994, Grandmother and Paul married. Paul and his wife were friends of my grandparents for more than twenty years. My grandmother helped him to end a fifty-year estrangement from his three children. Grandmother continued managing the household finances, cooking, cleaning, and exercising until age eighty-one, making it difficult for my family to accept the grim news of her physical condition in the summer of 1999.

DESCRIPTION OF CAREGIVING EXPERIENCE

The Phone Call

When I received the call from my mother, age sixty-one, my heart sank. Mother said that Grandmother, who lived in Orlando, Florida, was hospitalized with a third occurrence of colon cancer and unable to attend to my wedding. After surgery to remove more colon, she was taking cancer-fighting drugs to prevent its spread. Each physician treated a different part of her body, prescribed multiple medications, and rarely communicated. Her current symptoms—bruising, vomiting, weakness, confusion, and combativeness—probably were caused by the side effects and interactions of potent medications. The medical staff planned to restrain or transfer Grandmother to a nursing home unless someone constantly stayed with her. Predictably, Grandmother was angry that the hospital workers were not listening or explaining anything to her. The hospital discharged her, soon after she kicked a nurse who was attempting to put a needle in her arm, without referrals to or mention of community resources. We were on our own.

For the first time since she was a child, Grandmother relied on a team of family caregivers. Exhausted and coping with health problems, Mother needed my help. Grandmother, usually strong-willed with a commanding presence, was completely helpless, dependent, and confused. Before beginning graduate school in the fall of 1999, I drove the twelve hours from Virginia to help three people—Paul, Grandmother, and Mother—for several weeks.

My Role as Caregiver

Grandmother's small, lethargic, colorless body shocked and frightened me. She allowed only Paul to move, dress, or bathe her. I cleaned and prepared meals, although she was often unable to eat. Mother and I cared for her during the night to let Paul rest. The round-the-clock care was physically and emotionally exhausting for all, but none realized formal support was an option. In time for me to begin school, Grandmother improved—no longer needed a walker, performed some regular household chores, and was cognitively alert. She was diagnosed with diabetes, a side effect of a medication, we later learned. Her improvement supported our contention that her erratic behavior and downward spiral while hospitalized and undergoing chemotherapy were related to the hospital environment and medication side effects. Later, we would wonder whether heart failure, a diagnosis that emerged several months later, was also a factor.

Downward Spiral

By January 2000, Grandmother could walk only a couple of feet without becoming breathless, and her nausea returned with a vengeance. Having been a several-mile mall walker, she was frustrated, and she did not understand the reasons for her deterioration. After hospitalization and more tests, Grandmother learned she had congestive heart failure. The hospital discharged her with oxygen, more medications, and, for the first time, home health nurses to help her with the oxygen and medication set-ups in the home. Paul sometimes forgot to administer her medications. Mother brought meals biweekly. Not wanting to burden others, she never asked for or accepted additional help. Fortunately, Grandmother performed her own personal care.

By summer's end, Grandmother had lost 50 pounds, was sleeping constantly, and had little energy. Her third hospitalization lasted more than two months. There, she became insulin dependent, and ulcers covered her stomach. Thinking she was home, she tried to make pies; other times, she tried to rip the IV from her arm and leave the hospital. Therefore, someone had to stay with her at all times. She endured interventions such as drinking substances that gagged her and frequent diagnostic blood samples. She spoke briefly when I called, yet it was imperative to communicate directly with her. No staff discussed her medical condition or interventions with Grandmother or family members. When she had renal failure in September, she pointedly asked staff several times whether she was going to die, and they replied only that they could do nothing more for her. Therefore, she still thought she could beat the odds, as she had so many times before.

She stayed at the hospital until insurance no longer paid. The hospital released her with a walker, although she could barely walk 10 feet and had four major diagnoses: renal failure, type II diabetes, congestive heart failure, and stomach ulcers (these are the diagnoses I knew of). The hospital discharge planner told Paul only that she would arrange a nurse to help with her twelve medications, insulin injections, and bath. Now, Grandmother needed help with all her activities of daily living: bathing, feeding, dressing, grooming, and walking. Unable to ingest water or food, Grandmother was more depressed, confused, and ill. Mother stayed for long stints to help nurse her back to health. Paul had seen the doctor only once during the hospitalization, but he didn't think to ask any questions, so no family knew her prognosis.

Mother was overwhelmed with the caregiving challenges and lack of medical information and her inability to ease Grandmother's suffering. I spoke with Mother frequently, each time offering to return to Florida to help. Mother said there was nothing I could do and preferred I stayed in school for my second year. Mother sometimes wished for respite but knew she would face tremendous guilt if something happened to Grandmother in her absence. I felt completely helpless, especially because I was the social worker in training and I had no answers.

The Final Weeks

After Grandmother collapsed to the floor, an ambulance returned her to the hospital she detested. She spent the next two weeks growing weaker. She pleaded for hospital staff to stop hurting her, but they continued to poke and prod. Mother felt guilty about allowing the ambulance to bring her back there and helpless watching Grandmother writhe in pain. Again, no one shared information with the family about what was wrong. By this time, Paul was severely depressed and forgetful. Knowing the healthcare system better than anyone, Marie contacted the doctor. For the first time, he said Grandmother had an inoperable pancreatic tumor and finally told my grandparents. Grandmother cried and said, "I just wanted to die at home."

Marie knew about hospice from previous caregiving experiences. She asked a hospital nurse about hospice so Grandmother could go home. The discharge planner discouraged discharge because of limited staff over Thanksgiving. Marie persisted, and Grandmother, limp as a rag doll, was discharged that night on a stretcher with a catheter. The planner said the hospice person would visit Grandmother and complete her paperwork that evening, the day before Thanksgiving. With no explanation, hospice came the next morning.

Thanksgiving Day

Having last seen Grandmother in summer, Rod and I arrived on Thanksgiving Day. She was thin and her face was gray as she slept while sitting up in a chair. The fluid running through her catheter was brown. Paul told me she had spent most of the evening talking with her relatives who were long since deceased, but in the morning she seemed more alert, asking when I was coming with the turkey. From the situation and her appearance, I knew she did not have much longer to live. With a big smile on her face, she said how happy she was to see me and that her mother made the new booties on her feet, although her mother had died years before. The family said she was in and out of reality, partly because of the morphine she took for pain. Minutes after I saw her, I was shocked, overwhelmed, and grief stricken over how much my strong grandmother had endured. I had to step outside to collect myself. It was then that Marie came out of the bedroom to say Grandmother had passed away. What happened next was horrific.

In order to make Grandmother more comfortable when she came from the hospital, we removed her "do not resuscitate" (DNR) bracelet. Nobody at the hospital told us to leave it on until hospice arrived. Thinking the paramedics would need the living will when they arrived after Grandmother's passing, we searched for it, unsuccessfully. Paul, in a fog, was no help. In the absence of the bracelet and living will, the paramedics attempted to revive my grandmother, despite Paul's request that they not resuscitate her. The paramedic selected this action in direct violation of Florida's regulations and statutes permitting a surrogate or spouse to verbally request DNR orders (Sabatino 1999). I submitted a complaint letter to the paramedics involved that explains what transpired at my grandmother's house (see the appendix).

Caregiving Supports and Challenges

Our move to Richmond was stressful particularly for Rod, who had always lived in his birth city. We were adjusting to marriage and new employment positions and later my becoming a graduate student. In addition, I was helping Mother with her emotional responses to Grandmother's illness. My grandmother's declining health surfaced some of the unresolved feelings Mother and I shared about my father's premature death. In helping my mother, I struggled with the stress related to role reversal. Instead of the usual situation of receiving help, I was aiding Mother, my step-grandfather, and my grandmother. My role reversal was identical to what Mother faced with Grandmother and stressful for all. I battled it by exercising more and turning to Rod, friends, and resources at school. My friends and schoolmates helped me to set limits. One instructor gave me an extension on a paper, and another excused me from the class on death and dying, held at a mortuary. As a social work student, I learned about community resources and secured lists of questions one should ask prospective home health aides, knowledge I could share with my mother and Paul.

Rod was an excellent, attentive listener and my best friend, with whom I shared my feelings, frustrations, and anger. Rod and Grandmother loved each other. His resemblance to her brother-in-law endeared him even more to her. After Grandmother's death, Rod felt particularly guilty. He thought that if he had not moved her from the chair to the bed, as she requested, Grandmother would have lived.

ANALYSES

The experiences with my grandmother were chaotic, confusing, and emotionally exhausting. My family thought incorrectly that the healthcare system would guide us. Healthcare had changed significantly since my grandmother's previous illness, and our family was unprepared. Insurance companies and managed care were the ultimate decision makers, usurping physicians' power, authority, and expertise.

Because of managed care, patients with chronic illnesses are discharged quickly, often needing complex home equipment. Medical staff often does not share important medical information or community services after discharge. Therefore, family becomes caregivers; most are working women, and many are long distance (Family Caregiver Alliance n.d.). These factors, in addition to a shortage of qualified, trained personnel, create more barriers to effective healthcare, resulting in additional stress.

The social ecological system perspective states that individuals and environmental systems reciprocally influence each other. The theory posits that the satisfaction of human needs entails the availability of adequate resources in the environment and positive transactions between people in their environments (Hepworth et al. 1997). Using this framework, I examined the communication patterns between family members, physicians, hospice staff, nurses, and emergency medical service (EMS) personnel (Marks and Lambert 1997). The healthcare system provided a detrimental environment. It addressed no needs—social relationships, appropriate activities, goal achievement, adequate planning, medical and community resources, knowledge, and behavioral expectations (Coulton 1979). It was as if Grandmother were in a foreign environment, and staff expected her to function without diagnoses, prognoses, instructions, and education. She reacted with intense agitation and anger.

Role Theory

The confusion among my family can best be understood using role theory. The medical staff or social worker should have assessed family caregivers for proximity, available time, financial constraints, prior experience, role assignments, flexibility, clarity, and external influences (Hepworth et al. 1997). Assessments, if made, had no positive benefits.

The family, Paul, and the hospital staff expected Paul to occupy the primary caregiver role. Discharge planners assumed he could successfully perform the unexplained tasks. Feeling he was failing, he was unable to ask for help. However, what he experienced was role overload: too many responsibilities. One might have expected the discharge planner to ask a seventy-eight-year-old spouse whether he alone could care for his wife. However, if he answered "no," the planner would have had to identify needed resources.

Fearing additional responsibilities, Mother, the inexperienced and unprepared secondary caregiver, hesitated to question Paul's abilities. Moreover, she would have violated role expectations by questioning an elder and father figure. Role reversals made caring for Grandmother a challenge for all. Like many frail older adults, she was uncomfortable receiving care, and our family members had difficulty adjusting to directing and delivering the needed care or its supervision (Plowfield et al. 2000). Maintaining the dignity of the elder, identifying role reversals, resolving family boundary confusions, and validating caregiving challenges are essential interventions. Seeing Grandmother become dependent was particularly difficult for Mother to accept and respond to. No professionals helped Mother or any family members increase their comfort and skills with the novel roles. Like others (Hauser et al. 2006), my grandmother and the family caregivers were concerned more about issues that affected the other person than we were about issues that affected ourselves. In this way we, including my grandmother, were all involved in caregiving roles.

Role strain occurs when there is confusion about who does what (Hepworth et al. 1997). My sister and I had assumed that my mother and Paul would be the advocates for Grandmother's healthcare because they had opportunities to communicate directly with the medical providers. Ambiguous role assignments meant no one knew to advocate and take charge until it was too late.

Finally, my grandmother's story showed that communication within and between the family and environmental systems, such as healthcare, is essential to effective caregiving.

Poor Medical Care

The many physicians did not tell us that Grandmother had a baseball-sized tumor in her pancreas until the week before her death. Today, we still wonder why the diagnosis was given so late and only after Marie's unrelenting questioning. What happened with Grandmother was not rare. Lack of communication with and between physicians and the resulting medical errors annually cause hundreds of thousands of deaths (Reiland 2004). The United States is among the worst culprits, with one-third of patients reporting at least one medical error, including incorrect medication or dosage and delayed or incorrect test results (Arias 2005). Poor coordination between multiple doctors is a significant factor. Almost half of patients are unable to discuss the prognoses with their physicians (Marshall 1995). Medical professionals, trained to preserve life, have difficulty acknowledging and accepting death. The General Accounting Office reports that in 1998, more than one quarter of Medicare recipients received one week or less of hospice care (Pear 2000). The physicians may have thought that telling us they could do nothing more for my grandmother informed us that she was dying. However, medical providers had used these exact words on two previous occasions when she had cancer. Therefore, my grandmother and the family perceived this to mean it would again be up to this strong woman to overcome the odds. As our population ages, effective intervention strategies and hospice and palliative care must become an integral part of professional education.

Medical Staff Shortages

My grandmother constantly endured inappropriate and inadequate care at the hospital; she waited hours for nurses, developed bedsores because the staff did not turn her frequently enough, and received toxic levels of medication. By her accounts, her hospital experiences were a nightmare. Healthcare suffers from nurse shortages, a lack of skilled workers, long hours, professional burnout (Benjamin 2000), inadequate management of dementia patients, and patient errors (Przymusinski 2003; Rait and Walters 1999). Unfortunately, the future supply will not keep up with the nursing demand as youth and current RNs select more lucrative professions (Przymusinski 2003).

None of Grandmother's formal caregivers was a gerontologist or geriatrician. These professionals, trained in the important nuances of providing services to older adults, are familiar with community resources beneficial to the geriatric population and their families, such as hospice. They are concerned with both preserving life and promoting its quality. Currently, we have less than one-half of the needed geriatricians and will need five times more by 2025. Sadly, the number has declined 29% since 1998, and U.S. medical schools have only one-third of the requisite professors (US Newswire 2002; Willging 2004). Lack of institutional financial support and practitioners' preference (to heal the sick—not heal those in decline nor to help them have good quality of life during a terminal illness) are the crucial factors.

There is also a need for more professional social workers, especially with gerontological expertise. Many are baby boomers and readying for retirement (Whitaker et al. 2006a, 2006b, 2006c, 2006d, 2006e). Simultaneously, there are recruitment challenges, partly because of lower salaries than in other helping professions. At a time when the U.S. population is aging and needing additional services, there are insufficient gerontological professionals to meet the need (Whitaker et al. 2006a, 2006b, 2006c, 2000e). The current and expected labor shortages exist despite the commendable Hartford Foundation funding and the National Association of Social Work's free continuing education units, teleconferences, and certificates in gerontology and end-of-life care (Whitaker et al. 2006a). Social workers can attend teleconferences and continuing education courses via their computers. To serve the needs of older adults, more funding—from government and private sources, to recruit, train, and pay commensurate wages—is essential. Cost containment, the original goal of managed care, has not been realized. Instead, patient and staff dissatisfaction, malpractice payments, and poor-quality care have all increased. Increasing the number of experts in gerontology is a win–win proposition.

Validation Therapy and Dementia Training Needed for Hospital Staff

Although I had been personally involved with medical providers all my life because of my cerebral palsy, I did not think that the healthcare system lacked empathy until my grandmother was involved in it. While she was in the hospital, doctors talked over her as if she were not there. If there were another family member in the room, they would address that person but ignore my grandmother. They wanted to restrain her and place her in a nursing home because they thought she was aggressive and out of control. Hospital personnel made little effort to understand why she was trying to escape. Because they did not

ager. The healthcare system expects discharge planners to discharge quickly and efficiently, which means that families usually have less than twenty-four hours' notice before a loved one is discharged. In that short period, discharge planners give patients and family members a list of resources, such as nursing homes or home health facilities, and expect the family to call that list to arrange an adequate plan themselves. Often, the discharge planner spends little time helping overwhelmed families understand what is really needed to care for their loved ones. Within this timeframe, it is impossible to arrange for a posthospital plan other than family caregiving, even when the patient's health status necessitates community facility placement. The hurried in-home placement results in stress and failure. In turn, caregivers take on much of the responsibility to move their loved ones home, but many find out that they cannot adjust after the loved one has moved in with them. The hospital saves money through the hurried discharge only in the short term; prematurely discharged patients usually return because of inadequate discharge planning. These results suggest the need for discharge planning staff to begin assessing the situation with the family and medical staff and considering discharge options when the patient enters the hospital.

Many discharge planners do not accurately assess the disabilities and needs of patients at time of discharge. They also often assume that patients know more about their discharge plans than they actually do. Retrospective studies show that discharge planners underestimate the needs of recently discharged patients (Reiley et al., 1996). This could be because of the time constraints placed on discharge planners, which limit their ability to complete a thorough, accurate in-hospital assessment of the patient and caregivers to provide a plan that meets the needs of all involved. Furthermore, discharge planners have no method to monitor families after the discharge to ensure that no one slips through the cracks.

Medicare pays a large portion of the physician, hospital, and prescription charges for seniors and those with disabilities. However, the program has had some unintended consequences. The federal government introduced the Medicare Prospective Payment System (PPS) to control costs of medical care charged by hospitals. Under PPS, hospitals are paid a flat rate for each patient according to his or her diagnosis, regardless of the actual services performed. Studies document that since the introduction of the Medicare PPS, patients have been discharged in less recovered states (Kahn et al. 1990; Kosecoff et al. 1996; Moore et al. 2007). Older adults are going home more vulnerable and more dependent than they were a decade ago, and informal caregivers and primary care physicians have to provide more care to sicker people (Moore et al. 2007; Proctor et al. 1996). Assessment protocols to address these situations meet several implementation problems (Hawes et al. 2007).

Ethical Decision Making and EMS Personnel

I received a letter of response from the letter I wrote to EMS. The response stated that they had encountered such situations in the past and would look into it. I never heard back from them again. It was unsettling to hear that what I assumed was an atypical situation was not rare at all. It seems that further paramedic training in ethics would prevent paramedics from adding stress to their daily crises.

I have spoken with paramedics from various states since then and have researched their training requirements. The requirements to become a licensed paramedic vary from state to state (Hall 2005). There is no standardized national curriculum. One state may delve deeply into important issues such as ethics, communication with families in crisis, durable powers of attorney, and do not resuscitate orders; others may not require any of these. States do require ongoing training to maintain the paramedic license, but ethics is not required. Even without the ethical training, state EMS programs could easily implement policies and strategies to address the problems that occurred with my grandmother. However, our situation showed that the implementation of those policies and strategies may be insufficient. EMS was supposed to accept Paul's consent for a DNR order, but they did not. Thus, they did not follow procedures already in place.

IMPLICATIONS

Because situations such as the one I encountered with my family are so complex, it is difficult to identify how future problems can be prevented. Some social workers may feel that they are working against the odds, facing what may seem like insurmountable barriers. Charting and diagramming delineate the systems affected, how they are affected, and strategies to overcome the problems. They help simplify even the most complex issues. This section is based on social ecological system theory (Beckett and Lee 2004; Hartman 1995; Hartman and Laird 1983) and will serve as a guide to social workers as they work with families in these types of crises. The discussion is summarized in table 4.1.

Table 4.1 Implications

	Issues and Problems	Strategies for Change
Individuals	Caregiver is unable to take care of care receiver. Information on care receivers' needs and healthcare is inadequate.	Request help. Request information. Advocate for yourself.
Families	Information is not exchanged between family members. Families are unaware of resources available.	Have family meetings in times of crisis. Plan ahead.
Communities	Number of geriatricians and nurses is insufficient.	Increase media exposure.
Practitioners and educators	Geriatric and dementia education in professional schools and acute care settings is insufficient. Emergency medical personnel are not adequately trained.	Mandate geriatric and dementia training in professional and medical schools. Increase training in ethics.
Institutions	Discharge plans are based on incorrect assumptions from poor assessments. Patients have high readmission rates.	Make discharge assessment procedures patient-centered. Include postdischarge follow-up in discharge procedures.
Researchers	Valid data are needed to make systemic change.	Conduct research on impact of training on outcomes and impact of care management on hospital readmission rates.

Microsystem: Individuals and Families

Microsystems are informal systems in which people have face-to-face contact. These include individuals, families, and intimate small groups.

Request Help When the Caregiver Experiences Role Overload

Caregivers need to be educated that it is okay, even essential, to ask for help and must know ahead of time whom they can turn to for relief. Many area agencies on aging currently have grant funding from the National Family Caregiver Support Program that will help educate caregivers on options and resources available. Geriatric social workers, often called geriatric care managers, also provide helpful information and resources for family members. You can locate one near you by calling the National Association of Professional Geriatric Care Managers at 520-881-8008 or visiting the national Web site at www.caremanager.org.

Request Information When Feeling Lost in the Healthcare System. Advocate for Yourself

Individuals and caregivers need to learn to question everything. If there is something about their medical care that they don't understand, they need to ask. Many treatment options are available to the terminally ill, but options for the patient always are limited to those that the physician offers when he or she is ready to offer them. This also means that a conversation *must* occur between the physician and patient or family. Physicians are fallible, and patients and caregivers need to recognize this and take responsibility for asking the important questions to reduce the risks of mistakes and explore options. A second opinion, and if necessary a third, can provide additional information and support for your previously made decision.

Conduct Family Meetings to Facilitate Better Communication During Crises

Family meetings are very important during times of crisis. They will help clarify the roles of all caregivers involved, reducing confusion and stress. In some cases, family members assign roles such as grocery shopper, medication reminder, healthcare power of attorney, bill payer, and helper with personal tasks. When responsibilities are delegated to as many members as possible, role overload can be prevented. Knowing what I know now, we should have had a family meeting about my grandmother's care, and everyone should have selected a caregiving role and tasks. This would have alleviated role strain and reduced the role overload Paul and the rest of us felt.

Plan to Avoid a Crisis in the Future

Clients need to be aware that the healthcare system will not advocate for patients. Discharge planners cannot recommend one or two high-quality facilities; they can only provide extensive lists of facilities for families to wade through and often do not provide information to families and patients after discharge. If at all possible, older adults should plan ahead with their families before a hospitalization occurs and discuss important issues such as the living will, long-term care options, respite services, medical care, financial affairs, and home- and community-based programs (e.g., home-delivered meals, personal emergency response systems, transportation, and friendly visitor programs). Although these issues may not seem important to many families now, having a plan in place that incorporates becoming familiar with community resources could avert a crisis.

Macrosystems

Macrosystems are social institutions in the individual's or family's environment that influence their lives, such as religion, government, education, and social welfare. They include links between microsystems and between microsystems and larger institutions. Examples include interactions between the family (a microsystem) and the medical system or the social security system. The mass media are an example of a macrosystem that influences the culture, subculture, and physical environment of microsystems.

Communities

Increased Media Exposure of Geriatricians to Increase Enrollment and Demand

Many people have never heard of geriatricians or do not fully understand what nurses and other medical staff do, despite the many medical shows on network television. Doctors such as plastic surgeons, cardiologists, and neurosurgeons are the heroes and heroines on television medical shows, whereas nurses are portrayed as grouchy and incompetent and geriatricians are excluded. Social workers usually are cast as social welfare eligibility gatekeepers or foster care workers. These are often the positions that a person occupies with any bachelor's degree; the media rarely show trained bachelor's- and master's-level social workers. The media can be an ally and change agent by creating shows that introduce medical staff, social workers, nurses, and other helping professionals who are trained to work with geriatric populations. Programs and newspaper articles can concentrate on the good works they do for the public. Because of increased understanding, more students will be attracted to geriatric training programs.

Practitioners and Educators

Mandate Geriatric and Dementia Training in Professional Schools and for Hospital Personnel

There is a serious lack of formal training of healthcare professionals to care for the unique needs of older adults. In turn, healthcare providers overmedicate many older adults by prescribing dosages appropriate for younger people. Many senior citizens have so many different problems that physicians do not consider or address all of them. The healthcare of seniors and the medical care system are both complex. Seniors usually have multiple medical challenges; few physicians can address all. Because medical practice is so specialized, these seniors find themselves seeing multiple specialists, sometimes one for each diagnosis. Unfortunately, too often the necessary communication between treating physicians fails to occur. The result may be that physicians are working at odds with each other. Another factor is that a single symptom can have many causes. For example, overmedication, the process of recovery from heart surgery, and mental illness can cause hallucinations. I have seen many doctors misdiagnose clients with dementia. This resulted because the doctors confused delirium (restlessness, confusion, and sometimes hallucinations) derived from overmedication with dementia (loss of cognitive functioning and sometime hallucinations caused by damage to brain tissue). With an accurate history, this error would not occur. Although both diagnoses can include similar symptoms, the course of each illness is quite different. Delirium has a sudden onset (a few hours or days) and usually is temporary, whereas dementia is a progressive, irreversible cognitive deterioration. Furthermore, many doctors do not understand the continuum of care and how it affects older adults. The continuum of care stresses the provision of appropriate care for the changing health conditions and needs of older adults. In my grandmother's case, the doctor did not recognize the need and preference for hospice. He did not adjust his medical interventions to her terminal condition.

There are few innovative geriatric programs. Some medical schools are training medical students by having them role-play as older adults with disabilities. This gives students the opportunity to learn what it is like to be in the shoes of a disabled person. In the Public Broadcast Service documentary *And Thou Shalt Honor* (Bell and Wiland 2002), the University of Minnesota Medical School taught students in this manner. The students faced problematic situations similar to what my grandmother encountered. The person role-playing the physician talked over the students, did not explain what was happening to them, served them foul-tasting fluids, and exposed them to many other offensive situations that many people with disabilities endure. These experiential learning opportunities were beneficial. They served as eye-opening experiences for students who, subsequently, were better able to empathize with their patients.

These programs not only should be available in more medical schools, they also should be taught to any professional who interacts with older adults with disabilities: social workers, nurses and nurses' aides, and physical, occupational, and speech therapists, among many others. Furthermore, they should include validation communication dementia training. This would help to make any environment more nurturing for patients who need patience and understanding and reduce agitation for those who are confused. The population of the United States and the rest of the world is getting older. If healthcare workers and other professionals are untrained in how to meet the needs of older adults and those who have dementia, they will create more stress for themselves and for the patients they are attempting to serve.

EMS Paramedics Should Have a Standardized Curriculum and Ongoing Ethics Training

The standards for paramedic certification vary from state to state. In most cases, students have to complete approximately 2,000 hours of classroom training and internship before they can be paramedics. There are also continuing education requirements to renew the paramedic certification. Again, the numbers of hours and types of courses required vary from state to state. Matt Kauffmann is a paramedic from Illinois. He states that in his training program a very small percentage of his time was focused on ethics. He also indicates that role-plays involving family situations, such as the one I experienced, would be helpful in teaching deescalation skills, dealing with ethical dilemmas, and helping EMS personnel understand better how to respond effectively in situations that could bring potential lawsuits (M. Kauffmann, personal communication, June 21, 2006). With a greater focus on ethics, many paramedics would improve their empathy, communication, and problem-solving skills to deal with the public effectively. For example, they would be able to determine when a durable healthcare power of attorney would supersede a DNR order, or vice versa, and avoid future lawsuits.

Unfortunately, my situation was not unique. It is important that a national standardized curriculum be created for all paramedics that ensures that basic standards are met. Paramedics from all over the country would respond to natural disasters and other crises with the same standardized comprehensive training that covers not only the medical issues of their jobs but the emotional issues as well. They are intervening in highly emotional circumstances. National curricula that include ethics and role-plays would prevent the many families like mine from falling through the cracks.

Institutions

Change Discharge Procedures and Assessments to Be More Patient-Centered

Literature has shown that adequate discharge planning can decrease inpatient costs, improve patient outcomes and satisfaction, reduce readmission rates, and facilitate continuity of care (Anthony and Hudson-Barr 1998; Haddock 1994; Matt-Hensrud et al. 2001; McGinley et al. 1996). Unfortunately, many hospital discharge planners are under pressure from insurance companies to discharge patients as quickly as possible, regardless of whether a safe plan is in place when patients leave. A follow-up study of discharged patients found that almost all (97%) reported one or more needs for care, and one-third (33%) had at least one of these needs unmet (Potthoff and Kane 1997). Another study found that social workers rated their discharge plans as generally adequate. Yet they also acknowledged that in a large percentage of these cases, the plans would not withstand many changes in the patient's condition, the family support system would prove inadequate, or the patient would be unable to manage the regimen because of cognitive or physical limitations (Potthoff and Kane 1997). Patients and caregivers have many things to worry about in the hospital, producing high stress levels. Many times information about diagnoses or plans of care is given verbally. However, patients' and caregivers' stress levels make it almost impossible for them to understand and retain the information. Realizing this, some staff members resort to providing brochures, which do not really convey to families what they need to know about caregiving.

Several steps can be taken to ensure that the right discharge plan is selected. It is imperative that upon admission, discharge planners give families referral sheets, which contain a list of pertinent community resources. The discharge planner might develop a list of questions frequently asked by family members and their answers and share it with the patient and family. Second, training that requires discharge planners to role-play some of the situations family caregivers face will help them to better understand the frustration caregivers experience. This experiential learning would graphically demonstrate how important communication is between the family and hospital staff. Next, before discharge, planners, along with family members, should complete an in-hospital assessment of the patient to identify the current needs. Then the planner can help the family identify resources for each residual patient challenge. This process ensures that some agency or person addresses the remaining needs.

Finally, the discharge planner or other healthcare provider must obtain patient or primary caregiver consent and notify at least one other contact of the diagnoses and discharge plans for the patient, especially if the primary caregiver is frail. This ensures that there is no communication gap between hospital personnel and the caregiving team and that medical and resource information is disseminated to all responsible parties. When a patient is discharged, it is important that the caregiver receive proper training over a forty-eight-hour period to ensure that he or she understands everything that is expected. Healthcare professionals can be very helpful in this process (Messinger-Rapport et al. 2006; Miestiaen 2007). Testimonials of other family caregivers may also be helpful, illuminating what is involved in caring for a loved one after discharge.

Hospital Systems Should Incorporate Care Management After Discharge

The experiences with my grandmother and my clients have clarified for me how dire the need is for follow-up by a care manager to ensure that the patient and caregiver are both safe. Forty percent of patients with congestive heart failure who were discharged from the hospital did not follow one or more components of their discharge plans (Proctor et al. 1996). A care manager is a professional social worker who can visit the home and if needed train the caregiver, answer any questions that come up, and help link the family to resources if caring for the patient has proved to be more difficult than expected. This will reduce repeat hospitalizations for the patient and family. Some hospitals have recognized this need and have set up care coordination units in hospitals. Some patients are assigned the same case managers when they are readmitted to improve continuity of care. Care management will help hospitals by cutting costs, promoting quality, and improving effectiveness. These types of systems will also fix discharge plans that may be inadequate. This type of system would have demonstrated to hospital workers that the caregiving system my grandmother had was ineffective.

Enrich Nursing and Geriatric Programs

Medical schools should give geriatric medicine the attention it deserves by creating new programs and improving existing ones (Ascribe Higher Education News Service 2002). Credentialing of medical schools should require that each school have a geriatric medicine program in place. These programs should be held to strict accreditation standards. If the American Medical Association does not take a strong stand on this issue in the years to come, future physicians will not receive the specialized training needed to treat aging baby boomers. Without geriatric education programs, there may be more medical errors and lawsuits than ever before.

In order to attract nurses into the field, many programs are partnering with hospitals to offer tuition reimbursement programs and large signing bonuses. Although this has brought some new nurses into the profession, ultimately the nature of the industry needs to change to attract the numbers that are needed. Many hospitals are recognizing that younger people do not want to work long hours in a high-stress environment. Therefore, some settings offer eight-hour workdays and smaller patient caseloads per nurse (Przymusinski 2003). These types of changes are needed to ensure that future generations are attracted to and remain in the nursing field for decades to come.

Researchers

Much more research is needed to ensure that healthcare settings are fully addressing the needs of patients and caregivers. Although recommendations were made throughout this chapter based on available research and literature, more research must be conducted to validate the findings. Some areas where more research is warranted are measured outcomes of dementia training on hospital staff and reduction of restraints, effects of postdischarge care management on hospital readmission rates, correlation of graduation from geriatric education programs and medical error rates, and effects of ongoing ethics training on the number of complaints and lawsuits against EMS personnel. Through repeated validated research, practice can follow, and change can finally occur.

REFLECTIONS AND CONCLUSIONS

By the end of my grandmother's journey, she was weak and mild mannered. She looked like my grandmother, but she did not have the fire and spirit of my grandmother. Looking back, I now understand why she lost some of her spirit. She not only fell prey to the disease that ravaged her body, she lost much of her fight in the hospital system. Her experience shows that we need reform within the system to make caregiving less chaotic and hospitalization less painful for both patients and families.

My grandmother and family went through a very traumatic experience because of the ineffectiveness of our hospital system. It was very difficult for me to relive this experience while writing this chapter. I had enormous feelings of guilt for not having done more, especially because I am a social worker and that is my role. However, I also realize that as a student social worker, I was overwhelmed by my grandmother's healthcare situation. I was just learning about services for seniors and had never before dealt with the hospital system. After the experience with my grandmother, I learned more about caregiving and elder care issues than I ever could learn from a textbook. As a geriatric care manager, I relayed what I had learned to the caregivers I served through articles, presentations, and direct counseling.

Now that this chapter is complete, the journey of reliving the terrible experience with my grandmother and my family is almost over. When I volunteered to contribute my experience to this book, I never took into account how many different emotions I would experience or the amount of pain the process would cause my family. At first, I was excited to write this chapter. I wanted to share my story with others so that they would not repeat the same mistakes my family made. However, as soon as I sat down to write, I was plagued with doubt. Could I really do this? I realized I had only a patchwork quilt of what happened in the caregiving of my grandmother. I was afraid of getting a detail wrong, thereby upsetting my family. I would have to do a lot more research into what happened. The thought never once crossed my mind that I would not complete this chapter. Therefore, it became a challenge to me.

I called Paul, my mother, and my sister several times. Each time we had to recount what happened to my grandmother. Each time we cried. This was the most difficult part of writing the chapter. As I delved more and more into the situation, I realized that no one really had a clear idea of what my grandma's medical needs were or the resources available. It was an extremely frustrating, gut-wrenching process. Looking back, I now realize that during the caregiving, everyone was in a fog because no one had all the facts. It was a new realization; each person had a completely different take on the situation. Paul never thought to question the hospital. My mom thought Paul knew what he was doing, and my sister and I thought my mom was asking all the right questions. We all dropped the ball in our own way. It was at this point that I realized how poor our communication was. I was extremely depressed and felt that we had all ultimately failed my grandmother. I had completed the hardest phase of my book chapter, the narrative and analysis, after completing these family interviews.

In order for me to complete the recommendations phase, I had to conduct a literature review to learn more about the current medical system, state statutes for DNR orders, and social work theories that I could apply to my family. I became aware of the gigantic cracks in our healthcare system into which many families fall. A vast amount of literature was available on the ineffectiveness of discharge planning, poor treatment of patients in hospital settings, doctors who prescribe medications instead of hospice, and poor communication patterns in role-defined families. I was also able to find a statute that stated that the EMS personnel could have allowed Paul to make the DNR decision. I had stopped feeling guilty and began to feel angry and empowered. I knew what the problems were and read about innovative remedies.

The easiest part of writing this chapter was making the recommendations. I did not have to relive my grandma's dying or my mother crying. The only emotions I experienced were hope and excitement for the future. I found that I was not alone in what we had experienced and felt comforted, especially after reading about postdischarge planning, increased training for hospital staff, and many other industry-wide recommendations.

I used what I learned in my first professional post-master's position as a geriatric care manager for a nonprofit home service agency based in St. Louis, Missouri. Caregivers routinely contacted me after experiencing a crisis with a loved one. Some common situations I intervened in were "Mom is living alone with multiple health problems, and I'm worried about her ability to take care of herself" or "Dad is being discharged from the hospital, and I don't think Mom can take care of him safely." After meeting with the family caregivers and care receiver, we developed a feasible plan to ensure the safety and well-being of the care receiver and caregivers involved. I strove to ensure that they had the information and resources they needed to feel confident about any decisions they had to make. This position enabled me to use advocacy to prevent numerous families from going through the nightmare we experienced.

I took only a small role in caregiving for my grandmother: adviser to my mother and respite worker for Paul. I was ill equipped for both roles, knowing so little about the situation. I did not really understand how many barriers were involved. In order to perform effective long-distance caregiving, a person should know the questions to ask and the resources available to help. Writing this chapter helped me see the whole situation so that I will be better prepared in the future.

I encourage anyone who has encountered an emotional caregiving situation to write out exactly what they experienced and to get the reactions of others involved. It will help you not only to validate your own feelings but to outline clearly what happened, why it happened, and how the situation could have been avoided. Writing forces one to be objective. You will find that the convoluted situation will begin to make sense when you look at things from both a micro and macro perspective. Empowerment soon follows, and guilt recedes. We are all human. Writing forces us to recognize that no one can be perfect, but we can surely all learn from our mistakes.

REFERENCES

Andrews, K. 1986. Relevance of readmission of elderly patients discharged from a geriatric unit. *Journal of the American Geriatrics Society* 34: 5–11.

Anthony, M.K. and Hudson-Barr, D. C. 1998. Successful patient discharge: A comprehensive model of facilitators and barriers. *Journal of Nursing Administration* 28 (3): 48–55.

Arias, D. 2005. Medical errors, costly care a concern for American patients. *Nation's Health* 35 (10): 6.

Ascribe Higher Education News Service. 2002, Nov. 12. *As Elderly Population Explodes, Study Published in* JAMA *Calls for Increase in Geriatric Training Programs in U.S. Medical Schools.* Retrieved March 9, 2003, from InfoTrac Expanded Academic database.

Beckett, J. and Dungee-Anderson, D. 1998. Multicultural communication in human service organizations. In A. Daly (Ed.), *Diversity in the Workplace: Issues and Perspectives,* 191–214. Washington, D.C.: National Association of Social Workers.

Beckett, J. and Dungee-Anderson, E. 2000. Older persons of color: Asian/Pacific Islander Americans, African Americans, Hispanic Americans, and America Indians. In R. Schneider and N. Kropf (Eds.), *Gerontological Social Work: Fundamentals, Service Settings, and Special Populations,* 2d ed., 257–301. Pacific Grove, Cal.: Brooks/Cole/Wadsworth.

Beckett, J. and Lee, N. 2004. Informing the future of child welfare practices with African American families. In J. Everett, B. Leashore, and S. Chipungu (Eds.), *Child Welfare Revisited: An Africentric Perspective,* 93–123. New Brunswick, N.J.: Rugters University Press.

Bell, D. and Wiland, H. (Executive Producers). 2002, Oct. 9. *And Thou Shalt Honor* [Television documentary]. Arlington, Va.: PBS.

Benjamin, G. C. 2000. The nursing shortage: A crisis in health care. *Physician Executive* 26 (5): 77–80.

Coulton, C. 1979. A study of the person–environment fit among the chronically ill. *Social Work in Health Care* 5: 5–17.

Family Caregiver Alliance. n.d. *Selected Caregiver Statistics.* Retrieved June 18, 2006, from www.caregiver.org/caregiver/jsp/content_node.jsp?nodeid = 439.

Finnema, E., Droes, R., Ribbe, M., and Tilburg, W. 2000. The effects of emotion-oriented approaches in the care for persons suffering from dementia: A review of the literature. *International Journal of Geriatric Psychiatry* 15: 141–161.

Gooding, J. and Jette, A. M. 1985. Hospital readmissions among the elderly. *Journal of the American Geriatrics Society* 33: 595–601.

Graham, H. and Livesley, B. 1983. Can readmissions to a geriatric medical unit be prevented? *Lancet* 1 (8321): 404–406.

Haddock, K. S. 1994. Collaborative discharge planning: Nursing and social services. *Clinical Nurse Specialist* 8 (5): 248–252.

Hall, C. 2005. Riding to the rescue. *Louisville Magazine* 56 (7): 27–30.

Hartman, A. 1995. Diagrammatic assessment of family relations. *Families in Society* 76: 111–122.

Hartman, A. and Laird, J. 1983. *Family-Centered Social Work Practice.* New York: Free Press.

Hauser, J. M., Chang, C. H., Alpert, H., Baldwin, D., Emanuel, E. J., and Emanuel, L. 2006. Who's caring for whom? Differing perspectives between seriously ill patients and their family caregivers. *American Journal of Hospice & Palliative Medicine* 23(2): 105–112.

Hawes, C., Brant, E., Fries, M., James, L., and Guihan, M. 2007. Prospects and pitfalls: Use of the RAI-HC assessment by the Department of Veterans Affairs for home care clients. *The Gerontologist* 47: 378–387.

Hepworth, D., Ronney, R., and Larsen, J. 1997. *Direct Social Work Practice: Theory and Skills.* Pacific Grove, Cal.: Brooks/Cole.

Kahn, K. L., Keeler, E. B., Sherwood, M. J., Rogers, W. H., Draper, D., Bentow, S. S., Reinisch, E. J., Rubenstein, L. V., Kosecoff, J., and Brook, R. H. 1990. Comparing outcomes of care before and after implementation of the DRG-based prospective payment system. *Journal of the American Medical Association* 264: 1984–1986.

Kosecoff, J., Kahn, K. L., Rogers, W. H., Reinisch, E. J., Sherwood, M. J., Rubenstein, L. V., Draper, D., Roth, C. P., Chew, C., and Brook, R. H. 1990. Prospective payment system and impairment at discharge. The "quicker-and-sicker" story revisited. *Journal of the American Medical Association* 264: 1980–1983.

Marks, N. and Lambert, J. 1997. *Family Caregiving: Contemporary Trends and Issues* (NSFH Working Paper No. 78). Madison: University of Wisconsin at Madison.

Marshall, P. 1995. The SUPPORT study: Who's talking? *The Hastings Center Report* 25 (6): S9–12.

Mason, W., Bedwell, C., Vander Zwaag, R., and Runyan, J., Jr. 1980. Why people are hospitalized: A description of preventable factors leading to admission for medical illness. *Medical Care* 18: 147–163.

Matt-Hensrud, N., Severson, M., Hansen, D. C., and Holland, D. E. 2001. A discharge planning program in orthopaedics: Experiences in implementation and evaluation. *Orthopaedic Nursing* 20: 59–75.

McGinley, S., Baus, E., Gyza, K., Johnson, K., Lipton, S., Magee, M. C., Moore, E., and Wojtyak, D. 1996. Multidisciplinary discharge planning. *Nursing Management* 27 (10): 55–60.

Messinger-Rapport, B. J., McCallum, T. J., and Hujer, M. E. 2006. *Annals of Long-Term Care: Clinical Care and Aging* 14(1): 34–41.

Miles Away: The Metlife Study of Long-Distance Caregiving. 2004. New York: National Alliance for Caregiving and Zogby International.

Mistiaen, P., Francke, A. L., and Poot, E. 2007. Interventions aimed at reducing problems in adult patients discharged from hospital to home: A systematic meta-review. *BMC Health Services Research* 7: 47.

Moore, C., McGinn, T., and Halm, E. 2007. Tying up loose ends: Discharging patients with unresolved medical issues. *Archives of Internal Medicine* 167: 1305–1311.

National Institute on Aging. 2006. *Long Distance Caregiving.* Retrieved June 18, 2006, from www.nia.nih.gov/HealthInformation/Publications/LongDistanceCaregiving/chapter01.htm.

Oktay, J. S., Steinwachs, D. M., Mamon, J., Bone, L. R., and Fahey, M. 1992. Evaluating social work discharge planning services for elderly people: Access, complexity, and outcome. *Health and Social Work* 17 (4): 291–298.

Pear, R. 2000, Sept. 18. More patients in hospice care, but for far fewer final days. *The New York Times on the Web.* Retrieved March 28, 2003, from www.nytimes.com/2000/09/18/national/18HOSP.html.

Plowfield, L., Raymond, J., and Blevins, C. 2000, July. Wholism for aging families: Meeting needs of caregivers. *Holistic Nursing Practice* 14 (4): 51.

Potthoff, S. and Kane, R. L. 1997. Improving hospital discharge planning for elderly patients. *Health Care Financing Review* 19 (2): 47–63.

Proctor, E., Morrow-Howell, N., and Kaplan, S. 1996. Implementation of discharge plans for chronically ill elders discharged home. *Health and Social Work* 21 (1): 30–41.

Przymusinski, L. 2003. Nursing: A humanistic profession. *Humanist* 63 (1): 45.

Rait, G. and Walters, K. 1999. The diagnosis and management of dementia in primary care. *Generations* 23 (3): 17–24.

Reiland, R. 2004. The state of hospital care: Worse today than during World War II. *Humanist* 64 (6): 5–6.

Reiley, P., Iezzoni, L., Phillips, R., Davis, R., Tuchin, L., and Calkins, D. 1996. Discharge planning: Comparison of patients' and nurses' perceptions of patients following hospital discharge. *Image: Journal of Nursing Scholarship* 28 (2): 143–148.

Robinson, B. C. 1983. Validation of a caregiver strain index. *Journal of Gerontology* 38: 344–348.

Sabatino, C. 1999. Survey of state EMS-DNR laws and protocols. *Journal of Law, Medicine, & Ethics* 27 (4): 297–321.

US Newswire. 2002, Feb. 21. *Urgent Need for More Geriatric Training for Healthcare Professionals Focus of Senate Special Committee on Aging Hearing.* Retrieved March 9, 2003, from InfoTrac Expanded Academic database.

Whitaker, T., Weismiller, T., and Clark, E. 2006a. *Assuring the Sufficiency of a Frontline Workforce: A National Study of Licensed Social Workers. Executive Summary.* Washington, D.C.: National Association of Social Workers, Center for Workforce Studies.

Whitaker, T., Weismiller, T., and Clark, E. 2006b. *Assuring the Sufficiency of a Frontline Workforce: A National Study of Licensed Social Workers. Special Report: Social Work Services for Children and Families.* Washington, D.C.: National Association of Social Workers, Center for Workforce Studies.

Whitaker, T., Weismiller, T., and Clark, E. 2006c. *Assuring the Sufficiency of a Frontline Workforce: A National Study of Licensed Social Workers. Special Report: Social Work Services for Older Adults.* Washington, D.C.: National Association of Social Workers, Center for Workforce Studies.

Whitaker, T., Weismiller, T., Clark, E., and Wilson, M. 2006d. *Assuring the Sufficiency of a Frontline Workforce: A National Study of Licensed Social Workers. Special Report: Social Work Services in Behavioral Health Care Settings.* Washington, D.C.: National Association of Social Workers, Center for Workforce Studies.

Whitaker, T., Weismiller, T., Clark, E., and Wilson, M. 2006e. *Assuring the Sufficiency of a Frontline Workforce: A National Study of Licensed Social Workers. Special Report: Social Work Services in Health Care Settings.* Washington, D.C.: National Association of Social Workers, Center for Workforce Studies.

Willging, P. 2004. Better geriatric care isn't an "impossible dream." *Nursing Homes: Long Term Care Management* 53 (10): 16–20.

APPENDIX

This is a letter to the paramedics who tried to revive my grandmother, Elizabeth Wilson, on Thanksgiving Day, November 23, 2000.

November 29, 2000

My grandmother had been battling illness for the past year. The last couple of months have been the most horrific for her, my mother, her husband Paul, and the rest of my family. We have all helped to take care of her. She was a very independent lady who hated to depend on anyone. The last month she has had to depend on everyone. She suffered immense pain with pancreatic cancer, renal failure, an ulcerated stomach, and an enlarged heart. She could only eat a spoonful of food at a time without vomiting, and the last week that she lived she could not even hold her head up. She wanted to "go home to be with Jesus" & she stated this repeatedly.

She was in and out of the hospital. It was here that we found out after she died where she had specific DNR orders that would not transfer out of the hospital. However, she went into home hospice care on the evening of November 22, 2000 when the doctors stated she only had a week to live. She was released from the hospital that evening. Hospice staff said they would send someone out to the house that night to fill out the paperwork. No one came. The next morning someone was also supposed to come. Still, no one came.

I arrived to my grandmother's around 11:20 Thanksgiving Day. I had not seen her since August when she was feeling good. She was frail looking, deathly pale, and haggard. Her face looked like a skeleton. My sister woke her up when I arrived, because she said my grandmother was looking forward to my arrival. She was sitting up in a chair. She had a huge smile on her face & said "Hi Edith. I didn't think you were going to make it." I hugged her, but she did not have enough strength to lift up her arms to hug me back. We spoke for 5 minutes. She said she was tired of fighting and wanted to go home. She kept falling asleep sitting in the chair & wanted to be moved to her bed. My husband lifted her up to lay her on the bed. She was as limp as a rag doll. She lay in bed & started moaning and saying, "Blessed Jesus" with her eyes closed. I asked her if she was in any pain. She said "No." At that point, I left the room to cry, because it hurt me to see such a strong lady look the way she did. She looked so tired and frail.

Not more than 5 minutes passed when my sister ran out to tell me she was gone. I ran back inside. Her mouth was hanging open, her eyes were shut, but her skin was still warm. I couldn't believe that she was just there, and now she was gone. Most of her family was there with her. My sister was holding her hand, and we were all crying and in shock, but we were happy she was finally free from the prison her body had become. The air was thick leading me to realize that there was indeed a spiritual presence in that room. My husband even was moved to tears . . . something he didn't even do at our wedding.

I was to call the hospice to get info on what to do next. They stated that since she was "pending," I was to call 9-1-1. The woman on the phone told me nothing else. I called 9-1-1 & told them my grandmother had just passed away & that she was a home hospice patient. They said to call them, & I told her what the hospice told me. The dispatcher told me nothing about what to do, what to expect, or how to prepare for the paramedics. I told her it wasn't an emergency, so we were expecting for the paramedics just to take her body to the funeral home knowing that she was a hospice patient.

Not 10 minutes lapsed before there was banging on the door. I hadn't gotten to the door yet when it flew open. Several paramedics came rushing in. They asked where she was & started asking questions like "How long has it been?" "Where are the DNR orders?" The family was still in shock from the loss & had difficulty answering the questions that were shot at them. So the paramedics started yelling the questions. This created more stress and anxiety for the family and the paramedics. We told them her status with the hospice. "We have to resuscitate her without DNR orders." Mind you, few of the family in the room registered what they were talking about because they never said "do not resuscitate" orders. Everyone's mind was clouded from losing my grandmother & EMS' abrupt and military-like invasion.

One paramedic was nice enough to help us look for the papers, the rest were busy strapping my grandmother down, shocking her, pushing on her chest . . . making the whole experience harder on her (if she was revived) and her family. We couldn't find the papers. One of the paramedics (female) yelled at her co-worker to "call the police and have this woman arrested!" about my sister, because she was asking the paramedics questions like "Is this necessary? She wanted to die at home! Leave her alone!" My sister fell apart.

The police showed up soon after & really helped us out a lot. He knew all 5 of us were frantic, so he helped us to get the DNR orders. He called & spoke to the hospital. They explained to him the DNR order she had applied only in the hospital. He knew that hospice never made it out & he put two & two together that we were never able to get the DNR order.

Meanwhile, my sister was talking to one of the paramedics standing by outside. She asked him if they could ever use discretion. He stated, "they could" . . . yet for some reason they weren't.

EMS got my grandmother's heart started twice. We were sick with worry and fear about what she would have to go through if they revived her. They disregarded our wishes to leave her alone & put us all through the torment and trauma of trying to revive her. The quiet, spiritual moment was long gone at this point.

EMS got my grandmother's heart started and were taking her to the ambulance. We said a family prayer to the Lord for Him to not let her go. The policeman said we would need to follow the ambulance down & her husband could give power of attorney to not resuscitate her. We did, but she was already gone when we got there. It was the worst, most painful day of our lives.

So my question is: Why was discretion not used in this case? There would've been no lawsuit, because a slight amount of research by EMS would've shown that she was not supposed to be resuscitated. The policeman discovered that in 5 minutes. There were 3 paramedics available to help, but none extended themselves to find out really what my grandmother's wishes were. Why was there not more empathy shown by the personnel? They were yelling, telling us they couldn't do anything without a DNR order, yet they wouldn't help get at the bottom of the truth & put the family through hell. What began as a peaceful moment at my grandmother's house looked like something out of a war zone by the time they took her off away from us to die again & again after several failed attempts to revive her. Her husband was in shock, my sister was crying. Her husband could've given power of attorney at the hospital . . . why couldn't he have done this at his own house?

A week later . . . we are angry, upset, & deeply saddened by the whole incident. Don't worry, we do not want to sue you, but something should be done to ensure that this doesn't happen to anyone else. We respect the very difficult jobs paramedics have, and we realize that you are heroes, because you save lives of those who want to be saved. My family & I understood that you were trying to do your jobs, but the situation could've been handled much better than it was. Most family members are in shock and are grieving when you get there, and may need a little help to get the info you need, in order to carry out the wishes of their loved ones. Please, try to understand that if this circumstance should ever happen again . . . God forbid.

Thanks for your time. I hope you will take what I have written to heart.

Sincerely,
Erica Edwards

FIVE

Not an Option but a Duty

Caring for My Mother

YVONNE HAYNES

DESCRIPTION OF CAREGIVER

Trinidad is off the coast of Venezuela. South American Amerindians originally settled Trinidad, and Columbus visited it in 1498. First the Spanish, then the French, and finally the British ruled Trinidad until 1962, when it obtained independence, and in 1976 it became a republic (Carmichael 1961). Like the British, most Trinidadians display politeness, reserve, strength, modesty, adaptability, determination, a sense of humor, reverence for tradition, and a stiff upper lip (New Research 2004). Trinidad is the home of calypso and soca music and the place of my birth. My godfather named me Yvonne, and my mother provided my middle name, Patricia. I am the only child of my mother and oldest of my father's five children, and singularity and birth order together determined my fate as a caregiver from birth.

Even though I was not reared in the my father's household, that kind, easy-going man, speaking only in whispers, was always significant in my life and desired the best for me. He was the only child of his mother and was reared in a pristine household that included his mother, a never-married aunt, and his grandmother. He was their primary caregiver until their demise, in their nineties. My father has four other children—a son and three daughters—and I am the oldest daughter. Yet the words *step* and *half* are not in our vocabulary. In the West Indian tradition, I am their big sister, although I caution them about using that word.

My mother, the second of four siblings, was reared with her mother, an older sister, and her two younger brothers. Her father was the captain of a boat that traveled between the many West Indian islands, with infrequent visits home. My mother moved to another town to work when I was five and left me to enjoy the benefits of being reared by my very warm and saintly grandmother, who showered me with love and many of my core values. These included respect for all people, honesty and truth, a love of reading, and an abiding faith in God. My maternal side also had family caregiving responsibilities for my grandmother, performed in the United States rather than Trinidad. However, after my grandmother became blind, she immigrated to the United States and alternately lived with my mother and her sister. They dutifully shared caregiving until she died, ten years later.

I always felt that my future as an adult lay beyond Trinidad's shores. After completing high school, I chose to attend Howard University in Washington, D.C., having been accepted to universities in England and Canada, choices that many islanders made. Howard University enjoys an international reputation as a premier institution. Little did I know that my flight into Washington, D.C., coincided with the historical evolution of African Americans. People of color were fighting for equal citizenship and attempting to break the shackles of segregation and Jim Crow. What culture shock, from the rustic calm of a small island, where I knew who I was and most islanders, to the bustling metropolis of Washington, D.C., where everything was too fast and too loud and no one knew your name. The change from living where most looked like me to the United States, where others considered me a minority, was novel and sobering. Despite the palpable rage, the marches, and the destructive burnings, I was exposed to some of the most brilliant minds of professors and students—Roberta Flack, Donny Hathaway, Jessye Norman, Phylicia Rashad, Debbie Allen, and Richard Smallwood—which added an indescribable level of richness. I plan to captivate my grandsons with my description of my experience of meeting a young and militant Muhammad Ali when he visited Howard.

While a student at Howard, I met a man, a U.S. citizen, and married him shortly after my graduation with a degree in nutrition. In addition, my mother moved to the United States, and we shared an apartment until I married. Despite our physical separation after my marriage, my mother was a constant in my life. We maintained closeness through regular visits and phone conversations. Having hitched my future to my husband's rising star, I resided in three different states while he fast-tracked in his career. I gave birth to three children, a son and two daughters, and within five years I was a stay-at-home mom until they were all in school full time.

At that point, 1985, I decided to return to graduate school. Social work was an easy decision. I had already had the experience of corporate employment and gladly ran away from it. My comfort with and desire for involvement with people pointed to a helping profession. A part-time, three-year graduate program in our new home of Richmond, Virginia, allowed me to integrate a rigorous educational program with my family and home responsibilities. How could I have known that my second-year student placement at the local Veterans Administration Hospital or my postgraduate work as coordinator of social work on a community hospital's behavioral health unit would help prepare and train me for the caregiving responsibilities I would undertake with my mother fifteen years later? Who could have predicted that when I began caregiving, I would be divorced after almost thirty-five years of marriage, my three children would be married, dual-degreed adults residing in other states or countries, and that I would be enjoying grandmotherhood?

DESCRIPTION OF FAMILY MEMBER CARED FOR

It was December, my favorite time of year. Christmas 2004 was fast approaching, and I was looking forward to pulling out my Christmas tree and ornaments, many collected from my travels around the world and others from dear friends and family aware of my passion. This was to be the first Christmas spent in my new house in Richmond, Virginia. A few days away, on Sunday, I planned to host a large reception to commemorate my second grandson's baptism. The excitement was great because the proud parents—my older daughter and her husband, residing in Cleveland, Ohio—were expecting friends from around the country. My two oldest family members, my seventy-eight-year-old mother and my eighty-two-year-old aunt, were visiting from Maryland and assisting with the preparations.

On Thursday morning, my mother reported being unable to sleep because of excruciating pain in her left leg. On Friday, she reported sleeping less the previous night as the pain and leg spasms grew less responsive to the medications her physician in Maryland had prescribed. By Saturday morning, when it was apparent that the medications were ineffective, my younger daughter and her girl friend decided to accompany my mother to the emergency room of a nearby hospital. While preparations for the party continued, a low level of anxiety permeated the house as my aunt repeatedly remarked that she missed her sister. After about four hours, my mother returned home with a prescription for more painkillers and a recommendation to see her doctor when she returned to Maryland.

The baptism service was sacred; the brunch was festive; the food, catered by a friend, was exceptionally good. The day belonged to my seven-month-old, hazel-eyed grandson and his parents. However, my eyes never left my mother, who sat in one place and, when she walked, leaned heavily on her cane. My normally affable, talkative, and charming mother was withdrawn, on the perimeter of the festivities and wincing from unbearable pain. By 6:00 P.M. Sunday, the reception ended and everyone left, my mother for Maryland, promising to see her doctor the next day. I called my mother twice on Monday and learned she had decided to wait until Wednesday for a previously scheduled appointment with another physician. Furious, I called a friend in Maryland and urged her to take my mother to an emergency room. A little past midnight, my friend reported that my mother had been admitted to the hospital. Grateful to my friend, I returned to sleep, postponing my concerns for another five and a half hours.

My mother's history as a West Indian immigrant to the United States began some thirty-five years before. Since she was widowed, she lived independently in Washington, D.C., worked in a large hospital, and managed her affairs remarkably well. Although she worked in the healthcare industry, she never followed the professional advice she gave others about the need for regular doctor visits, exercise, and sound healthcare practices. An example of her noncompliance was leaving her 3:00–11:00 P.M. shift on a medical-surgical floor and driving home, some 15 miles away, with her neck wrapped in towels because she suffered neck spasms and hypertension. She drove home to her mother, who was totally blind and unable to care for herself, instead of going to the emergency room, located four floors beneath the unit on which she worked. So by the time my mother was diagnosed with cardiac problems in 1998, necessitating a quadruple bypass and aortic valve replacement, she was gasping for every breath and unable to walk a block. Her arthritic knees aggravated her difficulties. Unbelievably, my mother continued to work as a caregiver in an assisted living facility. In reality, she was depending on assistance from the younger African immigrant women workers, who greatly respected her.

DESCRIPTION OF CAREGIVING EXPERIENCE

The morning after my mother's admission to the hospital in December 2004, my aunt and I had a lengthy phone conversation recounting my mom's descent into fragile health and my recent caregiving. I am a woman of color who is in the upper range of what Erickson describes as middle adulthood and other life course theorists describe as the sandwich generation (Robbins et al. 1998). I am immersed in the task of generativity, which Erickson also describes as a passing on of values, traditions, and norms. In many ways, I feel as if I am a card-carrying member of the sandwich generation because I am the only remaining functional member of my generation in my family. I am my mother's only child and the mother of three adult children. I am also the grandmother of four grandsons, with the oldest being two. My aunt's adopted son, the other occupant of my generation, experienced severe disability, secondary to chronic type II diabetes. My ex-husband was well liked and respected by my family members, whom he embraced as his own; before our divorce, we were always able to share responsibilities in meeting the needs of family members. His absence left a void that I was required to fill. I remember stating during that conversation with my aunt that I was grateful for what I did for a living. As a licensed clinical social worker with a specialization in aging and having taught courses on human behavior in the social environment, I approached and accepted my role as a caregiver in accord with my culture, family values, education, and professional experiences.

Nevertheless, we talked about my caring for my mother for approximately thirty-five years, since her arrival in the United States. The second girl of four, my mother was well protected and supported as a child and was given the nickname Babygirl. Her only child, I was very close to this warm, wonderful, and strong West Indian woman. We had experienced a lot together, so it was not surprising that after my migration to the States, she joined me two years later. I was her daughter, front-runner, expert on everything, and friend. As is typical of West Indians, we lived together until I married and moved to another city.

My mother's health story began at the time of her cardiac bypass in 1998. I was fortunate to employ an old friend, visiting from the West Indies, who lived with and nursed my mother to stable health, relying on a cane and with diabetes. Because of her excellent care, I visited Mom in Maryland biweekly from Virginia. Her condition began an odyssey of doctors' visits, stress tests, unaffordable medications, inadequate insurance coverage, transportation difficulties, unexpected hospitalizations, and dependence on family members, old friends, and an extremely well-developed community support system. My son and his family reside in Southeast Asia, and I had a trip scheduled for early 2005. Two weeks before my departure, my mother was admitted to the hospital and scheduled for a left leg arterial bypass. Although Mom's recovery was slow and painful, I was able to enjoy visiting with my first grandson. A college roommate and my uncle assumed responsibilities for my mother, even after her discharge.

My mother's current situation was precipitated by failure of that 2004 leg surgery. After a summer of daily outpatient physical therapy, Mom needed a below-the-knee amputation and was discharged to a pleasant rehabilitation facility the week of Christmas. Driving from the rehabilitation center to Mom's second-floor walk-up apartment, I knew life was changing but not its new direction. Having a deep, abiding faith in God, I knew that all would be well.

Christmas morning 2004 dawned bright and cold. As I was preparing to leave my Mom's apartment to spend the day with her at the rehabilitation center, the phone rang. My son's mother-in-law asked whether I had heard about the killer tsunami in Thailand, where our children and grandchildren were. She anticipated that all were dead. At that point, the stress of the previous few weeks surfaced. I screamed a barrage of words, speaking simultaneously to God and her: "I cannot handle another thing; I am on the verge of losing my mind." I abruptly hung up the phone and rushed out to meet my aunt for our visit with my Mom. My aunt refused to receive the news that my son and his family were lost, so at a street corner I stopped the car, and we held hands and prayed that all would be well with our family members.

The next ten hours proved to be the longest of my life. When we arrived at the rehabilitation center, Mom, oblivious to the devastation in Southeast Asia, was showing pictures of my son and his family to friends who were visiting with her. As friends kept calling my cell phone inquiring about my son, I managed a calm exterior and left Mom's room for each call. I did not tell Mom about the tsunami, fearing it would inflate her anxiety. It was 10 P.M. when we received an e-mail from my son stating that they had been spared. Fortunately, my son's brother-in-law had encouraged them to vacation on another side of the island instead of their regular spot, now destroyed. Grateful for a miracle, I slept that night, but I already accepted that my mother would be unable to return to her apartment. I split the remainder of the 2004 Christmas holiday between visiting Mom and searching for alternative housing for her in Maryland.

Discharge Planning

Visits to my mother were numerous and regular, often coinciding with meetings with the social worker for discharge planning and meetings with the other professionals. I was blessed by my education and experience teaching graduate human behavior courses and working as the clinical coordinator of the behavioral health unit of a midsized community hospital. Those experiences helped me understand what our family was going through. The meetings helped me exert some influence over Mom's care, yet no one gave useful assistance for discharge planning. I was told both that the care my mother needed did not exist and that it would be extremely expensive. So they recommended that Mom return to her second-floor walk-up apartment. They provided a catalogue of suburban, resort-like facilities. It was obvious they had not explored Mom's financial situation and postdischarge needs. Fortunately, I comprehended Mom's needs, but it would have been helpful to have practical recommendations about needed community resources, which were omitted from the glossy catalogue.

This lack of information about residential resources in the Washington, D.C., and suburban Maryland area forced me to turn to trusted mentors and coworkers, whose experience was diverse, and old friends who were long-time residents of that area. My aunt, whom I dubbed "Old Soldier" because of her total involvement and support, slowed my "clinical social worker push" for my mother's placement in a more residential facility. After speaking with my mother, my aunt recommended a smaller apartment in the complex where my Mom resided. This practical suggestion kept my mother in her current complex near her extensive support system, developed over the past twenty years.

Mom never lived in her new apartment. In March 2005, four months after her admission to the rehabilitation center, my Mom was discharged to my newly built Richmond home, barely able to make a few stumbling steps with her new prosthesis. After my divorce, I built a barrier-free, single-story house to accommodate my changing needs and those of older family members who might live with me at some point. My mom moved into the bedroom that I had previously identified as being hers someday. The next day, a nurse selected by the rehab facility social worker visited and determined that Mom needed several services, including physical and occupational therapy and skilled nursing. This was a stressful time because, as through most of her life, Mom tended to see obstacles instead of possibilities, and her fear of change reduced her rational thought. So her days were filled with tears and hesitancy to move her legs. Her childhood nickname, Babygirl, aptly described the paralysis and despondency her fears created. She initially placed her prosthesis in a corner and ignored it.

The physical therapist insisted that Mom wear the prosthesis all day long to increase familiarity with it and to walk into the bathroom to perform her activities of daily living without assistance.

The occupational therapist and the nurse said Mom would be unable to care for herself adequately in her Maryland apartment and that she needed an assisted living facility. Without consulting me, they made a referral for their social worker to meet with Mom to discuss unaffordable residential options in which my mother had no interest. That evening, through her tears, Mom recounted the discussion. Concerned about offending me, she clarified that she had not complained about her care in my home or requested to move to an assisted living facility. I was furious because the staff knew that I was my mother's power-of-attorney and disrespected me by excluding me from the planning.

I clearly understood what was occurring and the cultural differences that precipitated these events. Researchers have discussed the difference between people of color and European American cultures in the sense of duty inherent in providing custodial care to parents and other family members (Carter and McGoldrick 1999). Historically, people of color have always taken in family members who needed assistance. Some consider these flexible family boundaries a strength in African American families (Hill 1972). So I reassured my mother that I was not angry with her and understood. I decided to ignore this major affront and told Mom to visit with the social worker, who turned out to be a former student, peruse the glossy catalogues, and simply say "no, thanks" to the offer.

Approximately one month after my mother's discharge from the rehabilitation center, two large lesions appeared on the toes of her right foot. Because of the residency constraints of her insurance, we were forced to travel from Richmond to Maryland to visit her physicians. Many times, we visited five different physicians in two days because of Mom's various health problems. Providentially, because we still maintained her new apartment in Maryland, we had a place to stay when visiting. Despite the medications and treatment, the lesions enlarged, and we both worried.

Simultaneous Caregiving to Multiple Family Members

In the midst of this, my aunt's only child, an adopted son, who was diabetic and a bilateral amputee with a deteriorating heart condition, was admitted to the hospital. In December 2004, in response to my Mom's situation, I encouraged both my aunt and my cousin to prepare advanced directives including health-care proxies giving me authority to act on their behalf. As a result, I had been managing all of my mother and cousin's financial, medical and pharmaceutical, transportation, and residential affairs.

In May 2005, after the placement of his pacemaker and defibrillator, I transported my cousin to the same rehabilitation center from which my mother was discharged one month earlier. Within two days, he passed away. His mother collapsed in the hospital where my cousin was taken to confirm his demise. A thorough medical examination showed that her shortness of breath was related to a cardiac arterial blockage necessitating immediate attention. Because of advanced age, she was a poor risk for a bypass and needed angioplasty with stenting. Again, I was forced to sit still and contemplate. How was I going to get through the many stressors that faced me: a disabled mother having trouble ambulating with the possibility of losing her toes, a funeral to plan for my cousin, and an aunt in a cardiac unit awaiting a high-risk procedure?

Once again, I felt the stress of being the only person of my generation in my family (see Bengtson et al. 1990). In the midst of my grief for my brother-cousin and concern for my mother-aunt, I commiserated with my mother about effectively handling all the situations. She recommended that I contact my ex-husband, who had remained extremely close to her and my aunt, and ask him to be with my aunt during her procedure and her period of mourning. Because of my power-of-attorney status, I was legally able to plan and execute a funeral and take care of my aunt's hospitalization and discharge needs.

The fictive kin, aunts, uncles, cousins, and godmothers helped with all of the necessary tasks (see Boyd-Franklin 1989). My ex-husband traveled the two hours from Richmond and was my chauffeur for three consecutive days as I made funeral arrangements. His involvement probably reflected his personality style, some guilt over our estrangement, and his loyalty to my family members. It also exemplified the importance of extended family relationships, particularly evident in Caribbean families, which my ex-husband embraced when we married (Chamberlain 2003). Even though we were divorced, he remained a family member who expected and was expected to continue to carry out tasks needed for family well-being.

By June 2005, despite expert home health care, my mother was admitted to a Richmond hospital for amputation of two toes on her right foot. After weeks of rehabilitation, Mom returned home needing more home healthcare. However, Mom suffered unabating, excruciating pain accompanied by loss of appetite, inability to sleep or focus, and constant tears. My mother's condition worsened, and nothing helped. Despite all medical interventions, Mom's toes clearly were not healing.

In August 2005, Mom returned to the hospital for her second below-the-knee amputation. Although the daily hospital visits took their emotional and physical toll, I was relieved that the surgery removed her pain and my feeling of helplessness as I watched her suffer. During this time, I was regularly visiting my aunt in Washington, D.C., supporting her in her grief. It is surprising that I never missed work, which provided solace from my many caregiving responsibilities and the support and comfort of my supervisor and coworkers.

Mom's Permanent Move to Our Home

With the second amputation it was clear Mom would be unable to move to the Maryland apartment, where she had never permanently resided. Although she had begun to get used to having one prosthesis, and her ambulation improved, we both accepted that she was unable to function independently. While she was hospitalized, with her permission I terminated the lease on her apartment and made my address permanent for her. During our discussions, Mom expressed relief that we had come to that decision. Because Mom's Maryland medical and pharmaceutical insurance did not adequately cover her expenses in Virginia, it became necessary for Mom to apply for a Virginia Medicaid waiver. The hospital discharge planner and the finance office worked tirelessly to ensure that Mom received coverage for her extremely large hospital bills and provided information about county services and resources.

On her return home in September 2005, a ramp was constructed in the garage and other minor renovations were made to the house to accommodate Mom's wheelchair. Six months later, Mom was fitted with a second prosthesis and discharged from home health. She now manages a few steps, but an arthritic knee prevents more mobility. Mom manages some of her activities of daily living with my assistance. She selects what she tries and has numerous excuses for unattempted activities. Sometimes, she is paralyzed by a baseless fear. For example, she refused to open the blinds for fear of falling out of her wheelchair. Because she loved the sunshine, my refusal to assist motivated her to open the blinds. My clinical experience, knowledge, and support have helped me to support her independence. Sometimes this angers her, and she says that I can never understand her situation. Although this is true, I still urge her to consider the adage that there is nothing to fear but fear itself.

In addition to her diabetes and cardiac difficulties, Mom is blind in one eye and receives care for glaucoma. Her doctor visits are numerous, and I am grateful to a supportive and empathetic supervisor and coworkers. I have a flexible schedule, accommodating the many doctor visits. Yet thoughtful and effective planning is essential. I schedule medical visits at the end of the day so we can retire early after the strenuous lifting of Mom's wheelchair. My greatest caregiving challenges are having balanced meals always prepared and planning for coverage when I am out of town. I manage by cooking many meals on the weekend and having Mom prepare accompaniments when needed. She fixes her lunch every day. When I am away for a few days, my neighbors take turns sharing meals with Mom and ensure that she is securely locked in for the night. My ex-husband calls her twice a day and is her guaranteed weekend visitor. In my absence, he functions as her first responder.

Because of inadequate insurance coverage, increasing medical costs, and her unstable health, Mom's medical expenses are great, easily $1,000 per month for medications. Consequently, I have supplemented her living expenses. This is not new but is more acutely felt because my expenses have doubled now that I have a roommate. In the West Indian community, there is the saying that succinctly describes this situation: "Cattle horns must never be too heavy for it to carry." It is expected that when the need arises, one will care for aging parents and kin regardless of the ensuing hardships. This perspective mirrors that of Africans (Dilworth-Anderson et al. 2005; Hill 1972). The caregiving my mother and aunt provided my maternal grandmother for more than twenty years was my model.

Children and Grandchildren: A Different Kind of Caregiving

I recently returned from North Carolina, where my third grandson was born. It was a different kind of caregiving. Leaving the stress of my job and my home caregiving responsibilities, I embraced the arrival of new life and felt the responsibility to be there for my daughter and her family. When one is confronted with continual care of the disabled family members, other normative caregiving continues (Carter and McGoldrick 1999). This reduces preoccupation with the disabled family member and the possible feelings of ill will. So when my original plans for coverage for my mother failed, my girl friend, ex-husband and neighbors volunteered; a community of support was in place. I am exhausted but content. I will recover. Life, as I live it now, will go on.

ANALYSES

During my tenure teaching human behavior in the social environment, I developed an appreciation for Erickson's life stages and attendant development tasks

(Robbins et al. 1998). So I believed that generativity, the passing on of values, norms, and culture, would be my successful resolution of my current stage. Consequently, I had an obligation to be available to my adult children in the establishment of their families and households. As a member of the sandwich generation, I had responsibilities for both parents and children (Zastrow and Kirst-Ashman 1997). According to family life cycle theories (Carter and McGoldrick 1999), the disability of parents, and more recently grandparents, exacerbates the sandwich phenomenon. I feel compelled to meet the needs of whichever generation has the strongest need at any given time. This is why I arranged for others to care for my mother and went to my daughter's when she gave birth, without any feelings of guilt or remorse.

The central themes of life are acknowledgment and acceptance of change. Personal growth and maturation throughout the life cycle coupled with positive, supportive personal relationships help one embrace change with creativity, growth, and resilience. Consistent with the strengths perspective, I never despaired throughout my caregiving but always searched for blessings in every challenge.

The strengths, or perceived lack thereof, of African American families have been the focus of many scholarly writings (Bradley et al. 2004; Burton and Dilworth-Anderson 1991; Hill 1972). One strength was kinship bonds. Peculiar to African American families is the concept of fictive kin: people not biologically related who provide emotional, economic, and other support (Boyd-Franklin 1989). It can range from my great-grandmother's best friend to my first child's godmother. Unlike the majority culture, African American families have historically taken in other people, including children, grandchildren, parents, and members of the larger fictive kin network. The ravages of slavery precipitated this practice, and later on the necessity of surviving in a hostile society mandated caring for each other and community cohesion. In addition, given my Caribbean history and traditions, as my aunt repeated, "It is not an option but a duty."

Significant parallels exist between the slave history experience and core values of African Americans and people of the Caribbean in terms of family, kinship ties, and veneration for elders. For example, one author reports that newly arriving slaves to the Caribbean considered themselves adopted children and called the slaves who took them in and cared for them parents (Bush 1990). The support of family and kin protected the slaves from the uncertainties of plantation life. The elders were collectively honored and cared for by the wider community. These preindustrial practices provided the basis for the extended family form and caregiving behaviors that are still prevalent in the West Indies today. As a young person growing up in the West Indies, I never knew of any place where sick, infirm, or elderly family members were sent for indeterminate custodial care. Family members graciously provided long-term care. It was common for elderly parents to rotate between their children's households or for one child, generally a daughter and her family, to move back into the parent's home. Given that legacy, I had to care and support my family members.

Like kinship ties, religion originating in the African experience is the acknowledgment of a higher power. So whether it is practiced as organized religion or expressed as a personal belief, central to the existence of the African American is the acknowledgment of a higher power. The practice of religion has been both a coping mechanism for stress reduction and principles that African Americans live by. For the caregiver, religion lowers depression and raises self-acceptance, particularly among African Americans (Drentea and Goldner 2006; Morano and King 2005). I have relied on my abiding faith in God throughout my life. During times of additional stress, such as my divorce and family caregiving, my faith helped me navigate the awesome challenges. With regard to the need for stress reduction in the face of caregiving, religious beliefs provided the mechanism for reaching in. Richmond Hill, an ecumenical retreat center housed in a convent setting perched on the highest peak of Richmond, periodically provided refuge. I could physically withdraw from the world, pray, read scripture, meditate, center, and focus. Away from external problems, these refreshing retreats strengthened my inner core, providing the peace and inner strength I longed for.

There were also the mechanisms of reaching out to others. Growing up in Trinidad, where requesting help was expected and sanctioned, may have taught me this skill. The church services and Bible classes, the ladies' prayer circle, and telephone prayer provided social, emotional, spiritual, and physical support. I reached out to my grounded "sistah friends," who lovingly anticipated my need for respite by caring for my mother or completing essential chores. Colleagues and friends at work listened to my concerns, prayed for me, offered personal and professional assistance, and shared their caregiving experiences and helpful practices. Religions also promise that good deeds result in rewards. Religion and spirituality consequently solidify the faith and belief system and impart strength for the difficult tasks of caregiving (Boyd-Franklin 1989; Dilworth-Anderson 1998).

Research concludes that people of color provide more family caregiving and display greater satisfaction and less stress than members of the predominant culture (Dilworth-Anderson et al. 2002). Other findings state that when families view caregiving as normal rather than burdensome, they experience less stress (Carter and McGoldrick 1999). In addition, the strength-based perspective proposes that if we view aging with pride, value our history and life experiences, and adjust courageously to change, the task of caregiving is less traumatic (Robbins et al. 1998). This perspective reinforced our family's earlier shared caregiving for my maternal grandmother. Battling many hardships because my grandmother was an immigrant and received no benefits, my aunt and mother never considered institutional care. Although I lived hundreds of miles away, as a stay-at-home mom with three young children, I brought my grandmother to my home for four to six weeks at a time several times per year. The benefits included: respite for my aunt and mother; more opportunities for interaction between my children and their great-grandmother, an alert, intelligent woman; and an opportunity to learn about the family caregiving roles. So we did what was culturally normative, thereby lessening stress for all involved (Chamberlain 2003).

Trends indicate that a daughter or daughter-in-law usually had the primary caregiving responsibilities for elderly parents (Family Caregiver Alliance 2001). Also, more than 50% of women can expect to become a parental caregiver, with 20% providing in-home care. Increasingly, these women are also in the workforce (Ginzler 2006). Employment has significantly reduced the number of women available for extended, full-time home care. Women who are caregivers and employees often face conflicting demands and have to work part time, resulting in lost wages (Martire and Stephens 2003; Wakabayashi and Donato 2005). Family mobility results in potential caregivers no longer residing near the family member needing care. Additionally, the phenomenon of the verticalized family, with multiple generations and fewer members to share caregiving tasks, has emerged (Bengtson et al. 1990). Creative responses notwithstanding, the norm remains for women to continue to assume the major responsibility for or the total care of frail older adults, and society has erected few supports for male caregivers.

Even with the assistance of family members or paid household help, the physical and emotional toll of caregiving is phenomenal. Muscular strains, backaches, sleeplessness, and even depression tend to be a constant in the caregiving experience. One study (Kiecolt-Glaser et al. 1995) reports that stress causes slower physical healing for caregivers. Thus, self-care is essential for strength and resilience. Unfortunately, many women of color, for whom paid help is not an option, meet the physical, emotional, or economic needs of all around them. Ignoring their own needs, many develop hypertension and other stress-related disorders (Dilworth-Anderson 2004; Mintz 2002). Time to enjoy walking, jogging, bowling, and other aerobic exercises and regular respite are essential. I have a standing weekend appointment for a 6-mile aerobic hike with my friend Karen. This provides physical activity, along with emotional release through our sharing. During the week, I maintain a regular schedule at the gym.

The ecological perspective in social work assists in the development of a holistic view of people and their environments, particularly helpful to explaining the interactions between individuals, organizations, communities, larger social systems, and their environments. Stress occurs when the fit between the person and the environment is problematic (Gitterman and Germain in Robbins et al. 1998). In my caregiving, this was evidenced by the lack of reciprocity for service between states. Maryland's nonresponsive and unwieldy insurance system refused to honor out-of-state medical claims. This necessitated 100--mile trips for medical care and thousands of dollars in uncovered medical and pharmaceutical bills in Virginia. Given the exploding numbers of older adults, especially frail and mobile ones, flexible regulations about basic medical care services are essential. Baby boomers will demand more and better-integrated services.

IMPLICATIONS

The ecological perspective emphasizes the dynamic interaction individuals have with each other, environmental systems, and their environments (Zastrow and Kirst-Ashman 1997). This perspective best explains the current phenomenon of aging, the changing dynamics in the family system, and the complexity of caregiving. It suggests the following proposed implications for the various societal levels of interaction, including the family, summarized in table 5.1.

Individuals

Because "sandwich generation" generally refers to the middle-aged woman, daughter or daughter-in-law, who feels squeezed and burdened by her intergenerational caregiving responsibilities, she must initiate an early conversation with the elders and family members. The discussion should begin before the first sign of illness or any disability and when the elders can make sound decisions. The primary purpose is to heighten awareness and plan for certainties. For example, Medicaid regulations stipulate that a three-year period must elapse after a property transfer before one is able to meet eligibility criteria. As parents age, the first significant change in physical ability might become a benchmark for decision making. This subject should be revisited frequently and include trusted and respected friends of involved parties until consensus can be reached. It took three years for my aunt to agree to sign power-of-attorney papers. In her eighties she said, "Who's going to die now?," believing her death was far enough in the future to delay planning and power-of-attorney issues. The unexpected death of her son led her to change her mind. In reality, executing a power of attorney is a legal issue, not an age issue; if it is commonly viewed in this manner, maybe more people will execute a power of attorney early in adult life, as a rite of passage into adulthood.

In some instances, there is a gradual onset of diseases such as Parkinson's and Alzheimer's, giving potential caregivers time to plan. In contrast, the sudden onset of illnesses such as strokes and heart attacks produces individual and family disorganization and confusion, leaving the potential caregivers with only reaction time and minimal information. With a plethora of health plans, Medicaid waivers, and new medications with myriad side effects, caregivers face an overwhelming amount of information. Aging issues including diminishing health benefits are a primary public health concern. Fortunately, copious amounts of relevant information are available through the click of a mouse or through printed materials from sources including the American Association of Retired Persons, Senior Navigator, Senior Connections, and the neighborhood public library. Peers, as in my case, or others who have had similar experiences can also provide help.

Whether they are caregivers out of love and duty or as the only option, all can testify to the physical and emotional toll caregiving sometimes takes. At best, caregiving is extremely difficult work, particularly when one is providing acute care, depleting emotional energy and dissipating physical strength. The caregiver must recognize his or her limitations and ask for assistance, recruiting each family member to bring whatever assistance they can. For example, I have rotated caregiving for my mother between family members and fictive kin when I travel. Also, when I moved Mom to my home in Virginia, my sister, who was visiting from the West Indies, assisted with packing Mom's belongings; my son's godmother made arrangements for the movers; my daughter came from Florida to help drive the truck; her girl friend came from New York to stay with Mom in Virginia while the rest of us went to suburban Maryland; and my ex-husband came to drive and do whatever else was needed. I have cheerfully turned to my neighbors to check on Mom when I work late or have other commitments.

Informal or professional respite care must be used, benefiting the caregiver and recipient. Respite care can include housekeeping, transportation to numerous physician appointments, and simply playing cards with the disabled person. Inherent in the act of asking often is the caregiver's sense of failure, personal guilt, shame, or inadequacy, sometimes coupled with the care recipient's refusal to accept assistance from others. Of course, this makes it more difficult to request help from others. Growing up as an only child, I quickly acquired comfort in asking for help for things, such as time to play, from peers. Also, people have always been there for me; therefore, it was easy to reach out to fictive kin, neighbors, and others. Living on a Caribbean island where the community is the family conditioned my mother to accept help from many people. Scheduling exercise, long walks and relaxation, and regular times of separation from the care recipient are strategies I found acceptable and essential.

Families

Reduced hospital stays make the family the primary source of treatment for both chronic and acute illness. Therefore, together the family must maximize its resilience and reduce individual and collective sources of stress. This includes using religious principles and beliefs to gain unity and strength, drawing on prior experiences with illness, grief, change, loss, changing family dynamics, and role reversal. Culture, traditions, ethnicity, and history can be elements of support when the family makes plans for the future and manages grief over the loss of life as they knew it. When my mother moved to my home, my youngest daughter mourned the loss of the only phone number for her grandmother that she had ever known, remarking that the life she had always known with my mother was over.

Additionally, family members must work deliberately to maintain healthy relationships through regular communications, develop problem-solving skills and flexibility in the face of overwhelming situations, and draw strength and courage from each other. This may be easier in immigrant families, like mine, in which the family members usually develop a close bond in their new country. My ex-husband's continued involvement with my mother since she moved to Richmond is a source of support for her and a resource. During my mother's acute illness, she first notified my ex-husband, then me, that she needed to go to the emergency room. When I arrived home, he was there ready to assist. Despite my grief and anger about ending a thirty-five-year marriage, with the help of friends and family I have learned to appreciate his love, caring, and help with my mother and to set boundaries in our relationship.

With longer life expectancies and increasing numbers of people eighty-five years and older, the chronic illness phase may need to be an integral part of normal family life. Therefore, when confronted with the disability of older adults, the family system should not be forced to sacrifice its development as a system (Carter and McGoldrick 1999). Accommodating this new conceptualization may lessen family guilt. For example, graduations, weddings, vacations, and bat and bar mitzvahs must still occur in the face of the disability of a parent or grandparent. This was demonstrated during my caregiving experience when on two occasions I decided to execute my roles as parent and grandparent while my mother was hospitalized. I also planned for Mom's alternative care when I was away assisting my daughter after childbirth. Acknowledging and including caregiving of family elders in the family life cycle should increase awareness, prompt education, and decrease guilt that generally plagues family members.

Communities

Advanced medical technology has increased life expectancy by eradicating many serious diseases. However, most other societal areas have not kept pace. Community-based services are a prime example and can be a source of significant stress (Canda 1998). Because of the burgeoning numbers of older adults and the consequent demand, community-based services are extremely limited, and this tends to be a source of extreme stress for people with disabilities, older adults, and caregivers. For example, in the area where I reside, there is one nurse and social worker for the whole county, so a family member could spend two or more months waiting to be assessed for services such as adult day care. An exponential increase in flexible, affordable services that encourage and maintain independence and meet the myriad needs of a diverse disabled and elderly population is needed.

Community integration in the least restrictive environment is an emerging ideal for people with disabilities (*Olmstead* 1999). Its achievement requires wraparound services. Specifically, people with functional disabilities need low-cost, accessible transportation to maintain independence and reduce caregiving. Reports on some community services have been dismal. For example, the newspapers have been replete with stories of transportation services dropping off disabled people in strange places other than their homes or forgetting to pick them up after appointments (Sun 2006). A one-size-fits-all concept of community service provision fails. Instead, accommodating diversity in financial status, levels of disability, available supports, and the disabled population is essential. Research shows that caregivers need additional culturally appropriate and accessible services (Whittier et al. 2005).

To influence service delivery, caregivers must become active and loud advocates on the local, state, and national levels. This can be done through participation in organizations such as the American Association of Retired Persons, local departments of aging, and voluntary, grassroots groups. Social policies must be written in support of family caregivers so families can be responsible for their own. Therefore, social service systems must financially compensate family caregivers, especially because unrelated and in many instances uncaring people often are paid to provide substandard care. Funds that communities save on institutional care can finance these initiatives.

The Bush administration has encouraged the proliferation of faith-based organizations to provide community services. Although there has been public resistance, these services could provide valuable respite care. A partnership between private, faith-based, and community organizations, in which not only finances but also necessary resources such as "friendly visitors" are shared, could significantly increase the number and quality of available services. For example, my church and others in the city have educational support groups for caregivers. Churches, synagogues, temples, and other religious and community institutions are a natural place to establish programs for caregivers and care receivers. Unfortunately, this is seldom the case; for example, I am unaware of support groups, sponsored by such organizations as the Alzheimer's Association, held in African American churches and community centers in Richmond. From my personal and professional experiences, African Americans are hesitant to venture into the larger society for such support groups and welcome church-housed programs.

Practitioners

As the baby boomers turn sixty and the fastest-growing cohort of the population is eighty-plus years old (Mintz 2002), clinicians pioneer in the untapped arena of gerontological social work. This challenge is complex and includes preparing students and providers to understand and meet the needs of older adults and their families and increasing the number of gerontological professionals. In an age of shrinking resources and overwhelmed family members, practitioners must increase their sensitivity to those who are grappling with sometimes insidious and unexpected life changes. In many instances, what is most needed is the empathetic listening ear as opposed to directions to the nearest assisted living facility or forms needed to apply for benefits. As mentioned earlier, I received little useful assistance from the workers at the first rehabilitation facility. However, my mother spoke fondly of the social worker who comforted her when she cried. Underpaid and overworked practitioners also need greater financial, educational, and emotional support.

According to the U.S. Census Bureau, the 45.8 million uninsured members of the population and an even greater number of underinsured are from families of diverse racial and ethnic backgrounds and, most often, lower socioeconomic levels (DeNavas-Walt et al. 2005). For instance, 11.3% of European Americans are uninsured, whereas a much larger percentage, 19.7%, of African Americans are uninsured (DeNavas-Walt et al. 2005). It is likely that these people will be included in some social worker's caseload. Uninsured people usually have had limited access to healthcare and have suffered from some form of discrimination. The current explosion of the Hispanic community is an important reality. Every practitioner must assess ethnicity, culture, and religious practices, elements that define and support resilience. A social worker interviewing Mom prefaced her question about religious beliefs as, "Here's a silly little question." My mother's religious and spiritual beliefs are a large and integral part of her being.

The increasing diversity of the U.S. population mandates that clinicians be familiar with the culture, traditions, and customs of their clients to prevent minimizing, misunderstanding, or pathologizing normative cultural patterns (Boyd-Franklin 1989). Unfortunately, members of the majority culture tend to use themselves, their practices, and their traditions as the standard and subsume anything that is different. The need for members of certain Southeast Asian tribes to follow the directions of the shaman and the Western medical doctor; the practice of some Caribbean people to use herbs, rubs, and folk medicine before consulting a medical practitioner; and that of African Americans to take in and care for family members and fictive kin in the face of daunting odds must be recognized, validated, and incorporated in the clinician's assessment and interventions. Because families draw on prior experiences with caregiving, illness, loss, and their own history, clinicians must acknowledge the attributes individuals and families bring to difficult situations. These attributes, possibly different from those of the clinician, are possible strengths and supports.

Social Work Educators

As with many other disciplines, social work education, current theory, and practice have focused mainly on issues related to the young. With the proliferation of older adults and the impact of their needs on families and society, teaching the life course must include value, meaning, stability, independence, wisdom, respect, role change, and the like for later life stages. Because of increased mobility, budding practitioners may have not interacted with older family members.

When I brought older adults to class to share their life journeys, it was a powerful experience for the students because they had few models to assist their understanding of change and development over time. Priceless in my experience was my mother's change from independently managing her complex life in a large metropolitan area over a long period to her insistence that she needed extraordinary amounts of assistance to perform basic tasks. Chronic illnesses, numerous hospitalizations, and a seeming loss of control over one's life can cause the strongest people to lose hope and doubt their ability to survive.

As people live longer with chronic illnesses that strain the family, social workers must be taught that the greatest weapon in their service arsenal is the family. I have seen far too many clinical situations in which the family member or designee was not consulted or informed about treatment plans. To address this gap in education, the social work department at Middle Tennessee State University has developed an online course in family caregiving designed to teach students how to support family caregivers and gain an understanding of caregiving issues (Taylor 2004). Students in the class develop both personal and professional skills. Further strategies for strengthening families, family development and the chronic illness phase, maintaining healthy family relations in later life, and maintaining respect for the demented parent are all conceptualizations that need to begin in the classroom.

REFLECTIONS

I assumed my current position as director of adult mental health seven years ago. The project I was hired to manage was a segment of a larger statewide research project that involved several localities. Eighteen months after the project began, I had accumulated significant data that included outcomes and implications to fulfill my professional goal of writing an article and having it published in a scholarly journal. Unfortunately, personal difficulties, life changes, and transitions forced that ambition to be deferred. Because the desire remained just under the surface of my professional activities, when I was asked to write this chapter I was stunned; it was like a gift being handed to me. The desire of my heart was standing ready to be fulfilled if I was willing to work frenetically. I quickly said "yes" amid a barrage of words about my present schedule, my already planned out-of-state work trips, and other projections of time constraints in the two-month timeframe I was given. I also realized that my ever-present caregiving responsibilities were not going to go away, either. I apprehensively agreed, with the awareness that I was going to

Table 5.1 Implications

	Issues and Problems	Strategies for Change
Individuals	Caregiving duties typically rest on women. Caregivers often lack relevant information. Caregiving is emotionally and physically stressful.	Initiate caregiving and end-of-life conversations with elders and family members. Include trusted friends and collaterals until a decision is reached. Become knowledgeable about caregiving responsibilities and healthcare information relevant to the care recipient. Recognize limitations. Ask for assistance. Involve family members and seek informal assistance for respite.
Families	Families are the primary source of treatment for acute and chronic illness.	Work together to maximize resilience and reduce stress. Use religious practices and beliefs to gain unity and strength. Draw on prior experiences with loss, grief, change, role reversal, and family dynamics. Work to maintain healthy relationships through regular communication to develop problem-solving skills and flexibility in the face of overwhelming situations. Draw strength and courage from each other. Chronic illness phase must become a part of normal family life. Family system must not be forced to sacrifice its development in the face of the illness of one member. Prepare for the caregiver role through education.

(*continued*)

Table 5.1 (continued)

	Issues and Problems	Strategies for Change
Communities	Communities often are unable to provide services.	Increase flexible services to encourage and maintain independence. Change from one-size-fits-all to flexible services. Caregivers need to participate vocally and loudly. Social policies must be written in support of families. Financial compensation for family members must be considered. Share resources between all entities; collaborate and coordinate efforts.
Practitioners and educators	There is little or no interest in working with older adults and their families.	Provide opportunities to be a pioneer. Increase sensitivity to those experiencing significant life change. Include culture, ethnicity, and religious practices in every assessment. Explore with honesty. Practitioners must familiarize themselves with the cultural customs and traditions of their clients.
Social work educators	Educators focus on the young, with little or no experience with older adults. Educators do not focus sufficiently on family members.	Begin tracking the life course to include value, wisdom, meaning, stability, independence, respect, and role change. Expand classroom opportunities to meet and interact with older adults. Teach strategies for strengthening families and family relations in later life and for maintaining respect for those with dementia. Teach new conceptualizations of caregiving and its effects on families.

have to produce quickly but confident that the recording of my caregiving experience would be worthwhile.

As I hung up the phone, the realization of what I had just committed to overwhelmed me. I had just agreed to tell readers exactly how I feel about having to care for my mother and the role reversal that entails. I would have to describe feelings and behaviors that were nobody's business, really. I would have to tell about family transitions and difficulties from which I was just emerging and was still unhealed. I was no longer sure that I could do this because I certainly did not feel the need to expose my family and our difficulties to the world. In this state of doubt, I called my older daughter and confessed my feelings. She commented that everything I was concerned about and wanted to omit was integral to the story. Simply stated, I had to tell it all. She confirmed for me what I inherently knew, so I continued to hold on to the conviction that this assignment was indeed a gift. Conversations with my younger daughter further convinced me that my story was worth telling only in its entirety. For many days, I contemplated, perseverated, and recounted in my head events, places, conversations, and feelings in preparation for recording.

One evening, without planning or preparation, I sat down with pencil in hand and began to write, purely in a stream of consciousness, how I got to this place in my journey of caregiving. This manner of recording allowed me to write during plane rides, in hotel rooms, anywhere and everywhere, during every free moment I had. I described the actual experience of caregiving first because it was the easiest for me; reflections on the process and the literature search followed in that order. Writing about the caregiving experience was the easiest because of the catharsis it provided. The bulk of the writing took place near the first anniversary of significant events related in the chapter (i.e., the passing of my cousin and my mother's second amputation). Also, every phone conversation I had with my children was filled with reminiscences of specific events related to my caregiving and the admonition not to omit certain events and situations that would add depth to the story. My older daughter also clipped newspaper articles and mailed them to me to ensure inclusion of current trends and similar life stories. Finding the time to research information and review pertinent scholarly literature presented a formidable challenge. Obtaining access to certain information systems proved to be daunting. As the deadline for submission approached, I became extremely apprehensive as to whether I would be able to meet it. However, because I had made a commitment, I cleared all my weekends for two months and focused on nothing else.

Process recordings, a narrative-type writing assignment, are an exercise that is vital to the supervision of social workers and ultimately the development of sound clinical practice. Writing this chapter returned me to the times when I was a graduate social work student at the local veterans' hospital, and process recordings were used to analyze my application of theoretical and practice concepts to the therapeutic relationship and situation. Writing this chapter forced me to focus on my perceptions of my caregiving experience. My first response to my perceptions of my caregiving experience would be that it is not bad, primarily manageable, surprising, and extremely stressful at times. This response is first because the literature is replete with horrific examples of adult children caring for demented and acutely ill parents and the personal and familial toll it takes on everyone involved (Drentea and Goldner 2006; Sorensen and Pinquart 2005; Williams et al. 2003). Having worked in both medical and behavioral health environments, I am fully aware of the difficulty involved in caring for acutely ill family members who fall into any of those categories.

My mother, though somewhat forgetful at times, needs a hearing aid but is fully oriented most of the time; her thoughts are coherent, and her speech is clear. With assistance, she manages her activities of daily living and can be left alone for periods. She is not a danger to herself or others, and in her own way she tries extremely hard not to create work or cause difficulty for me. She does all that she can to be self-sufficient with her physical care and the maintenance of her immediate surroundings. In general, my mother's sense of self-awareness and her motivation not to be a burden to me have been instrumental in easing the responsibility of caregiving and making it somewhat manageable.

Caregiving is a complex phenomenon and means different things to different people. Literature and research report that people of color, as a group, tend to display greater caregiving satisfaction and experience less caregiving stress than the majority population (Dilworth-Anderson 2005; Roff et al. 2004). Other studies show that a more thorough understanding of how African American caregivers experience caregiver burden is needed. Although African Americans may experience positive aspects of caregiving, they also experience of variety of stress-related symptoms (Drentea and Goldner 2006; Williams et al. 2003). My perceptions of myself as a caregiver can be described as typically warm, caring, and humane.

Because my mother's disability was fairly sudden, she is still trying to make sense of her current predicament and in many ways continues to mourn her acute loss. At times I provide supportive counseling as she bemoans what she perceives to be her almost total dependence on me. During those times I have to remind her that when I signed on for this tour of duty, I knew what I was getting into, but I signed on for the long haul nevertheless. During those times we discuss my almost total personality change when I walk in the door from a long, hard day at work, absolutely exhausted, and she calls repeatedly for me to perform some task that is not essential at that moment. I know that my voice assumes a "leave me alone and don't call me again" edge. I am fully aware of my behavior when I'm exhausted, and I try to get my mother to recognize those signs, to pay attention to what I say when I describe my feelings, and then to prioritize her needs, distinguishing what is essential and what is not.

True to her name, Babygirl, there are times when my mother, out of apprehension, intimidation, or lack of motivation does not attempt a task and looks to others to help her or do it for her. Because my mother also tends to have a pessimistic outlook, when she attempts to give credence to her views, I experience an array of emotions that range from support to anger. Furthermore, I tend to verbalize and act on my feelings. For example, when my mother refuses to move dishes in the refrigerator to locate a specific item already prepared for her and responds that she does not feel like being bothered, I feel frustrated. Although I understand that the task might be difficult, her failure to try and her propensity to wait until I get there are disconcerting. In an attempt not to infantilize or demean my mother, I attempt to meet her physical needs in a supportive, uplifting manner. Nevertheless, given her proclivity for dependence, there are times that I walk away, attempting to help her maintain that which she so desperately needs: her independence.

CONCLUSIONS

Writing my story helped me to see myself as a very humane caregiver who performs this service out of a sense of love and duty. In discharging my responsibilities as a primary caregiver, I become tired, angry, supportive, upbeat in the face of uncertainty, and irritable when exhausted. I see myself as a sure thing: a dependable, very loving, dutiful daughter determined to do all possible for this warm and caring woman who has experienced so much tragedy within a short timeframe. Because of this sense of love and duty, I see myself as no better or worse than the next person who commits to honor and care for a parent. The fifth commandment is the only one that comes with a promise: "Honor thy father and thy mother: that thy days may be long upon the land which the Lord thy God giveth thee" (Exodus 20:12).

REFERENCES

Bengtson, V. L., Rosenthal, C. J., and Burton, L. M. 1990. Families and aging: Diversity and heterogeneity. In R. Binstock and L. George (Eds.), *Handbook of Aging and the Social Sciences,* 3d ed., 263–287. New York: Academic Press.

Boyd-Franklin, N. 1989. *Black Families in Therapy: A Multi-Systems Approach.* New York: Guilford.

Bradley, E. H., Curry, L. A., McGraw, S. A., Webster, T. R., Kasl, S. V., and Andersen, R. 2004. Intended use of informal long-term care: The role of race and ethnicity. *Ethnicity & Health* 9 (1): 37–54.

Burton, L. and Dilworth-Anderson, P. 1991. The intergenerational roles of aged black Americans. *Family & Marriage Review* 16: 311–330.

Bush, B. 1994. *Slave Women in Caribbean Society (*1650–1838*).* London: James Currey Ltd.

Canda, E. 1998, April. Spirituality, religious diversity, and social work practice. *Social Casework* pp. 238–247.

Carmichael, G. 1961. *The History of West Indian Islands of Trinidad and Tobago* 1498–1900. London: Alvin Redman.

Carter, B. and McGoldrick, M. 1999. *The Expanded Family Life Cycle: Individual, Family & Social Perspectives,* 3d ed. Boston: Allyn & Bacon.

Chamberlain, M. 2003. Rethinking Caribbean families: Extending the links. *Community, Work, & Family* 6 (1): 63–76.

DeNavas-Walt, C., Proctor, B., and Lee, C. 2005. *Income, Poverty and Health Insurance: Coverage in the United States:* 2004. Washington, D.C.: U.S. Census Bureau.

DeNavas-Walt, C., Proctor, B. D., and Lee, C. H. 2006. *U.S. Census Bureau, Current Population Reports, P*60-231, *Income, Poverty, and Health Insurance Coverage in the United States:* 2005. Washington, D.C.: U.S. Government Printing Office.

Dilworth-Anderson, P. 1998. Emotional well-being in adult and later life among African Americans: A cultural and sociocultural perspective. In K. Warner Schaie and M. Powell Lawton (Eds.), *Annual Review of Gerontology and Geriatrics: Focus on Emotion and Adult Development,* Vol. 17. New York: Springer.

Dilworth-Anderson, P. 1999. The contexts of experiencing emotional distress among family caregivers to elderly African Americans. *Family Relations: Interdisciplinary Journal of Applied Family Studies* 48 (4): 391–396.

Dilworth-Anderson, P. 2004. Can culture help explain the physical health effects of care giving over time among African American caregivers? *Journals of Gerontology: Series B: Psychological Sciences and Social Sciences* 59B (3): S138–S145.

Dilworth-Anderson, P. 2005. The cultures of caregiving: Conflict and common ground among families, health professionals, and policymakers. *Journal of American Medical Association* 293: 104–105.

Dilworth-Anderson, P., Brummett, B. H., Goodwin, P. Y., Williams, S. W., Williams, R. B., and Siegler, I. C. 2005. Effect of race on cultural justifications for care giving. *Journals of Gerontology: Series B: Psychological Sciences and Social Sciences* 60B (5): 257–262.

Dilworth-Anderson, P., Williams, I. C., and Gibson, B. E. 2002. Issues of race, ethnicity, and culture in caregiving research: A 20-year review (1980–2000). *The Gerontologist* 42: 237.

Drentea, P. and Goldner, M. 2006. Caregiving outside of the home: The effects of race on depression. *Ethnicity & Health* 11 (1): 41–57.

Family Caregiver Alliance. 2001. *Selected Caregiver Statistics* (Fact Sheet). San Francisco: Author.

Ginzler, E. 2006, May 15. When Mom or Dad moves in: A few things to discuss. *USA Today*, p. A1.

Hill, R. 1972. *The Strength of Black Families.* Washington, D.C.: National Urban League, Research Department.

Kiecolt-Glaser, J. K., Marucha, P. T., Mercado, A. M., Malarkey, W. B., and Glaser, R. 1995. Slowing of wound healing by psychological stress. *Lancet* 346: 1194–1196.

Martire, L. and Stephens, M. A. P. 2003. Juggling parent care and employment responsibilities: The dilemmas of adult daughter caregivers in the workforce. *Sex Roles* 48 (3/4): 167–173.

Mintz, S. G. 2002. *Love, Honor, and Value. A Family Caregiver Speaks Out About the Challenges of Care Giving.* Hernodon, Va.: Capital Books.

Morano, C. and King, D. 2005. Religiosity as a mediator of caregiver well-being: Does ethnicity make a difference? *Journal of Gerontological Social Work* 45 (1/2): 69–84.

New Research Characterises "Britishness." 2004. Retrieved September 27, 2006, from http://www.rsa.org.uk/news/news_closeup.asp?id=1237.

Olmstead, Commissioner, Georgia Department of Human Resources, et al. v. L. C. (98–536) 527 U.S. 581 (1999).

Robbins, P. S., Chatterjee, P., and Canda, E. R. 1998. *Contemporary Human Behavior Theory: A Critical Perspective for Social Work.* Boston: Allyn & Bacon.

Roff, L. L., Burgio, L. D., Gitlin, L., Nichols, L., Chaplin, W., and Hardin, J. M. 2004. Positive aspects of Alzheimer's caregiving: The role of race. *The Journals of Gerontology Series B: Psychological Sciences and Social Sciences* 59: 185–190.

Sorensen, S. and Pinquart, M. 2005. Racial and ethnic differences in the relationship of caregiving stressors, resources, and sociodemographic variables to caregiver depression and perceived physical health. *Aging and Mental Health* 9 (5): 482–495.

Sun, L. H. 2006, June 16. Metro access rules are eased. *The Washington Post*, p. B03.

Taylor, J. 2004. Teaching university students family caregiving online. *Educational Gerontology* 30: 423–431.

Wakabayashi, C. and Donato, K. 2005. The consequences of caregiving: Effects of women's employment and earnings. *Population Research and Policy Review* 24: 467–488.

Whittier, S., Scharlach, A., and Del Santo, T. 2005. Availability of caregiver support services: Implications for implementation of the National Family Caregiver Support Program. *Journal of Aging and Social Policy* 17 (1): 45–62.

Williams, S. W., Dilworth-Anderson, P., and Goodwin, P. Y. 2003. Caregiver role strain: The contribution of multiple roles and available resources in African-American women. *Aging and Mental Health* 7 (2): 103–112.

Zastrow, C. and Kirst-Ashman, K. 1997. *Understanding Human Behavior and the Social Environment.* Chicago: Nelson, Hall.

SIX

"My Last Born Shall Care for Me and Mine"

Caring for Siblings and Mother

JOYCE E. EVERETT

"My last born shall care for me and mine." My mother spoke these words to an aunt when I was only eleven years old. Mentally, I protested fervently, thinking there were family members far more capable of effective caregiving. The youngest of my mother's four children, I always assumed an older sibling would become my mother's caregiver. I was the only child of my mother and father. My mother was the fourth oldest of ten children, five boys and five girls. Born, educated, and married in South Carolina, my mother moved to Philadelphia with her first husband in 1938 in search of better employment opportunities. My father was also a transplant from the South. He was born and reared in North Carolina.

Each of my parents had been married previously and was widowed. Each had three children from the previous marriage. My father's children from his first marriage were adults when he married my mother. Some were about the age of my mother. Although these siblings participated in the life of our family, even after my father died when I was four, they never lived in my household. My mother's oldest child was a son, eighteen years older than I. My maternal grandmother raised him. Although he never lived with us, he was an important part of our family. Mother's second child was a daughter, who was ten when I was born. Another son was nine when I was born. I was very close with my maternal siblings, even though they were much older. Even after they left the household, they remained a part of our close-knit family. After my mother's oldest daughter completed high school and later married, I spent most weekends with her. I never differentiated between my mother's three older children and me by referring to them as half siblings. They were always just my brothers and sister.

The closeness of our family involved many members of our extended family and community as well. Five of my mother's nine siblings lived in our hometown of Philadelphia, where I spent my entire childhood. Like many families in west Philadelphia, we lived in a brick row house in a working-class neighborhood that had many children. Ours was a household of evolving composition; some member of the extended family always lived with us. For example, Uncle John, one of my mother's brothers, lived with us most of his adult life. My cousin and her daughter lived with us for a couple of years, and my mother's other brothers lived periodically with us throughout my childhood. Our home was the center of the maternal side of my family. My mom maintained a leadership position with her siblings, and we regularly visited my aunts, uncles, and cousins. We had close relationships with our neighbors, and I remain in contact with my childhood friend and her mother. Although they have moved, her mother still writes notes and sends me birthday cards each year.

DESCRIPTION OF CAREGIVER

Some Africans Americans would consider me an "old folks' child" because of the age of my parents when I was born. My mother was nearly forty and my father was in his fifties at my birth. Even though I was very young when my father died and retain few memories of him, I do recall that he was active in our church, where he served as a deacon. On Sundays, our family spent a good part of the day at church, attending Sunday school and morning service and occasionally an evening service. After my father's death, my mother remained very active in church. This level of religious involvement provided a firm spiritual foundation for me. Nevertheless, I now think that the large amount of time my family spent in church may have contributed to my current pattern of attending church irregularly.

I attended public school, enjoyed learning, and had some inspirational teachers who took a special interest in me. When I completed high school, I wanted to go away to college. In addition to an emphasis on the importance of church and family, my mother believed in the importance of education, and she saved money for each of us to attend college. Despite this focus, I was the only one of my siblings to attain a college degree. Although my mother would have preferred that I attend a local college, she gave me her blessing when I decided to attend Morgan State University, a predominantly African American college in Baltimore, Maryland. At seventeen, I left Philadelphia for college and never returned to live there. While at Morgan, I met Paulette, who became a lifelong friend and support. Paulette and I were among a group of five students from Morgan who attended the preparatory program for students interested in graduate social work education. Upon graduating from Morgan, Paulette and I attended and graduated from the University of Michigan School of Social Work. Years later I attended Brandeis University for my doctorate in social policy, while Paulette remained at Michigan for her doctorate. After receiving my doctorate, I worked as the student coordinator for the National Association for Social Work and taught at the University of Tennessee at Knoxville for four years in the human services program. After receiving my doctorate, I completed a postdoctorate at the school of social work at the University of North Carolina in 1987. I then joined the faculty at Boston University.

Currently, I am in my fifties and am a social work professor and co-director of the doctoral program at a private university in New England. Despite my earlier expectation that an older sibling would care for my mother if the time came, I have become my mother's caregiver. Within a three-year period, because of a series of unexpected tragedies, my mother's earlier expressed wishes became a reality. Before becoming a caregiver for my mother, I was a caregiver to my brother and sister. These early tragedies opened the door for many teachable moments about aspects of caregiving, managing stress, attending to the emotional needs of others, interacting and advocating with healthcare professionals, gathering information, and galvanizing family supports when tough decisions must be made. Now I am the primary caregiver of a ninety-five-year-old mother who until 2006 lived independently in another state. Some of those teachable moments are described in this chapter along with my analyses about what should have occurred.

DESCRIPTION OF CAREGIVING EXPERIENCE

Caring for My Brother Sam

The first of three major incidents occurred in 1986. At the time, Sam, age forty-five and the younger of my two brothers, had retired from the military and was living in another state. I was then thirty-six years old, single and living in New England working as an assistant professor at a private university. A drunk driver traveling on the wrong side of the road collided head-on with the vehicle in which Sam was a passenger, instantly killing the driver. Sam survived the crash. He was conscious but critically ill when he arrived, by helicopter, at the shock-trauma unit at the university hospital in Baltimore. I learned of the accident later that day while at work and immediately called Sally, his wife, and my mother to indicate that I would meet them in Baltimore at the hospital. Fortunately, the family of my best friend's sister lived in Baltimore, and she was kind enough to provide overnight accommodations. They were wonderful: They met me at the airport, drove me to the hospital, and later drove my family to their home, fed us, and allowed us to stay with them for as long as we needed.

Traveling to Baltimore, I reminisced about times when Sam and I were children. He and I were very close, possibly because I was his little sister. He often teased me as big brothers do, and I loved the attention. Mother doted on Sam, partly because she was so impressed with his "go get 'em" attitude. At an early age, he worked hard outside the home. He had a paper route and completed it early enough to attend church with the family on Sundays. All in the community and church admired him for his fortitude and spunk. He was jovial and outgoing. He managed to get a coveted position in a neighborhood butcher shop. Because of this position, all in the neighborhood knew him.

Sally, Mother, and I waited in the hospital to learn more about Sam's condition. That evening, the doctors explained that while they were beginning their examination, his heart burst, and he suffered from a lack of oxygen to the brain (hypoxic brain damage). However, the extent of the brain damage could only be determined later, when and if he came out of the coma. The doctors wanted to know whether we wanted them to exercise heroic measures to keep him alive if he experienced seizures or other complications associated with head injury. Our eyes turned to my mother, who in fear of losing her son responded affirmatively. Had she known what was ahead, I know she would not have made this decision.

Perhaps this was the first teachable moment. Feeling helpless and distraught, we were asked to make such a decision in an emergency room filled with lots of activity and other patients. We knew little about this type of injury and had insufficient information to make an informed life or death decision. The doctor admitted that when my brother arrived in the trauma unit, he was able to indicate where he experienced pain and that the medical staff may have responded too slowly. Suddenly, he went into cardiac arrest, and when they opened his chest, his heart burst. We assumed that the impact of the collision and the associated physical traumas to the body accounted for the bursting of the heart muscle. Had we been allowed the time to integrate and adapt to the information we had just received, my mother might have responded out of reason rather than emotion. We were allowed to visit him in the intensive care unit for a few minutes. He was in a coma and on life supports. His head was wrapped in gauze and swollen, and he was hooked up to what seemed like a million machines. It was a very scary sight.

The next day, Paulette's mother drove us to the hospital. My brother's condition was unchanged, and because there was little we could do there, Sally and Mother returned to Philadelphia. I remained in Baltimore one more day and then returned to Boston. Because I had a more flexible schedule and could afford it, I made several additional trips to the area to check on him. Neither Sally nor my mother was able, because of age in my mother's case and finances in Sally's case, to get to Baltimore regularly. At first, I would fly into Baltimore from Boston about once every two weeks and, after each visit, would call my mother and sister-in-law with what little information I had obtained about my brother's condition. Sometimes I would drive from Boston to Philadelphia to drive the two of them to Baltimore to visit him. Sally was in contact with his doctors on a regular basis. Her concerns were not only about him but about their two children, who were seventeen and twenty-one years of age. Neither his children nor my siblings were able to visit him while he was in the hospital.

He remained in a coma for weeks. We didn't know at the time that the longer a patient remained in a comatose state, the less favorable the outlook. He eventually regained consciousness, and the life supports were removed. He recognized me when I visited and could speak my name, but he wasn't able to communicate very much more. Doctors performed computed tomography scans and determined that significant brain damage was present. It was difficult to believe. My brother was such a vibrant person, always playing practical jokes on others and laughing. He made friends easily. It was especially difficult for my mother to comprehend that her son would never be like he had been; she had to believe that with prayer he would get better. Sally had arranged a meeting with a neurologist at the hospital. The doctor conveyed his opinion in a cold, direct, and definite manner. His words were chilling. I silently wept because I knew I would never develop the type of relationship with my brother that I so wanted. Sam was nine years older than me and had enlisted into the military when I was only ten years old. He always seemed to be out of the country as I was growing up. Despite his absence from the household, though, we remained close. He frequently sent me letters, and when he was home he played with me and lovingly teased me. I grew up idealizing our relationship. As an adult, I always spent a few days with him in Maryland after he retired (he and Sally separated before the accident) on the drive between Tennessee and my family home in Philadelphia. Sam's retirement meant that we could finally relate to each other as adults and perhaps be able to spend longer periods together. Although it was possible that physical therapy would help, the doctor left us with little hope that his condition would improve significantly. He would never walk, be able to feed himself, or exercise the level of attentiveness, perception, or communication skills he once had.

In retrospect, I realize this would have been the most appropriate time for a social worker's intervention—another teachable moment. We needed support and, more importantly, information about what to expect, the types of future decisions we would need to make, and the possible implications of these decisions. There was no one there to help us understand that head injury, regardless of its cause, simultaneously strikes the physical and intellectual functioning of the victim and the victim's personality. I don't think any of us fully grasped what the doctor's chilling words actually meant. I later learned that victims of head injury experience physical, cognitive, psychosocial, behavioral, and emotional impairments. Although the intellectual abilities of a brain-injured patient might not improve over time, the social and behavioral abilities and memory can improve with time and early therapeutic intervention.

After hearing this devastating news, I returned to Boston to hear additional bad news. The dean of the school of social work could offer me only a part-time faculty position for the next year. I had taught at the school for two years in a tenure-track position that had been vacated by a colleague who was pursuing a law degree. I had simply been substituting in her tenure-track position while she was away, and now she was planning to return. In the mist of such emotional turmoil and the seriousness of my brother's condition compared with my own, I gave little thought to what I needed to do. I began sending out résumés and interviewing for jobs between April and May, the end of the academic year. My trips to Baltimore were limited to monthly visits. My best friend's family was very helpful during these times, continuing to provide housing and emotional support. Fortunately, I had some choices in searching for another position; however, most of them were far more distant from my family. By happenstance, I ran into a friend from the doctoral program we had both attended who suggested that I apply for a position in another Massachusetts school. With her support and advice, I managed to get through the interview and received an inviting offer for employment. What a relief: I would continue to be financially secure.

Meanwhile, weeks later my brother was transferred to Walter Reed Hospital. During my first visit to the hospital, I was pleasantly surprised to find my brother in a wheelchair next to the nursing station, talking and observing all the activity around him. The attending doctor had been a physical therapist and consequently attempted to apply less traditional and more comprehensive approaches to my brother's care. Placing my brother in a wheelchair in front of the nursing station provided constant audio and visual stimulation, which the doctor hoped would improve his cognitive impairments. And it appeared that there was some improvement. As I walked down the hallway, I could hear my brother joking and chatting with the nurses (in hindsight I now realize they were joking and chatting with him). Having lost oxygen to the brain, my brother had limited short-term memory. He could barely remember what he had had for lunch two hours earlier, but his memories of the distant past were quite vivid. This was another teachable moment: Advocate for the best treatment approaches, even those that are not the customary treatments. In order to do this, of course, one has to be knowledgeable about the possible nontraditional interventions.

After this initial visit, I began searching for information about how patients who experienced anoxia, illnesses produced by the lack of oxygen to the brain, should be treated. At that time, before the Internet, there was very limited information about anoxia that a layperson could access. Trying to understand and interpret information from medical and rehabilitation journals was difficult; however, from these sources I learned that only an eighth of the 400,000 people who suffered a serious head injury survived, and even then they were unlikely to return to a normal life. Most head injury victims were men between the ages of eighteen and thirty, and motor vehicle accidents caused most of these injuries. With some luck, I learned about the national head injury foundation and its chartered state associations. The foundation provided an information and referral network for families and professionals about rehabilitation facilities, offered support groups for survivors and families of head-injured patients, and advocated for additional services for the victims of head injury.

Armed with more information and an information referral source, I tried to provide a realistic appraisal to my family, especially Sally, of what was happening to my brother and what needed to happen to ensure adequate care. I learned that the rehabilitation of victims of head injury required a team approach consisting of the services of occupational therapists, physical therapists, speech pathologists, cognitive therapists, recreational therapists, neuropsychologists, rehabilitation nurses, and sometimes dietitians and special education teachers. In many ways, rehabilitation of a brain-injured patient resembles that of a stroke victim. Most importantly, those working with brain-injured victims must be patient, flexible, and willing to discuss and accept creative ideas from other team members. The traditional, discipline-specific approaches do not work with the brain-injured population because the illness involves so many aspects of their functioning.

During his stay at Walter Reed Medical Center, the staff gave Sam rehabilitation treatments that by far outmatched any other he would receive over the next five years. In a subsequent visit to the hospital, I learned that the doctor actually had my brother standing up. My brother seemed so proud to tell me he had been standing up, if only for a few minutes, with the support of mechanical devices, of course. I was so hopeful that with the right type of rehabilitation services, the quality of his life would improve. But alas, this sense of hope was short-lived. Sally and I returned for another visit and spoke with the hospital social worker, who was anxious to begin the discharge planning process. Neither of us was prepared to talk about discharge planning. We had hoped that as a twenty-two-year veteran, Sam would be able to remain at Walter Reed. Our hopes quickly faded. Having found the information I received from the national head injury foundation helpful, I used their information and referral network to locate a rehabilitation center that specialized in the treatment of head injury victims. There was a very good facility located in Camden, New Jersey, not far from Philadelphia. I passed this information on to Sally, who was legally responsible for decisions about my brother's care. She referred this information to the social worker, who attempted to follow up, only to find that the costs of the rehabilitation were prohibitive for the family.

Looking back, I realize this could have been a teachable moment. One lesson was that we should have pushed the social worker to strongly advocate for the best possible discharge plan. Because she knew I, too, was a social worker, I think she took a stronger interest in the case but felt her responsibility was to the next of kin, Sally. The second lesson had to do with who could make decisions about his care. Legally, Sally was responsible, so whatever my mother or I wanted we had to negotiate with her. In order to make the best discharge plan, the three of us needed to agree on what we thought were realistic expectations for the possible outcomes for my brother. We didn't. My mother had unrealistic hopes that Sam would fully recover; Sally, the realist, had few illusions that he would recover; and I hoped that with the right type of rehabilitation his condition would improve. Because the three of us didn't or couldn't come to a consensus about our expectations and thus the type of care Sam needed, it was easier to later place blame on other people, such as the medical staff, for the outcome.

We also had to face the fact that providing appropriate care for my brother would be expensive. Despite the fact that he was a twenty-two-year veteran, medical coverage was limited. In the years before his retirement, the federal government began to reduce healthcare coverage for veterans, and neither Sam nor Sally had the resources to supplement the Veterans Administration (VA) Champus insurance coverage. This was the third lesson: the importance of social policy and its effects on individual lives. Given the financial limitations and geographic considerations (Sally wanted him to be near the neurologists who had cared for him), Sam was transferred to a VA hospital on the eastern shore of Maryland.

My first visit to the VA facility on the eastern shore of Maryland was disappointing. The facility was located in an isolated area; it took nearly an hour and a half to get there from Baltimore. It was an old, dingy, unfriendly place. Few nurses or attendants seemed to know much about Sam's case. Nurses and other hospital staff rushed down the hallways, apparently very busy, but none seemed to be attending to Sam. Instead of being in therapy, Sam was in his room alone, with no visibly stimulating sounds or sights. When I inquired about his care, the staff told me that the doctor assigned to his case was unavailable that day. Once again, Sam recognized my face and asked a number of questions about events that occurred when he was an adolescent living at home. His memory had deteriorated.

The information I had gathered about the symptoms of brain injury prepared me for Sam's memory lapses, but after the progress he had made at Walter Reed, the situation seemed bleak. In the weeks after his transfer to this VA hospital, my brother began to exhibit the behavioral symptoms of brain injury. He had constant mood swings, was aggressive and uncooperative, and became agitated quickly. On my subsequent visit to the facility, an attendant told me that when my brother was taken to physical therapy, he was placed in a corner alone because of these behavioral symptoms. The therapists found him difficult to work with and therefore left him alone. He remained in the VA facility for only a few months. Sally decided to have Sam transferred to a nursing home in Philadelphia sometime that summer so he would be closer to my mother and the rest of the family. Her decision was an acknowledgment of both the hopelessness of his condition and the condition of the facility.

From May through August, I was preparing to leave the teaching position in Boston to assume another faculty appointment some 100 miles away. However, I spent my summer commuting 200 miles once a week to teach two classes at my current place of employment. This period, then, included commuting to teach, traveling several hundred miles to visit a brother who was deteriorating, and planning for a move and a new job.

Caring for My Sister Joan

In September 1987 I relocated, and later that month a second incident occurred. Joan, my maternal sister, and I had always been very close; she had been my confidante since childhood, and I always discussed important things with her before discussing them with my mother. Our special relationship continued across the miles after I left home. Joan was a tall, confident, well-spoken person, with distinct views about life and her goals. She was so attractive that she did some part-time modeling when she was younger. Although Joan and my mother disagreed often, in some ways I would say my mother worshipped Joan. At age twenty-four, Joan married, probably to get away from our intrusive and overprotective mother. Joan was an assembly line worker for electronics companies for many years. She had one son and later separated from her husband.

Late that September, I learned that Joan, who was forty-eight at the time, had been diagnosed with mouth cancer, probably caused by cigarette smoking. Had she sought medical care earlier, she might not have needed surgery. When she had the surgery to remove part of her tongue in October, I was sitting at her side when she awakened. With my mother's help and emotional support, my sister successfully underwent radiation treatment and the subsequent physical therapy. Because of the surgery, it was difficult to understand her when she talked, so I seldom spoke with her by phone. I periodically sent her money because she was unemployed and receiving only a small welfare payment. My letters continued for nearly six months before I began calling her again. By then James, her adult son and only child, had moved back into her house to care for her. During this stressful period, my caregiving responsibilities were limited to simply driving to Philadelphia to provide emotional support to my mother and sister and to visit my brother Sam.

However, in 1988 Joan died from a stroke. It was ironic and surprising that my sister, who had been healthy until the diagnosis of mouth cancer, died before Sam, who had been seriously ill for several years. At her funeral, the church was packed with family, neighbors, friends, and coworkers. After Joan's death, I withdrew emotionally from most of my friends and especially James, who was in his twenties. I resisted becoming a substitute parent for him when I was still grieving. I found it difficult to grieve with my family, although I continued to travel to Philadelphia at least four times a year for long visits that were depressing for me but reassuring to my mother. She needed to feel the closeness of her youngest child. Moreover, my friends, those geographically closest and distant, had difficulty understanding the depth of my grief.

This too was a teachable moment. Although friends can empathize with one's loss, unless they have experienced the loss of a sibling it is difficult for them to sustain that level of emotional support over time. Mourning is an idiosyncratic experience that has no time limit. One does not recover from loss in a day, a month, or a year. Consequently, I learned that it was not feasible to rely so heavily on friends for emotional support. I also learned that caregivers need respite in order to care for themselves. In situations that involve grief it is sometimes difficult to rely on others for care; instead, one must grieve in isolation. One can deal with the demands of caregiving and being a professional only for so long without taking time for self-care. I took the time, but it had a cost. Because I resisted becoming a substitute parent, my nephew suffered. He needed his aunt to grieve with him and to guide him during this time of transition.

In addition to grieving and avoiding caregiving responsibilities, I needed to prepare for the long, agonizing contract renewal process. For anyone in academe, this is a long, daunting, and stressful process. I had worked extremely hard in the school, teaching more courses than required, assuming an administrative position as chair of a curriculum area, and taking on a heavy advising load. I had been teaching in other schools for more than five years before assuming this position as an assistant professor and had decided I would request a promotion at the same time as a contract renewal. At this college, no one had ever requested a promotion at the end of the first contractual period, but given everything else, I took the risk. I found the process extremely stressful, although I felt supported by colleagues. The withdrawal from the problems of my family made it possible to get through the contract renewal and promotion process. As I think about it now, maybe my decision for an early review for promotion gave me an acceptable reason to withdraw from the family and friends.

I was not the only family member who withdrew after my sister's death. My mother also withdrew. The loss of her child was more burdensome than losing her first and second husbands after prolonged illnesses. After their deaths, she rebounded quickly for the sake of her children. She had retired in 1978 and to my surprise developed a fairly active life, attending a senior center regularly, baking sour cream pound cakes for the center, teaching quilting, attending church services, and taking trips with the church. By 1989, three years after my brother's accident and one year after my sister's death, she no longer went to the senior center, nor did she attend church services regularly. Instead, she devoted her time to making visits to the nursing home to care for my brother. She was becoming increasingly dependent on me for companionship and emotional support, although I increasingly resisted taking her dependency needs seriously.

One summer during one of my regular visits home, I realized how much the isolation had affected her memory, and immediately, without giving it much thought, I enrolled her in another senior center that provided transportation. Although she protested, she began attending the center twice a week, enjoying the company of other older adults. Things were beginning to take on the appearance of normalcy for her. A routine had been established. Mondays she paid bills, Tuesdays and Wednesdays she spent at the senior center, Thursdays she and one of my uncles visited my brother in the nursing home, and Fridays she did her grocery shopping.

Caregiving for My Mother

The third incident, which prompted my direct involvement in caregiving, occurred on Christmas day in 1991 when Sally called to inform the family that my brother had died early that morning. My mother answered the phone. I was in the kitchen preparing part of our holiday dinner (we were expecting several aunts, cousins, nephews, and friends later that afternoon) when I heard her call out my name. When I came into the living room, my mother was sitting at the bottom of the staircase in tears. Until this moment, I had never seen her cry. She was devastated. She had lost one child already and now another. Although we decided not to cancel the holiday dinner, it was certainly a very sad celebration. Sally, Mother, and I began making funeral arrangements the next day. Peter, my older maternal brother, lives in South Carolina and because of the distance and his poor health could not visit Sam and is unable to fully participate as a caregiver for our mother. However, Peter attended Sam's funeral. After the funeral, my eighty-year-old mother admitted Sam's death was a relief. Concerned about Mother, I extended my holiday visit into the New Year, and my extended family sat with my mother every day for weeks. Sam's death and previous losses—two husbands, her parents, five siblings, and a daughter—seemed more than she was prepared to handle. It is often said that the passing of a child before a parent is unnatural.

In the years after my brother's passing, my mother, then age eighty, became increasingly frail. Once 150 pounds, she dropped to only 115 pounds, she had difficulty remembering things, and she had little patience for her seventy-nine-year-old brother, who had always lived in her home. Mother aged quickly after Sam's death. We talked by phone once a week, and I drove to

A contextual approach assesses "the sociocultural, situational, interpersonal, temporal, and personal context in which African Americans give care" (Dilworth-Anderson et al. 1999:391). The contextual approach assumes that the broader environment directly influences the caregiving experiences and outcomes, including emotional distress.

Sociocultural Context

The sociocultural context examines the cultural beliefs and attitudes that "reflect the caregivers views on filial obligation, duty and reciprocity" (Dilworth-Anderson et al. 1999:391) and influence family processes, perceptions, explanations, and responses to illness and dependency within specific groups. Studies comparing caregiver burden consistently show that African American caregivers report less burden than their European American counterparts (Calderon and Tennstedt 1998), even though older adults of color have higher levels of disability and need more hours of care (Hinrichsen and Ramirez 1992). Explanations for the differences in caregiver burden are numerous. The sense of familial obligation for the care of the young and the old presumably is higher among people of color than among European Americans. Reliance on larger extended family networks among people of color may reduce some of the responsibilities of the primary caregiver. Ethnic differences in caregiver burden may also be the result of measurement errors caused by differences in definitions of burden, approaches to measuring burden (i.e., objective vs. subjective burden), and "the applicability of different measures to different populations" (Calderon and Tennstedt 1998:162). Their qualitative study suggests that caregivers of color experience burden by expressing frustration, anger, isolation, somatic symptoms, and differences in coping styles. Certainly, in my own case the frustration, anger, and isolation have been enormous and sometimes are alleviated by assistance from extended family members.

Situational Context

The situational context, the second level of conceptual analysis, consists of factors directly relating to caregiving duties (the recipient's level of physical dependency, mental status, cognitive impairment, and behavioral problems) and other caregiving stressors (Pinquart and Sorensen 2003). The double-jeopardy hypothesis suggests that higher levels of stressors (not burden) among ethnic caregivers result from their greater risk for poor health, resulting from lifelong economic disadvantage and discrimination (Wykle and Kaskel 1995). Fortunately, Mother, now ninety-four, needs no assistance to bathe, dress, walk, or eat. Because her cognitive skills are deteriorating, she needs help correctly dispensing medications and preparing meals, which the home health aide does.

Other factors such as role strain, role reversal, and long-distance caregiving cause much more stress than Mother's physical dependency. The role strains of having a professional life, working outside the home, and parenting in combination with caregiving all contribute to stress and burden. One study examining role strain, role demand, and role conflict among a sample of European American and African American female caregivers found higher levels of role strain among European Americans and higher role demand among African Americans (Mui 1992). Poorer physical health and unavailability of respite support predict role strain among African Americans, and poor parent–daughter relationships predicted role strain among European Americans.

Women, especially in their middle years, provide the bulk of elder care. They are the sandwich generation, simultaneously managing work, child rearing, and adult caregiving. Just when most women expect to realize a reduction in tasks, they sacrifice their time, emotional well-being, earnings, and employment benefits to assist their elders. One scholar suggests that competing demands have more influence on when they help their parents than on how much (Finley 1989) because women, unlike men, extend their work week to provide care to their parents after work and on weekends (Stoller 1983).

According to some (Simon 1986), families often view never-married women, like me, as free-floating resources because they can't use commitments to spouse and children to counterbalance family claims (Davis and Strong 1977:124). A study of never-married female caregivers for elderly parents revealed the high price of caregiving: emotional costs of suppressing feelings, physical exhaustion, depleting finances, and social isolation (Simon 1986). Although these women "derived satisfaction and legitimacy from their role of nurturer" (Simon 1986:29), they paid a high emotional, physical, social, and financial price. Because I am a single woman without children and with a flexible schedule and more education than most in my family, there is an unspoken expectation that I should be able to assume caregiving responsibilities for my mother, my siblings, and others. After all, I had left the area to pursue my own goals, and now it was time to give back. The struggle to balance work, family, and friends remains physically exhausting and emotionally draining.

One scholar citing Emily Abel (1991) indicated that "the process of caregiving demands that adult children and aging parents redefine their roles vis-à-vis each other" (Lan 2002:816). For most adult children the change in dynamics and the need to exert authority in the relationship with a parent are unwelcome, often denied and avoided for as long as possible. Parents often feel ambivalent about this power shift, evidenced by their attempts to exercise self-determination and hold children accountable. Increased family tensions, resentments, and reduced contact are results (Pyke 1999). Some elderly parents consider care an intrusion into their lives; they resist help. According to one scholar (Tronto 1993), the practice of caregiving consists of four phases: (1) caring about, (2) taking care of, (3) caregiving, and (4) care receiving. "Caring about (recognizing the necessity of care) and taking care of (assuming some responsibility for the identified need and determining how to respond to it) are the duties of the powerful, while caregiving (the direct meeting of needs for care), and care receiving (the subject of care responds to the care he or she receives) are the duties of the less powerful" (Tronto 1993:114). No question, I am in a more powerful position to care for my mother's needs. Appreciating my help, she finds it difficult to relinquish complete control. I find it refreshing that she still wants to exercise some power because it means she has not completely given up.

Caring for elderly parents significantly differs from the care of other family members with disabilities such as mental illness or mental retardation. With mental illness, caregiving rarely begins before adolescence or young adulthood. Mental retardation, usually diagnosed in childhood, requires a lifetime of caregiving (Lefley 1997:443). The need for care of older adults usually begins later in the lives of both the caregiver and the care receiver and increases with age.

Long-distance caregivers face unique challenges. Caring from a distance makes it difficult to assess needs, especially if no significant critical event, such as a recent hospitalization or accident, has occurred. The functioning of older family members tends to decline gradually over time, and without consistent and direct observation it is difficult to evaluate needs or determine the onset for caring. Elderly parents often do not disclose their health or care needs, for fear of worrying an adult child or being hospitalized or placed in a nursing home. Another complication is relatives, neighbors, and aging parents who exaggerate the situation or postpone reporting beyond the availability of help. After a need has been identified, long-distance caregivers have difficulty locating and monitoring services. This was the situation with my brother Sam. Unanticipated delays in service delivery occur for many reasons, including the need to establish the receiver's eligibility for services, arrange transportation services, or wait for placement slots. Communicating with formal service providers complicates the situation further; sometimes they dismiss the opinions of long-distance caregivers, especially when the caregiver has not developed a relationship with them.

Still another challenge is the strain on family relationships. Research shows that local siblings or relatives sometimes resent out-of-town siblings for being inconsiderate or not doing enough (Hooyman and Lustbader 1986). Some experts suggest that "long-distance care often causes more psychological stress," whereas caring for relatives nearby often results in more physical exhaustion (Wagner 1997:iii–5). Long-distance caregivers have other strains (costs of travel, long-distance calls, time away from work) and guilt because they are not always available (Koerin and Harrigan 2002). I experienced psychological stresses as a long-distance caregiver to my brother, sister, and mother and physical exhaustion as I managed two households, my mother's and mine. My caregiving experiences suggest it may not be a question of either psychological stress or physical exhaustion but instead a combination of both.

Interpersonal Context

The third aspect of a contextual approach involves an examination of the interpersonal context or the quality of relationships caregivers have with others in their support networks. According to research, the number of support network members is less important than the caregiver's perception of social support. In their study of 187 elderly African American care recipients and their primary caregivers, one group of researchers found that increased satisfaction with social support reduced the likelihood of emotional distress among caregivers (Dilworth-Anderson et al. 1999). Thus decreased satisfaction with social supports increases the likelihood of emotional distress among caregivers. Other researchers have found that adverse social contacts with daughters, sons, friends, and neighbors were associated with increased caregiver strain, but positive contacts with these same social supports were insignificant (Spaid and Barusch 1991).

It is generally assumed that the strong kinship ties among African Americans decrease caregiver vulnerability to depression and distress. Several studies have shown that African American caregivers have more people in their support networks (including family and friends) than their non-caregiving counterparts (Haley et al. 1995; Wallsten 2000). These secondary caregivers are a significant part of a caregiver's social support network. They are often a source of respite for primary caregivers, are a potentially valuable resource if something happens to the primary caregiver, and sometimes are major sources of adverse contact with primary caregivers (Spaid and Barusch 1991).

Previous research indicates that older adults report assistance from on average two secondary caregivers, usually spouses, children, and siblings (Horowitz and Dobrof 1982; Tennstedt et al. 1989). Some research (Bullock et al. 2003) found that employed primary caregivers were more likely than the unemployed to have help from secondary caregivers. Moreover, research indicates that the care secondary caregivers provide supplements rather than complements that offered by primary caregivers (Tennstedt et al. 1989). How primary caregivers perceive the support and pattern of care provided by secondary caregivers is likely to affect the level of emotional distress they experience. Research also shows that "the amount of help from secondary caregivers is influenced more by their own characteristics than by the characteristics of the elder" (Tennstedt et al. 1989:682). The relationships between the amount of help from secondary caregivers, patterns of care, and emotional distress experienced by primary caregivers have not been examined and represent an important area for future study.

As a caregiver for my mother, I was fortunate. A host of family members, neighbors, friends, and church members easily moved from the role of primary caregiver to secondary caregiver as needed. They provided primary care when I was not in Philadelphia and secondary care when I was. The large social network our family developed over time provided a ready-made cadre of helpers. In providing both primary and secondary care for Sam, friends were there to provide emotional support, seek medical information, and offer a place to stay and transportation. I pulled away from friends as I grieved the injuries my brother faced and the death of my sister. Paulette, my best friend, and her entire extended family continued to be available for whatever I needed. Eva, Paulette's sister, would pick me up at the airport, provide lodging, and transport me to the hospital to visit Sam and helped with other things. Many of my other friends did not understand the salience of my relationships with my siblings. In addition, although my friends had difficulty understanding my obsession in obtaining every detail of Sam's accident and his illnesses, they remained supportive. If one has not experienced these types of losses, it is difficult to understand what the other may be going through.

Temporal Context

Temporal context, the fourth aspect of a contextual approach to analyzing caregiver distress, focuses on the timing of caregiving in the life cycle of the caregiver. For example, caring for other dependent elderly relatives simultaneously and full-time employment are secondary stressors that increase caregiver distress. As the number of care recipients increases, caregiver distress is likely to increase as well. Of course, certain mediating factors might reduce or increase caregiver distress, such as income, social supports, severity of care recipient illness, coping processes, and appraisal of the caregiving experience.

Evidence suggests that employed caregivers are more likely than unemployed caregivers to purchase assistance (Enright 1991). In a study of 119 elder–caregiver dyads (Bullock et al. 2003) report that employed caregivers changed their work schedules, reduced their work hours, or changed jobs to accommodate their caregiving responsibilities.

Being an academic affords a great deal of flexibility in scheduling the completion of work, yet the pressure and insecurities associated with the tenure process are constant. Today's American college faculty consists largely of European American men, especially in universities and in the higher ranks. Women and faculty of color are less likely than their European American male counterparts "to hold full-time faculty positions, be promoted to full professor or receive tenure" (Trower 2002:25). Another study indicates that women represent 36% of full-time faculty, compared with 23% in the early 1970s (Trower and Chait 2002). Twenty-four percent of faculty women were ranked at the full professor level, and 55% were ranked as lecturers in 1998. According to these authors, women are more likely than men to hold lower academic ranks and work at less prestigious institutions. Female college faculty members tend to receive promotions at a slower rate, and their earnings generally are lower than those of their male colleagues. Women also find that tenure policies collide with the biological clock, thereby making them choose between having an academic career and having a family. One author suggests that women's access to institutional resources and rewards may be limited because their legitimacy as academics is questioned (Aguirre 2000). A lack of mentoring and collegiality often impedes women's progress.

Despite affirmative action policies, people of color continue to be underrepresented in academic institutions, and their retention rates are lower. The percentage of full-time faculty of color has remained consistent (12%) between 1989 and 1999 (Trower 2002). People of color are less likely to be tenured than European American faculty (Trower and Chait 2002) and more likely to hold the rank of lecturer or instructor. One study (Carter and Wilson 1997) indicated that faculty of color represent only 9.2% of full professors.

The factors that account for these trends include the organizational features of the academic workplace. The academic culture has been "characterized by group struggles over the definition of knowledge and about what it means to be a knowledgeable person" (Aguirre 2000:3). In this culture, women and people of color, if hired, often are burdened with heavy teaching, advising, and service responsibilities that distract them from engaging in research and publication. They are also expected to perform roles that will advance the institution's pursuit of diversity on campus. Their research and publications often are perceived as less legitimate than those of European American men (Aisenberg and Harrington 1988). These data suggest that although an academic appointment has advantages in terms of flexibility, it also imposes multiple levels of stress on caregivers.

Personal Context

The personal context refers to the resources caregivers use when providing care. Coping styles and feelings of mastery in the caregiving role along with the caregiver's income, employment status, and health status are examples of these resources. African American and European American caregivers differ in their use of spirituality and religiosity to cope with the demands of caregiving (Dilworth-Anderson et al. 2002). A twenty-year review of caregiving among diverse groups suggests that several studies link higher levels of spirituality and religiosity with lower depression and burden (Dilworth-Anderson et al. 2002). African American caregivers use prayer, faith in God, and religion to cope with the difficulties of caregiving. One study (Wood and Parham 1990) reports that African American caregivers, unlike European American caregivers, indicate that God is a part of their informal support.

Others report that African American caregivers use cognitive (i.e., positive reappraisal) and emotion-focused coping (e.g., distraction, avoidance, and venting of emotions) more than European Americans. Several studies show that African American caregivers use more positive reappraisal than European American caregivers in dealing with the difficulties of caregiving (Farran et al. 1997; Knight and McCallum 1998: Knight et al. 2000). By using positive appraisals of the caregiving situation, African American caregivers reportedly had different levels of depression and burden than European American caregivers. Although African American caregivers have been found to fare best psychologically, they are at a disadvantage in terms of physical health (Pinquart and Sorensen 2005) and have fewer financial resources to assist them in their caregiving functions and less education.

From a simplistic perspective caregiving is the act of providing for or the giving of services, whether concrete or abstract, to another. As some scholars suggest, however, "caregiving is not only a form of labor; it constitutes a relationship" (Garey et al. 2002:709), with a multiplicity of emotional dimensions ranging from anger, guilt, resentment, love, pity, sympathy, embarrassment, frustration, shame, grief, and disappointment—all of which cast forbidding shadows over the caregiver and the care receiver. Caregiving also captures the relationships between the people giving and those receiving care and reveals the complexity of their interdependence. The caregiver feels anger, fear, and guilt about the reversal in roles, whereas the care receiver experiences shame, grief, anger, and fear about the loss of independence. To view this relationship as one of dependence and independence alone is far too simplistic. In actuality, over time a degree of interdependence occurs between caregiver and care receiver that neither is prepared to fully acknowledge or deal with. Caregiving transforms relationship dynamics, and the greatest challenge is that of establishing a healthy balance between the care receiver's sense of independence and the care provider's sense of dependence.

IMPLICATIONS

Although politicians and others have extolled the virtues of family caregiving, few have heeded studies that reveal the personal costs for family care providers. Increasing amounts of funding are appropriated for elder services in the form of housing, nutrition, medical care, and home health services, but gaps in services remain. Most of these services are geared to older adults who have physical aliments that limit their mobility and functioning. However, for those who do not suffer from such impairments, the selection of elder services is restricted. As the number of older adults increases and the number in the oldest age group, those eighty-five years and over, grows, the service gaps have widened and become increasingly problematic to those who care for them. The implications of these demographic changes for the care of older adults and for caregivers necessitate change on multiple levels.

On a societal level, financial support for frail older adults is always needed. Ensuring the continuation of government policies and programs that provide basic services such as financial support, healthcare, nutrition, transportation, and housing is vital, especially for the baby boomer generation. Besides these basic needs, older adults also have spiritual needs that might be met through religious organizations such as churches. Some religious denominations, such as the Catholic Church, have established senior centers; others might form senior companion groups or organize teams of members who regularly visit sick and elderly members to offer Bible classes, Holy Communion, or other religious rituals. For older adults and for those with severe disabilities, home maintenance and safety, especially for homeowners, are serious concerns. Area offices of aging have attempted to address some of these concerns by mounting campaigns to provide low-cost home modifications and assistive devices in the homes of older adults. Many of these offices also provide transportation, but even more could be offered, such as information about home repair services and respite care for family caregivers. Hospitals are increasingly recognizing the need for specialized services for older adults, and specialized training is also offered to physicians interested in geriatric medicine. Extending hospital social services to family caregivers as a specific component of geriatric care has not yet been done.

The plight of older adults living in low-income urban areas is particularly concerning because services, especially routine services such as shopping areas, are become increasingly difficult to reach. In my mother's case, for example, there is no grocery store within a ten-block radius, and abandoned houses surround the neighborhood, making safety another major concern. Communities and neighborhoods could play a significant role in protecting older adults by organizing neighborhood watch groups to patrol the neighborhood and periodically check on elderly neighbors.

As a vulnerable group, older adults living in urban and rural areas are likely to experience isolation, loneliness, physical impairment, poor nutrition, financial strains, and fears about their safety. Attending church activities, senior centers, and adult day care programs places an elderly family member in regular contact with other active older adults. Joining these types of programs is also empowering. For those who are physically impaired, visiting nurses and senior companions are invaluable resources who sometimes identify the need for home modifications, prepare meals, offer assistance with light housekeeping and shopping, or provide information and referrals for Meals on Wheels. Obtaining assistance from legal or investment counselors helps to address concerns about finances.

Long-distance caregiving has some unique issues. "Family relationships may become strained by caregiving responsibilities in any situation, and particularly for long-distance caregivers" (Koerin and Harrigan 2002:67). When possible, every effort should be made to share caregiving responsibilities with extended family members, such as asking extended family members to organize visits by service providers. Regular telephone contact with the elderly and disabled increases communication and reduces their isolation. Arranging regular family meetings to discuss caregiving may also reduce the amount of conflict between family members. For the primary family caregiver, joining support groups and seeking respite care are recommended approaches for reducing caregiver burden.

Case management is another needed service, especially for older adults being cared for by distant relatives, who otherwise attempt to negotiate, manage, and coordinate a wide range of service providers from afar. When they are locally available and affordable, many long-distance caregivers enlist the assistance of geriatric case managers to oversee the provision of services. Social work practitioners in the field of gerontology and healthcare are in a strategic position to incorporate information about the needs of family caregivers into their daily practice. Progressive healthcare providers have begun to employ social workers in private practice to holistically attend to patients' needs. These social workers sensitize healthcare providers to the needs of patients and caregivers. For example, when physicians know that transportation is not available for an elderly patient, they are less likely to refer them for weekly physical therapy. Social workers can attain needed services and offer psychoeducational interventions and support groups to reduce caregiver burden and family strain. Finally, additional research is needed about long-distance caregiving that studies racial, ethnic, and socioeconomic differences between long-distance caregivers. Further examination of the role social work can play in the treatment of the brain injured is also needed.

REFLECTIONS AND CONCLUSIONS

When initially asked to write about my caregiving experiences for this book, I hesitated to disclose personal information about the losses I had experienced. Only my closest friends were aware of the number of losses in my family. I didn't want to mentally relive these tragic events for fear that the pain, sorrow, sadness, and anger I felt would reveal the inadequacies of my caregiving. Nor did I want others to feel pity for me. I couldn't imagine how writing about the experience would be helpful to others or to me, yet in many ways it was a healing experience.

Although I talked with close friends about the opportunity to write about caregiving, I had concerns about how my family would respond and about whether the writing would be perceived as exploiting a personal situation. In the end, I realized no one in the family would be harmed. Overcoming these initial reactions was a slow process. It began with rereading newspaper articles about my brother's accident, followed by an attempt to write a description of the event. I asked a friend to read the first seven pages of the description to be sure the information was presented clearly. I had tried to blur my memories of these tragedies and didn't feel confident that I could describe them accurately and clearly. Interestingly, I did not confer with other family members about the accuracy of my recollections throughout the writing process. The comments from my friend helped me to clarify the people and events I was attempting to

Table 6.1 Implications

	Issues and Problems	**Strategies for Change**
Society	Financial assistance Housing Nutrition	Provide Social Security and disability coverage. Provide health and drug insurance. Increase housing for older adults. Supplement long-term care services. Support Meals on Wheels.
Institutions	Responding to the spiritual needs of older adults Providing auxiliary services to older adults Providing specialized health services to older adults	Form senior companion groups, groups that visit the sick, and senior centers. Provide low-cost home repairs, home modifications, assistive devices, transportation to doctors' offices and grocery stores, respite care, and information and referral services. Establish specialized services for older adults and their caregivers.
Communities	Safety	Organize neighborhood watch groups. Establish food delivery services through grocery store chains.
Families	Caregiver burden Conflict with other family members over care	Share caregiving responsibilities with extended family. Organize home visiting and telephone trees to enhance communication between older adults and family members. Arrange regular family member visits. Join support groups. Seek respite care.

(*continued*)

Table 6.1 (continued)

	Issues and Problems	Strategies for Change
Individuals	Isolation and loneliness Physical impairment Poor nutrition Safety Financial management	Attend church.Join senior centers.Attend adult day care programs. Hire visiting nurses or senior companions. Sign up for Meals on Wheels. Use neighborhood watch groups. Secure assistive devices or home modifications. Obtain assistance from investment and legal counselors.
Practitioners	Coordination of services	Provide case management. Provide geriatric care managers. Offer psychoeducational groups for caregivers. Offer support groups for caregivers.
Researchers	Lack of knowledge about long-distance caregivers Need for additional research on the treatment of the brain injured	Examine the racial, ethnic, and socioeconomic differences between long-distance caregivers. Examine social work's role in the care of the brain injured and their caregivers.

describe. Finding literature on caregiving was a secondary process—one that took time—but it did not influence the direction of the chapter. I searched for literature after I had written the descriptions of the caregiving experiences. The events remained primary throughout the writing process.

Writing this chapter was emotionally traumatic, so much so that I called the editor to discuss what I was feeling and struggling to convey. For example, describing my brother's condition was painful and provoked anger toward healthcare providers and certain members of my family. Describing the instrumental activities of daily living (Koerin and Harrigan 2002) that I performed for my mother and sometimes other members of my extended family felt overwhelming and exaggerated. If there was anything easy about writing this chapter, it was identifying the sparse pieces of literature on the topic.

Did writing the chapter change my perceptions of the caregiving experience? If anything, I began to realize that by caring for my mother, I had slowly begun to care for her siblings and other extended family members as well. My family has become increasingly important in my life. Even when I am not with them, I still worry about them and appreciate their help in assisting my mother. My perceptions of myself as a caregiver also changed. I was able to acknowledge how much I use my observational skills to assess my mother's needs and to anticipate what may be needed in the future. For example, on one visit I created a memory board to hang in the kitchen to make it easier for her to find important telephone numbers in case of an emergency.

Reading the literature, especially articles on long-distance caregiving, normalized the experience for me by confirming the difficulties of caring for someone from a distance. I also found the literature that described caregiving in terms of the relationships between people very affirming. It seemed to capture the complexity of the interdependence between caregiver and care receiver more accurately than the literature on caregiver burden. Reading about the research that examined the caregiving experience in diverse groups was extremely enlightening. This literature suggested that culture may play a role in meditating emotional distress.

Were there things that I did not convey in this chapter that would have helped the reader to understand the situation? Yes! For example, in the description of my sister's illness there is no mention of teachable moments about the care of cancer patients, their recovery, and the role of a family caregiver in this process. Although the types of problems experienced by cancer victims and their caregivers are similar to those of older adults, there are distinct differences that should be recognized. I have not described the deep feelings I had for my siblings or the impact of their personal tragedies on my life. The loss of a sibling, like that of a parent, is something one never gets over. There's no one to reminisce with about one's upbringing or special events during childhood, no one to rely on when one worries about a parent or another family member. Knowing such things might explain what motivates a family caregiver. Finally, I made no attempt to describe how I managed the stress of each of these experiences. Much of what is described in the "Implications" section is suggestive of the various ways caregivers manage stressful situations.

Using narratives about caregiving is one way to make meaning out of a personal experience. Although I have been writing this narrative in my head all along, the meaning I attached to my caregiver role was not fully realized until I began to describe the events on paper. Caregiving is about the relationships between the caregiver and the care receiver and the interdependence between them. The bond between my mother and me was strengthened because of my caregiving role. What a magnificent unanticipated consequence!

Writing this chapter, I also learned something that another social worker said in a recent article: "I was especially impressed by the ways in which professional training both did and did not prepare me to cope with the personal experience" (Swenson 2004:459). It did enable me to seek information about my brother's condition and its treatment, to access and advocate for available services, and to use my observational and listening skills in making assessments of situations. However, there is a difference between professional knowing and personal knowing that professional training cannot provide. Until one lives it, one doesn't really know it. Professional training did not teach me that there is a dearth of services available to care for physically able older adults.

Unquestionably, it would be extremely difficult to perform caregiving functions if I did not have a highly flexible work situation, a tolerant employer (Swenson 2004), and financial security. Being in reasonably good health reduces the physical strain of traveling so frequently to visit family. Without these resources, it would be extremely difficult to provide care or to manage the stresses associated with caregiving. Being the last to be born in the family afforded opportunities that were not available to any of my siblings. With opportunities come responsibilities. So, despite the difficulties that sometimes come with caregiving, I realize that I should be the one to take care of others. In doing so, I have learned a great deal about my family and myself and enriched my own life with the rewards attendant with giving to others.

REFERENCES

Abel, E. 1991. *Who Cares for the Elderly?* Philadelphia: Temple University Press.

Aguirre, A. 2000. Women and minority faculty in the academic workplace: Recruitment, retention and academic culture. *ERIC Digest* ED445723 2000-00-00.

Aisenberg, N. and Harrington, M. 1988. *Women of Academe: Outsiders in the Sacred Grove.* Amherst: University of Massachusetts Press.

Bullock, K., Crawford, S., and Tennstedt, S. 2003. Employment and caregiving: Exploration of African American caregivers. *Social Work* 48 (2): 150–162.

Calderon, V. and Tennstedt, S. 1998. Ethnic differences in the expression of caregiver burden: Results of a qualitative study. *Journal of Gerontological Social Work* 30 (1/2): 159–178.

Carter, D. and Wilson, R. 1997. *Minorities in Higher Education*. Washington, D.C.: ACE.

Cook, J., Lefley, H., Pickett, S., and Cohler, B. 1994. Age and family burden among parents of offspring with severe mental illness. *American Journal of Orthopsychiatry* 64: 435–447.

Davis, A. and Strong, P. 1977. Working without a net: The bachelor as a social problem. *Sociological Review* 25: 109–129.

Dilworth-Anderson, P. and Anderson, N. 1994. Dementia caregiving in blacks: A contextual approach to research. In E. Light, G. Niederehe, and B. Lebowitz (Eds.), *Stress Effects on Family Caregivers of Alzheimer's Patients*, 385–409. New York: Springer.

Dilworth-Anderson, P., Williams, I., and Gibson, B. 2002. Issues of race, ethnicity, and culture in caregiving research: A 20-year review (1980–2000). *The Gerontologist* 42 (2): 237–272.

Dilworth-Anderson, P., Williams, S., and Cooper, T. 1999. The context of experiencing emotional distress among family caregivers to elderly African Americans. *Family Relations* 48 (4): 391–396.

Enright, R. 1991. Time spent caregiving and help received by spouses and adult children of brain-impaired adults. *The Gerontologist* 31: 373–383.

Farran, C., Miller, B., Kaufman, J., and Davis, L. 1997. Race, finding meaning, and caregiver distress. *Journal of Aging and Health* 9: 316–333.

Finley, N. 1989. Theories of family labor as applied to gender differences in caregiving for elderly parents. *Journal of Marriage and Family* 51: 79–86.

Garey, A., Hansen, K., Hertz, R., and MacDonald, C. 2002. Care and kinship: An introduction. *Journal of Family Issues* 23 (6): 703–712.

Haley, W., West, C., Wadley, V., Ford, G., White, F., Barrett, J., Harrell, L., and Roth, D. 1995. Psychological, social, and health impact of caregiving: A comparison of black and white dementia caregivers and noncaregivers. *Psychology and Aging* 10: 540–552.

Heller, T., Hsieh, K., and Rowitz, L. 1997. Maternal and paternal caregiving of persons with mental retardation across the life span. *Family Relations* 46: 407–415.

Hinrichsen, G. and Ramirez, M. 1992. Black and white dementia caregivers: A comparison of their adaptation, adjustment, and service utilization. *The Gerontologist* 32: 375–381.

Hooyman, N. and Lustbader, W. 1986. *Taking Care of Your Aging Family Members: A Practical Guide*. New York: Free Press/Macmillan.

Horowitz, A. and Dobrof, R. 1982. *The Role of Families in Providing Long-Term Care to the Frail and Chronically Ill Elderly Living in the Community*. Final Report, Health Care Financing Administration, Grant No. 18-P-97541/20-02. New York: Brookdale Center on Aging.

Knight, B. and McCallum, T. 1998. Heart rate reactivity and depression in African American and white dementia caregivers: Reporting bias or positive coping? *Aging and Mental Health* 2 (3): 212–221.

Knight, B., Silverstein, M., McCallum, T., and Fox, L. 2000. A sociocultural stress and coping model for mental health outcomes among African American caregivers in southern California. *Journal of Gerontology: Psychological Sciences* 55B: P142–P150.

Koerin, B. and Harrigan, M. 2002. P.S. I love you: Long-distance caregiving. *Journal of Gerontological Social Work* 40 (1/2): 63–81.

Lan, P. C. 2002. Subcontracting filial piety. *Journal of Family Issues* 23 (7): 812–835.

Lefley, H. 1997. Synthesizing the family caregiving studies: Implications for planning, social policy and further research. *Family Relations* 46 (4): 443–450.

Mui, A. 1992. Caregiver strain among black and white daughter caregivers: A role theory perspective. *The Gerontologist* 32: 203–212.

Pinquart, M. and Sorensen, S. 2003. Association of stressors and uplifts of caregiving with caregiver burden and depressed mood: A meta-analysis. *Journal of Gerontology: Psychological Sciences* 58B: P112–P128.

Pinquart, M. and Sorensen, S. 2005. Ethnic differences in stressors, resources, and psychological outcomes of family caregiving: A meta-analysis. *The Gerontologist* 45 (1): 90–106.

Pyke, K. 1999. The micropolitics of care in relationships between aging parents and adult children: Individualism, collectivism, and power. *Journal of Marriage and the Family* 61: 661–672.

Simon, B. 1986. Never-married women as caregivers to elderly parents: Some costs and benefits. *Affilia* 1 (3): 29–42.

Spaid, W. and Barusch, A. 1991. Social support and caregiver strain: Types and sources of social contacts of elderly caregivers. *Journal of Gerontological Social Work* 18 (2): 151–161.

Stoller, E. 1983. Parental caregiving by adult children. *Journal of Marriage and the Family* 47: 335–342.

Swenson, C. 2004. Dementia diary: A personal and professional journal. *Social Work* 49 (3): 451–460.

Tennstedt, S., McKinlay, J., and Sullivan, L. 1989. Informal care for frail elders: The role of secondary caregivers. *The Gerontologist* 29 (5): 677–683.

Tronto, J. 1993. *Moral Boundaries: A Political Argument for an Ethic of Care.* New York: Routledge.

Trower, C. 2002. Why so few minority faculty and what to do?: Diversifying the region's professoriate. *Connection.* (Fall). New England Board of Higher Education.

Trower, C. and Chait, R. 2002. Faculty diversity: Too little for too long. *Harvard Magazine* online. www.harvard-magazine.com/online/030218.html.

Wagner, D. 1997. *Caring Across the Miles: Findings of a Survey of Long-Distance Caregivers*. Washington, D.C.: NCOA.

Wallsten, S. 2000. Effects of caregiving, gender, and race on the health, mutuality and social support of older couples. *Journal of Aging and Health* 12 (1): 90–101.

Wood, J. and Parham, I. 1990. Coping with perceived burden: Ethnic and cultural issues in Alzheimer's family caregiving. *Journal of Applied Gerontology* 9: 325–339.

Wykle, M. and Kaskel, B. 1995. Increasing the longevity of minority older adults through improved health status. In Gerontological Society of America, *Minority Elders: Five Goals Toward Building a Public Base*, 32–39. Washington, D.C.: Gerontological Society of America.

SEVEN

Caring for My Mother

Four Phases of Caregiving

SHIRLEY BRYANT

This chapter traces major phases of caregiving for my mother: while she was in her own home in Indianapolis, Indiana; in my home in Temple Hills, Maryland; in her apartment in Oxon Hill, Maryland; and, at the end of her life, in a nursing home in Adelphi, Maryland.

DESCRIPTION OF CAREGIVER

In 1988 I, a forty-five-year-old social work faculty member, for the first time faced responsibility for caring for another human being: my mother. A never-married adult, I had focused primarily on my education, obtaining a baccalaureate degree from Hanover College in 1965, a master's in social work in 1969 from Fordham University in New York City, and a doctorate in social work in 1985 from Howard University in Washington, D.C. Nurtured by several teachers who exposed me to wider opportunities, I graduated valedictorian of my elementary and high schools. My parents were not unusual in welcoming my teachers' input. One scholar notes, "Black families have a passionate commitment to education and will cooperate with the schools to insure their success"

(Billingsley 1992:175). Another reports that more than half (64%) of support systems in African American families are nonrelatives, the largest group teachers and professors (Manns 1981). Graduating during the height of the civil rights movement, a classmate and I desegregated our college.

Upon graduation I moved to New York and worked in the Department of Welfare. Later I became a parent involvement coordinator in a Harlem Head Start program, followed by social work graduate school with a community organization focus. I spent the next twelve years working for various agencies organizing local African American communities in the Midwest, North, and Southeast to advocate for basic rights ranging from tenant rights and welfare to healthcare and educational entitlements. Whether a staff member, president and CEO of my own human services consulting firm, or executive director of an innovative child abuse and neglect agency, I always intervened with macrosystems: groups, organizations, and communities. Yet I was keenly aware of daily pressures individuals faced trying to meet their needs.

After receiving my doctorate, I began teaching the skills I had learned and practiced at the National Catholic School of Social Service in Washington, D.C. Ten years later, in 1995, I became the director of Virginia Commonwealth University's School of Social Work Northern Virginia Campus, a position I held in Alexandria, Virginia, until 2003, when I began teaching full time.

DESCRIPTION OF FAMILY MEMBER CARED FOR

Mother was born in Richardville, Oklahoma, in 1911 to a young and inexperienced mother who often left my mother and her younger brother to fend for themselves. So my mother grew up protecting and caring for herself and her brother. Nurturing others became a major theme of her life. When my grandmother migrated to an Indiana metropolitan area for employment, she sent my mother to her uncle and aunt, Oklahoma farm owners. Her new caregivers initially forced her to pick cotton and assume major housekeeping responsibilities. Because they considered Mother too slow in the fields, her uncle and aunt physically abused her, underscoring that her value lay in her ability to complete household chores. Because of these chores, Mother had sporadic education. Yet Mother loved learning—another lifelong theme—and was the star pupil in the little one-room schoolhouse she attended until the beginning of the eighth grade.

At age fifteen and weary of the abuse, she asked to join her mother in Indiana. Again, she was forced to leave school, this time for earnings. With my grandmother, she worked as a hotel maid and continued day work until her 1970 retirement. My earliest memories of my mother are of her always taking self-improvement courses. Whether in a cooking, sewing, Bible, or upholstery class, she always found time for learning. Reading voraciously or discussing history and current events, a progressive thinker and open to new ideas, she also spoke her mind. Once she told me an employer asked her whether my brother, James, would amount to anything. Without considering job security, she replied that her son could and would be whatever he set his mind to because he was smart and ambitious enough to succeed at anything. Such behavior earned Mother both respect and genuine affection. Years after she retired, for example, several former employers called and sent pictures and gifts annually. Mother's expectations for my brother also illustrated African American parents' socializing a child for and "combating the negative aspects of minority status" (Manns 1981:242). Mother made certain that we went weekly to the children's library, where we read books about different careers, among other subjects. One scholar indicates that education is a preeminent source "of survival, achievement, and viability of African American families" (Billingsley 1992:174).

Mother had strong beliefs about the importance of family and helping those less fortunate, yet another major life theme. A woman of deeds, she purchased and prepared food for the homeless and visited and cared for the sick, never expecting repayment. Mother's helping was a historical African tradition. One study notes that "historically black women have always been in the forefront of care giving . . . [undertaking] the burden of caring for the sick, the elderly, the infirmed, the orphaned, the mentally ill, the children, the men, the entire Black community, and a great portion of the White community as well" (Martin and Martin 2002:165).

Trusting God to give her no more than she could bear, Mother was a woman of great faith, dignity, prayer, and pride, all of which permeated everything she did. Belief in God's goodness was perhaps her most fundamental life theme. She read her Bible constantly, made certain that my brother and I went to Sunday school and church every Sunday, and referred me, even as an adult, to particular passages in the Bible for problems in my life. Mother also believed deeply there was a season for all things, including dying, and never feared "going home." Mother had high self-esteem and infused in her children the notion that they were somebody. Self-acceptance—the essence of ego integrity and identity—started early and became more profound with age.

My mother's marriage to my father in 1942, at age thirty-one, was her second. Her first was fifteen years earlier, ended with a divorce, and produced a daughter, Ima. From a Georgia sharecropper family, my father migrated to Indianapolis to live with his sister and have a better life. Because of his limited education, only low-wage jobs were available. However, his strong work and family ethic undergirded his endurance. At age fifty-five, he died on his job of a heart attack in 1965, shortly after my graduation from college and after twenty-four years of marriage.

My niece, Beverly, Ima's daughter, is three months older than I and has a younger brother, Jimmy. Ima died in 1949, shortly after Jimmy was born. Subsequently, Jimmy grew up with his father's relatives, and my maternal grandmother took charge of Beverly. Our initial household included my mother, my father, my maternal grandmother, Beverly, James, and me all together in a middle-class home that my grandmother purchased with her meager savings as a hotel maid. In this extended family arrangement, my brother, niece, and I were more like siblings than anything else. When we became teenagers, my parents moved us into our own home, within walking distance of my grandmother.

After my brother and I had grown up and moved away and after my father's death, Mother tried to maintain our home, but because of financial challenges, she was forced to a smaller, federally subsidized house and eventually to a senior citizen's apartment. I was concerned that she had to give up her beloved dog, Bertha, in order to reside in senior housing; I feared she might become depressed because of the loss of her long-time companion. In her typical practical manner she accepted the facts and found Bertha a perfect home. Although I talked with her by phone every week and she phoned family, including a cousin, Hughsie—my father's nephew—and occasionally saw James and his children, clearly she missed us and wished we had more time with her. In her later years, Mother's only regret was that she never became a pediatric nurse, a lifelong dream. However, she felt good about her life, viewing the successes of her offspring as evidence of a life well lived.

DESCRIPTION OF CAREGIVING EXPERIENCE

Caregiving in My Mother's Home

In 1988 I received a call saying Mother, then seventy-seven years old, was hospitalized with heart failure. Unable to get to Indiana to directly attend to her, I knew she had immediate family attention. Hughsie, in his sixties, took initial responsibility and kept me informed. Then Beverly, a nursing assistant from

Detroit, provided emotional support, administered medications, and performed housekeeping chores, with Jimmy's aid, in Mother's home. My mother's minister and the church she co-founded in 1988 were there with prayers, meals, and frequent visits. The church fulfilled its role of contributing to the well-being of African American elders (Walls and Zarit 1991). Conspicuously missing from the caregiving circle was James and his wife and six children, who lived only minutes from Mother. Everyone, except my mother, considered his lack of response negligence. She always found ways to forgive and excuse his behavior. The fact that my mother expected less from James than me conformed to a historical tradition: "Among blacks . . . the male children often have greater value to the parents and are reared to expect certain advantages over women" (Staples 1982:156). After a long history of strong bonds between my mother and brother, he curtailed visits with Mother after his 1969 marriage to a woman who resented their close relationship; he accepted church doctrine, which defined the marital relationship as primary and exclusive. In the acute response to illness that our family faced, all facets of family functioning—cohesion, adaptability, communication, emotional support, and conflict—affected Mother's stability (Bowles and Kington 1998). Therefore, we compensated for my brother's absence.

My role in my mother's care was largely emotional, reassuring her despite the miles that physically separated us, mobilizing social supports, and later solving problems with the healthcare system. For example, I learned that her cardiologist, serving also as her primary physician, had prescribed improper medications for my mother's recovery, resulting in persistent nausea and vomiting and necessitating several additional weeks of recovery. The doctor's incompetence became more obvious when in early 1990 I visited home only to find that Mother's plants, her "children," were dying. Alarmed by her lack of awareness of their condition, I thought perhaps she was depressed. Instead, I learned she had a year-old breast lump; she had been unconcerned and had not told me because the doctor had told her it was nothing to worry about.

Gripped by disbelief, fury at the doctor, fear, and guilt, I immediately thought Mother had breast cancer, which had worsened in a year without treatment. Her doctor's improper response supported findings that African Americans are less likely than European Americans to get appropriate and vital health information or referrals to specialists for diagnostic procedures (Hall et al. 1988; Harel et al. 1990; Mouton 1997) and highlighted the persistence of race- and age-based inequities in the quality of healthcare ("Inequities exist" 1991).

Caregiving in My Home

I immediately got my mother to accompany me to my Maryland home. After the ten-hour drive, she was excited and back to her usual self. The next day we visited a geriatrician, an appointment a colleague had arranged, highlighting the importance of personal references and social and professional networks. I was impressed with how the doctor listened to Mother's medical issues and her demonstrated interest in Mother as a total being. She established an instant rapport and elicited our immediate trust, important dimensions for the results: Mother had breast cancer and needed immediate surgery.

As I recovered from this jolt, my first thought was to comfort and reassure my mother and make sure she understood, hoping I would not have to sell her on the surgery. She was ready to have it immediately, which meant it was my own fear that I most needed to quell: At seventy-nine, she might not survive the surgery or might face untreatable cancer. However, my mother adhered to a major theme of her life: faith that God will not give you more than you can bear. This theme is consistent with literature based on analyses of life stories of elderly African Americans (Nye 1993). Religion is a major continuous life theme, unlike developmental phases and tasks (Erikson 1963). Continuity theory (Kaufman 1986; Melia 1999) suggests that identity formation is a lifelong process and that one reaches ego integrity by looking back and recognizing and acknowledging one's life themes.

I didn't know how to tell the rest of the family. In the end, Mother did, reassuring each with the strength in her voice. The family showed obvious concern, and James immediately made plans to fly in for the procedure, making my mother's day. My brother acknowledged that his new responsiveness was a result of his sudden recognition of Mother's vulnerability. On the day of her surgery, my brother, my best friend Joan, and I stayed in the room with my mother as long as we could. Mother regarded Joan as her daughter and often introduced her that way. Using family titles, such as *daughter,* for nonrelatives or fictive kin is common in the African American community (Martin and Martin 1985:5). Just before she was wheeled out for the procedure, we joined hands, and James prayed. Fearlessly, she faced her surgery.

The bad news was that the lump was malignant and the largest the surgeon had ever removed, but the good news was that they had gotten all of it. Mother would not need radiation or chemotherapy. Apparently, if any cancer remained, it would metastasize much more slowly, given her age. Returning to her room,

Mother looked up at us and gave us a thumbs-up and a smile. Our prayers had been answered. My mother came to my home and had a perfect recovery, aided by occupational therapy.

Later, I had my mother wait in the car while I stood in line along with others for hours outdoors, in the cold, waiting to be admitted to the Department of Social Services to apply for Medicaid and the state pharmacy program. I telephoned the director of the program, complained about these unacceptable circumstances, and suggested that all wait in the atrium. Realizing I was a social worker and professor, he returned my call, saying they were in the process of changing the procedures. The next time we went to the office, we were able to wait inside. The lesson was that one's position can have an impact on organizational change and social policy. After helping to complete the mountains of paperwork, I realized most seniors could not negotiate this system without assistance. Fortunately, because my mother had qualified for Medicaid in her home state and had documentation of her income and resources, the process of proving eligibility, though time consuming, was successful despite her out-of-state residency.

Mother's acceptance of a breast prosthesis was a sign that her self-esteem was still intact and she was anticipating the future. She joined the local senior center, where she met new friends, became involved in their arts and crafts program, and visited various points of interest and recreation around the state. She became the principal caregiver of my two dogs, a task she loved. She and Joan designed and built a dog run in the house. Mother and I spent time talking and re-bonding during these days.

In 1991, after living with me for six months, Mother wanted to return to Indianapolis to get her belongings and secure an apartment in my city. My feelings were hurt, but I realized that I had not considered her needs. I wanted to nurture our deeper connection because during my childhood, my mother was closer to James. Our living in the same house had finally provided the deeper and closer relationship I longed for. These desires illustrated the sometimes competing needs of caregiver and recipient.

After recognizing the importance of having her own home to Mother's sense of autonomy, I located a nearby senior apartment, with guidance from a friend, the U.S. commissioner on aging. After getting a lovely one-bedroom apartment with a view, Mother, Joan, and I went back to Indianapolis to pack. Joan and I were unprepared for the challenge we faced: Mother had enough in her apartment to fill two houses. Deciding what to keep and what to throw away became a major task, which Mother supervised. Staying up late for several nights, Joan and I discovered in the mornings that Mother had brought half the discarded items back into the apartment, accusing us of throwing away her good things. Mother gave away and sold some things and, most importantly, said goodbye to her friends. Mother usually masked her feelings, and this event was no different; she displayed no sadness, instead focusing on her excitement about her new apartment.

The Move into Her Maryland Apartment

An ample-sized dwelling, the new apartment was overcrowded, without remedies. I finally accepted Mother's need to be surrounded by all her memories: At eighty she left the place where she had lived since she was fifteen. Mother settled into her new space and established a routine: cooking, cleaning, attending her senior center, going to church, talking with friends in Indianapolis, and getting acquainted with new neighbors. She visited me regularly, and we always made a big celebration of Christmas and her birthday, video recording her opening her gifts and cutting her cake. Beverly and Hughsie often called. Hughsie had provided a cozy, safe alternative mode of transportation, compared with Mom's use of the slow city bus, for shopping, doctor's appointments, and other places in Indianapolis. She often talked about how appreciative she was of him.

Gradually, over the next year, my mother stopped attending her senior meetings, preferring instead to stay at home and watch television, something she had never done. I thought that this change might be a sign of depression, as confirmed by her doctor, who prescribed medication. I thought infrequent contacts with her small circle of Indianapolis friends and medical stressors—high blood pressure, arthritis, and her recent mastectomy—accounted for the depression, as some research indicates (Husaini 1997). She reassured me that she was all right. Nevertheless, I tried to get her out of the house, one day suggesting that we go to a movie. I was shocked to find out that she had never been to a movie, and I asked what she and my father did when they were dating. I was glad to introduce her to this art form and happy that we saw one of my favorites: *Sister Act*. She loved it, and I loved learning more about my parents' early life.

Joan and I did whatever we could to keep Mother interested in life. She and Joan repaired household items, planned my surprise birthday party, and visited displays of national and state holiday trees and lights. As a result, Mother snapped out of her malaise, which supported findings that increasing older adults' levels of involvement and activity increases their level of life satisfaction (Havighurst 1968).

In 1994, for the first time, I heard my mother express fear. This followed a diagnosis of cataracts and the necessary laser surgery resulting in temporarily blurred vision. She could handle almost any other loss except sight. After this experience, Mother began discussing her mortality and reassuring me she had no fear of dying. Ironically, whereas she was fearless about and comfortable with her mortality, these discussions frightened me. We talked about her many losses, such as the death of her first daughter; her divorce from her first husband; the deaths of her mother, my father, and her eight-year-old brother, whose funeral her mother could not afford to return home to attend; raising children and having them leave home; and her inability to become a pediatric nurse. She talked about her pride in her accomplishments despite setbacks in her life, including childhood maternal neglect and helplessness when her brother died of malaria. She discussed her closeness to her mother, wisely understanding that her mother loved her and simply lacked good parenting skills. After her first marriage at sixteen, she moved out of her mother's home. They again shared a home when my parents and grandmother merged households, creating the extended family I grew up in.

Our discussions eventually turned to estate planning and medical and final directives. These were difficult, necessary, and helpful discussions. For example, she was adamantly against the use of a respirator. Mother finally agreed to hire a housekeeper. Using her professional housekeeping standards, Mother was never quite satisfied, and we eventually let the housekeeper go, so these tasks became my responsibility. Conscious that caregiving burden increased with increasing hours of care and decreased when well-being increased (White-Means and Thornton 1996), I tried to be efficient. For example, I simultaneously washed my and my mother's clothes. My responsibility for providing her meals (partly because of her forgetfulness on a few occasions, resulting in burned food) also offered a novel and pleasurable experience for Mother: eating out. Mother continued to be active, alert, and eager to converse, especially sharing jokes during phone calls with Beverly.

For her eighty-third birthday and in recognition of her resilience during the last year, I gave Mother a surprise birthday party. My brother, his wife, and four of their six children came for this gala celebration. Mother was thrilled when she saw them, and she nearly fainted. I learned a valuable lesson: Don't surprise octogenarians! But the result was exactly what I had hoped for, and her spirits soared for weeks to come. From a health perspective, she did fine for the next couple of years, while continuing to see her doctor for routine examinations.

Mother's Diagnosis of Renal Disease

Between 1995, when I made a major job change, and 1997, when she passed away, Mother began to have stomach problems and was diagnosed with end-stage renal disease. After other medical interventions were unsuccessful, she had dialysis three times per week. Her nephrologists recommended a center near her home. Because both subsidized transportation and I were unavailable (because of my work schedule), I was referred to a reputedly reliable taxi company to transport her to and from her treatments. Later, I found that the dialysis staff sometimes failed to follow the medical orders, resulting in post-treatment weakness and disorientation. I wrongly assumed that the nephrologist had developed strategies to prevent future mistakes. After another occurrence, however, Mother had her first stroke and lay for hours unattended until I came home from work to a concerned neighbor's voice message, frantic after unsuccessfully trying to contact Mother. I found Mother on the bedroom floor, unable to explain what had happened. I was able to reconstruct the events in a discussion with the taxi driver. He knew she was incoherent when he picked her up from the center, yet he left her home alone, without alerting anyone. More disoriented during the stroke, she was unable to summon help with her lifeline alarm. I felt betrayed by all in whose care I had entrusted my mother. After learning of additional egregious problems, I lodged a formal complaint against the dialysis center, suggested that the nephrologists use other facilities, and identified a center located at her regular hospital, near her doctors. I was equally angry with the taxi driver, who sounded so caring about my mother when we interviewed him. I assumed his negligence reflected his fear of losing a regular fare. I was dismayed that my best planning skills had resulted in inadequate care for my mother.

Mother in the Hospital

After calling an ambulance and getting her admitted to the hospital, I insisted that doctors examine Mother for evidence of a stroke, although her nephrologist insisted that malnutrition caused the fainting. A computer tomography scan revealed several recent transient ischemic attacks (TIAs), resulting in problems walking, a temporary stutter, memory loss, inability to eat without assistance, and medication-resistant hypertension. I visited Mother daily, reassured her and myself that she was safe, and learned all I could about her diagnosis and prognosis. She gradually regained some functions but continued needing help walking, which occupational therapy addressed. When checking on her apartment while she was hospitalized, I thanked her friends, gave each my phone numbers, and suggested they contact me and the building manager, who had a key, if future concerns emerged when she returned home. These changes formally increased my caregiving network. Wondering why I overlooked these safety precautions, I accepted that considering all safeguards is one caregiving challenge. Miraculously, Mother returned to her apartment after three weeks to welcoming neighbors and friends. Subsequently, we selected a wheelchair that her Social Security purchased, and I began personally transporting her to the new dialysis center three days per week.

Caregiving in My Home

Adequately managing for a time, Mother began to have a series of TIAs, which returned her to the hospital in 1996. During her hospitalization and brief stay in a rehabilitation hospital, I packed and transported her belongings to my house, fifteen minutes away, keeping everything that fit into the three-room, aboveground apartment on the lower level of my home. Hanging her favorite pictures, I cheerfully decorated to help her feel at home. Realizing that moving in with me signaled yet another loss, I knew it was important to have her own space. She was pleased with her new home and especially liked looking out to see street events, deer in the woods, and rabbits in the yard. The one thing she missed was cooking facilities, a loss I also regretted because of my meager culinary skills. I still keenly regret that I was unable to get her cornbread quite right, despite her instructions.

Reliance on a hospital-arranged homemaker service was problematic, and we curtailed it after trying several replacements. Soon we settled into a routine: We got up at five o'clock, dressed, and had breakfast, and I prepared a snack for her to have at the center and a lunch for her return. We left the house by six o'clock in order to arrive promptly for treatment. I went to work, returned to pick her up at noon, took her home, and then returned to work for the afternoon. In the afternoon, I called and checked on her. Mother had my work telephone number, along with a list of emergency telephone numbers, in case she needed help. I equipped her room with a speaker system for her use during the night to contact me, but I found that she was never quite able to master it. Therefore, I decided to rely on the telephone because she had her own telephone with large numbers and print and could use that to call me. I encouraged her to call her friends in the area and in Indianapolis so that she would have someone to talk to during the day. She rarely did so, but she was always glad to receive a call from friends and family. To her great disappointment, my brother rarely called to see how she was doing, a pattern of behavior that was somewhat surprising given his newfound recognition of her increased need for support at this stage of her life. However, in looking at this in the context of male behavior, I was reminded of research showing that males find it difficult to provide psychological support (Staples 1982). These studies claim that men are more accustomed to providing instrumental support—being breadwinners. Moreover, my brother was accustomed to receiving emotional support from my mother and probably found it difficult to reverse the roles.

When I came home I prepared Mother's dinner and joined her in her dining room because she rarely felt like coming upstairs. Sometimes my friend Joan joined us, which my mother always liked. I never needed to say a word when the two of them were together. They could always find something to talk about, with my mother periodically saying that Joan reminded her of herself when she was younger. She was referring to Joan's enormous energy, drive, and interest in everything around her. I had purchased a large pillbox for my mother with spaces for morning, afternoon, and evening dosages of medicine, but I soon discovered that she was not taking them as prescribed. This system seemed too complex for her, so we settled on my making sure that she received her morning dosages and then got the rest when I first arrived home and just before bedtime. She was clearly finding it increasingly difficult to master the activities of daily living. She was also losing interest in even watching television, a favorite activity, and had almost stopped reading or listening to her music. She loved gospel music, and I had bought her a number of tapes and a tape recorder, but she rarely listened to them. It was clear that she was beginning to need a level of care that could not be provided in the home, but I was reluctant to place her in a nursing home. I held onto the hope that I could care for her, attempting to prevent her from spending the end of her life away from the warmth of her family.

After she had lived with me for several months, Mother called me on the telephone one night to let me know that she was having trouble breathing. I summoned an ambulance, which took her to the nearest emergency room. I followed in my car and remained at her bedside after her initial examination. Doctors diagnosed her with heart failure and expressed concern about the fluid buildup around her heart and her elevated blood pressure, which they could not bring under control. The medical staff decided that Mother needed to be hospitalized, at which point I arranged for her to be transported to the hospital where her doctor was located in Washington, D.C. She was alert throughout the process but not always coherent. This condition indicated that the heart failure probably had been accompanied by another stroke.

Caregiving in the Nursing Home

After she spent a month in her regular hospital, it became increasingly clear that we were at another important decision point in Mother's care. I conferred with James and Beverly and discussed the nursing home option with Mother, and she decided to go directly from the hospital to a skilled nursing care unit. Because of her previous stays, my mother and I were familiar with the facility. It was nearly an hour away, but it had an on-site dialysis unit. In addition, one of my former students was the head social worker. Because Mother's entire life was spent in the African American community, it was very important to ensure her comfort, acceptance, and appropriate treatment in this integrated environment. How my mother felt about the way people at the nursing home treated her was far more important to me than anything she or I could read about the institution in its brochure.

Once she left the skilled nursing unit, Mother moved into a room with two other residents, wait-listing a double room. Mother easily made friends with the residents and their families. She participated in all available activities, phoned friends and family, and took pictures of the rabbits and the scenery outside her window. She told me if anyone had behaved inappropriately with her, and we could discuss how to handle it. Mother and I regularly attended meetings with the staff to learn their perspective about her progress. I washed her clothes and advocated when needed; for example, the staff immediately honored my request not to puree her food. It was fortunate that an African American beautician was available because European American beauticians usually are untrained in African American hair care. I also took Mother to her regular dentist and ophthalmologist. Joan and I took her out to dinner and on visits to my home whenever possible, and Mother spent all holidays at my home.

Final Good-Byes

My mother lived in the nursing home for about six months before passing away. One evening after work, Mother was taken to the hospital because of dialysis problems and was expected to return to the nursing home the next day. The next day, Mother was disoriented and complained of bleeding all night. My immediate call to her doctor and subsequent questions brought no definitive answers. She rapidly declined, refusing to eat and sleeping a lot. I went at meal times to feed her, but it didn't forestall the inevitable.

After my call, James and one of his sons arrived the next day, and we visited her the next morning. My nephew and I went to the nursing home to pick up some of her clothes while my brother stayed at the hospital with Mother, who was noncommunicative. Upon my return, she was alert, wide awake, smiling, and talking. She was happy her friends from the nursing home asked about her. Then she called me from the foot of her bed and told me that she had something to tell me, but by the time I reached the head of the bed, she just as suddenly fell silent and went to sleep. I kept asking Mother what she had wanted to say.

Later, when the family was preparing to go to feed Mother dinner, the hospital called saying we needed to get there right away. By the time we arrived at her room, the medical staff had already moved her to the intensive care unit. Apparently, Mother had stopped breathing, and they had resuscitated her against her stated wishes. This meant that the family now faced the ordeal of deciding to honor her wishes, although the hospital ignored them, and have the respirator disconnected. Before they could disconnect it, Mother expired and spared us the agony of living with the fact that we had ended her life. We all held hands, my nephew sang Mother a song, and we prayed together and thanked God for giving her to us for as long as he had and for letting us be there to walk with her the last earthly mile of the way.

ANALYSES

The actions I took during my caregiving experience were informed by multiple theories and perspectives. For example, one perspective that I used to assess the formal caregiving institutions with which I interacted included the availability, accessibility, and acceptability of their services. From her physicians to the hospitals, skilled nursing care facilities, dialysis center, and nursing home, most of my mother's expenses were covered by Medicare or Medicaid, making all these services affordable and available to her. Mother's out-of-pocket expenses for pharmaceuticals were mitigated by a state-subsidized pharmaceutical plan for which she was eligible. Mother's situation was different from that of many older Americans, who have high out-of-pocket expenses. One author notes, "The average out-of-pocket health bill per year for a person 65 or older is over $3000 . . . a bill many aged persons cannot afford to pay" (Schiller 2004:116).

Had I not been available to transport my mother to the various health and human service facilities, she would have found the majority inaccessible because of the paucity of public transportation. Furthermore, the one private taxi service that we employed to transport her to and from dialysis appointments proved unreliable, making that resource equally inaccessible. Access to services was an important dimension of my mother's care.

Acceptability of services was another important factor in her care. Motivated by the desire for the most competent care available, I spent time investigating provider options and interpreting my findings to my mother for her input and approval. My decision to act on these choices was further informed by my perception of conditions that constituted a good therapeutic relationship. I was interested in skilled, competent, capable practitioners who could demonstrate warmth, empathy, genuineness, and cultural sensitivity in their interactions with my mother (Monte 1995).

My understanding of organizational dynamics and the propensity for worker burnout in large formal organizations caused me to be hypervigilant about the quality of my mother's care, particularly in the nursing home. One scholar defines burnout as "a process in which a previously committed worker disengages from his or her work in response to stress and strain experienced in the job" (Hutchison 1999:320). I visited and telephoned my mother regularly in the nursing home and hospital to get her interpretation of how her care was being handled and to see in person how she was being treated, in part to guard against the effects of worker burnout.

Other perspectives that informed my caregiving included resilience, empowerment, and strengths. Researchers define resilience as "the ability to bounce back from a difficult or trying situation" (Ross et al. 2003:84). Resilience was my mother's potential to rebound and emotionally cope with the health crises she experienced. A strengths perspective helped me to assess her in terms of her abilities rather than her deficits. An empowerment perspective helped me to understand that Mother was capable of making many of the decisions that affected her, such as whether and when she should live independently in her own apartment and when it was time to transition to a nursing home. Therefore, I included Mother in the decision-making processes, knowing that her input was essential.

The concept of resilience also helped me understand my own ability to cope with the stresses of caregiving. In retrospect, I am able to identify with some of the characteristics researchers cite as common to resilient caregivers (Ross et al. 2003). The first is distancing both physically and emotionally from the caregiving situation, which takes the form of doing something just for oneself. I engaged in this process by going to the movies or reading. Second is physical exercise, which I did less of than I should have, but which usually took the form of walking. Third are hobbies, which I did not use. Fourth is support, including confiding in another as a means of venting emotions. I was fortunate to have my friend Joan, who was always available for me to discuss my problems. Fifth is religion, which took the form of regular prayer and abiding, unshakable faith that God was in charge and that everything was in divine order. Sixth is a philosophical belief, such as that caring for others is a commandment or expectation. Caring for family members in time of need was rooted in both the African American culture and my family's history, representing an immutable imperative for me. The seventh and final characteristic is humor, which I used frequently. Often, I reminisced with my niece or Joan about something my mother had done or said that transformed a serious moment into something much lighter. Each of these strategies was an effective way to meet my challenges and helped me appreciate the opportunity for caring for my mother in her declining years.

IMPLICATIONS

This chapter began with a portrait of my mother and the major themes that shaped her life. This information was provided as a framework for understanding how she viewed the world and handled the events of her life, including her illnesses. I have chosen to view her life through the lenses of continuity theory (Melia 1999) as opposed to a stage theory of development. As I recalled her life, the themes spoke more to her ego integrity and identity than did any special point in time or stage of life. Those themes—faith in God, the importance of family, nurturing and caring for others, a demand for respect, self-knowledge, a love of learning, and the belief in a season for all things—only deepened as she matured.

I believe it is important for children to encourage their elders to share their personal histories and life stories so that the texture of their lives becomes the fabric of the children's memories and not just their elders' demographics. History provides perspective, and so it is important to spend time thinking about and trying to understand the meaning systems or worldviews of our elders in order to more fully understand what sustained them through difficult times. That information will provide more guidance about how to manage the fundamentals of their aging process than any textbook on aging. For example, knowing the value my mother placed on nurturing and caring for others helped me eventually to understand why she needed to accumulate and keep furniture she didn't need and other items that eventually had to be placed in storage. She needed to be able to help a family member or friend in need at a moment's notice. In the interest of her well-being and self-esteem, it was important for me to understand her need to accumulate and to cooperate with her in her efforts to follow through with this important theme of her life.

Furthermore, from a systems perspective it is important to evaluate the impact of institutions within the environment on the lives of people as they age. Using the employment system as an example, the system perspective allows us to examine how hiring practices of various employers adapt to changes in the social, political, and cultural environments. For African American elders, there is a need to advocate for more affirmative action programs that open the doors of employment opportunities and to insist on equitable compensation for their labors. Women still receive lower wages than men for the same jobs, and African American men and women receive less than European American men and women. Some statistics indicate that African Americans make less than European Americans in the same occupational category. According to the Bureau of Labor Statistics, African American men working full time have a median income of only 79.1% of that of their European American counterparts, and African American women working full time have a median income of only 84.0% of that of European American women (Bureau of Labor Statistics 2007). Advocating for equity in employment practices should allow people of color to enjoy the benefits of their more appropriately compensated labors in their latter years. My mother received Social Security from my father's account, providing a higher income than her own account. But for many women who spend their young lives in domestic employment, if their employers did not pay Social Security taxes for them, they receive only the lowest benefits from the system. Many African American women have experienced this problem, making their survival during their golden years even more difficult.

According to some researchers, logic suggests that those who earn better incomes in their preretirement years should have larger incomes, larger net worth, and better health in retirement (Ozawa and Choi 2002). However, their research shows that this result depends on the person's race. In a comparison of African Americans and European Americans, higher income before retirement did not translate into better health for retired African Americans but did result in better health for European Americans. They speculate that for African Americans, "money did not necessarily create better access to health care—especially high quality care" (Ozawa and Choi 2002:34). The authors suggest that money might not buy good healthcare for African Americans. These findings show that even with adequate preretirement income, older African Americans also need improved healthcare services. For instance, findings demonstrate that African Americans and other people of color are less likely to be referred for more complicated, needed interventions for serious conditions such as heart disease and lung cancer (Alliance for Health Reform 2006). Other barriers exist as well, such as communication problems between medical providers and people of color and a lack of healthcare providers in areas that are populated primarily by people of color (Alliance for Health Reform 2006).

Social Policies

In addition to healthcare disparities, it is imperative to consider changes in Social Security and other systems that will benefit low-income and aging people of color (Ozawa and Choi 2002). For example, one researcher suggests that a system of privately invested accounts within the Social Security system might benefit African Americans more than the current system (Tanner 2001). African Americans have lower average incomes than European Americans, yet their Social Security tax rate is the same rate as that of European Americans. This results in African Americans and other ethnic groups paying a larger percentage of their income for Social Security. This economic inequality leaves little or no money in the paychecks of African Americans for savings, investment, or wealth acquisition. The expectation continues to be that such wealth in the latter years of one's life contributes to less stress and a higher quality of life because of the greater variety of options it affords, such as assisted living care facilities instead of nursing homes and the ability to pay for prescription drugs. However, privately invested accounts rely on financial investment expertise. This is a skill that few African Americans and others of all income levels have. Possible changes in Social Security and other social programs are complex. The expected and possibly undesirable consequences must be considered as one proposes policy changes.

Another lesson from my caregiving experience was the need to acknowledge the racial differences in the treatment of older adults by medical practitioners and hospitals and to demand that those differences be eradicated. In 1990, the overall amount of doctor and hospital care African American and European American older adults received was about the same with the advent of federal healthcare programs such as Medicare and Medicaid (Wallace 1990). Interestingly by 2000, disparities emerged despite the federal benefits. Current legislation is not enough to ensure equitable provision of healthcare services. Noting that politicians are not eager to address barriers to high-quality healthcare because of the racial implications, one author suggests that African American seniors will receive the quality of care they need only when they organize and turn their problems into policy issues (Madison 1991). Some refer to rights that reduce discrimination as procedural rights, such as the right to equitable provision of healthcare services (Stone 2002). These rights have to be sought sometimes through a paradoxical civil rights strategy: "In order to be treated as individuals, people first have to organize and make demands as a group" (Stone 2002:328).

Social Work Curricula

The social work profession is uniquely positioned not only to influence quality of care issues in institutions that serve aging populations but also to address family system issues that affect the quality of interactions between family members and their elders. In relating to African American families, this means incorporating spirituality as a tool of intervention in social work practice with African American elders. The introduction of the Africentric paradigm of human services into the curriculum in schools of social work is one way to achieve this goal. This Africentric paradigm of human services focuses on culture, which is inextricably connected to spirituality. It views the soul as an "unexplored source of power and self-affirmation" (Schiele 2000:35) that can be used to help clients attain their highest good. The principles underlying the Africentric paradigm can and should become a central part of social work curricula. In the last half of the 20th century, scholars (e.g., Ab'kar 1984; Asante 1988; Baldwin 1985; Nobles 1972, 1980) began to identify an Africentric approach to philosophy and human behavior that emerged into the Africentric paradigm. This paradigm led to the Africentric intervention perspective, an innovative, culturally sensitive, and empowering social work practice model for African American clients. Various helping professionals have shared this model.

One proponent of the Africentric model in the field of social work (Schiele 1990, 1996, 1997, 2000) uses propositions from Africentric theories to transform social work intervention with African Americans. Using characteristics from the African culture, this model's goals include empowering African Americans to take an active part in identifying strengths and making necessary changes in self, family, community, and the larger society. The central propositions of the Africentric intervention model are that all things are connected, so prosperity occurs when people and nature are in harmony; the individual is important, but the collective group is paramount and shapes the individual in profound ways; spirituality is a necessary component of the human experience; and the use of language and storytelling is powerful and therapeutic. Furthermore, the Africentric model acknowledges the concept of difference and encourages "cultural pluralism in both the knowledge base of the human services, and wider society" (Schiele 2000:13).

These propositions are quite different from those of the Eurocentric perspective, such as rugged individualism, and support African American behaviors that are different from those of European Americans as positive coping mechanics rather than pathology. Much of the Eurocentric perspective denies strengths in the various forms of African American families. Some unrecognized strengths include the following: Extended family networks provide emotional and economic support; a large number of relatives, fictive kin, older children, and close friends share child rearing; families have adaptable roles and elastic boundaries, strong kinship bonds, and a strong work and achievement ethic; men and women value assertiveness; compared with European Americans, men are more accepting of women's employment and more willing to share in the in-home responsibilities; and despite racism, sexism, and other prejudices, families instill self-esteem in their children (Beckett and Dungee-Anderson 1996; Daly et al. 1995; Robins et al. 2002; Twenge and Crocker 2002).

Social work curricula should also incorporate more content on the caregiving structure of African American families, which has historically included immediate and extended family members: children, grandchildren, nieces, nephews, and even fictive kin or augmented family members (e.g., "play" children, godchildren, and godparents). Greater knowledge of the role of informal care by family members will produce more sensitive practitioners who are better able to appropriately involve pertinent members of the family structure in treatment decisions for African American elders. One study shows that critical functions are performed by second- and third-generation adult kin in caring for and supporting low-income African American older adults (Luckey 1994).

Another study of racial and ethnic differences in caregiving arrangements found a difference in the structure and size of caregiving networks among European American, African American, and Hispanic households (Lum 2005). Caregivers for African American elders often include siblings, relatives, and friends. Furthermore, scholars found that people of color view caregiving by family members as a cultural tradition—"not a choice but a duty" (Chadiha et al. 2002; Scharlach et al. 2006:50). In the case of my mother, it would have been important for the formal healthcare and social service systems to involve my niece and nephews in healthcare decisions while Mother lived in Indianapolis because they were intimately involved in her care.

In addition to curriculum content on African American caregiving patterns, there is a need for gerontology content in schools of social work. In their assessment of gerontology curricula in social work schools, some scholars have found that "social work education has not been responsive to the demographic data that indicates a dramatic growth in the aging population" (Rosen et al.

2002:27). With the aging of baby boomers, more gerontological social workers will be needed just as a large proportion of social workers are preparing to retire. Fortunately, more recently social work has become more responsive to issues of aging. For example, the Council of Social Work Education has identified gerontology as an area for growth and funded a number of projects to infuse gerontology in the curriculum and attract more students to that field. The National Association of Social Workers (NASW), the largest professional social work organization, has targeted gerontology as an important area for growth. To encourage current professional social workers to enter the gerontological field, NASW has developed free computer teleconferences, continuing education courses, and certificate programs (Whitaker et al. 2006). Unfortunately, greater efforts are needed, especially funds to make the salary of social workers commensurate with that of other helping professionals with similar education.

Other concerns related to my mother's situation that require attention include the need for hospitals to be held accountable for honoring end-of-life directives. In my case, the hospital neglected to follow the directive it had on file for my mother and caused needless suffering for the family as we prepared to make the painful decision to remove my mother from life support. Similarly, there is a need to federally regulate the quality of care offered in dialysis centers. After discovering the lapses in care provision at the center where my mother was a patient, I explored several other centers and heard horror stories about the care patients received. This type of negligence will continue to happen until these centers are federally regulated and the regulations are enforced. I was able to move my mother to a better center, but not everyone has that luxury.

My experiences with the social service department reinforced the need to staff social service offices with personnel who can help older adults apply for Social Security and other benefits. The procedures and forms are so complex that neither elders nor their primary caregivers can navigate them without professional help. Additionally, all social service offices should be required to have accessible waiting areas. Having seniors wait in line outside offices in the cold of winter, rain, or heat of summer is unacceptable and completely contrary to social work principles and values of treating clients with dignity.

There is a need to educate older people of color about breast cancer prevention, with doctors sharing a large part of this responsibility. As some have observed, African Americans expect their doctors to be knowledgeable, open, and willing to listen to them and give them information about their illness (Mouton 1997). Had my mother's doctor listened to her and exercised the requisite knowledge and skills, her cancer might not have progressed as far. Literature demonstrates that African Americans are more likely to develop and die from cancer than any other racial or ethnic group, and this disparity is caused by many factors, including income level, access to medical care, and inadequate medical care (Miller and Garran 2007).

Finally, there is a need to better compensate homemaker service providers in order to improve their quality. We had to let my mother's homemaker go because of her unreliability. Usually female, these employed caregivers receive low wages for important work, which may provide less incentive for them to provide high-quality service or observe normal work expectations, such as arriving at work on time and spending the full time engaged in activities for which they are being compensated. Their low wages often mean that they depend on unreliable or nonexistent public transportation. Their wages indicate to them that society does not value them or their work. Because most of these homemakers are women, the elimination of gender discrimination is another goal.

The lessons I learned from my caregiving experience were many, but foremost was that being a professional social worker did not make me feel any more certain that my mother's needs would be addressed than if I had not held that credential. A major case in point was the failure of my mother's dialysis center to provide adequate care for her and the reluctance of her physicians to examine her for a stroke when I indicated my suspicions of this possibility. I had to insist on the examination. The results confirmed my suspicions: She had experienced TIAs. My professional expertise on social welfare policy helped me secure entitlements for my mother. It was interesting that no one provided information about the benefits. Had I not known, I may never have applied for these entitled benefits.

My knowledge of the social service system helped me negotiate it. For example, I was able to identify the director of a social service agency and suggest new procedures that would prevent applicants from standing outside rather than entering the building. Knowledge of the aging process was useful, but trial and error were my best servants in actually knowing how to use knowledge on behalf of my mother. Empathy and the ability to listen with the third ear went a long way in keeping me in touch with my mother's needs, which she did not always verbalize. For example, when Mother stopped contacting her friends, I knew something was wrong, and I began to search for reasons for this new and rare behavior. Caring for loved ones is a daunting task that must be approached with humility and love. It must also incorporate flexibility and the willingness to experiment with new ways of doing things. For example, when my mother was unable to use the two-way speaker system to contact me during the night, we decided to rely on her telephone, an appliance with which she was familiar.

Self-care for the caregiver must be a major part of this formula. This is an essential component of the caregiving experience for people of color (Scharlach et al. 2006). In some research, caregivers "mentioned the need for in-home respite care, primarily as a mechanism for enabling them to provide better care over a longer period of time" (Scharlach et al. 2006:154). Respite care gives caregivers an opportunity to rest, reflect, and refuel. I involved my brother, my niece, and Joan in my self-care. Both my brother and my niece took time to come to Maryland to be with my mother for one week each to give me time to get away and just take care of myself. Joan, my ever-present rock, patiently listened to my frustrations and fears and always offered support and caring. My faith held me in good stead as well, so that in the end all systems came together to make this experience as good as it could be for my mother as the care recipient and for me as the primary caregiver. Religiosity often serves as a protective factor to mediate the strain and stress of providing care (Morano and King 2005). I more deeply embraced my faith and religion in my caregiving experience.

Table 7.1 lists the various issues related to my caregiving experience and their implications for various levels of society and the profession of social work. It further delineates strategies for resolving each issue.

REFLECTIONS AND CONCLUSIONS

Writing about one's own life is very different from reporting findings from empirical research. This section attempts to capture my reactions to writing this very personal chapter. My reactions to being asked to write about my caregiving experiences for a book that many may read began with my worrying about whether I could handle the emotions that reliving the caregiving experience would evoke. I wondered whether I could even accurately recall all the events. I handled my reactions by discussing them with both a close friend and a family member, who had also taken part in the caregiving experience. It was important to get their approval to write this chapter because it would reveal personal information about the family that had not been exposed to the public before. I needed to feel certain that the overall goal of this book justified talking about private matters involving my family. I also sought spiritual guidance on what my mother would have wanted in this matter. In the end, I believed that she would approve of something that would help others—one of the major themes of her life.

Table 7.1 Implications

	Issues and Problems	Strategies for Change
Individuals, families, and practitioners	Understanding individual meaning systems, worldviews, and values of the care recipient	Caregivers should listen to the stories care recipients tell about their lives and derive life themes from them; observe what they emphasize in their lives. Incorporate these preferences and values in the plans you make with them about meeting their daily needs. Ensure that their life themes and worldviews are honored by formal caregivers.
Practitioners and educators	Discriminatory employment policies against women and men of color	Schools of social work should teach students about the need to advocate for equity in employment practices for their clients, especially clients of color. Teach students how to help clients advocate for themselves.
Individuals, families, communities, and practitioners	Social Security system inequities	Social workers, community advocates, and clients themselves should advocate for changes in the Social Security system, including exploring private investment accounts for persons of color, who typically receive less wage compensation than nonminorities but pay into the Social Security system at the same rate, thus having little or no leftover income for wealth accumulation for use in later years.

(continued)

Table 7.1 (continued)

	Issues and Problems	Strategies for Change
Communities, practitioners, and educators	Racial differences in treatment of elders by doctors and hospitals	Schools of social work should include this information in the curriculum on aging and teach students to advocate as professionals with their clients to eliminate differences in delivery of health-care services. Political activism is essential in this process.
Individuals, families, practitioners, and educators	Failure to recognize caregiving structures of African American families	Schools of social work should include curriculum on the presence of extended family structures in the African American communities and the importance of including extended family members, including fictive kin, in caregiving decisions.
Practitioners and educators	Failure to recognize the importance of religion in caregiving for African American elders	Schools of social work and practitioners should learn the importance of opportunities for religious expression by elder African American care recipients and make such opportunities available to them.

The process I used to write the chapter began with my writing the description of my experiences and then gathering the literature. As I wrote the various sections, I submitted them to the two people whom I had consulted about writing the chapter: my friend Joan and my niece, Beverly. This helped me recall the facts and process my emotions while writing about each phase of the caregiving cycle.

I did not find this an easy task on any level. But the things I most enjoyed writing about were my mother's strengths and the themes of her life. I worked hard to communicate clearly and compassionately the courage and love she demonstrated in her life. Challenging things about writing the chapter included remembering and writing about the multiple physical struggles my mother experienced toward the end of her life. I also found it challenging to recall and write about the failures of the various systems to support my mother throughout her illness and my inability to protect her as effectively as I wanted to. The failure of the dialysis center to care for her properly, which led to her first stroke, is an example. Unresolved problems such as this made me realize that I could not anticipate all her needs and provide for them as, I felt, she always provided for my needs when I was a child.

This chapter influenced me by helping me learn about my own tolerance levels and finding out that I was much stronger than I had ever imagined. My caregiving experience was occurring at the same time that I had taken a new job as the director of a branch of a school of social work. I had the awesome responsibility of becoming familiar with my new academic surroundings and responsibilities and for meeting all the requirements for tenure in a short time (four years instead of the usual six). I found that I could multitask effectively but also that I was not always as sensitive to my mother's needs when I arrived home from a hard day at the office as I wish I had been. My insensitivity produced feelings of guilt that I eventually overcame by understanding that I was only human—and not superhuman, as I had wanted to be.

I understood on a deeper level what mothering must be like, never having had children. I wanted only the best for my mother and felt as if I could not always control whether she would receive that from the institutions and systems that were in charge of her care. As a result, I became a greater advocate for changing those systems. Reading about the research on caregiving in African American families made me realize how similar my family was to many others. It also helped me conceptualize some of the feelings I had as I went through the experience. From this literature, I was also able to better understand my mother's experience as a care recipient. I omitted nothing that I think would have helped the reader.

Finally, I think narratives are good tools for understanding the experience of both the caregiver and the care recipient. The "Implications" section allowed me to consider the meaning of my experiences on a more detached level and help the reader find value in my experiences. I hope readers will take helpful information from this and other chapters for the increasingly important role of caregiving.

REFERENCES

Ak'bar, N. 1984. Afrocentric social services for human liberation. *Journal of Black Studies* 14: 395–413.

Alliance for Health Reform. 2006. *Covering Health Issues: A Sourcebook for Journalists.* Washington, D.C.: Disparities.

Asante, K. A. 1988. *Afrocentricity.* Trenton, N.Y.: Africa World.

Baldwin, S. 1985. *The Costs of Caring: Families with Disabled Children*. London: Routledge & Kegan Paul.

Beckett, J. and Dungee-Anderson, D. 1996. A framework for agency-based multicultural training and supervision. *Journal of Multicultural Social Work* 4: 27–48. Reprinted in Y. Asamoah, (Ed.), *Innovations in Delivering Culturally Sensitive Social Work Services*. New York: Haworth.

Billingsley, A. 1992. *Climbing Jacob's Ladder: The Enduring Legacy of African American Families*. New York: Simon & Schuster.

Bowles, J. and Kington, R. S. 1998. The impact of family function on health of African American elderly. *Journal of Comparative Family Studies* 29 (2): 337–345.

Bureau of Labor Statistics. 2007, Jan. 19. *Usual Weekly Earnings of Wage and Salary Workers: Fourth Quarter* 2006. Washington, D.C.: Author.

Chadiha, L. A., Adams, P., Phorano, O., Ong, S. L., and Byers, L. 2002. Stories told and lessons learned from African American female caregivers' vignettes for empowerment practice. *Journal of Gerontological Social Work* 40 (1): 135–144.

Daly, A., Jennings, J., Beckett, J., and Leashore, B. 1995. Effective coping skills of African Americans. *Social Work* 40: 240–248.

Erikson, E. 1963. *Childhood and Society*, 2d ed. New York: Norton.

Hall, J., Rater, D., and Katz, N. 1988. Meta-analysis of correlates of provider behavior in medical encounters. *MedCare* 26(7): 657–675.

Harel, Z., McKinney, E., and Williams, A. (Eds.). 1990. *Black Aged: Understanding Diversity and Service Needs*. Newbury Park, Cal.: Sage.

Havighurst, R. 1968. Personality and patterns of aging. *The Gerontologist* 8: 20–23.

Husaini, B. A. 1997. Predictors of depression among the elderly: Racial differences over time. *American Journal of Orthopsychiatry* 67 (1): 48–58.

Hutchison, E. D. 1999. *Dimensions of Human Behavior: Person and Environment*. Thousand Oaks, Cal.: Pine Forge Press.

Inequities exist in health care for elderly blacks. 1991, Feb. 25. *The Brown University Long-Term Care Letter* 3 (4). Providence, R.I.: Manisses Communications Group.

Kaufman, S. 1986. *The Ageless Self: Sources of Meaning in Late Life*. Madison: University of Wisconsin Press.

Luckey, I. 1994. African American elders: The support of generational kin. *Families in Society: The Journal of Contemporary Human Services* 75 (2): 82–90.

Lum, T. Y. 2005. Understanding the racial and ethnic differences in caregiving arrangements. *Journal of Gerontological Social Work* 45 (4): 3–21.

Madison, A. 1991. The social contract and the African American elderly. *Urban League Review* 15 (2): 21–28.

Manns, W. 1981. Support systems of significant others in black families. In H. McAdoo (Ed.), *Black Families*, 238–251. Beverly Hills, Cal.: Sage.

Martin, E. and Martin, J. 2002. *Spirituality and the Black Helping Tradition in Social Work*. Washington, D.C.: NASW Press.

Martin, J. and Martin, E. 1985. *The Helping Tradition in the Black Family and Community*. Washington, D.C.: NASW Press.

Melia, S. P. 1999. Continuity in the lives of elder Catholic women religious. *International Journal of Aging and Human Development* 48 (3): 175–189.

Miller, J. and Garran, A. 2007. The web of institutional racism. *Smith College Studies in Social Work* 77 (1): 33–67.

Monte, C. 1995. *Beneath the Mask: An Introduction to Theories of Personality*, 5th ed. Fort Worth, Tx.: Harcourt Brace Jovanovich.

Morano, C. L. and King, D. 2005. Religiosity as a mediator of caregiver well-being: Does ethnicity make a difference. *Journal of Gerontological Social Work* 45 (1): 69–84.

Mouton, C. 1997. Special health considerations in African American elders. *American Family Physician* 55 (4): 1243–1254.

Nobles, W. 1972. African philosophy: Foundations for black psychology. In R. L. Jones (Ed.), *Black Psychology*, 18–32. New York: Harper & Row.

Nobles, W. 1980. African American family life: An instrument of culture. In H. P. McAdoo (Ed.), *Black Families*, 77–86. Beverly Hills, Cal.: Sage.

Nye, W. P. 1993. Amazing grace: Religion and identity among elderly black individuals. *International Journal of Aging and Human Development* 36 (2): 103–113.

Ozawa, M. N. and Choi, Y. 2002. The relationship between preretirement earnings and health status in old age: Black–white differences. *Journal of Gerontological Social Work* 38 (4): 19–37.

Robins, R., Trezesniewski, K., Tracy, J., Gosling, S., and Potter, J. 2002. Global self-esteem across the life span. *Psychology and Aging* 17 (3): 423–434.

Rosen, A. L., Zlotnik, J. L., and Singer, T. 2002. Basic gerontological competence for all social workers: The need to "gerontologize" social work education. *Journal of Gerontological Social Work* 39 (1): 25–36.

Ross, L., Holliman, D., and Dixon, D. R. 2003. Resiliency in family caregivers: Implications for social work practice. *Journal of Gerontological Social Work* 40 (3): 81–96.

Scharlach, A. E., Kellam, R., Ong, N., Baskin, A., Goldstein, C., and Fox, P. J. 2006. Cultural attitudes and caregiver service use: Lessons from focus groups with racially and ethnically diverse family caregivers. *Journal of Gerontological Social Work* 47 (1): 135–158.

Schiele, J. H. 1990. Organizational theory from an Afrocentric perspective. *Journal of Black Studies* 21: 145–161.

Schiele, J. 1997. The contour and meaning of Afrocentric social work. *Journal of Black Studies* 27 (6): 800–820.

Schiele, J. H. 2000. *Human Services and the Afrocentric Paradigm.* New York: Haworth.

Schiller, B. R. 2004. *The Economics of Discrimination and Poverty,* 9th ed. Upper Saddle River, N.J.: Prentice Hall.

Staples, R. 1982. *Black Masculinity: The Black Male's Role in American Society.* San Francisco: Black Scholar Press.

Stone, D. 2002. *Policy Paradox: The Art of Political Decision Making.* New York: W. W. Norton.

Tanner, M. 2001, July. Social Security shortchanges African Americans. *USA Today,* p. 130.

Twenge, J. M. and Crocker, J. 2002. Race and self-esteem: Meta-analysis comparing whites, blacks, Hispanics, Asians, and American Indians and comment on Gray-Little and Hafdahl (2000). *Psychological Bulletin* 128: 371–408.

Wallace, S. 1990. The political economy of health care for elderly blacks. *International Journal of Health Services* 20: 665–680.

Walls, C. T. and Zarit, S. H. 1991. Informal support from black churches and the well-being of elderly blacks. *The Gerontologist* 3 (4): 490–495.

Whitaker, T., Weismiller, R., and Clark, E. 2006. *Assuring the Sufficiency of a Frontline Workforce: A National Study of Licensed Social Workers. Special Report: Social Work Services for Older Adults.* Washington, D.C.: National Association of Social Workers.

White-Means, S. I. and Thornton, M. C. 1996. Well-being among caregivers of indigent black elderly. *Journal of Comparative Family Studies* 27 (1): 109–129.

EIGHT

Aunt Doris's Moves

F. ELLEN NETTING

DESCRIPTION OF CAREGIVER

My name is Florence Eleanor Netting, but few people know that. For some reason (which has died with them) my parents called me Ellen. It is ironic that they shortened the lovely name they gave me, although as a young person I thought it was anything but lovely. But as I've aged I've come to appreciate just how lovely it is. I was named for my father's mother, Florence, and my father's mentor, Eleanor. Eleanor was the head of library services at the University of Tennessee when my quiet, studious father was an engineering student there. He worked in the library, and he greatly admired this older librarian. Thus, I was named after the two women he most admired.

I was destined to be a caregiver because my parents had only me. In addition, my father had five siblings who lived to adulthood, and only one of them had children. Thus, I had a ready-made caseload of older aunts and uncles who would live to old age without children. My mother's family, on the other hand, gave birth to many cousins—except for one sister, Doris. It is her story that I tell in this chapter.

As I write this chapter, I am fifty-eight years old. I am at the stage of life in which one begins to see less time ahead than one has traversed. I tinker with the concept of generativity, giving to the next generation, which seems to be the stage I am rapidly approaching, and because I do not have children of my own I find it in other ways. As a professor in a school of social work, I chaired the search committee this year, and I enjoyed the fact that we were hiring the next generation of educators. I suspect that is what generativity is all about. I also find myself not having to get credit for things these days, and maybe that is an indicator that I have reached a point where it is simply relationships that matter, not the status that comes with recognition. At least that's what I'm aiming for these days.

I have been married thirty-eight years in August to Karl, the man I fell in love with at first sight. He was a football player in his senior year at Emory and Henry College in southwest Virginia, a small United Methodist school. I was a freshman. I schemed in every way possible to get his eye, as I knew he'd be graduating and I had to work fast. He is now a hospice chaplain, having served in churches for more than a decade and done hospital chaplaincy for more than a decade. We live in Richmond, Virginia, where he works for a large healthcare system, and I teach B.S.W., M.S.W., and Ph.D. programs at the School of Social Work.

I never thought of myself as a caregiver. I just knew that as my father's siblings aged, as he aged, and as my mother's sister aged I would be the person they would turn to if they needed help. I felt almost as if I'd been born primarily to shepherd them through the last episodes of their lives, and they figured it too (without our having really talked about it). Because I studied gerontology in undergraduate school, maintained that focus in my graduate work, and eventually worked in the aging network, it was assumed I would know something about caregiving and aging. I gained a reputation among my extended family as one who could do anything. This expectation put quite a burden on me, given how hard it is to navigate the nonrational system of services we have in this country. But I gave it my best effort because they were counting on me, and I was fortunate enough to have their confidence, which went a long way in their thinking I was able to do more than I felt I actually did. In the process, I discovered that confidence in a person could go a long way, even when that person is totally perplexed about what to do next.

Moving into My "Senior Year"

My mother died in 1967, the month that I turned seventeen. It was the last week of summer school, and I was literally sweating it out in the era before buildings had central air in my hometown of Kingsport, Tennessee. Because I was an only child, when she died I was left with my father, a very quiet engineer. The house was silent. No one talked of my mother's death. We were supposed to go on with business as usual. I finished summer school the week after my mother's funeral, having been allowed to take an incomplete. The next week my mother's mother (my grandmother) died. She had been very frail, and when she heard of her child's death, she seemed to just give up. The two most important women in my life were suddenly gone.

I entered my senior year of high school. My father and I pretended that business would indeed go on as usual. It was during this time that I realized the implications of having nurturing women in my life. During my senior year and continuing into my college years, a special bond transcended space and time between my Aunt Doris and me. Perhaps it was enhanced by the fact that she was the only of my mother's siblings who was childless, and I was looking for traits that reminded me of my mother and maternal grandmother. Possibly, I reminded her of what she had lost in the characteristics I brought to the relationship as I entered adulthood. For whatever reasons, we grew emotionally closer over the years.

DESCRIPTION OF FAMILY MEMBER CARED FOR

I had always been close to Aunt Doris, as one of my mother's older sisters. She lived 350 miles away on Grove Avenue in Richmond, Virginia. Her story was one of the most romantic and touching of any in my mother's family. All eight children in my mother's family were unique and interesting people, but Aunt Doris was special. As a child, I noticed a sense of protectiveness and what I perceived to be mystery that surrounded any conversation about Aunt Doris and Uncle John. Only later did I learn why.

Driving to Richmond: An Easter Ritual

My mother, father, and I drove to Richmond every Easter. We usually took my maternal grandmother with us. She lived in Gate City, Virginia, my mother's hometown. Several years ago, I gathered up all the 8-millimeter films my father made during those sojourns and had them transferred to videos. These silent films reveal an annual ritual in which my mother, my grandmother, Aunt Doris, and I donned Easter gear and posed as my father used his movie camera. We paraded up and down Grove Avenue, and then the film switched to Byrd

Park, where we stopped and gazed at the swans on the pond and stood next to early spring flowering bushes. The places in the films remained the same, but the clothing and my height changed with each sequel. The year my grandmother was dressed all in black (1952) revealed the year my grandfather had died, when I was three.

Aunt Doris and Uncle John lived in a two-bedroom, first-floor apartment in the historic fan district of Richmond. A wooden ramp had been constructed in the narrow passageway between the side-by-side walk-up apartment buildings, and this ramp was Uncle John's only route in and out of the apartment. There were at least six high steps in the front of the brick building, the route I used as a child. However, if Uncle John had to leave or enter the apartment, he used the ramp. The ramp led to a back alleyway, where his car was parked. It was one of the first hand-controlled cars in the city, having been made especially for him. When it snowed, my aunt and uncle put on heavy clothes, rolled out the back ramp, got into the car, and drove around the city in the snow. They loved snow. I always marveled at how such a small woman could collapse a wheelchair so quickly and put it into the back seat.

I was less than a year old when I first crawled into Aunt Doris and Uncle John's apartment. I have no idea whether I was curious or afraid or even aware of the fact that Uncle John moved on wheels instead of walking upright. No doubt it didn't matter because Uncle John was one of the most wonderfully loud and boisterous people I had ever encountered (quite a contrast with my father, the engineer), and he would swoop me up in his lap; sitting atop the wheelchair, I would clap as he sang what he affectionately labeled "Buchanan County Love Songs." He was from the hills of Buchanan County, Virginia.

Aunt Doris's Move to Richmond

Their story unfolded gradually as I grew old enough to comprehend what happened to Uncle John. He and Aunt Doris met in southwest Virginia, where they were both newly minted teachers. He was an outdoorsy person who hunted, fished, and played semiprofessional baseball. She was a genteel Southern woman. One night in 1936, he was in a local tavern and was shot when he suggested to another man that he shouldn't clean his gun inside. John Pleasant McCoy was shot in the spine by an escaped convict and paralyzed from the waist down that night. It was never clear to me whether this was an accidental shooting or whether the man had gotten angry and intended to shoot him. (Years later I found the bullet in Aunt Doris's jewelry box.) Regardless, he lay in a local hospital, pressure ulcers forming rapidly. Well-meaning friends told Aunt Doris that no one would feel badly toward her if she "let the boy go." Others reminded her that he shouldn't have been in a tavern at all. They had just been engaged before his accident. She was heartbroken. He was probably going to die.

She mourned, grieved, and then mustered the stamina to mobilize every resource she could. Her brother (my uncle), who was stationed in Norfolk, Virginia, told her of a surgeon at the Medical College of Virginia (MCV) in Richmond who was having some success with spinal cord injury. Aunt Doris had looked at the x-rays showing that the bullet was lodged against the spinal cord, but the cord wasn't severed. Having no medical training, she assumed that if the spinal cord was not severed, he might stand a chance of regaining mobility. In 1937 she arranged to have John moved, via train, to Richmond. She went against all the advice of everyone she held dear, but her father and mother (my grandparents) drove her to the train station when they finally realized she was going to do this regardless of what anyone thought.

When the surgeon in Richmond saw the x-rays, he explained that if he had seen them in advance, he would not have agreed to see John. The impact had done just as much damage as if the bullet had severed the cord. Later Aunt Doris remembered that it was her ignorance in interpreting those x-rays that gave her hope, resulting in John coming to Richmond. And once he was in Richmond, he remained at MCV Hospital for more than a year. There they treated the pressure sores, and he lived. She described how changing the dressings on these open wounds was a continual and tortuous process.

Discharged to the Home for the Incurables in Richmond, John lived there for six years. There, people with various conditions, for whom others had little hope of recovery, lived in a large mansion that had been donated to the cause. It was near beautiful Byrd Park. Both he and Doris showed the stress they had been under; both were thin and exhausted. She supported herself by doing secretarial work and would go to the home every evening. Eventually, he began to write his first novel while lying in bed. She would take the handwritten copy and type it up at night, returning each piece to him as he gave her the next. He used his background in southwest Virginia to craft his story. His first book was published just as he left the home (McCoy 1944). After years of John's being institutionalized, they married and moved to the apartment on Grove Avenue. He purchased an old typewriter, went back to school in literature at the University of Richmond, and continued to write. She worked outside the home as an administrative secretary, supporting them on a daily basis. He wrote during the day. This was the life they led.

Moving Despite a Wheelchair

Caregiving was a part of Aunt Doris's adult life, yet anyone who met Uncle John would have immediately recognized the vitality and spirit of this very capable man. He rolled around in his wheelchair, drove his car, and fully participated in life. When they were confronted at a local theater by a manager who said that they did not allow wheelchairs, they pushed forward. They existed in a pre–Americans with Disabilities Act world without curb cutouts, required elevators, or sensitivity to accommodation. Like some other oppressed groups in the South, they were refused service in restaurants because he was in a wheelchair. They lived in a world before "normalization theory, the predominant philosophy that . . . has helped establish the belief that all people with disabilities should have the opportunity to live normalized lives to the extent their disabilities allow" (Dudley 2000:449).

As a child, I was unaware of the barriers Aunt Doris and Uncle John faced. I had an idealized view of how they lived, thinking it was not unusual. They welcomed me with open arms, and the fact that he could not move his legs in no way diminished his capacity to be totally engaged in life. I loved visiting them in Richmond, and I took every opportunity to do so. As a child, I knew Uncle John wrote books, but when my parents received copies, they carefully placed them on high shelves out of my reach. For their time the books were considered racy, although years later, when I was old enough to read them, they didn't seem very racy at all. But they were definitely full of life and gregarious language, much like Uncle John (McCoy 1950, 1954, 1971).

When Uncle John had a stroke in the 1970s, he was in his late sixties. Somehow, I knew that I needed to get to Richmond. During the time I spent in Richmond, I vividly recall how Aunt Doris and I walked to the hospital from the apartment each morning and stayed with Uncle John at the hospital until after suppertime. He died in 1973, six years after my mother and maternal grandmother. At his death, Uncle John was sixty-nine and had been married for almost thirty years.

Aunt Doris Moves Back Home

After John's death, Aunt Doris seemed to know what she needed to do. At age sixty-five, Aunt Doris was just retired, and her three brothers were still alive in southwest Virginia. She moved back to Gate City in 1975, leaving Richmond after thirty-seven years. For several years after her return, she rented an apartment where she could walk to the library and to the small downtown area in the little Virginia town in which she had grown up.

When she heard that a high-rise condominium was being built in an adjacent Tennessee town, she put her deposit down and became one of the charter members to move in. The high-rise was part of an established campus that had studio and garden style apartments attached to a nursing wing. At that time, it was a modified life care community (Netting and Unks 1984) in which residents paid for their units using a life lease arrangement. They could live in the unit there until they didn't need it anymore, and the life care corporation would then resell the unit. The residents could also move to the smaller apartments in the same building with the nursing wing or even move to the nursing wing without an increase in cost. A small maintenance fee was paid monthly as well, no matter which living arrangement the resident had.

A number of people in the family did not encourage this move. Several family members called it "going to a nursing home," even though it was independent living in a continuing care retirement community (CCRC). A CCRC is a campus-like setting in which a continuum of care is provided (Netting and Wilson 2006). This CCRC had independent living apartments, congregate living (smaller apartments) with meal plans, and a nursing wing. I was totally supportive, even though I was in the early days of doing research on the regulation of the CCRC industry and fully aware of the financial and legal difficulties a number of these communities had been facing (e.g., bankruptcies, failure to place funds in escrow, and assumptions about religious sponsorship) (Netting and Wilson 1994). Yet this community seemed to be financially solvent according to the reports of its annual audit, and the guarantee of care across levels of need, without additional costs, was rapidly disappearing in the industry. Just as she had made up her mind to move to Richmond, then to move back to southwest Virginia, Aunt Doris did not look back. She moved into a two-bedroom condo on the sixth floor in Johnson City, Tennessee.

Moving Around the Condo

For more than twenty years, Aunt Doris lived in her condo unit at the CCRC. During that time the community's leadership developed and matured as well, eventually recognizing that selling life care contracts was not financially feasible. Soon Aunt Doris became one of the charter members with one of the old life care contracts. Costs for buying into the community rose rapidly as actuarial tables revealed just how long older residents would live in these types of settings. Aunt Doris and I giggled together about how she had gotten her money's worth. The longer she lived, the more she benefited from her decision to move into the CCRC just as they had built the new condo building. She shared tidbits about life in the condos when I visited. I visited every three or four months, enjoying the chance to live in her world for short episodes of time. We laughed together about those episodes as being "Ellen's laboratory experiences" in the real world of gerontology.

Aunt Doris was no stranger to disability. As the years passed, she had a number of chronic conditions: arthritis, macular degeneration (a progressive eye condition), congestive heart failure, mini-strokes, and several broken bones due to falls. She and I had long conversations about the implications of each condition and the medications (and their side effects and interactions) that were accumulating to counter her symptoms (Feinberg 2000–2001). She had always been a planner, so it was very common for us to include in our conversations plans for her future. These plans included Aunt Doris's appointing me the executrix of her will and her power of attorney. And she decided and shared with me how she wanted to be buried next to Uncle John and what she wanted sung and read at her memorial service. I took notes, then typed them on my computer, and sent her a hard copy, and she added and changed things over the years. In some ways, I had taken on Aunt Doris's earlier role with Uncle John; I was now the typist of her wishes and stories. I did not think there was anything morbid about discussing her death; it was just what one did. We were always very practical in recognizing the inevitability of death. Perhaps it was the fact that we had experienced deaths together—of my mother, her mother, and Uncle John. Perhaps I was so used to death as a subject, because my husband is a hospice chaplain, that this seemed normal parlance.

One year she decided to ask family members what items they wanted from her apartment. As requests came in, she labeled these items with the name of the person to whom it was promised. I went through the apartment with her, writing down each labeled item so that I would have a master inventory. I typed up an inventory and sent her a copy, updating it periodically when we met. She remarked about how she used to type all the time yet had never learned to use a computer. For years, her old typewriter sat unused, covered with cards and letters stacked on a sturdy typing table in her guest room.

There were a lot of family members, and the letter that Aunt Doris sent out raised a number of eyebrows. I suppose she received every conceivable reaction, from horror that she would consider the option of eventually dying, to fear of being greedy in saying what one would like to have, to concern over one's own mortality brought on by the request. But eventually, approximately twenty-five people (nieces, nephews, grandnieces, grandnephews, and a few cousins) had their names attached to various pieces of furniture or smaller items that they admired. In recollection, I suspect that family members felt awkward about making their desires known because Aunt Doris was still very much alive.

Years later I found a study titled "Gift Wrapping Ourselves: The Final Gift Exchange," which reinforced what we had experienced. The authors wrote, "When a person gives an object, which is an extension of the self, to friends, family members, or charity, s/he expects in return that the object be appreciated in ways consistent with her/his own definitions of the object's nature and value" (Marx et al. 2004:S274). As we recorded who wanted what, Aunt Doris seemed to find joy in telling me how she had acquired these treasured items, tethering them to a memory often tied to Uncle John.

DESCRIPTION OF CAREGIVING EXPERIENCE

The year Aunt Doris turned eighty-five was pivotal in testing every social work, gerontological, and organizing skill I could muster. She had had several falls in the past. She was predisposed to falling, being a slight woman who tipped over easily. She had broken a wrist, an ankle, and her nose and chipped teeth in various falls over the years. But in 1997, she broke her hip. I knew enough from the gerontological literature to know that "a fall is often a seminal event for an older person. Many older people describe a fall as a dreaded event that could precipitate a cascade of problems that will rob them of their independence" (Tennestedt 2002–2003:5). I knew that Aunt Doris was facing a cascade of problems, and so did she. Neither of us was naive about the potential for this fall to be the beginning of a prolonged encounter with the healthcare community.

Aunt Doris's Move to and from Rehabilitation and the Nursing Home

Aunt Doris had surgery the second day that she was in the hospital, and they pinned her hip. Four days later, the hospital transferred Aunt Doris to the rehabilitation facility. My greatest fear was that Aunt Doris would become invisible as a person, and this fear was quickly realized. The case manager at the rehabilitation hospital told me, "Given your aunt's age, we'll recommend she go to assisted living." This recently hired case manager said this before she had even met Aunt Doris, without any assessment. I knew that Aunt Doris was in jeopardy of being stereotyped as just another old gray-haired woman and that

I needed to act quickly. The pervasiveness of ageism in medicine and in the larger society has been written about for years (Cole and Thompson 2001–2002), so it was not surprising that Aunt Doris was encountering ageism.

I talked with Aunt Doris daily while she was in rehab. She was cognitively intact but was weak and exhausted. I had a lot going for me because she understood the concept of rehabilitation better than I; she had lived it with Uncle John. She knew that it would be painful and tiring—there were no illusions—but she was willing to work hard. The indignities she suffered during this process made me cry but also motivated me through anger. For example, to help her practice walking, the rehabilitation staff took her to the same mall where her friends walked every day, but she did not have appropriate clothing. When she asked not to go, they labeled her "resistant." When she asked for a hat because the wind was cold, they wrapped her head in a towel.

Aunt Doris was in the rehabilitation hospital for almost two weeks. The team wanted to send her to an assisted living facility because that was the "safe" thing to do. I called her primary care physician, who intervened with the medical director at the facility, asking that she be sent to the nursing wing at the CCRC. I knew that she would not lose her independent living unit if she could move from the nursing wing back to her apartment within three weeks. She was in the nursing wing for over two weeks, and her primary care physician assessed her as being able to move back home (Netting and Williams 1996). Aunt Doris got back to her apartment, but it took constant vigilance. I remained in close contact with her physician, knowing that he had the power to discharge her from the nursing wing and knowing that we had to keep him aware of how important it was for her to go home. In the process, Aunt Doris and I had long conversations about the concerns of well-meaning professionals that she be "safe" by being in a more sheltered environment and how their concerns were valid (Netting 1998). I would ask her, "Are you willing to take the risk of being alone in your apartment?" "Are you afraid if you are alone?" The week that she returned to the condo, we hired a companion aide to come in several hours a day and to be there at critical times, such as when we got up in the morning and took her shower.

Aunt Doris's Move to the Residence

Aunt Doris stayed in the condo for almost four years after her hip surgery, until she was eighty-nine years old. She used a walker for safety and wore a Lifeline in case she had a fall or needed help. The Lifeline was my idea because I was concerned that she was alone much of the time. But she continued to fall, sliding down off the bed when she was getting up and not being able to get up from the floor. The risk factors for falls, such as medications, weakness, gait imbalance, and age-related frailty, were all very relevant in this situation (Rubenstein and Josephson 2002–2003). We worked with her primary care physician and his physician's assistant on an ongoing basis, attempting to identify a medication that was causing dizziness or weakness. We also explored possible medication interactions and the fact that the same medications can affect older and younger people differently (Beers 2000–2001). During this time, she got so weak that she could barely get up. I consulted with one of my dearest friends, a social worker who works in a geriatric clinic, and she suggested it might be her thyroid. It was.

Once she was on thyroid medication, much of her strength returned. However, she recognized her own increasing frailty, and we talked about when it would be time to move to the residence. I suspected it was my own reluctance for her to give up the condo and some denial about her inability to continue to live there that held up the process. I didn't want to say, "I think it's time for you to go" any more than she wanted to make the move. We had conversations in which she asked whether it was time to leave, and I said that I wasn't sure. For the last year she was in the condo, we recognized that we were probably moving closer to a decision for her to leave, but she had good weeks in which she got along very well. We kept the companion aide we had hired earlier, and she came in every day for a few hours. Aunt Doris and Gertie became friends, sharing news about their families. Gertie did grocery shopping and light housekeeping. In a way, we developed a modified assisted living environment in the context of an independent apartment unit. On days when Aunt Doris did not feel well for any reason, Gertie kept me informed. I found myself feeling very comforted by having Gertie there.

During the holiday season, I brought a friend to meet Aunt Doris. When we arrived, she had just fallen off the edge of her bed. Gertie, who had become a trusted companion, was helping her dress so they could take her over to the nursing wing, where she could have an x-ray of her ribs, which were hurting. We borrowed a wheelchair and took her across the street. She had two cracked ribs. She agreed that it would be best to stay in the nursing wing for a few days. Gertie continued to visit her while she was there.

It was shortly after this visit that Aunt Doris and I agreed it was time to move to the congregate living apartments located in the same building as the nursing wing. The critical episode that had made this decision easier was her last fall. Gertie was helpful in this decision-making process because she had actually been in the apartment when Aunt Doris had fallen. She felt responsible even though she could not have prevented it. Having a companion aide present while Aunt Doris did some things for herself, having privacy as she bathed, toileted, and dressed, did not prevent her from falling. Gertie kept saying, "I was right in the next room. I could have prevented this." I found myself reassuring Gertie that this was not her responsibility and that the fact she was there meant that Aunt Doris did not lie on the floor alone for a long time. Gertie had been at her side right away. Aunt Doris and I had conversations about what it would mean to live in another setting and that falling could happen as easily in a more sheltered environment as it could in her condo. It was during these conversations that I began to realize that the size of the condo (two bedrooms with a living room and small kitchen) was becoming almost too much to handle. A studio apartment appealed to Aunt Doris, a space that was manageable and where everything was in closer proximity. She called it "cozier," which became symbolic language for the studio apartment being more controllable, not so overwhelming.

The moves in Aunt Doris's life had been highly symbolic: leaving home to go to Richmond with the mission of getting help for John against all the odds, moving back to southwest Virginia to be near siblings before they died, and moving to the condo as a recognition that this was an opportunity she should take. This move represented something different. It was an admission that living independently (even though Aunt Doris and I knew that she had not fully been living independently in recent years) was no longer an option. Even Gertie was relieved, as she feared that Aunt Doris would be at risk of falling on her watch. The privacy and comfort of her condo would be replaced by a much smaller studio in the residence. She was gracious about this move, probably more gracious than I. Even though she didn't know it, I was grieving the loss as if I were the one moving. I had spent so much time fighting for her right to remain in these surroundings that I found myself having difficulty changing direction. I was no longer encouraging her physician and others to let her remain at home, pushing against the rehabilitation team to see her as a person. I was actually assisting in a move that took her away from her condo, which the CCRC and others called an independent living unit.

Moving from the Residence to "Camping Out" in the Nursing Wing

Aunt Doris adjusted well to being in the residence, and the size of the studio apartment seemed to suit her. She had a number of medical emergencies in the almost three years she was there, probably related to mini-strokes. A pattern developed in which a nurse was called from the nursing wing (in another pod of the residence), came over, checked her blood pressure, and called me to confer, and I talked with Aunt Doris. If she felt she needed to go to the emergency room, she would say so. But we both dreaded each of these episodes because once she was in the emergency room, she would almost surely be admitted to the hospital. Once she was in the hospital, a series of events would occur: first the bladder infection, then the antibiotics and other medications, then a medication interaction with the drugs she was already on, and then a spiral into trying to sort out what had gone wrong.

The residence offered a home aide service that we could purchase for several hundred dollars a month. Gertie had worked briefly for this service but had gone to sit with another woman in the larger community. The aides would check on Aunt Doris every two hours and oversee her medication management. They would walk with her as she pushed her walker to the dining room. I knew that I could check with their supervisor at a moment's notice if anything went wrong.

Then the inevitable letter arrived. Because the residence was technically considered independent living, and because they could no longer afford to run a home aide service, residents were required to contract for home services outside the CCRC. A list of existing agencies was provided. At this point, Aunt Doris and I had a serious conversation about what to do. We both knew that the aides who checked on her did more than just check. There were times when she had had an accident and they had cleaned her up. They knew her habits, her preferences, and her routine. She *knew* them. When she was not feeling well, they stopped in more often as they went down the hallway to check on others. They were in-house, and they could do those extras without broadcasting what they were doing. Their kindness and the fact that they liked her meant that she was actually getting more than they were supposed to be doing. If we hired a home aide agency, they would have to come for blocks of time, and they would not be in-house. In short, her support system of in-home providers was being stripped away. We knew that we had been living on borrowed time with these arrangements and that there were about seven other residents in the same situation; they had been able to remain there because the aides had covered for them by not reporting just how much care they were actually receiving. The other seven had decided to move to the nursing wing.

We knew that Aunt Doris could always move to the nursing wing because her life care contract would cover the cost of her care there. We also knew she needed extensive oversight and care, but she needed assisted living, not nursing care. We also knew that the CCRC was building an assisted living unit on the premises, but it would not be completed for another six to nine months. We talked with the marketing person from assisted living. I'll never forget that day because Aunt Doris made what I considered the only safe decision she could make, but it was not an easy one. She would move to the nursing wing and live there until assisted living was available. We put down a deposit that very day for assisted living and began to plot our course of action.

I called the local movers and asked whether they could store furniture for several months. I asked the management whether we could leave Aunt Doris's things in her apartment by paying an extra month's fee until I could get everything taken care of. Aunt Doris moved downstairs to the nursing wing while her apartment was still intact. As she needed things in the small nursing home room, we took them down. Gertie agreed to return for a few hours a day, and she came over and hung several pictures. We took her favorite chair, but she was reluctant to put too much in this room because it was temporary. I packed up everything she could do without for several months, and the movers took her bed, couch, table, chairs, end tables, TV, winter clothes, and assorted other items to a storage unit. We were officially "on hold" at that point, and we never once suggested to ourselves or anyone else that this was anything but a temporary living situation.

The best way I could frame this plan was to liken it to camping. It was spring, and the weather was getting warmer. I told Aunt Doris that she would be camping out in the nursing wing, but by winter she would be in assisted living. We laughed about this metaphor throughout her stint there. I sent her camping clothes in the form of jogging suits and tennis shoes. Whenever we talked, she said that camping food wasn't what it was cracked up to be, alluding to the most talked-about problem in nursing homes: the food. To keep her spirits up, she continued her habit of reading every large-print book she could get her hands on. To do so, she had to use a magnifying glass, given her progressive macular degeneration. She would lose herself in her reading, devouring fiction and nonfiction alike. I would come to the door of her room and see her in a pink jogging suit and white tennis shoes, with her head lowered over a book as her hand-held magnifying glass scanned the pages. She was a vision of concentration in a sea of chaos as the woman across the hall cried out a repetitive refrain and as men and women tethered to wheelchairs shuffled their feet up and down the corridor.

Moving to Assisted Living

There were times during this process that I was fearful that Aunt Doris would not live long enough or would have a serious decline that would not permit her to move to assisted living when and if the units were finally finished. At one point, someone came to administer a mini–mental status test and Aunt Doris couldn't remember the day. She was petrified that she had failed the test and had already tried to convince herself that she could manage to live out her days in the nursing wing. We had a frank talk about why she couldn't remember. Before this episode, I had asked her repeatedly whether she'd like to have her calendar on the wall. She didn't want to know the days. She had determined not to mark off days but to read her way to assisted living, losing herself in her literature. After she had not been able to remember whether it was Tuesday or Thursday, she commented to me that all days were the same here but that she now wanted a calendar if that was what it took to get her into assisted living. After that I called and quizzed her about the day, and she always knew what day of the week it was.

The completion of the assisted living facility was delayed, but she was the first occupant on the very first day it opened, the week before Christmas. I finished up the semester, raced to Tennessee, met the movers, and set up her new assisted living apartment in two days. It was a beautiful facility, with all the smells of newness and a lovely window looking out onto a courtyard. We told people that Aunt Doris was being sprung out of the nursing wing. And then the unthinkable happened: She was not sure she could manage assisted living. We had long conversations about what happens to people when they become institutionalized. She told me stories about Uncle John and how he didn't think he had become institutionalized but that he had after staying in the Home for the Incurables for those long years. We used him as an example, and we worked through how he had managed to be deinstitutionalized. The first thing was to move her bed so that it faced the same way the nursing home bed had faced. She couldn't seem to maneuver her walker to get in and out otherwise, even though there was plenty of room. Going to the dining room was exhausting because food had always been brought to her. She practiced the walk to the dining room, taking breaks along the way to rest. She saw that her nice winter clothes had been hung in her closet, but she didn't have the energy to dress up. She decided to wear her "camping" clothes even in her new apartment. For a few months, I struggled with the possibility that she might not be able to adjust to this more independent environment. She told me that she felt like the Israelites when Moses had led them out of bondage and how they had complained when it wasn't all they had hoped it would be. We laughed at how appropriate this seemed.

Three months into assisted living, I had just visited with Aunt Doris and she seemed to be adjusting better. The next day, her blood pressure spiked on a Sunday afternoon. The nurse practitioner was so worried that she rode in the ambulance with Aunt Doris to the hospital. It was flu season, and all hospital beds were full. Aunt Doris spent three days in the emergency room, waiting for a bed. She told me that she wished she could die, that it was her time. The nurse practitioner prepared for the worst. After two weeks in the hospital, she was sent to the nursing wing at the CCRC. Only semiprivate rooms were available, and her roommate had a severe dementia. Aunt Doris decided that she needed to go home. She mustered enough strength to walk up and back down the corridor under the supervision of the physical therapist. He told her that if she could do that, then she could return to assisted living. And she did. She had weathered another storm, and when she returned to her assisted living apartment, this time it felt like home.

ANALYSES

In this chapter, I began with the historical context that brought Aunt Doris and me together. In my adult life, we have become more like mother and daughter, given that my own mother died early and that Aunt Doris did not have children. No one in the family questioned why we were as close as we were, and my other two remaining aunts called me whenever they were concerned about Aunt Doris just as they might call a daughter if she had one. I have wondered whether anyone resented my relationship with Aunt Doris; if so, the resentment was deeply hidden. Before Aunt Doris broke her hip, I thought of myself more as an anticipatory caregiver. It was in her eighty-fifth year, when she broke her hip, that I became recognized by Aunt Doris, others, and myself as her caregiver. It was not insignificant that she was eighty-five and entered the chronological period called the "old-old" (Wang 2004). At the time, I was increasingly aware that social work departments were disappearing in various healthcare facilities throughout the country (Netting and Williams 1998). In 1997, when I received a call that Aunt Doris had been taken to a hospital, I began to calculate whom I might find in a case manager type of position. I remember asking for the social work department, then hearing silence. I then knew to ask for case management and discharge planning because I had been conducting research that involved working with large healthcare systems. The names of units, departments, and positions were always in flux, and even if I wanted to locate a social worker, I was aware that she or he might not be in what used to be called a social work department.

My work in the gerontology and health fields had taught me to know that Aunt Doris, like others in her situation, would be given as short a time as possible at the hospital because of reimbursement constraints. Medicare reimbursement was less than that of private insurance, so her use of the bed was costly to the medical center. Therefore, I needed to immediately develop a relationship with the person who would be writing her discharge plan, and I would have to develop this relationship long distance, given that I was not living in Johnson City. I realized that any information I could communicate about Aunt Doris would help this discharge planner and future professional caregivers understand her better and provide her with better care. Her hip was surgically pinned, and I pushed for her discharge to a rehabilitation hospital rather than to a nursing home, hoping that they would provide more aggressive care. This hope was based on multiple conversations with colleagues in the aging field about the different organizational cultures of rehabilitation hospitals and nursing homes. Some theorists (Morgan 1986; Schein 1992) indicate that organizations, like other groups, have distinct cultures. According to them, organizations have cultural norms such as valuing client input, teamwork, or professional-led decision making. Organizational cultures often dictate how programs in the organization view and treat seniors. Most of my colleagues and friends and I thought that the culture in a rehabilitation setting was better for Aunt Doris.

I was 350 miles away and drove down the first weekend Aunt Doris was in rehabilitation. As a college professor, I could stay only three days because it was it was the busiest time of spring semester. And then I struck upon a plan, remembering a question that a colleague of mine had asked students in doctoral comprehensive exams: "What would Saul Alinsky do in this situation?" Alinsky was the father of a powerful grassroots social movement, community organization, and a passionate believer in social justice. I remembered that in *Rules for Radicals* (1971), one strategy he advocated was to go outside the experience of one's targeted audience, and I decided that I had to move outside the experience of the rehabilitation team to get their attention. They were probably not used to having nieces fax long messages to each team member, and I was determined to make them see Aunt Doris as a person in context. I also knew the importance of patients having an outside advocate, someone in the larger community to watch and monitor their experiences (Cherry 1993). Therefore, I began the letter by referring to vast number of relatives interested in her care. I also recognized the importance of the primary care physician and looped him into the situation by copying it to him. I drafted a letter to raise their consciousness, using persuasion as the primary tactic (Ezell 2001; Schneider and Lester 2001). I read the letter to Aunt Doris over the phone to receive her approval and faxed her a copy so she would have it when the team received it. I then faxed the letter to every member of the rehabilitation team, copying her primary care physician. The team members were so taken aback that they decided to postpone their decision-making process on her situation until the next week. Not only did this buy us time, but everyone knew who Mrs. McCoy was. (See the appendix for a copy of the letter.)

The importance of understanding historical context not only is important to this chapter but also has become important to me when I have encountered professionals in the service delivery system. The letter I wrote to the rehabilitation team when they were seeing Aunt Doris as "just another blue-hair" (a phrase a colleague in geriatric medicine introduced me to) included information about her earlier life in an attempt to convey her personhood and her uniqueness. It was this tendency to stereotype and to name "blue-haired ladies" as a category that motivated me to act (Rosenblum and Travis 2000). Professional staff needs to individualize clients. Each client is unique, and the professional is responsible for making sure they have the expertise and knowledge to sensitively and effectively intervene with the client. For instance, when Aunt Doris was labeled "resistant" for not wanting to go to the mall in inappropriate clothing and was then given a towel to cover her head, her behavior was improperly construed as problematic. If staff had developed an understanding of her particular worldview, behavior patterns, and preferences, her objections probably would have been correctly interpreted and respected.

In addition to the episode in which Aunt Doris was in danger of being targeted for assisted living sight unseen, I have learned repeatedly that there is no substitute for informal care. Even being in a CCRC in which she could move between levels of care did not protect Aunt Doris or anyone else from what occurred when they needed hospital, subacute, rehabilitation, or skilled nursing care. The nursing wing at the CCRC was not skilled care. It was more of an infirmary setting. Therefore, as needs changed, residents could move on and off campus to receive the care not available within the security of the campus setting. These services were not covered by their life care or continuing care contracts, and their insurance would not cover these services beyond short-term, temporary stays. Having informal caregivers as advocates, to work with CCRC staff, is critical if they are to be included in the decision-making process (Penning 2002). Also, having Gertie as a companion was critically important to keeping me, as an informal caregiver, aware of what was happening.

The literature suggests that representation and influence are two fundamental skills needed to perform an advocacy role. Representation has three dimensions: exclusivity, mutuality, and use of a forum (Schneider and Lester 2001). As I reflected over the years since Aunt Doris originally moved into the

CCRC, these dimensions were evident throughout. *Exclusivity* means that the advocate is focused on the client's needs as primary. *Mutuality* means that there is a relationship between the advocate and the client. The forum is the arena in which the needs of the clients are advocated. Aunt Doris was not my client, but I have tried to represent her with respect for her needs (exclusivity), enhanced by the relationship that binds us (mutuality), and within various forums, including hospitals, rehabilitation hospitals, and the CCRC. Influence, the second set of skills, is fundamental to an advocacy role, and it requires one to gather facts and plan one's approach to change in a way that can make a difference (Schneider and Lester 2001). In Aunt Doris's situation, I have had wonderful teammates in the gathering of facts. Gertie served as my eyes and ears for three years. A close cousin in Gate City was always willing to make a trip over if something was awry and I could not get there right away. She made numerous hospital visits when I was unable to get there. Other cousins kept in touch by phone with Aunt Doris and with me. Other people who lived at the residence would let me know when Aunt Doris was not feeling well or if they thought she needed me. Staff in the assisted living unit called me if anything was not going well. In short, the ability to influence means having resources on which one can count.

As Aunt Doris and I reflected on her move to the residence apartment, we talked about the many aspects of making such a move. I tried to always use an empowerment- and strengths-based approach (Chapin and Cox 2001), and she gently let me know that being included in the process was important up to a point. Decisions about personal items of value and what things to take from the condo required her concentrated attention, but going through drawers crammed with everything she had saved from the past twenty years was not at all what she wanted or could do. Learning to discriminate between what to talk with her about and what to omit was important. She assured me that if I had asked her about everything, it would have worn her out. She also trusted me to do this, and therefore I was empowered to use my best judgment. It is important to know that this was unique to Aunt Doris's wishes and the situation and that other people may want to be more involved in the details of the process.

A study of decision making in long-term care (Nakasima et al. 2004) was particularly helpful in my thinking about the processes Aunt Doris and I encountered in the multiple moves she made. The findings revealed three approaches to decision making: autonomous, collaborative, and delegated. Until Aunt Doris broke her hip, she engaged in autonomous decision making. As soon as she entered the hospital, we entered a phase of collaborative decision making in which options were provided but mutual communication had to occur between us in making decisions. After her discharge, Aunt Doris and I entered into a mixed process of collaborative and delegated decision making. For example, when Aunt Doris moved to assisted living, she delegated me as the decision maker in all aspects of her move. We still collaborated and we always communicated, but it was typically around very personal decisions such as bodily care and socioemotional concerns. Our ability to communicate well across these approaches also reflected the mutuality that had always existed in our caregiving relationship.

My caregiving experience continued to underscore difference. Other people in the family called me and said things like, "You helped Aunt Doris make that move. I want to talk with you about . . . ." I always told them that there are no hard-and-fast rules, that each situation is unique. I certainly shared with them what I have learned, but I say these are guidelines that worked for me, and they may not work as well in other situations. Aunt Doris and I often reflected on her multiple moves. We agreed that it was very important to be organized and to manage time well in the process (my engineering father's influence worked well here) but that there was also an interpretive, emerging process (Rosenblum and Travis 2000). In this emergent process, we co-constructed our joint reality (found our personal meanings) of what each move meant and how we would view it. We had not rehearsed the process, but together we symbolically analyzed it as it happened. For example, I'm convinced that framing the move to the nursing wing as a camping experience helped us both maintain a sense of continuity between the residence and assisted living in the face of uncertainty. Because camping typically is a temporary condition, it helped her get through the time spent in the nursing wing.

IMPLICATIONS

I had moved many times in my life. I knew the drill. But I had never moved another person with whom I did not live. What is curious about the moves with which I assisted Aunt Doris is that they were not a matter of cleaning out Aunt Doris's condo or studio apartment after she had died. She was very much alive, albeit somewhat frail.

Several years ago, she had a large two-bedroom condo full of furniture. Every drawer was packed to overflowing, and she had saved papers from the twenty years she had resided there. An approach to the process began to emerge as I obsessed about how to do this long distance. I knew I would have to be efficient in managing the time I would be in Johnson City because I had to work around breaks in the academic schedule. I would stay awake at night, thinking about possible guidelines.

- Work with the CCRC staff to determine dates when another living unit is going to be available. If possible, negotiate to keep the current unit for a month thereafter.
- Recruit other family members (if they are available) to participate in this process. Although you may serve as the point person, others will want to be involved. Determine clear tasks they can assist you in doing.
- Call a local moving company (recommended by others who have had similar moves) and coordinate two moving dates. The first move is to get your relative settled into her or his new apartment. This entails moving only the things that will go to the new residence. The second move (possibly a month later) is to move everything else out of the former unit.
- If you need to distribute items, ask the moving company about the possibility of storing items that may be too large to ship by mail, and ask whether they take individual items to other parts of the country as they have room on other loads.
- Talk with your relative about what pieces of furniture need to go to the new apartment and tag every item with a colorful sign so the movers will know which pieces to take over.
- Measure the space carefully in advance and then measure the items that are tagged so that whatever is taken will fit in the new space. Draw a rough floor plan, based on the actual floor space that your relative feels comfortable with.
- Be sure your relative is in a safe place away from the moving process.
- Wait for a few weeks, even if it costs a little to keep the former place of residence a bit longer. In this way, your relative can determine what she or he has forgotten or what is not wanted in the new place.
- Inventory everything in the old living space once the first move to the new living space is complete. Methodically go room by room, keeping a running list. When you run across an item that is not labeled, put an asterisk on it to remind yourself to check with your relative.
- Check with your relative about what she or he wants to do with the asterisked items.
- Notify all the relatives whose names appear on any item, and if your relative is not taking it to the new home, make shipping arrangements.
- Pack up anything that will be shipped, and take these items to a local shipping center with complete addresses and phone numbers. Get tracking numbers for each item.

- Be prepared to make decisions about the contents of drawers. Use discretion about items that appear to be valuable or papers that should be kept, but don't overload your relative with details of contents that can be discarded or given away.
- If there are personal items such as journals, photographs, or letters that your relative has no room for, put these items in a box and take them to your own home to sort through later so that you can be reflective and thoughtful about them. Let your relative know that you are keeping these items in a safe and secure place.

As these instrumental guidelines emerged, there were accompanying socioemotional feelings. Aunt Doris was very much alive, admittedly weak and frail, but very aware of what was happening. I found myself worrying about the process and asking myself, "What right do I have to do this?" "How can I include her in this process without wearing her out?" and "Will it break her heart to see the condo one more time, or should she go back?" These questions revealed how I managed to project a number of feelings onto her: that she might question my right to do this, that she might be wearing out, and that her heart was breaking. Ironically, I learned through conversations with her that none of these feelings was hers; they were based on my fears of what she might be thinking. I never worried about whether I could manage the tasks. Later I realized I had pushed myself to the physical limit.

I probably erred on the side of including Aunt Doris in everything until she clued me in to her own mode of thinking. Yes, she wanted to see the condo one more time, but only to point out where things were and to give practical instructions. She had no need to be there during the process, especially because watching was as tiring as doing it herself. I had been wearing her out, and she told me this in her characteristically gentle way.

I encountered a new dimension to extended family dynamics once this process began. Almost by default, the larger family system (consisting of two other maternal aunts who were living in New Mexico and California, nine nephews, five nieces, and twenty-seven grandnieces and grandnephews) rose to the top of my priority list. I knew the fourteen nephews and nieces well because they were my first cousins, many of whom I hadn't seen in years. However, there were grandnieces and nephews I had never met. I knew that Aunt Doris was the oldest of the remaining living children in her family of eight siblings and that she had recently assumed the matron's role within the larger family system. Everyone was interested in the progress of her move, and everyone had her or his own reasons.

With Aunt Doris's permission, I alerted a key member in each nuclear family about the move. I was prepared for family dynamics to emerge in process, dynamics about which I had not been privy up until then. A cousin with whom I had had minimal contact volunteered immediately to drive from three states away, hoping to pilfer whatever was available. Others warned me about the motives of this person. I had managed to avoid having this knowledge for many years. Fortunately, Aunt Doris and I could talk about these dynamics. We agreed that these dynamics typically would arise at someone's funeral as her possessions were distributed, but she was still very much alive. She told me stories that my mother would have been privy to, along with the historical significance of who had what feelings within the family. It was like having an inside track, when under typical circumstances I might have been cleaning out her apartment after her death.

In the moving process, I discovered very quickly that I had to use my best time management skills. I was there for nine days to accomplish the second move (a month later, after Aunt Doris was in the residence apartment). During that time, I stayed in her condo, which had piles of items everywhere, sleeping in the remaining twin bed that was to be shipped at the end of the week (she had taken one twin bed to her new place). My routine was quickly established. I would get up at dawn, take out trash from the previous night's work in a cinch garbage bag, and head for the dumpster behind the condos. I would take a particular room, clear out anything in closets or drawers in that location and inventory anything of value. I separated items into three piles: those that could be thrown out (e.g., old wrapping paper and bows, dated coupons), those that could be given away, and those that I needed to ask Aunt Doris about. I kept a running list of the latter. I quickly realized that I needed to set a schedule to meet with her twice a day at her new residence. I would go around lunchtime and eat with her, and we would go over my list. I'd then exit for the afternoon, returning right after dinner to check in with her. If I made more frequent trips, we would engage in conversation, and the time would fly by. I did not want to ignore her, but I also knew that I had to work quickly.

My trips across the street to her apartment became like a refuge from the chaos I was encountering in the condo as I dumped out the contents of every box, drawer, cabinet, or container. Every drawer was packed to the brim, and I began to muse about what I had read about hoarding behavior (Franks et al. 2004; Thomas 1997), recognizing that Aunt Doris was a controlled hoarder (on the surface everything was neat, but when one opened a drawer it was like opening a jack-in-the-box). Aunt Doris and I talked about this, and she revealed that this was a lifelong pattern, that she had always saved things and been somewhat of a pack rat. This tendency increased as she accumulated items throughout her life. This was a little surprising to me because she did not like clutter and was extremely neat, so that anyone coming into her home would not necessarily know that she was putting so many things away.

Whenever items on my list were viewed as valuable in an emotional sense to Aunt Doris, I relegated them to the box I was taking home with me. In this way, she knew that her journals, letters, and sentimental items were with me if she wanted to see them again. Table 8.1 summarizes the moving process from the vantage point of the key stakeholders in terms of relevant images and perceptions and the strategies used.

As I originally wrote this chapter, Aunt Doris was ninety-four years old, and she has been settled in her assisted living apartment for half a year. I visited her about every three to four months, more often if needed. She said that her residence was very comfortable, and until her last hospital stay (last month), she spent hours reading large-print books with a magnifying glass. Her greatest loss at that point was that her macular degeneration had progressed so that she couldn't see to read, even large print. She continued to use her walker. With the help of professional friends (social workers, nurses, and pharmacists) I consulted, medication interactions had been caught early. Her physician was cordial but probably saw me as "*that* niece in Richmond," given the number of times I suggested medication changes. He always complied with these requests, and Aunt Doris found it amusing that he might think of me as "*that* niece." Gertie still came in to check on Aunt Doris for me, even though she worked elsewhere most of the time. Aunt Doris had someone to check on her every few hours, and one of "the girls" helped her shower and dress in the mornings, just as Gertie used to do.

At age ninety-four Aunt Doris suffered another health crisis and returned to the intensive care unit at a local hospital. She kept repeating over and over again, "Please tell my story." In the wee hours of the morning, she had the nurse call me so that she could tell me her story. There was an urgency in her voice, and I assured her that I would share her story with others. This is Aunt Doris's story, and I have been fortunate to have lived part of that story with her.

The charter members of the condos with whom Aunt Doris entered the campus years ago have either died or moved to the apartments where she resided as they have aged in place. A new generation occupies the condos, and their contracts are much less liberal in their provisions. Aunt Doris took pride in her decision to move there early on because she could not have afforded the current market prices. And when I visited with her, we reminisced about the times I

Table 8.1 Implications

	Issues and Problems	Strategies for Change
Individuals	Include your relative in the process, but try not to overwhelm and tire the person out. Use discretion in what must be discussed and what can be discarded. Frame the process symbolically in meaningful language.	Talk with your relative about what to keep and label accordingly. Use a floor plan to discuss preferences about where things might go. Inventory everything. Asterisk items requiring checking with your relative. Package up anything to be shipped and make arrangements. Sort through drawers and cabinets. Be certain your relative is in a safe place during the move. Secure cherished items.
Families	Include others who want to help. Expect some trepidation from others about the symbolic nature of the move.	Notify all relatives whose names appear on any item and notify about shipping options. Recruit other family members to be part of process. Identify well-defined tasks for each person to do.
Communities	Communication with facility staff is critical. If you are from another community, respect the norms of this community and be flexible.	Work closely with staff to coordinate and show appreciation for what they do. Negotiate to keep current unit for a month after move. Call local moving company and coordinate two dates. Ask about storage possibilities and identify local shipping options.

(continued)

Table 8.1 (continued)

	Issues and Problems	Strategies for Change
Practitioners and educators	Recognize different forms of decision making and uniqueness of each caregiving situation. Learn to hear symbolic language and observe human behavior.	Prepare practitioners to recognize differences and draw from research on decision making and choice (see Nakasima et al. 2004). Be as sensitive to what is said as to what is not said. Observe the interactions between caregiver and recipient about the meaning of things (see Marx et al. 2004).
Researchers	Consider complexity of caregiver–care recipient relationships. Recognize that staff may have perceptions of how moves are conducted and that they may influence how they perceive and treat residents.	Study the logistics of moving in light of the decision-making process. Explore perceptions of staff on how moves are conducted.

spent in Richmond as a child when Uncle John sang me songs about Buchanan County. I also told her about the Richmond of contemporary times because I teach at the Virginia Commonwealth University (VCU) School of Social Work, right around the corner from her old apartment on Grove Avenue. The Medical College of Virginia where Aunt Doris moved Uncle John is now part of VCU. See table 8.1 for a summary of this discussion.

REFLECTIONS AND CONCLUSIONS

I was eager to respond to the invitation to write a chapter for this book. It never occurred to me to react in any but a positive way. I think this goes back to the fact that I expected all my life to be there for my older relatives. Because I was an only child, I spent a lot of time with adults. When I became an undergraduate at Duke University, a number of initiatives were bubbling up in gerontology. As a senior I was allowed to take a graduate-level seminar on retirement, my adviser was a gerontologist, and there were a number of the early aging experts there. I was intrigued that I could take these courses and that I could study something I considered a personal interest. Thus writing about caregiving, like studying aging, was as natural as anything I've done in life. My reactions were that it would give me a wonderful opportunity to tell Aunt Doris's story. I always tell my students that the older I get, the more credible I get because I'm a gerontologist.

I wrote the chapter in a stream-of-consciousness mode, allowing myself to tell the story without being hampered in any way. Because this was to be a more informal style in a narrative format, this worked well. I also made the choice to be somewhat chronological in the process, allowing the early days of Aunt Doris's life with Uncle John to lead to her aging in the CCRC. Much of the literature was already familiar to me, and I tried to integrate references into the narrative in an unobtrusive manner. After writing the guidelines for moving Aunt Doris that appear in this chapter, I was very excited to see an article (Reuss et al. 2005) on moving a loved one, and I recommend it to the interested reader.

The easiest thing about writing this chapter was that the story told itself. Aunt Doris had always been very literary and loved the idea of my being able to use my experiences with her in a narrative format. For example, the story of her early days with Uncle John has been handed down verbally ever since I was old enough to understand the words. Reconstructing the story of what happened and how she moved to Richmond (where I live now) was the easiest part of the chapter to write because it was long overdue in its telling.

The most challenging thing about writing this chapter was trying to follow the guidelines provided by the editor. I trusted the emergent process. However, it did not always lead me to each section and to answer specific questions posed to the chapter writers. Thus at times I had to cut and paste to fit the format so that chapters would have parallelism.

Writing the chapter allowed me to sort out some things I had been pondering for some time. For example, I had not realized how much Aunt Doris and I shared metaphorical thinking until I realized how we both bought into the camping metaphor, no questions asked. I also realized that Aunt Doris had been very clear about me not overwhelming her with choices as she got older. For example, when she moved to the nursing unit temporarily, I knew enough to go ahead and make the decision to store her furniture and just say, "I'll call the movers to store your furniture," instead of saying, "Do you think we ought to store your furniture?" There were some times that she wanted to delegate the decision-making process and other times that she wanted to collaborate (Nakasima et al. 2004). We established a unique rhythm that does not necessarily translate to other caregiving situations, and these differences must be respected.

Both of us agreed that sometimes we really didn't want another choice to make, and it was a gift for someone we trusted to decide for us. Knowing when those times were (and were not) required a deep connection with one another.

I could have gone into more depth in a number of areas, but then this chapter would have become a book. I have just completed with three other colleagues a book on elder advocacy (Huber et al. 2008). Had I made this chapter longer, we could have delved into the larger issues of how the healthcare system doesn't work well (Vladeck 2004) and concerns about age-segregated communities, housing options, and case management. But an interesting addendum would be the many times I have used my professional knowledge base in helping Aunt Doris. For example, when the CCRC was considering building another condo, I was able to arm Aunt Doris and her friends with the latest research on life care regulation. Or when Aunt Doris explained how difficult it was to move from one facility to the next, I could tell her about concepts in the literature such as "transfer trauma" and give her words to use for what she was experiencing. As we named what was happening to her, she had the language to normalize her experiences.

From my experience in writing this chapter, I have found it very helpful to share the story Aunt Doris and I continued to live. I am glad that I've had the chance to write most of the story before she died because it is like a play that leaves the reader a bit up in the air, leaving it up to his or her imagination as to what will happen next. As I thought about the story, I remembered a conversation Aunt Doris and I had when she was still wondering about whether to move to the residence. It was about six months before she made the decision. At one point, she said she'd been a planner all her life and that at that moment she didn't know what the plan should be. Moreover, I used what I learned from a colleague at the School of Social Work who taught qualitative research. I said, "Aunt Doris, there's a name for that, and it's called trusting emergence." From then on, whenever we had to live one day at a time because we had no idea what would happen next, we would smile at one another and say, "Let's trust emergence today."

REFERENCES

Alinsky, S. 1971. *Rules for Radicals*. New York: Vintage.

Beers, M. H. 2000–2001. Age-related changes as a risk factor for medication-related problems. *Generations* 24 (4): 22–27.

Chapin, R. and Cox, E.O. 2001. Changing the paradigm: Strengths-based and empowerment-oriented social work with frail elders. *Journal of Gerontological Social Work* 36 (3/4): 165–179.

Cherry, R. 1993. Community presence and nursing home quality care: Ombudsman as a complementary role. *Journal of Health and Social Behavior* 34: 336–345.

Cole, T. R. and Thompson, B. 2001–2002. Introduction: Anti-aging—Are you for it or against it? *Generations* 25 (4): 6–8.

Dudley, J. R. 2000. Confronting stigma within the services system. *Social Work* 45 (5): 449–455.

Ezell, M. 2001. *Advocacy in the Human Services.* Belmont, Cal.: Brooks/Cole.

Feinberg, J. L. 2000–2001. Introduction: Ensuring appropriate, effective and safe medication for older people. *Generations* 24 (4): 5–7.

Franks, M., Lund, D. A., Poulton, D., and Caserta, M. S. 2004. Understanding hoarding behavior among older adults: A case study approach. *The Journal of Gerontological Social Work* 42 (3/4): 17–107.

Huber, R., Nelson, H. W., Netting, F. E., and Borders, K. 2008. *Elder Advocacy: Knowledge and Skills Across Settings.* Pacific Grove, Cal.: Brooks/Cole.

Marx, J. I., Solomon, J. C., and Miller, L. Q. 2004. Gift wrapping ourselves: The final gift exchange. *Journal of Gerontologist* 59B: S274–S280.

McCoy, J. P. 1944. *Swing the Big-Eyed Rabbit.* New York: E.P. Dutton.

McCoy, J. P. 1950. *Big as Life.* New York: Harper.

McCoy, J. P. 1954. *Love for a Stranger.* New York: Avon.

McCoy, J. P. 1971. *The Secret Doorways.* New York: Dell.

Morgan, G. 1986. *Images of Organization.* Newbury Park, Cal.: Sage.

Nakasima, M., Chapin, R., Macmillan, K., and Zimmerman, M. 2004. Decision making in long-term care approaches used by older adults and implications for social work practice. *Journal of Gerontological Social Work* 43 (4): 79–102.

Netting, F. E. 1998. Interdisciplinary practice and the geriatric care manager. *Geriatric Case Management Journal* 8 (1): 20–24.

Netting, F. E. and Unks, R. P. 1984. Life care: An emerging industry in need of professional scrutiny. *The Journal of Applied Gerontology* 3 (1): 20–33.

Netting, F. E. and Williams, F. G. 1996. Case manager–physician collaboration: Implications for professional identify, roles and relationships. *Health and Social Work* 21 (3): 216–224.

Netting, F. E. and Williams, F. G. 1998. Can we prepare the next generation of geriatric social workers to collaborate in primary care physician practices? *Journal of Social Work Education* 34 (2): 195–210.

Netting, F. E. and Wilson, C. C. 1994. CCRC oversight: Implications for public regulation and private accreditation. *Journal of Applied Gerontology* 13 (3): 250–266.

Netting, F. E. and Wilson, C. C. 2006. Continuing care retirement communities. In B. J. Berkman (Ed.), *Oxford Handbook of Social Work in Aging,* 667–675. New York: Oxford University Press.

Penning, M. J. 2002. Hydra revisited: Substituting formal for self- and informal in-home care among older adults with disabilities. *The Gerontologist* 42 (1): 4–16.

Reuss, G. F., Dupuis, S. L., and Whitfield, K. 2005. Understanding the experience of moving a loved one to a long-term care facility: Family members' perspectives. *Journal of Gerontological Social Work* 46 (1): 17–46.

Rosenblum, K. E. and Travis, T.-M. C. 2000. *The Meaning of Difference,* 2d ed. Boston: McGraw-Hill.

Rubenstein, L. Z. and Josephson, K. R. 2002–2003. Rick factors for falls: A central role in prevention. *Generations* 26 (4): 15–21.

Schein, E. 1992. *Organizational Culture and Leadership,* 2d ed. San Francisco: Jossey-Bass.

Schneider, R. L. and Lester, L. 2001. *Social Work Advocacy.* Belmont, Cal.: Brooks/Cole.

Tennestedt, S. L. 2002–2003. Introduction: "I've fallen and . . . ." *Generations* 26 (4): 5–6.

Thomas, N. D. 1997. Hoarding: Eccentricity or pathology: When to intervene. *Journal of Gerontological Social Work* 29 (1): 45–55.

Vladeck, F. W. 2004. Beyond one hip fracture at a time: Rethinking aging services. *Journal of Gerontological Social Work* 42 (3/4): 151–162.

Wang, D. 2004. Service delivery and research considerations for the 85+ population. *Journal of Gerontological Social Work* 43 (1): 5–17.

APPENDIX

Dear Ms. Jones:

Thank you so much for keeping in touch with me during the time that my aunt, Doris McCoy, has been a patient at your Rehabilitation Hospital. As you know, she has many friends, nieces, nephews and cousins who have been very interested in how she is doing. Your communication with me has provided an avenue for keeping us all informed of her progress, and we are most appreciative.

I spent this weekend with Aunt Doris and we were very encouraged by what happened. I asked her permission to write this letter so that you could share this information with the rehab team which meets on Tuesday. Since Tuesday is almost upon us, I'm faxing this to you, with copies to both her primary physician and her rehab physician. I hope that I have not left someone out (sometimes it is difficult to sort out who all the providers are), so please share this information with any other physician and with the rehab team members that are involved in her care.

Her primary care physician visited Aunt Doris on Saturday and he indicated that she would continue at the rehab hospital for awhile, then return to her apartment. We told him that the rehab team had recommended assisted living for Aunt Doris. Since Aunt Doris and I had spent a long time talking about this option prior to his arrival, we talked with him about the pros and cons of giving up her apartment. We agreed that Aunt Doris should remain in the hospital until she could be discharged to her apartment with the appropriate in-home services necessary to continue her recovery.

Let me hasten to say that this decision was not made lightly. We recognize the risks that being in an apartment may pose to anyone who has a history of falls, and we understand that the rehab team is focusing on her safety. However, we realize that a person can fall in assisted living units as well. Essentially, wherever Aunt Doris is, she will have to be extremely careful. Since everyone is concerned about her safety, it is essential to develop a plan that will transition her in as safe a manner as possible.

On a personal note, Aunt Doris is a very realistic person who has been very intentional about making hard decisions such as moving to a retirement community, getting hearing aids, giving up driving, etc. She has always done this with grace and courage, realizing that as all of us age these types of accommodations often have to be made. She also realizes that moving to assisted living is an option if she goes back to her apartment and finds that she does not feel safe there. Moving to assisted living and giving up her apartment is very symbolic, however, and her primary care physician and I felt that her wishes to return there must be honored.

Obviously, Aunt Doris is very capable of telling you all of this herself, and I am copying this to her in case I have misrepresented in any way. We decided, however, that is was easier for me to communicate this information to the rehab team, so that she can focus on her therapy.

When we talked last week you indicated that March 29 was the scheduled discharge date. That date is approximately 20 days post acute hospitalization which should be covered 100% by Medicare. In addition, I believe that there would be up to 80 additional days covered at 80% Medicare as long as at least three hours of skilled level care are needed per day. Since Aunt Doris has Blue Cross secondary, that should cover the 20% not covered by Medicare once her 20 days are up. We are assuming, therefore, that as long as she is making progress in the rehab hospital and that she has a documented need for at least three hours of skilled care per day that it would be possible to keep her longer than March 29 and that her care would be covered by Medicare and Blue Cross. If these assumptions are incorrect, please let me know.

In terms of discharge, it would be helpful to have a new projected date so that she will have an idea of when she would return to her apartment. Certainly we don't want to jeopardize her in any way and therefore need the discharge plan to cover the full range of services that she will need. I was not certain which physician would be signing the orders for the discharge plan, but assume that it will be her rehab physician in consultation with her primary care physician. I am assuming that it is the rehab physician who is responsible for setting the discharge date.

I am sure that there are additional considerations and issues that haven't been covered. Please let me know what we need to do at this point. Today and Tuesday it will be easier to catch me at my work number which is 804-828-0404.

We cannot thank you enough for your assistance. Please convey my sincere appreciation to all the rehab team members and the other staff who have and are continuing to provide care for Aunt Doris.

Sincerely,
F. Ellen Netting
(niece of Doris McCoy)
cc: Doris McCoy

NINE

Closing Muriel's House

Caring for My Mother

KING E. DAVIS

DESCRIPTION OF CAREGIVER

Until 1992, Mother lived alone in a midwestern state while I lived with my wife and three children just south of Washington, D.C. Mom came to live with my nuclear family near my fiftieth birthday, a milestone for me because few men in my family had lived to this age. When Mother became disabled, two of my children were attending college and the third was completing high school. Mom, age seventy-two, was a full-time seamstress. On leave from a state university school of social work, I was the state mental health commissioner. My wife was a private geriatric in-home consultant for clients with disabilities. We lived in a large suburban home with many large oak trees. We led very active lives in our community, church, and circle of neighbors and friends. Ours was a close family, and the departure of our older children was difficult and rewarding. My mother's need for care came suddenly at a period of transition for our entire family, but particularly for my wife.

Within just a few weeks of completing my doctorate in Boston in 1972, I accepted a position to manage the state's community mental health system. We had a two-year-old son, and my wife was in the third trimester of her second pregnancy. Our parents (although divorced) lived very independent and productive lives, many miles away. I don't recall discussing the possibility that one of our parents would become totally dependent on us.

I entered the doctoral program after a four-year tour in the Army Social Work Service. My wife was an occupational therapist and an Army officer. We worked in a large military hospital that provided acute health and mental health treatment and some rehabilitation to severely wounded Viet Nam soldiers and their dependents.

DESCRIPTION OF FAMILY MEMBER CARED FOR

Muriel's Heritage

Muriel was born on April 6, 1920, in a small wood-framed house with white-washed walls in Danbury, a dusty lumber mill town in the Petit Jean Mountains of south-central Arkansas. Muriel's extended family was brought to Danbury as slaves before Arkansas's statehood in 1840 (Banks 1959) and remained despite many traumatic economic and emotional losses. Mother's family moved to Townsend, Oklahoma, when the Depression closed the mill.

Muriel's mother, grandmother, and grandfather obtained service sector jobs in Townsend, and her older sister and other relatives soon followed. Subsequent joblessness and poverty pushed her parents toward a divorce, bitter in both the emotional and legal sense. The Depression took away the fragile but stable economic base that had sustained the large family for almost 100 years; they lost their rented home and most of their land and the spiritual moorings that had provided sustenance, endurance, and identity.

Muriel dreamed of owning a home, feeling that ownership guaranteed economic security and spiritual balance. Over time, emotional fissures developed between Muriel and her family members. She resisted the efforts of her youngest son to help her reconnect with her father, and when he died, she had not spoken to him for more than forty years. Muriel remained intensely bitter about her father's alleged failure to participate in the care of his children (see Bailey 1994; Barnett and Baruch 1987; Daly 1995; Dowd 2000; W. Johnson 1998).

Muriel Becomes a Wife and Mother

Muriel followed her mother and migrated to Ft. Allen in 1938 to seek work. She became pregnant within a year, married the child's father in 1940, and had their second child two years later. When her Army husband went to South Korea in 1942, Muriel and her sons moved to Townsend to live with her mother and seven other adult relatives in a two-bedroom duplex, across the street from other relatives. The overcrowding disturbed Muriel.

Muriel looked forward to her husband's return, expecting to purchase a home together in Townsend or Ft. Allen, Arkansas. This move would emancipate her from the dominance of her older female relatives. She dutifully saved the money her husband sent from his gambling, eventually collecting $7,000 she hid in her grandmother's home. Although his letters described his dreams of home ownership, when discharged Muriel's husband took the money and abandoned her and their sons. After several years of separation, depression, and failed efforts to reconcile, Muriel obtained a divorce without a legal petition for a financial settlement, alimony, or child support for her sons. Her ex-husband ignored her repeated personal appeals for financial assistance, but she did not seek legal assistance. She wanted a stable lifestyle for her family, but her meager salary of $18 biweekly afforded no opportunity to live independently.

Muriel's House

In 1950, she fixated on a newspaper story about the construction of a new housing area in Townsend and began to dream of living in a house away from the emotional and physical hazards of a crowded inner city on the outermost fringe of the colored community. Townsend had a long history of racial conflict that resulted in the burning of the entire colored sections of the city and all of its businesses (H. Johnson 1998). Muriel knew colored families who lived through this violence, and she thought that it would be safer to live further away from the restored sections. The closest bus stop was more than 3 miles away, a distance she walked twice daily.

Every house on the two streets of the new housing tract was the same, differentiated only by the color of the exterior paint selected by the contractor. The smaller homes sold for $5,200 and the larger homes for $7,200. The downpayment on the new two-bedroom house was slightly over $1,000. Muriel secured a loan on Monday, March 17, 1951, just two weeks shy of her thirtieth birthday. Rather than celebrating, she worked extra hours, cooking and cleaning for European American families so that she could earn extra. She wanted to prepare for her new home and its attendant independence.

The form of Muriel's downpayment brought forth much humor and suspicion. She used ten hundred-dollar bills with her loan application, each without presidential faces. On every bill her husband sent to her from Korea, he cut out the president's face to personalize and prevent their deposit. By the end of her bank transaction, Muriel had obtained a new house—the first in her immediate family—a thirty-year mortgage, and a reputation for the unusual form of downpayment.

The home allowed Muriel and her sons to break an inveterate cycle of renting that marked the lives of most low-income people in the United States, particularly people of color (Conley 1999). Importantly, the purchase of her own home brought Muriel a share of the nation's wealth, a higher standard of independence, an opportunity to borrow on her equity in times of financial shortages, and a source of financial and spiritual comfort for Muriel and her family for the next fifty-seven years. Muriel's home became the epicenter of her consciousness, spirit, sense of connection, and linkage to her neighbors and her church and the source of mutual linkages to new neighbors who became lifelong friends.

Muriel was an attractive African American woman, about 4-foot-11 and near 100 pounds. She took pride in her ability to maintain her small size, despite excess sweets, salts, and fats. Each morning she arose at 5:30 A.M., dressed herself in an excessively starched white uniform, and made a single cup of coffee. Within an hour, Muriel joined other service workers at the bus stop. She called this daily routine "catching the mule." The daily bus ride was marked by spirited conversations, news, stories, and humorous exchanges between passengers and the driver, fostering and enriching lifelong friendships.

With an elementary school education, Muriel read a copy of the local black newspaper each week and the local white daily paper that she obtained from her employer. Continuing the tradition among Arkansas migrants, she read everything—articles, editorials, want ads, and sales—displaying her appreciation for the recently gained ability and right to read.

Muriel's Health and Employment

Throughout her early years, Muriel's health appeared good, and she exuded energy that belied the excessive demands of caring for her employers' children and households and her own. She often remarked that she had two families—"one white and one black"—that shared dependency on her. As she aged, Muriel experienced a number of chronic health problems: severe periodontal disease, duodenal ulcers, hypertension, and high cholesterol. Although these diseases were not seen as related in the 1960s when they first appeared, by the 1990s medical literature began to identify numerous causal connections

(Windsor et al. 2005). For almost twenty-five years, Muriel saw the same physician, a Jewish internist. Their professional relationship developed over the years into a mutual friendship based on respect, with each seeing the other as a colleague. They would have been friends—a devout black Catholic woman and a reformed Jewish physician—had they met outside the doctor–patient relationship.

Muriel confided about various body changes—fatigue, loss of balance, bleeding gums, and a persistent problem with a hernia—details about her inner spiritual life, and details about a period of depression and a soured second marriage she believed caused many of her physical ailments. Dr. Levenson successfully repaired the hernia, offered her emotional support during her extensive periodontal surgery and recovery, and unfortunately did not recognize a causal connection between these health problems and her chronic ulcer disease (see Windsor et al. 2005).

Later, concerned about her exceptionally high cholesterol readings and hypertension, Dr. Levenson shared findings from the Framingham Heart Study (Dhingra et al. 2006; Kannel 2000; Seshadri et al. 2006). He believed that she could prevent some of her health problems if she stopped smoking. Muriel altered her diet and reluctantly accepted antihypertensive medication. For her subsequent increase in depression, Muriel accepted Valium and valerian root, a lower-cost antianxiety medicine. For more than two decades, Muriel and Levenson worked collaboratively to maintain her physical and emotional health with considerable success. When Muriel stopped smoking, so did Levenson, because he would not have anyone to borrow cigarettes from.

Dr. Levenson retired in 1989, transferred his practice to a young physician new to community practice, and moved out of state. Muriel was unable to establish a similar relationship with his replacement. She had bad feelings and judgmental interactions with the new doctor. He was too hurried and curt, accepted too many patients, required a larger copayment, and was unfriendly. There was no coffee together, no sharing snacks or family information, and no evening phone calls to remind her to refill a needed prescription. The new physician also replaced the office staff, stable for thirty years. The "new man" did not care about her well-being and could never replace Dr. Levenson as a physician or friend.

Without calls to remind her, Muriel missed her 1990 annual physical, her first missed appointment in nearly twenty-five years, nor did she renew her antihypertensive prescription medication or pay close attention to the factors exacerbating her duodenal ulcer. Gradually, Muriel slipped back into her former, less healthy pattern, except smoking, and did not seek medical attention for two years.

Muriel complained frequently of a weakened arthritic knee, blaming it for her clumsiness. Muriel had several minor automobile accidents and blamed the other driver and failed brakes. Differences in opinion about responsibility rekindled intense, usually dormant conflicts between Muriel and her aunt, reducing interactions and mutual support at a crucial time. Muriel did not share these accidents with her sons or make any associations between the accident and her own deteriorating health. Muriel also began falling down more frequently.

Muriel shared her deep emotional loss when Dr. Levenson retired and her frustration with declining health, particularly her inability to maintain her balance on a weakened knee, with a long-term female friend, who accepted her conclusions and interpretations.

Generally, Muriel believed that she was doing well both physically and economically in 1992. She enjoyed visits to her grandchildren every other year and her new and rewarding work as a cook, maid, and seamstress. With agile hands, she was highly skilled at making shirts and other apparel for her employer, elaborate robes for her minister, and dresses for neighbors. Recently purchasing a knitting machine, she made original outfits, selling to customers across the city. For her seventieth birthday, her employer gave her a new Ford Falcon. By age seventy-two, earning far more than she ever, she ignored her not-so-subtle health changes.

Muriel's Visit for Graduation

The complexity of the McCall's pattern that my youngest daughter selected had become a source of tension in our family. She concluded, "Grandma does this all the time, almost every day. She'll finish it in just a few hours, just in time for high school graduation. She won't even need a pattern." Unlike other years, when Muriel arrived in May 1992, she seemed excessively tired, somewhat disheveled, and emotionally flat. We drove the short distance from the airport in almost total silence. Previously, she complained about losing her way in the complex labyrinth of the Atlanta airport, where she changed planes. When she descended the stairs into the basement sewing room of our house, she was almost mute, visibly anxious, and unresponsive to the anticipatory glee her youngest grandchild expressed. She sought out a comfortable chair instead of approaching the sewing machine and managing the complex pattern. Muriel's absence of enthusiasm and energy was evident to everyone. We realized something was wrong with Muriel when we discovered she had brought no matching clothing.

After graduation was over and the dress, barely held together with pins, was put away, Muriel's employer called to share his concerns. She had gone to his house on two Sunday evenings in the past month, although she never worked Sundays; she had been unable to complete routine sewing; and she seemed unable to manage simple tasks. He was concerned about her and the severe alterations in her mood, behaviors, and attention to detail, formerly compulsive. Unsure what to do, he needed to share with her family. Within a few days, Muriel's best friend in Townsend also called with concerns about her friend's changing behavior: failure to lock her doors and put her car in the garage and heightened suspiciousness. The observations by Muriel's local support system, her family, and her employer convinced us to schedule an immediate physical examination and neurological assessment.

DESCRIPTION OF CAREGIVING EXPERIENCE

By default, I became the caregiver. I would have preferred another option, but few existed in her small Oklahoma community. Over several months I exhausted my search for an alternative means of caring for my mother. In her most lucid moments, my mother voiced strong opposition to available nursing care, where several friends lived their last years. I would not force her to live in an environment she found threatening and barren. Moving her to the East Coast became the best option but displaced her from the environment and the cultural nuances that sustained her for almost a half century.

In 1992, Muriel's two sons were ages fifty-four and fifty. Her older son, Jim, lived in California, had been divorced for nearly ten years, and had two adult sons. One son lived with him periodically, and the other was in the Navy. Jim had just recently been laid off by the company where he had designed store interiors for almost twenty-five years. He was devastated by the precipitous job and income losses. He considered bankruptcy because of the difficultly of obtaining a comparable position, which he attributed partly to age discrimination.

I, the younger son and a tenured social work professor at a local university in Virginia, was on leave while I served as the state mental health commissioner, a politically tenuous position. It was the second year of an intense four-year term. My wife and I were again in marriage counseling to solve a number of long-standing communication problems. Because the relationship between my wife and my mother weakened over the years, I recognized that any caregiving probably would increase the marital strain. However, I knew I would have to play a major supportive and financial role in Muriel's care.

Muriel also had extended family who could not or did not help. For example, an aunt had never forgiven Muriel for not lending her the military savings her husband sent. Muriel's older sister lived in St. Louis and was unable to assist because of poor health. My brother and I relied on church members and neighbors while we explored options for her long-term care.

Medical Care and Findings

As a geriatric occupational therapist, my wife immediately recognized many of Muriel's symptoms. Jim feared that Muriel, like our maternal grandmother, might have dementia and spend her final years in a nursing home. We agreed I would immediately make an appointment with a friend, a geriatrician, and Jim would convince Muriel to take a physical exam while she was visiting my family. We enlisted the support of our half-sister, who had a close relationship with Muriel. Muriel agreed and compensated well before the exam.

Dr. Southall, the geriatrician, had a kind, soft, and reassuring manner. His graying hair and dark eyes and interest produced memories of Levenson. Like many geriatricians, Dr. Southall gave her more time, asked her opinions, and invited her participation in the exam and planning. When he proposed she should get an immediate full medical and neurological exam, she willingly cooperated. Dr. Southall's older nurse was helpful in getting Muriel undressed because she could not follow the doctor's instructions. Muriel agreed to Dr. Southall's suggestion that I stay for the neurological and mental status exams. Dr. Southall recognized without blaming that our family exhibited patterns of delayed help seeking, typical in African American families (Ayanian 1994; Broman 1987; W. Johnson 1998; Neighbors and Jackson 1984; Snowden 2000).

The disappointing implications of the exams showed on Dr. Southall's face in less than half an hour. Muriel was unable to maintain her attention, had little short-term memory, and could not reason well. Unaware of the date or month, she was unable to follow instructions to remove her clothing or give her phone number or grandchildren's names. The signs of dementia were devastatingly clear.

Her computed axial tomography scans illustrated that Muriel had suffered a series of cerebral strokes over the years, their dates, duration, and number impossible to determine. Probably caused by untreated hypertension, they affected her cognitive functioning. He hypothesized that her falls, automobile accidents, and late evening confusion were all symptomatic of vascular dementia, the culprit of untreated hypertension.

Dr. Southall cautioned me that Muriel would be unable to live alone. We needed to make decisions fairly soon because the vascular dementia and its associated cognitive losses would advance at an unknown but steady pace. Muriel did not comprehend the severity of her health status, saying she wanted to return to her home, her job, and her church as soon as possible. She became slightly hostile when Dr. Southall said she could no longer manage these responsibilities alone. Dr. Southall stressed that we should immediately seek permanent help. I shared this information by telephone with Jim.

Short-Term Care

Based on the diagnoses and prognoses, we identified and discussed five issues that required our mutual consideration and collaboration:

- Honoring our mother's desire to remain in her home
- Locating and assessing in-home care in her community
- Identifying external sources to meet the cost of care
- Managing our mother's care from a distance
- Accessing retirement and disability benefits from her employers to help defray the cost of supportive care

We avoided discussing long-term plans because neither Jim nor I could handle the associated emotional pain. Nor were we ready for the imminent restructuring of our mother's life, which signaled a resounding change in our own lives. We sought a short-term solution.

Muriel compensated sufficiently to return home soon after her medical exam. Her best friend arranged follow-up healthcare and obtained daily support from an adult neighbor to help Muriel around the house. Neighbors provided transportation and assisted Muriel with cooking, cleaning, and personal care, and her friend checked on her daily. Within weeks of her return, Muriel's level of suspicion and accusations increased substantially. The presence and assurance of her widowed aunt and long-term friend helped maintain her fragile short-term support structure. Jim and I agreed that we should find support that would maintain Muriel in her own home. Once interested, Muriel's employer no longer called. As a social worker, I agreed to meet with various Townsend agencies to explore the availability of needed services.

Jim, emotionally closer to Muriel, was frozen by the demands associated with her illness and the major changes in her cognition. He kept in touch with her by telephone. I believed the major reason he didn't visit was his emotional discomfort with watching her degenerate. Distance probably helped him deny the painful severity and irreversibility of her illness. Jim's emotional needs translated into his excessive and financially impossible care standards, our Achilles' heel throughout our caregiving years. Jim seemed to need perfection in exchange for our inability to reverse Muriel's decline and our failure in seeing it coming. Both my brother and my maternal aunt seemed unwilling at times to accept the level of care that I could afford. My inability to meet their expectations gave rise to my incredible sense of guilt and failure. Here I was the mental health commissioner and a social worker, but I could not provide a higher level of care for my own mother. For years, I engaged in an intensive and exhaustive search for the best care, tempered by the reality of cost.

In-Home Services

The first issue became one of examining the existing public policies in Muriel's local community and state that might be helpful. Oklahoma had a series of public policies that offered older citizens a comprehensive range of in-home services. These services included wraparound services, such as in-home assistance with meals and activities of daily living, and day care services. Under these policies, Muriel qualified for a caregiver five days a week, but our family would be responsible for self-care on weekends. This policy offered clear benefits that would help keep Muriel in her own home. Muriel's close neighborhood friend offered to provide this supplemental care each weekend and to ensure that Muriel's house was secure each evening after the in-home worker left. Muriel's widowed aunt offered to allow her to stay in her home each weekend. In addition, our half sister, who lived in another city about an hour away, offered to allow Muriel to come to live with her. However, all of these care plans depended on whether the Oklahoma legislature would renew the legislation that covered these policies in July 1993. Without that supportive legislation, it would have been impossible for Jim and me to meet the costs of daily in-home care or obtain high-quality nursing home care.

Exploration began with Muriel and me visiting nearly ten in-home services and ten day care services. For me, it was important for Muriel to see each facility, have input, and meet the potential caregivers so I could assess their interaction with her. In my visits, I looked for a sense of warmth, caring, activities, skills, and knowledge of aging and dementia. Although I understood the progressive decline of the disease, I felt guilty for considering programs that did not offer rehabilitation services. In my interviews of prospective in-home service providers, I also considered how much they respected Muriel's home and lifestyle. I noticed whether they talked to her during the interview and asked about how they handled absences and their attitudes about toileting accidents.

The interviews clarified that long-distance caregiving carried a number of major risks, all of which made it more difficult for Jim to accept our previous decision to obtain help for Mother. Jim wanted guaranteed care with no risks. Balancing his desires with the obvious risks was stressful and difficult.

During the next several months, Muriel's local relatives and friends helped her with meals and safety while Jim and I explored a variety of long-term care options. I monitored her care, frequently conferring with Dr. Southall and her local physician. Month by month, Muriel deteriorated.

Planning for Long-Term Care

When the Oklahoma legislature allowed the in-home care legislation to expire, funding stopped, and our hopes and plans for in-home care vanished. Muriel would have to move from her home by June 1993. Now, Jim and I had to choose between her long-term care options. When we met in May 1993 at Muriel's, she announced it was time for her to go to work, although it was a Sunday evening. Muriel became agitated and tearful when we told her that it was the wrong day and time for work. In response to my suggestion that she consider retiring, Muriel said her employer depended on her. His needs took priority. The employer had had no contact with the family for several months. Efforts to obtain retirement, disability, or severance from either employer were unsuccessful, although Muriel worked for each for almost thirty years. Her Social Security was her only income, less than $300 a month.

In the next several hours, Muriel was unable to sleep, remained agitated, and lost cognitive functioning hourly. Throughout the night, Jim and I reviewed the various short-term options. What was eminently clear was that we could not leave our mother alone again. The risks were too great, and her needs exceeded what her neighbors and older friends could provide; therefore, she could not remain at home. By morning, Muriel decided to retire, and Jim and I agreed to declare her incompetent, seek a twenty-eight-day inpatient evaluation, and apply for Medicaid.

However, from the outset it was clear that the responsibility would fall more on my shoulders than Jim's. Jim did not feel that he could care for Mother in his home because his demanding new job forced him to spend several days and nights away each week. Because Jim was divorced, he insisted that I was in a better position to care for our mother. I felt caught emotionally and financially between the various needs and perceptions of my mother, my older brother, and my wife. It appeared at times that because I was a social worker, my family assumed that I was adept and comfortable in managing the diverse needs of my family without conflict or loss.

We both agreed that it would be in Muriel's best interest to move to Virginia to live temporarily with me. Because I was the commissioner of mental health, I had access to information about long-term care facilities licensed by the State of Virginia. I also asked my staff to recommend high-quality placements. To my dismay, few places were available that I could afford and that provided good-quality care.

After twenty-eight days of inpatient evaluation and care, I returned to Muriel's home to carry out the relocation plans. On a number of occasions, it was necessary to have our relatives be quite specific about their expectations, in light of what was realistic for me. When my older aunts expressed the expectation that mother receive private care around the clock, I had to explain why that was not possible. At the same time, it was important to show that the level of care would meet her needs and provide safety. Increasingly, my role was to identify, explain, explore, and share options—including the risks and benefits—with my relatives and my mother's closet friends. Ultimately, too, my role was to reach and pursue decisions that were in the best interests of my mother (see Draper 1998; Harris 1993; Lee 1992; Lutzky and Knight, 1994; Opie 1994; Parsons 1997; Winakur 2005). Here were roles that were congruent with my training and ones in which I could find comfort.

The family as a whole did not convene to reach a decision. Muriel's time in the hospital had ended. She had shown little progress and in fact had developed a heightened sense of suspiciousness, almost paranoia. She could not live alone again, and the only viable options that would have allowed her to live in her own home had evaporated. I expected that my mother's presence in my home would result in an incredible strain on an already weakened marriage, but I could not identify any other emergency options. I made the decision to move her into our home with great risk.

Muriel's Move to Our Home

My mother and I boarded a plane the next afternoon, heading toward Virginia. At the airport, Muriel told me that she needed to go to the bathroom. When she exited the women's bathroom, she was no longer wearing any clothing. She had removed all her clothing, and she had forgotten how to put it back on. Miraculously, I found a way to secure the bathroom door and help my mother with her clothes. This became the first of many challenges that reflected major role reversals between my mother and me. The major challenge was how to balance her fleeting hold on independence with her need for personal dignity and safety. The ghost challenge for me was how to balance Muriel's long-term needs with the needs of my spouse and our strained marriage. Other challenges included how to pay for care and involve my own children in caring for their grandmother. Within a few hours, we arrived in Rutherford and made the ride to my home, again in silence, reminiscent of her visit during my youngest daughter's graduation. This time, however, there was no greeting awaiting her arrival.

A local day care organization, owned by a social work professor, offered to help with Muriel's daily care. The agency staff member came at 7:30 A.M. and remained until 6:30 P.M. I provided care for my mother in the evenings and on weekends. Bathing and toileting my mother in the evenings became very difficult. I was fearful that she would fall in the shower and felt uncomfortable seeing her without clothing. She did not seem to notice. My reticence dissipated quickly. The most difficult problems came from the agency. Several times in two months, the agency staff member failed to arrive. As a result, I could not work or travel on those days because I could not obtain substitute care. I became angry with the owner and the staff member, who seemed unconcerned about her failure to appear for work.

Muriel's Move to St. Thomas

Within a few weeks, it was clear that I needed to search for a permanent placement outside my home. However, I was disappointed at the quality of care available and frustrated by the high costs. Within two months, my wife suggested a more permanent, high-quality placement. The Catholic Diocese of Rutherford operated a small home, St. Thomas, for adults with disabilities, where my wife had patients. Mom's long tenure in the Catholic Church was helpful in getting her quick admittance and a reasonable monthly fee. Most of the other people in this home were able to provide some degree of self-care, and others were recovering from accidents or injury. My mother was clearly the most disabled of all the residents and needed a high level of personal assistance. The home charged modest extra payments for this added care. In return, they provided a private room and gave her lots of attention and affection. The other residents also helped with her care, as did volunteers from the Catholic churches in the community. I later installed a telephone line in my mother's room so she could receive calls from Jim and her friends and relatives. The first night my mother stayed at St. Thomas was the first night I slept soundly and comfortably in several months. The stress of her care had been physically and emotionally exhausting, as described in the literature (Chesler and Parry 2001; Cook et al. 1997; Fuller-Jonap and Haley 1995).

Dr. Southall became Muriel's primary care physician and saw her on a regular basis for the next two years. She responded well to his approach and seemed to identify with him as she had with Levenson. He prescribed tacrine (Marks 2006), an expensive experimental drug, to help her with her memory loss. The improvements in her cognition were remarkable. For at least a few months, Muriel became more outgoing, paid greater attention to her appearance, and seemed more conscious of her surroundings. The quality of her speech improved, and her thoughts were clearer for the first time in several years. She remembered more and asked clear questions about where she was and what had happened to her. She knew the names of the staff, other residents, and the administration. She asked about her grandchildren and her friends. Remarkably, she was able to discuss the changes that had occurred in her life over the past year. Muriel stayed on tacrine until she experienced severe physical side effects (Marks 2006). After she went off the medication, she lost the cognitive, emotional, and behavioral gains and increased interpersonal skills. I wondered whether she realized that tacrine was the last hope for regaining a modicum of functioning.

In November 1993, I took Muriel to California to visit Jim for Thanksgiving. She handled the outbound flight with comfort and relative ease. During her stay, she seemed to communicate reasonably well with Jim. However, the extent of her cognitive declines was shocking to him. He was not prepared to help her with personal care, such as toileting, dressing, and grooming. The reversal of roles was too difficult for him to accept. He avoided these tasks whenever he could. At the airport in San Francisco, Muriel defecated in her pants. The odor was so strong that it was impossible to ignore. There were no accommodations in the airport for such problems. Traveler's Aid could not help. The American Red Cross seemed confused by the problem. With Jim guarding the door, I changed my mother's clothing in the changing station reserved for babies in the airport. This episode was humorous for my brother and me, and our shared experience seemed to bring us closer together around the realities of our mother's needs. I felt that he better appreciated and respected my efforts of the past year.

Muriel's Move to a Private Home

After two years at St. Thomas, Muriel's disability clearly exceeded their capacity, and the director and staff recommended that she move to another class of care. She then moved to a small private home operated by a middle-aged African American woman. Thirteen men and women lived in this woman's home, some distance out from the city. The environment was more personal and homelike than St. Thomas. There were more family visitors. Rapidly, Muriel adjusted to the personal attention she received there. Muriel lived there, much like a family member, until her death in 1998. At her funeral services in her "mother church," many of her neighbors, fellow church members, and friends came to give their support and praise. We buried her in a cemetery plot that she purchased in Townsend.

Closing Muriel's Home

Muriel had accumulated fifty years of furniture, appliances, utensils, and clothing in her house. After she moved to Virginia, Jim and I agreed to meet in Townsend in 1994 to clear the house and make decisions about her assets. Jim and his son did not keep their promise, leaving me alone with the monumental physical and emotional tasks of clearing and closing Muriel's house before the end of the summer in 1994. That full week was the most emotionally draining time of my life. It took a week to find and exercise the emotional reserves to complete these tasks alone. Social work skills and knowledge did not change my deeply felt emotions. My initial anger and disappointment toward my older brother transformed into greater empathy as the week wore onward. I realized that he had become financially bankrupt and emotionally drained by the decision to put our mother in a hospital and move her to my home in Virginia. In some respects, I began to interpret my brother's failure to arrive as a gift, my first opportunity to spend a week alone in my mother's house. Solitude was an opportunity to find peace and spiritual balance with the decisions that had been made.

During that week, I waded through fifty years of papers, letters, and old bills. Mom had started stuffing money in the oddest places; money showed up periodically under the couch and in magazines, Bibles, shoes, and coat pockets. Going through her things, I learned more about the length, character, and extent of her cognitive gaps. She left a clear map of her cognitive decline. Merchants cashed Muriel's checks when she wrote in larger amounts than she owed and pestered her when the amount was lower. She left many other bills unpaid.

She had not deposited or cashed many of her paychecks for several months. These events were congruent with the timing of the automobile accidents. Mail was not opened. Muriel had failed to renew her health and life insurance coverage. She paid higher interest rates because she failed to respond to letters from various creditors. These papers helped to identify the month and year when her functional impairment became most evident. The connection between the loss of Muriel's relationship with her trusted physician and her cognitive decline was clear. Evident too was her denial, or perhaps more accurately her inability to recognize, that the changes in her functioning were caused not by arthritis but by major vascular changes that had a long and deleterious history in our family.

Had I missed these connections, too? Was there something in my training that I had not used that might have changed this situation? Also evident was the relationship between Muriel's inability to make the transition to a new physician and her increased vulnerability and cognitive risk. Could I have intervened earlier to buttress the relationship between Muriel and the new physician? While her friends, neighbors, fellow church members, and employers noted the changes in her levels of functioning, the degree of change had been incremental. It was not until there was a significant accumulation of problems that they became aware of the extent of her decline. No pattern emerged early or clearly enough to give an adequate warning to Muriel's support system. By the time Muriel's symptoms became evident, the irreversible cerebral damages from the silent ischemic strokes had taken place. Tracing this very clear path of decline was emotionally wrenching. I wept uncontrollably for what seemed hours during my week alone in my mother's house (see Winakur 2005; Winstersteen and Rasmussen 1997). Many of Muriel's neighbors and friends inquired about her health during my stay in her home. They called. Many came by to see how she was doing. In response, I opened her house and gave each of them and her church something. In less than a week, Muriel's house was physically empty but filled with remnants of spiritual gifts to her neighbors. The sentiments and caring of her aging neighbors and their genuine interests in her health reminded me of my earlier life in this neighborhood and the support from these same people.

At the end of the week, I stuffed Muriel's remaining personal items in her small Ford Falcon and started the drive from Oklahoma to Virginia. In the car were articles of clothing, pictures, her vintage coffee pot, and other items that she might recognize. Her house was clear, cleaned, and closed. I had agreed to rent her home to an elderly relative of one of her neighbors. The rent payment would be helpful in offsetting the monthly cost of Muriel's care not covered by her Social Security. Importantly, her house remained instrumental in defining this new phase of her life. Closing the door to her house brought a flood of emotion and tears, but it also brought a sense of spiritual completion that Muriel's wisdom, creativity, persistence, and knowledge had come full circle. Her house was a metaphor for her life, values, spirituality, life force, and contributions. It lives on to influence the lives of others.

ANALYSES AND IMPLICATIONS

A retrospective analysis is helpful in identifying the implications for social work of my family's odyssey. During the intense crisis of care, it was not possible for me to think about social work or my role as a social worker. The tasks and demands were too intimate, immediate, and personal. However, several questions related to a retrospective analysis emerged:

- What factors explain the differences in the level of participation in family caregiving (Winakur 2005)?
- To what extent is participation in caregiving influenced by gender (Harris 1993; Hirsch 1996; Lee 1992)?
- What is the relationship, if any, between occupation and participation in caregiving? More specifically, are social workers more inclined to participate in caregiving for an ill relative than people who are in other non–human service occupations?

In my family, each of these issues was pertinent and is addressed to some extent in the scholarly literature. The final set of questions revolves around what specific personal learning arose from my efforts to reach decisions about obtaining care for my mother and how this knowledge influenced the decisions about my own life. My experiences have several implications for other men and social workers (table 9.1).

The most significant feature of the literature on caregiving is the failure to address the participation of men (Barnett and Baruch 1987; Bristol and Gallagher 1986; Brotherson et al. 1986; Chase-Lansdale and Vinovskis 1995; Chesler and Parry 2001; Daly 1995; Fitting et al. 1986; Greif and Bailey 1990; Lefley 1997). It is certainly clear from the literature that caregiving is the responsibility of women in America. Male caregivers are a rarity. The same literature is even more limited on the role of African American men (Furstenburg 1995, 2000). There is little scientific knowledge or study about how African American

Table 9.1 Implications

	Issues and Problems	Strategies for Change
Individuals	Unfocused communication	Plan attention to health matters. Engage parents in discussion of changes in health status. Teach men caregiving skills.
Families	Delayed help seeking	Schedule annual health exams as a family. Increase frequency of contact with age.
Communities	Accurate health information	Build health information into church activities and awareness campaigns.
Practitioners	Termination of long-term relationships	Increase awareness of importance of personal ties by elderly clients. Pay greater attention to impact of change.
Researchers	Knowledge of male caregiving	Conduct qualitative and quantitative studies of how men participate.
Public policymakers	Absence of retirement support	Require retirement plans for domestic workers beyond Social Security.

men conceptualize or experience illness in a close relative and related caregiving patterns (Zarit et al. 1986). A significant portion of the literature in the past decade has indirectly sampled the perspectives of European American men on caregiving through surveys of their spouses (Coley and Chase-Lansdale 1999). The narrow focus in the literature reflects the view that defines caregiving in almost exclusively feminine terms (McConachie 1982; McNeil and Chabassol 1984; Seligman and Darling 1989).

In addition, the literature tends to conceptualize caregiving in negative terms. Caregiving performed by women is described as a burden and a source of stress and depression (Aneshensel and Pearlin 1987; Belcher 1988; Cook and Pickett 1987; Heller et al. 1997; Mastroyannopoulou et al. 1997; Opie 1994; Parsons 1997). Part of the conceptualization in the literature suggests that caregiving is a natural rather than acquired role. Furthermore, because caregiving is more naturally affiliated with the nurturing role of women, participation by men could be considered contrived, acquired, forced, or a reflection of gender confusion. Some researchers conclude that women have a "gendered moral obligation" to participate in all forms of caregiving (Kazak 1987; Opie 1994). The role obligation for women is considered so prominent in American society that they are unable to resist such participation even when they incur disabling stress or burden.

Men do not have such a moral obligation in American society. Men are less likely to experience the related stress, sense of burden, or guilt if they do not participate in caregiving. One researcher (Opie 1994) concludes that other work-related (instrumental) responsibilities are substituted for the nurturance role for men. The forced obligation of women to provide caregiving could be a major factor in their perceiving such roles as burdens accompanied by high levels of stress and depression.

A small number of studies (Bailey 1994; Chesler and Parry 2001; Dowd 2000; Fuller-Jonap and Haley 1995; Harris 1993; Howard 1998; Johnson 1998; Lutzky and Knight 1994; McBride and Darragh 1995; Opie 1994; Parsons 1997; Winstersteen and Rasmussen 1997) have identified high rates of stress, depression, and physical health problems in men who care for an elderly relative. However, related studies suggest that part of the explanation for the participation by men in caregiving is their inability to accept the condition of their relative. Compared with women, men seem to have more difficulty adjusting to severe physical and mental illness (Essex 1999; McConachie 1982; Winstersteen and Rasmussen 1997).

Gender also appears to differentiate how individuals respond to the tasks associated with caregiving (White 1994). Whereas women appear to manage by releasing their emotions, men tend to find comfort in accomplishing practical tasks (Heru 2000; Hirsch 1996; Lutzky and Knight 1994; Mastroyannopoulou et al. 1997). Some studies also suggest that the way that men respond to an ill family member reflects a set of defenses different from those seen in women. Men seem to manage these emotional conflicts through denial, rationalization, and reactivity.

The gaps in the literature on caregiving and gender and race are reflected in similar gaps in professional support, services, and approaches (Daly 1995; Draper 1998; Germain and Gitterman 1995; Heru 2000; Winakur 2005; Winstersteen and Rasmussen 1997). Very often support groups for relatives of ill family members focus exclusively on issues experienced by women or mothers (Belcher 1988; Chesler and Parry 2001; Cook 1988; Winakur 2005). Men often are assumed to have found effective ways to manage their responses to the illness because society generally exempts them from active participation and from the sense of guilt. Some studies point out that professionals' use of terms may tend to exclude men, resulting in serious communication gaps (Daly 1995; Draper 1998; Fitting et al. 1986; Harris 1993). When my mother was admitted to the hospital for twenty-eight days, the admission social worker asked whether I had a sister she could contact to obtain personal information about my mother. After I gently let her know that I would be the contact and source of information, she questioned whether I knew certain things about her condition. Similar issues arose when I met with the admitting physician and participated in the family support group, comprised only of women. Most of the discussions were based on women as caregivers—a fact in the United States.

In other instances, meetings and hours of service are constructed to meet the schedules of middle-class European American women rather than the work schedule of men in general and African American men in particular (Sagi and Sharon 1984). Even when both parents are employed full time, the rate of participation in caregiving by men is less than that of their spouses (Culp et al. 2000; Markowitz 1984; Walker 1992). As a result, the structure of organizations that provide services to caregivers may work against the active involvement of men in general and, because of transportation and wage loss issues, against lower-income African American men in particular.

Because caregiving tends to be conceptualized as principally a natural obligation of women, men who participate in caregiving violate societal norms. In one sense this violation suggests that unmarried men or men without sisters will seek out a woman to provide care for an ill relative to avoid violating the societal standard. In other instances, married men may transfer the caregiving role of their own aged relatives to their wives. In other instances, people may view men who participate actively in caregiving as less masculine (Bem 1974; Chesler and Parry 2001; Draper 1998; Fuller-Jonap and Haley 1995).

Overall, the literature does not provide adequate guidance for men who have a caregiving responsibility (Hearn 2002; Kim 2005). The absence of literature combined with societal disdain may increase the anxiety and maladaptive responses of men when they are asked to participate in the caregiving of aged relatives, children, or spouses. Men lack guidance and assistance in assuming their caregiving roles. These are areas where social workers can be of assistance (Kim 2005; Kraemer 1999).

Social work research must address how men conceptualize illness and what factors influence their participation in caregiving (Earl 2005; Kim 2005).

Such studies must focus on caregiving across race and social class boundaries. Findings from such studies must be structured into viable programs, services, approaches, and techniques to facilitate caregiving by men. Social workers need to develop skills that are helpful to men who are responding to illness and caregiving in defensive ways that are condoned by American society. Social work agencies also need to examine and explore such structural issues as hours of operation and the focus of existing programs to determine whether they are erecting barriers to male participation in caregiving.

I used my social work skills almost unconsciously to structure the various phases of my mother's life and to structure the way in which she remained a vital part of her neighborhood. I made sure that her neighbors had mementos from her home, no matter how small. I also made sure that her friends had an address and a telephone number for her. I sent cards on special occasions to them from her over the years she was in my care. I used my advocacy skills to straighten out the insensitive creditors who threatened to confiscate her home because she had been unable to make her meager payments. Social work skills in negotiation, reconciliation, and advocacy became important in salvaging part of the significance of her home. Knowledge of social policy was also instrumental in helping me establish her entitlement to supportive services in Virginia. Transfer of property rights, power of attorney, and eligibility for federal programs became part of the policy base that proved helpful. Aside from these social work skills and attitudes, I also learned a number of bitter lessons.

As parents age, the frequency, depth, and focus of communication with them become critically important. Conversations that once were centered on grandchildren or generic issues must increasingly be focused on how one's parents are managing changes in their lives: the retirement of a physician, death of a friend, preparation for retirement, response to an illness, or loss of functioning in some area. Adult children must engage their aging parents in such a way as to help them take preventive healthcare steps. Where prior relationships have been strained, such intervention is not easy to establish or maintain. Even with the constraints of geographic distance, these issues are nonetheless important.

Conceptual Frame of Reference

Winakur, a geriatrician, concluded there are more than 35 million Americans over the age of sixty-five who are residents of various healthcare facilities. Because of their illnesses (acute and chronic), their families must make a range of care decisions that determine quality of life. In some instances, the need to make healthcare decisions can arise suddenly, as was the case for me and my family. These sudden decisions come immediately after a life-altering accident, stroke, surgery, disease, or a heart attack. In other instances, the onset of the disability may be gradual, but the impact is acute. Depending on the level of residual disability, families may be forced to consider long-term care without adequate input from the person most affected. Winakur made a series of critical decisions about his father's care in an effort to increase quality of life and to avoid a range of mishaps that occur in medical care settings and can be life threatening. Based on his knowledge of healthcare, Winakur decided that it was in his father's best interest to be discharged home from an inpatient setting. While his father was hospitalized, Winakur closely monitored all aspects of his care and ensured that a family member was present at all times. Although in-home care with supports would not reverse the physical and cognitive deterioration, it appears to have prolonged his father's life.

It is important to identify, examine, and understand the processes families go through to reach a healthcare decision for a relative with a disability. Figure 9.1 is a theoretical conceptualization that proposes that familial decision making (dependent variable) is influenced by the complex interaction of three clusters of independent factors: family characteristics, number of prior hospital admissions or health crises, and characteristics of the healthcare system.

Within the family cluster, it is proposed that familial decision making is highly dependent on the type, amount, and accuracy of information families have at their disposal. Information seems to be closely related to the quality of decisions families must make. Families need accurate, understandable information about their relative's health conditions and the prognosis. Theoretically, the greater the amount and quality of the information available, the better the decisions that a family can reach. When Dr. Southall completed his exam of Muriel, his assessment of her current and future functioning was instrumental in the subsequent decisions my family made. Had our family received information about Muriel's health much earlier, the nature of our decisions, and perhaps her health, would have been different. A second factor in the family cluster that influences decision making is the level of impairment of the relative. If the level of impairment is severe, it is likely that the family's decision-making pathways will differ from those where the impairment is mild and of short duration. Muriel's level of impairment from vascular dementia

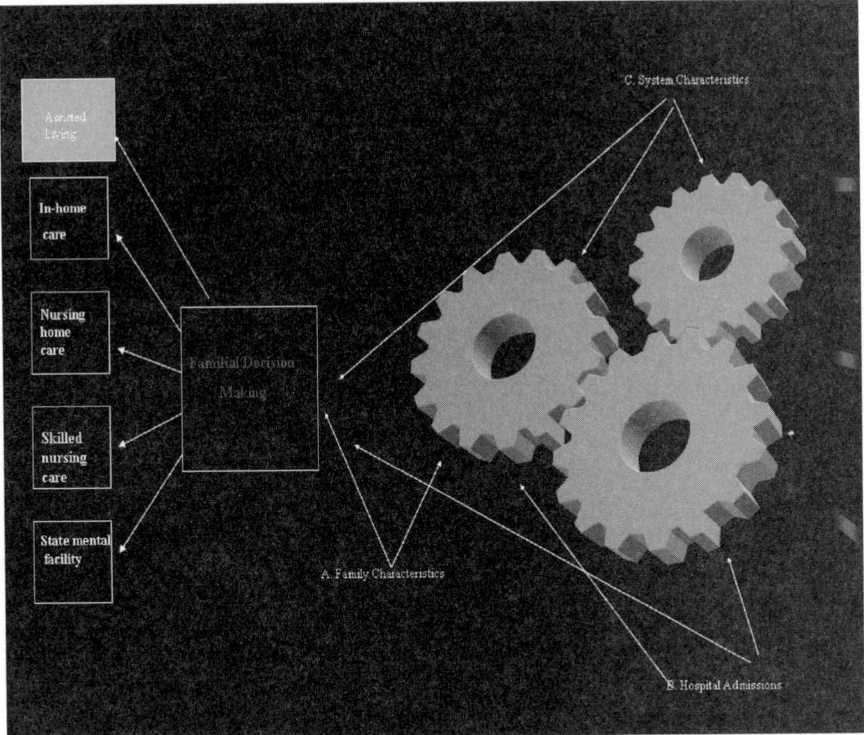

Figure 9.1 Conceptual Framework.

was profound, and the course of the ailment was progressive and unrelenting. This greatly influenced our decisions.

The third factor in the family cluster is the amount of resources juxtaposed with the prospective cost of care. I could not afford many of the optional services that were available to Muriel. She did not have any personal disability coverage, and her meager assets, including the value of her home, limited our choices.

Familial decisions are also affected by the extent of social support available. Although Muriel had a small number of relatives in her community, their health status and advanced age lessened their ability to offer her long-term support. The same conclusion was reached about her fellow church members, close friends, and neighbors. Each group provided much-needed short-term support but was unable to be a long-term support network. Neighbors, friends, and relatives all offered to take Muriel into their homes, but it was clear that other decisions were necessary.

When family members live in various parts of the country, decision making, even in crises, is complex. Had my brother and I lived in the same community as my mother, our care options and choices would have been different and perhaps easier. The Depression-era migration of my family to different parts of the United States resulted in a broad pattern of dispersal by the 1990s that will have an impact on future healthcare decisions, including my own.

Families that have a small number of members may also find that their decision making is affected. For example, Muriel's next-door neighbors were parents to a single child who lived in Illinois. As her parents aged and became disabled, their daughter found it increasingly necessary to travel to Townsend to arrange for their care. Having to make decisions about care alone was stressful. Family decision making appears to change based on the number of healthcare crises, admissions, and episodes they experience. As the number of health crises increases, families become more experienced, knowledgeable, and familiar with the process of making decisions. When St. Thomas's home indicated that Muriel's condition warranted a change, my family was much more confident about our ability to find an acceptable alternative. With each minor crisis she experienced over the years, our support network expanded to include other medical specialists, nurses, social workers, ministers, physical therapists, and nutritionists. Within each of these three clusters in figure 9.1 are a number of important factors. These are listed in table 9.2.

How these factors affect familial decision making is complex and varies across families as well as within the same families over a period. Changes in a family's annual income could greatly affect the range of healthcare choices they can exercise. For example, a business owner purchased private psychiatric care

Table 9.2 Clusters That Influence Family Decision Making

Family Cluster	System Cluster	Health Cluster
Information available	Costs	Prior admissions
Level of impairment	Location	Prior health crises
Resources	Services available	
Extent of support	Vacancies	
Help-seeking behavior	Public policies	
Number of members		
Geographic location		

for his young adult son until he recovered sufficiently to resume his college education. The cost of private care was significant, but a large proportion was covered by their health insurance carrier. Insurance coverage and a high level of income allowed the family to choose a costly healthcare alternative throughout a series of health crises with their son. However, after a long remission, the son suffered more psychiatric episodes at age thirty but was no longer covered by the family's health insurance. As a result, the family's range of choices narrowed greatly and had to include admission to a state mental hospital. In another family, it was learned that Medicaid funding could be used to provide six hours of in-home care when an elderly relative broke her hip. Although the relative also had dementia and lost her ability to walk without assistance after hip surgery, external funding broadened the choices available. After a short course in a skilled nursing facility, the family was able to avoid long-term custodial nursing home care.

REFLECTIONS AND CONCLUSIONS

Writing this chapter was more than a means of chronicling the issues related to the caregiving of my mother in the latter years of her life. Ultimately, as her life underwent various changes, so did the lives of everyone in her network of nuclear and extended family, close neighbors, friends, fellow church members, employers, and caregivers. The circle of caregiving extended broadly to encompass the lives of many people. Writing about her life allowed me an opportunity to identify, describe, and juxtapose these caregiving interactions in an ecological context. When I started giving away items from her home, I began to understand the connections between people as neighbors and the circular impact of caring, giving, sharing, and supporting. Although I grew up with these same neighbors, their visages became mirrors of my mother, and their needs for caregiving also were immense.

Furthermore, writing proved cathartic in that it allowed me to reflect on the personal emotionality of caregiving and how it increased my understanding of several complex issues:

- Subjective meaning of caregiving of a close relative
- Dealing with gradual loss
- Conceptualization of caregiving by culture and race
- Perception of male caregiving in society
- Impact of caregiving on relationships with others

- Skills needed in caregiving
- Personal planning

Initially, writing about these caregiving issues forced me to recall the range of very personal emotions, particularly loss, fear, helplessness, guilt, anger, sadness, elation, relief, and acceptance, that I experienced over a period of five years. Eventually, I grew to accept the changes in relationship between my mother, her extended network, and me. Various elements associated with caregiving can be very humbling. Could I have done more to help her manage her health? Repeatedly I asked myself whether and to what extent geographic distance and my focus on my career reduced my attention to the changes in her overall health. Did I ask the right questions? Was I conscious of the changes she was undergoing? Did we visit enough?

Through the writing, I have come to accept the subjective meaning of the events in Muriel's life and the extent to which I could and could not control the outcomes. Rather than remain constrained by the past, it became necessary to find a new equilibrium. It is clear that there were points where intervention was possible. Dr. Levenson's retirement was the ideal time to engage my mother in discussion about her reactions, feelings, and initial interactions with the new physician. However, part of establishing a new equilibrium was accepting Muriel's desire to be in full control of her life. Although our family wanted to offer guidance and support, Muriel had her own ideas about her health that made intervention difficult. Based on what I learned from the latter years of my mother's life, I ask more questions of my aging relatives, call more often, make more suggestions, help them make linkages, interpret symptoms and signs, and offer help in making appointments.

What is also important here is what I learned about my mother's approach to life. Through the process of writing this article I was able to find and appreciate more of the connections and patterns in my mother's life in ways that I had never done before. Earlier in my life, I did not consider the significance of her purchase of a home in the 1950s. As a single black woman in a neighborhood of two-parent families, she was unusual. However, when I read literature (Conley 1999) on the long-term economic import of home ownership, I marveled at what she accomplished and, more importantly, why she thought it was necessary. I regret that this was not something we discussed at length over the years. What I don't fully understand is the motivational wellspring from which her strength originated and the meaning of home ownership throughout her life. I believe that I took her ownership for granted and did not recognize just how meaningful it was to her. Perhaps her interest in home ownership will be influential in the lives of my children (Conley 1999). As I look at her influence, I see that my brother and I share her interest in home ownership. She had a persistence about her that allowed her to achieve against a number of stressful life events: divorce, abandonment, limited education, children, low wages, and restrictive policies. Despite these seemingly overwhelming odds, she achieved a high degree of success as a black woman, a parent, and a citizen.

Attempting to care for Muriel in the waning years of her life raised substantive issues for me in my relationship with my own children. What do I want from them in my aged years? How well have we communicated about our lives? How well have I helped them to honor my dignity while helping to ensure my health and longevity? How much sanction have I given to them to become involved in my end-of-life issues so that my burden to them is lessened? How prepared am I to enter into a new set of relationships with my network? I hope these brief reflections clarify the close relationship between retrospection, introspection, and how one plans for the future.

Since my caregiving of Muriel ended, my life has changed in several ways. My children are adults with graduate education and working in their various professions. I now have grandchildren. I am happily remarried and living in Texas. I occupy a chaired professorship in mental health and social policy at a school of social work and am the executive director of a foundation for mental health. My and my family's memories of Muriel and the many lessons she provided have grown more precious over the years. In closing her house and writing this chapter, I realized again what a phenomenal woman she was.

REFERENCES

Aneshensel, C. S. and Pearlin, L. I. 1987. Structural context of sex difference in stress. In R. Barnett, L. Biener, and G. Baruch (Eds.), *Gender and Stress*, 75–95. New York: Free Press.

Ayanian, J. Z. 1994. Race, class and the quality of medical care. *Journal of the American Medical Association* 271: 1207–1208.

Bailey, W. T. 1994. A longitudinal study of fathers' involvement with young offspring. *The Journal of Genetic Psychology* 155: 331–339.

Banks, W. 1959. *History of Yell County, Arkansas*. Van Buren, Ark.: The Press-Argus.

Barnett, R. C. and Baruch, G. K. 1987. Determinants of fathers' participation in family work. *Journal of Marriage and the Family* 49: 29–40.

Belcher, J. R. 1988. Mothers alone and supporting chronically mentally ill adult offspring: A greater vulnerability to illness. *Women and Health* 14: 61–80.

Bem, S. R. 1974. The measurement of psychological androgyny. *Journal of Clinical and Consulting Psychology* 42: 155–162.

Bristol, M. M. and Gallagher, J. J. 1986. Research on fathers of young handicapped offspring. In B. E. Robinson and R. L. Barret (Eds.), *Families of Handicapped Persons: Research, Program and Policy Issues,* 81–100. Baltimore: Paul H. Brookes.

Broman, C. L. 1987. Race differences in professional help seeking. *American Journal of Community Psychology* 15: 473–489.

Brotherson, M. J., Turnbull, A. P., Summers, J. A., and Turnbull, H. R. 1986. Fathers of disabled offspring. In B. E. Robinson and R. L. Barret (Eds.), *The Developing Father: Emerging Roles in Contemporary Society,* 193–217. New York: Guilford.

Chase-Lansdale, P. L. and Vinovskis, M. A. 1995. Whose responsibility? An historical analysis of the changing roles of mothers, fathers, and society. In P. L. Chase-Lansdale and J. Brooks-Gunn (Eds.), *Escape from Poverty: What Makes a Difference for Offspring?,* 11–37. New York: Cambridge University Press.

Chesler, M. A. and Parry, C. 2001. An integrative analysis of the experiences of fathers of offspring with cancer. *Qualitative Health Research* 11: 363–384.

Coley, R. L. and Chase-Lansdale, P. L. 1999. Stability and change in paternal involvement among urban African-American fathers. *Journal of Family Psychology* 13: 416–435.

Conley, D. 1999. *Being Black, Living in the Red: Race, Wealth, and Social Policy in America.* New York: Columbia University Press.

Cook, J. A. 1988. Who "mothers" the chronically mentally ill? *Family Relations* 37: 42–49.

Cook, J. A., Cohler, B. J., Pickett, S. A., and Beeler, J. A. 1997. Life-course and severe mental illness: Implications for caregiving within the family of later life. *Family Relations* 46: 427–436.

Cook, J. A. and Pickett, S. A. 1987. Feelings of burden and criticalness among parents residing with chronically mentally ill offspring. *Applied Social Sciences* 12: 79–107.

Culp, R. E., Schadle, S., and Robinson, L. 2000. Relationships among parental involvement and young children's perceived self-competence and behavioral problems. *Journal of Child and Family Studies* 9: 27–38.

Daly, K. J. 1995. Reshaping fatherhood: Finding the models. In W. Marsiglio (Ed.), *Fatherhood: Contemporary Theory, Research, and Social Policy,* 21–40. Thousand Oaks, Cal.: Sage.

Dhingra, R., Pencina, M. J., Wang, T. J., Nam, B. H., Benjamin, E. J., Levy, D., Larson, M. G., Kannel, W. B., D'Agostino, R. B. Sr., and Ramachandran, S. V. 2006. Electrocardiographic QRS duration and the risk of congestive heart failure: The Framingham Heart Study. *Hypertension* 47: 861–867.

Dowd, N. E. 2000. *Redefining Fatherhood*. New York: New York University Press.

Draper, P. 1998. Why should fathers father? In A. Booth and A. C. Couter (Eds.), *Men in Families: When Do They Get Involved? What Difference Does It Make?*, 111–121. Mahwah, N.J.: Erlbaum.

Earl, T. R. 2005. *Examining Caregiving Practices of Siblings Caring for a Brother or Sister Diagnosed with a Severe Mental Illness*. Ph.D. social work, the University of Texas at Austin.

Essex, E. A. 1999. Parental caregivers of adults with mental retardation: The experience of older mothers and fathers. *Dissertation Abstracts* 59: 3208-A.

Fitting, M., Rabins, P., Lucas, M. J., and Eastham, J. 1986. Caring for dementia patients: A comparison of husbands and wives. *The Gerontologist* 7: 99–119.

Fuller-Jonap, F. and Haley, W. E. 1995. Mental and physical health of male caregivers of a spouse with Alzheimer's disease. *Journal of Aging and Health* 7: 99–119.

Furstenburg, F. F. Jr. 1995. Fathering in the inner city: Paternal participation and public policy. In W. Marsiglio (Ed.), *Fatherhood: Contemporary Theory, Research, and Social Policy*, 119–147. Thousand Oaks, Cal.: Sage.

Furstenburg, F. F. Jr. 2000. Intergenerational transmission of fathering roles in at risk families. *Marriage and Family Review* 29: 181–201.

Germain, C. B. and Gitterman, A. 1995. Ecological perspective. In R. L. Edwards (Ed.), *Encyclopedia of Social Work*, 19th ed., 816–822. New York: NASW Press.

Greif, G. L. and Bailey, C. 1990. Where are the fathers in the social work literature? *Families in Society* 71: 88–92.

Harris, P. D. 1993. The misunderstood caregiver?: A qualitative study of the male caregiver of Alzheimer's disease victims. *The Gerontologist* 33: 551–556.

Hearn, J. 2002. Men, fathers and the state: National and global relations. In B. Hobson (Ed.), *Making Men into Fathers: Men, Masculinities and the Social Politics of Fatherhood*, 245–272. New York: Cambridge University Press.

Heller, T., Hsieh, K., and Rowitz, L. 1997. Maternal and paternal caregiving of persons with mental retardation across the lifespan. *Family Relations* 46: 407–415.

Heru, A. M. 2000. Family functioning, burden, and reward in the caregiving of persons with mental retardation across the lifespan. *Families, Systems, and Health* 18: 91–103.

Hirsch, C. 1996. Understanding the influence of gender role identity of the assumption of family caregiving roles by men. *International Journal of Aging and Human Development* 42: 103–121.

Howard, P. B. 1998. The experience of fathers of adult children with schizophrenia. *Issues in Mental Health Nursing* 19: 399–413.

Johnson, H. B. 1998. *Black Wall Street: From Riot to Renaissance in Tulsa's Historic Greenwood District*. Austin: Akin Press.

Johnson, W. 1998. Paternal involvement in fragile, African-American families: Implications for clinical social work practice. *Smith College Studies in Social Work* 68: 215–232.

Kannel, W. B. 2000. Incidence and epidemiology of heart failure. *Heart Failure Review* 5: 167–173.

Kazak, A. E. 1987. Families with disabled children: Stress and social networks in three samples. *Journal of Abnormal Child Psychology* 15: 137–146.

Kim, Y. R. 2005. *Fathers of Offspring with Severe Mental Illness: Key Factors Related to Fathers' Participation in Care giving.* Ph.D. social work, the University of Texas at Austin School of Social Work.

Kraemer, S. 1999. The fragility of fatherhood. In G. Dench (Ed.), *Rewriting the Sexual Contract*, 89–102. New Brunswick, N.J.: Transaction.

Lee, G. F. 1992. Gender differences in family caregiving: A fact in search of a theory. In J. W. Dwyer and R. T. Coward (Eds.), *Gender, Families, and Elder Care*, 120–131. Newbury Park, Cal.: Sage.

Lefley, H. P. 1997. Synthesizing the family caregiving studies: Implications for service planning, social policy, and further research. *Family Relations* 46: 443–450.

Lutzky, S. M. and Knight, B. G. 1994. Explaining gender differences in caregiver distress: The roles of emotional attentiveness and coping styles. *Psychology and Aging* 9: 513–519.

Markowitz, J. 1984. Participation of fathers in early childhood special education programs: An exploratory study. *Journal of the Division for Early Childhood* 8: 119–131.

Marks, J. 2006. *Tacrine and Alzheimer's Disease.* Medicinet. Retrieved January 3, 2007, from www.medicinet.com/tacrine/article.htm.

Mastroyannopoulou, K., Stallard, P., Lewis, M., and Lenton, S. 1997. The impact of childhood non-malignant life threatening illness on parents: Gender differences and predictors of parental adjustment. *The Journal of Child Psychology and Psychiatry and Allied Disciplines* 38: 823–829.

McBride, B. A. and Darragh, J. 1995. Interpreting the data on father involvement: Implications for parenting programs for men. *Families in Society* 76: 490–497.

McConachie, H. 1982. Fathers of mentally handicapped children. In N. Beail and J. McGuire (Eds.), *Fathers: Psychological Perspectives*, 144–173. London: Junction.

McNeil, M. and Chabassol, D. J. 1984. Paternal involvement in the programs of hearing-impaired children: An exploratory study. *Family Relations* 33: 118–125.

Neighbors, H. W. and Jackson, J. 1984. The use of informal and formal help: Four patterns of illness behavior in the black community. *American Journal of Community Psychology* 12: 629–644.

Opie, A. 1994. The instability of the caring body: Gender and caregivers of confused older people. *Qualitative Health Research* 4: 31–51.

Parsons, K. 1997. The male experience of caregiving for a family member with Alzheimer's disease. *Qualitative Health Research* 7: 391–407.

Sagi, A. and Sharon, N. 1984. The role of the father in the family: Toward a gender-neutral family policy. *Children and Youth Services Review* 6: 83–99.

Seligman, M. and Darling, R. B. 1989. *Ordinary Families, Special Children: A Systems Approach to Childhood Disability.* New York: Guilford.

Seshadri, S., Beiser, A., Kelly-Hayes, M., Kase, C. S., Au, R., Kannel, W. B., and Wolf, P. A. 2006. The lifetime risk of stroke: Estimates from the Framingham Study. *Stroke* 37: 279–280.

Snowden, L. R. 2000. Inpatient mental health use by members of ethnic minority groups. In J. M. Herrera, W. B. Lawson, and J. J. Smerck (Eds.), *Cross Cultural Psychiatry,* 261–274. Chichester, England: Wiley.

Walker, A. J. 1992. Conceptual perspectives on gender and family caregiving. In J. W. Dwyer and R. T. Coward (Eds.), *Gender, Families, and Elder Care,* 34–46. Newbury Park, Cal.: Sage.

White, N. R. 1994. About fathers: Masculinity and the social construction of fatherhood. *The Australian and New Zealand Journal of Sociology* 30: 119–131.

Winakur, J. 2005. What are we going to do with Dad? *Health Affairs* 24: 1064–1072.

Windsor, H. M., Abioye-Kuteyi, E. A., Leber, J. M., Morrow, S. D., Bulsara, M. K., and Marshall, B. J. 2005. Prevalence of *Helicobacter pylori* in indigenous Western Australians: Comparison between urban and remote rural populations. *The Medical Journal of Australia* 182: 210–213.

Winstersteen, R. T. and Rasmussen, K. L. 1997. Fathers of persons with mental illness: A preliminary study of coping capacity and service needs. *Community Mental Health Journal* 33: 401–413.

Zarit, S. H., Todd, P. A., and Zarit, J. M. 1986. Subjective burden of husbands and wives as caregivers: A longitudinal study. *The Gerontologist* 26: 260–266.

TEN

Social Worker Husband as Caregiver of Social Worker Wife

SAMUEL PETERSON

In this chapter I discuss my experience of caring for my wife after she suffered a stroke on March 1, 2000. I describe how this event affected our lives and our marriage and how we coped with the challenges of this new experience. Although I can describe my wife's afflictions, I cannot state with any certainty what she thought and felt, especially because the stroke limited her ability to communicate these things to others. Moreover, I am clearer about what I thought and felt; so I will focus primarily on my thoughts and feelings rather than those of my wife.

The purpose of this book is to bring professional social work insights to the family caregiving role and to subsequently derive some implications for other social workers. Literature on family caregivers of stroke patients already exists; in many ways, my experiences are similar to those of many others. Other reports describe such struggles of the caregiver as meeting his or her own needs while meeting the needs of the family member with the disability, adding the tasks that family member can no longer fulfill to his or her own, and advocating for that family member with many components of the health system (Han and Haley 1999).

For example, in a study of twenty-two caregivers one year after a stroke occurred, Kerr and Smith (2001) found that the main kinds of help required of these caregivers were physical assistance, emotional support, information, and help in finding appropriate social and health service providers. These authors also discovered that the emotional toll associated with caregiving was great and that the help and support provided by the health and social services often was inadequate, inappropriate, and poorly tailored to their needs.

Researchers have confirmed the importance of social support in a study of forty families in which the presence of social support, the adequacy of social support, and the extent of social support were the best predictors of caregiver life satisfaction (Grant et al. 2001). This finding was also confirmed in a larger study of 212 caregivers (Van den Heuvel et al. 2001). Because I am a male caregiver, it is important to note that the literature is less adequate in describing male caregivers than female ones. This is despite the estimate that 28% of the care for disabled older adults in the United States is provided by men (Wagner 1997). In addition, attention has been drawn recently to the deficiencies in studies that examine male caregivers (Houde 2002).

I cannot be sure that I would have handled this caregiving situation any differently had I not been a social worker. In fact, I experienced many emotions that probably were very similar to those of other caregivers. I will leave the reader to judge whether I was better able to deal with my situation by virtue of my profession. Nevertheless, my social work training and experience have given me the tools with which to describe my experiences as a caregiver and the tools with which to anticipate what might help others in similar circumstances.

DESCRIPTION OF CAREGIVER

At this time, I am seventy-seven years old. I retired five years ago from my position as a professor of social work at a major midwestern university, where I taught, wrote, and did research, mostly about direct practice. My special interest was in group work. I also taught about international social work. I taught doctoral and master's-level courses, and for a period of time I was the director of the doctoral program.

Currently, I am researching and writing on a nearly full-time basis; I have been married to my wife for forty-nine years, and we have three children, two of whom are social workers. We are grandparents of three, one an older adolescent, one a younger adolescent, and one an infant. We continue to live in the college town where we have resided for forty years. I received my master's degree in social work in 1951. I practiced social work for the next dozen years, first in a residential treatment center, then in the U.S. Army, and finally in community centers and settlement houses. After we married, my wife finished her M.S.W. I began my doctoral studies in 1963; while still working toward my doctorate, I began my academic career in 1965.

During the many years before my wife suffered her stroke, we were fairly equal marital partners. My wife probably would tell you that she had a greater responsibility for administering the household; this included cooking and planning. It was somewhat contentious that I assumed more control of our financial affairs, even though we both worked full time for most of our marriage. Nevertheless, she took charge of her own personal finances, had her own accounts, and made the decisions about her assets (including a modest inheritance), and she still does. I paid some of the bills, such as mortgage, food, and so forth, and she paid for vacations, her clothes, visits to the hairdresser, and so forth.

It is important to note that when she became disabled with the stroke six years ago, I knew all about our finances. I also had the good fortune of having learned how to cook when I was in college, although I cooked to a much lesser extent than my wife. Whereas my wife loved to cook gourmet dishes, I regarded cooking as a chore. We both did laundry, depending on who was free when the hamper was full, although, to be honest, she was always more careful than I about sorting things. As you can probably tell, I did most of my chores as quickly as possible.

If my memory serves me correctly, we shared the caregiving of our children. We diapered our children as infants, we disciplined them as they became school aged, we took them to their appointments and sat in on school conferences, and we supervised their activities as teenagers. It is important to note that I continue to be a worrier and have been diagnosed with an anxiety disorder. As a parent, I worried about childhood illnesses, school progress, teenagers driving, and teenagers staying out late. My wife probably was more sensitive than I to our children's feelings; she also could put our children's needs before our needs.

We were fortunate that neither of us had extensive caregiving responsibilities for aging parents. My father took care of my mother when she became fairly disabled. I lived in a different city than they did, and I did not take on many caregiving responsibilities for her. My sister lived in the same area as they did, so she functioned as a caregiver of my father when he became less competent. My mother-in-law died in her sleep when she was still fully able to care for herself. My father-in-law lived until he was ninety-one years old; he was able to function as a doctor until the day he died from a heart attack.

DESCRIPTION OF FAMILY MEMBER CARED FOR

Before my wife suffered a stroke, she had worked for many years as a medical social worker. Just before her stroke, she had worked for ten years at a medium-sized community hospital where many of her clients had suffered strokes. Before that, she had worked for about a dozen years for the state social services department; even then many of her clients had disabilities such as those stemming from strokes. Before that, she had several other positions. It is an interesting twist of fate that her first position in our city was at an agency providing intensive speech therapy to people with aphasia, which usually occurs as a result of a stroke.

My wife's stroke was the type that results from a clot in the blood vessels of the brain. Her clot occurred in the left side of the brain. This type of clot usually results in partial or complete paralysis of the right side of the body and in a speech disorder known as aphasia. My wife experienced these impairments, as well as an impact on her field in vision that obscured objects on the right side of each eye.

At the time my wife experienced her stroke, we were in Florida and packing to move from a motel into a condo we had rented for the month of March. I was on a phased retirement furlough, so I had that academic term off; I planned to commute to my university several times to carry on project responsibilities that I would otherwise handle by phone and e-mail. I came in from loading some luggage into the car and saw my wife slumped into a crouched position on the floor. I initially assumed that she had become faint, perhaps from the heat, but when she couldn't speak, I knew that the situation was much worse than heat exhaustion. I managed to help her onto the bed, although this was difficult because of her weight. I knew immediately that she had suffered a stroke because one side of her body appeared paralyzed, and the right side of her mouth drooped. She seemed partially conscious but dazed. I immediately called 911, and the paramedics were with us in a matter of minutes. She arrived at the emergency room about thirty minutes after the stroke.

This could have been lucky, but it wasn't. Many stroke survivors can be brought rapidly back to normal functioning through administration of a drug that immediately dissolves the clot. A computer axial tomography scan is always used to determine whether this is feasible. In her case, this was not an option. The stroke was massive, and in those circumstances this drug could have caused additional harm to her brain. She was immediately admitted to the hospital and placed under intensive observation, because some stroke victims can suffer life-threatening events for several days after the stroke. This did not happen.

Nevertheless, my wife was fortunate to have been treated at the hospital to which she went; this facility had extensive equipment and staff to meet the needs of stroke victims, including a substantial rehabilitation wing. After several days, my wife was moved there. At that time, she was completely paralyzed on her right side. She could repeat words that were said to her but initiated little or no speech. She used "yes" and "no" interchangeably, without conveying what she meant. However, she was conscious at the time of hospital admission and appeared to understand when hospital staff told her she had suffered a stroke. She could sit up in a chair when carried to it, and she fed herself. She knew who I was and who her children were when they arrived. Because many stroke patients lose the ability to swallow properly and may choke on food or drink, she was fed special foods to prevent this from occurring. This special food was pureed, shaped to look like the real thing, and given in thickened liquids.

I was quite frightened by all these events. Shortly before the stroke, we were a healthy, gradually aging couple. We looked forward to many years of travel, to other pleasures, and to continuing in our professions. Now, these plans were jeopardized. I previously had a wife who was a partner, who could converse with me about our plans. Now my wife could not speak, and I did not know how much she understood of what was going on around her.

Within days of admission to the hospital, she was admitted to the rehabilitation wing of the hospital. Most of the other patients there had also suffered strokes. She was given a schedule of several hours a day of speech, occupational, and physical therapy. She was moved about in a wheelchair that she couldn't control because one side of her body was paralyzed. Almost from the beginning, she fed herself and groomed herself (i.e., brushed her teeth, combed her hair, and applied makeup). But others showered her and dressed and undressed her. I was told she had expressive aphasia, meaning that she couldn't speak, but the staff did not yet know what she understood. However, she could comply with such demands as those to turn her head, close her eyes, and so forth.

I was depressed. When I returned to the apartment we had rented, I frequently found myself in tears. This is not an unusual reaction to this type of loss. One study found that caregiving spouses of aphasic patients are significantly more depressed than those of nonaphasic patients (Zak 1999). I was also very anxious and plied the hospital staff with dozens of questions. However, my coping style was to make whatever plans I needed to make with reference to my work, our travel arrangements that had to be aborted, the payment of bills, and so forth.

There were both hopeful signs about my wife's condition and scary ones. Within days, the paralysis in her right leg lifted (although this continued to be the weaker limb), and I was told this was more likely to occur in her leg than in her arm. She also suffered a blood clot in this leg, and she wears compression stockings to this day to prevent this from happening again.

Within a week or two, she graduated to more solid food as her control of swallowing improved. I soon saw her standing and walking short distances under the guidance of a physical therapist; I will never, never forget the huge smile on her face when she showed me she could do this. Our daughter lives a few hours' drive from the hospital, and she spent a good deal of time with me. Our son flew down for periods. My sister-in-law and a close friend from our hometown visited also. I found these support systems to be of great value.

The setbacks included the development of a severe blood clot in her right leg that was painful. This development limited her mobility for several days and necessitated wearing a support stocking around the entire leg. She continues to wear a support stocking that ends at the knee.

My wife remained in the hospital for almost two months. The hospital social worker and doctor strongly recommended that she remain this long. They asserted that Medicare rules in that state were more liberal than those in our home state and would allow this long a stay, whereas the authorities in our state would have moved her to outpatient status in less than half this time. They claimed the inpatient intensive rehabilitation program would be more likely to increase my wife's level of functioning than an outpatient one.

The two hours of speech therapy a day enabled her to regain the use of many words spoken singly. She received the same amount of physical therapy, and the therapist worked on strengthening her limbs, her ability to walk, and (unsuccessfully) to have some use of her paralyzed arm. The occupational therapist worked on her ability to engage in self-care, to go up and down stairs, to transfer from her wheelchair to her bed, and ultimately to go into a restaurant and indicate what she wanted from a menu.

I had thought my wife would return to our hometown and would reside for a period in a nursing facility. I was concerned about my ability to care for her, change her clothes, keep her from falling, arrange for her meals, transport her to appointments, bathe her, and do the countless tasks for her that she could not do for herself. The hospital doctor and staff argued that she would be better off at home. They convinced me that she would be happier at home and that with help we would be able to cope. The social worker helped us plan this (as a social worker I already understood the concept of discharge planning, something my wife had done for years for others). I knew that if the situation had been reversed, my wife would be much more capable of helping a couple develop the support systems they needed. I was enough of a social worker to know what I needed to learn more about, and I called my wife's social work supervisor and other social workers to learn about the resources that were available in our city.

The hospital social worker helped me access the following resources:

- Arrangements were made for my wife to attend a daily outpatient rehabilitation program.
- A contractor installed bars in the bathroom.
- A wheelchair was rented and a bath–shower transfer bench purchased.
- An agency was contacted that would provide a home health aide every weekday morning to help my wife bathe and dress.
- The visiting nurse association was contacted to supply a Lifeline, which is an electronic device worn around the neck that would summon help by dialing the Visiting Nurse Association on the phone.
- Various implements were ordered such as a knife that she could use to cut food by rocking it on the food and a pad that would hold a plate in place. This pad would provide a barrier so the food landed on the fork and not on the table. (My wife actually used very few of these aids.)
- An appointment with an agency that would inventory our house for dangerous obstacles and recommend ways of dealing with them.

Fortunately, our house was a single-story one with only two steps to navigate at the rear entry. There turned out to be few problems to be solved for a disabled person to reside there.

So, late in April 2000 we headed for the airport and our home. At this time, my wife had a modest single-word vocabulary, more often than not said "yes" and "no" when she meant these, could walk short distances with the use of a quad cane (a cane with four prongs at the end for stability), could use the toilet and feed herself, and could go out to restaurants and entertainment with appropriate help. She could enjoy watching TV and movies and appeared to understand most of what went on. She could at least scan the daily papers, whose perusal was always important to her.

Now, eight years later, my wife has made a good deal of progress and continues, albeit it at a slow pace, to make more. She can speak in short sentences and has a larger vocabulary. She still has difficulty expressing more complex ideas such as contingencies. For example, she would not be able to say, "If it rains I would like to go to the movie, and if it is clear I would like to go on a picnic." She still walks with a quad cane but hasn't fallen for several years. Before that, she had two bad falls that involved severe lacerations. She goes to a speech support group once a week, has a session with a speech therapy volunteer at home twice a month, and has an occupational therapist come to our house to work with her on maintaining an exercise schedule and doing more things for herself.

As of this writing, she has developed an irregular heartbeat. This has caused a clot to develop in the heart, and they cannot perform procedures to regulate the heartbeat until it dissolves. She takes anticoagulants for this purpose, and these must be monitored through blood draws.

Her comprehension is very good, and she enjoys going to retired adult classes, reading, and going to movies, theaters, and concerts, all of which she selects from ads and brochures. Because she can't get about outside our home by herself, I or someone else must accompany her. We pay a companion to go shopping with her once a week, and she seems to enjoy this. The good news is that she can do these things. The bad news is that she wants to go a great many places and can't do so on her own, and as a result she often feels bored and frustrated. I have a great many professional activities and can't take her places as often as she would like, and this makes her angry.

She has purchased an electric wheelchair so that she can navigate by herself, and she dreams of a day that we could live closer to businesses and she could go out by herself. With her speech problems, I do not believe this is realistic.

DESCRIPTION OF CAREGIVING EXPERIENCE

The literature indicates that caregivers of patients who have suffered a stroke have many needs. For example, an in-depth study of nine such caregivers found that their needs included many areas of support such as information, role change, and respite (Denman 1998). An interesting collection of narratives includes many very useful articles, most in the form of stories that describe the emotions of caregivers, the reactions of medical institutions, and the ways in which a variety of people coped with the caregiving experience (Levine 2004).

The reason why I took on this caregiving role was simple: I love my wife and want her to have the best and most loving care. I believed that I was the only one who could provide it. I could have hired others to do almost everything I did, but several things prevented this. First, this is extremely expensive. I did not want to deplete our assets, which we had saved for our retirement and for possible future long-term care expenses. We can afford a modest amount of service, such as the daily bathing and dressing help and the companion mentioned earlier.

For the first two months after my wife's stroke in 2000, my caregiving experiences were affected by the fact that she was in a rehabilitation program in a hospital. Therefore, I did not have to provide personal care because hospital staff provided it. My main caregiving responsibilities were to provide emotional support to my wife and to assist the hospital staff. I provided this support by telling my wife about what was happening with friends and family members and by spending time with her when she wasn't in the various therapies. I tried to be present for most lunches and dinners; I bought food at the hospital cafeteria and took it to the rehabilitation unit's dining room, where my wife was taken in a wheelchair at meal times. We spent evenings talking (I had to do most of the talking), watching TV, or walking around the hospital grounds with my wife in a wheelchair. When friends or family visited, they joined us for these activities.

Once we returned home, my specific caregiving responsibilities were as follows. I helped my wife select clothes she would wear that day; on weekdays, a health aide came to the house for about thirty minutes (paid for by us) and helped her dress and bathe. I helped her dress and bathe on weekends. She was able to walk to the bathroom to use the toilet, brush her teeth, apply cosmetics, and so forth, on her own. She has become increasingly able to obtain food and drink by herself. She recently has become able to place the dishes in the dishwasher and turn it on.

I transported my wife to all her rehabilitation activities, medical appointments, and similar things. She could not use a taxi service because she needed to be helped from the house to the car and from the car to the appointment site. I either took my wife shopping for personal items and clothes, or I bought these things for her. The companion now helps her with this.

I shopped for food, prepared all our meals, and cleaned up afterwards; we went to restaurants a few times a week. She helped set the table and moved the dishes to make clearing the table easier for me. She could also accompany me for grocery shopping, but I must secure a wheelchair attached to a basket for her. She is able to use the electric carts supplied by the stores. My wife used to do a lot of cooking and now often helps with food preparation. I did not understand why she refused to do so earlier.

I made sure that she took all her medications in the morning and afternoon, at dinner, and at bedtime. I arranged these in a pill organizer once a week that has twenty-eight little bins. She took nine different medications, and two of these were taken more than once a day. Sometimes when we went out, I forgot to take her pills with me. Then I calculated whether she could wait until we returned or whether I needed to dash home to get the pills. These pills included anticoagulants, anticonvulsives, cholesterol-lowering pills, thyroid pills, and osteoporosis preventives, as well as some others.

I arranged all social engagements. My wife was very reluctant to go to social gatherings where there was a lot of group conversation because she found it hard to follow the conversation or to join in. (Afterwards, she would describe such events as "talk, talk, talk.")

I helped her to get ready for bed by helping her remove her clothes and put on her nightgown. Occupational therapists have taught her how to take things such as blouses on and off with her one usable arm, but this is a time-consuming process and, perhaps unwisely, I have not pushed it. It is a struggle for me to patiently encourage her to do this and other tasks. I am a rather impatient person and feel driven to move on to other tasks I want to do rather than take the extra time needed to work with her on doing things for herself.

We have three grown children, but only one of them, a son, lives in the same city as we do. Our son occasionally does things for his mother such as driving her to appointments. However, he has a very busy life, and I think he is reluctant to do more than this, although I would find it helpful if he invited us to his home more often for a meal or took his mother out to lunch. I have not discussed this with him, which may well be a mistake. I would like more support from him, but instead he criticizes me for not being more emotionally supportive of him. I find it hard to deal with this for reasons I am not prepared to discuss here, but this is an area of tension in my life.

Friends are very important to me, and this has always been true. I am saddened by the fact that some friends have withdrawn from us. I suspect this is because of their discomfort with my wife's inability to be as interactive verbally as she once was.

Many services were provided at first by professionals. The major ones were rehabilitation specialists such as occupational, physical, and speech therapists. Their intensive services during the early months after the stroke were invaluable. As time passed and my wife's progress became slower, most of these professionals stopped their services because their protocols required that significant progress must be possible for them to continue. Insurance providers also demanded significant progress because such care is very expensive. I also did not experience any professionals as paying much attention to my needs as a caregiver.

ANALYSES

Caregiving Challenges

Insurance Coverage

This has been a mess! Not the least of the problems is that we had Medicare, my policy with the university, and my wife's policy as a retired state employee. There are various rules as to which one is primary, secondary, and tertiary, which refers to the order in which they are to be billed. Most of the social workers did not understand how this worked and gave us a good deal of incorrect information. This resulted in unpaid bills, threats, and actual actions to turn us over to collection agencies, calls and threats from collection agencies and billing personnel, and many confusing bills and letters. This continues to this day. I now understand a good deal more than I did before. I can only conclude that health coverage in our society, even for those with insurance, is abysmal.

Communication

My wife has continued to improve in speech, thanks to continuing speech therapy, although largely because of insurance rules this was reduced from five days a week to three, to two, then to one. She now has a pretty good store of words and short phrases. Nevertheless, she is unable to communicate more complex thoughts and opinions, and this leads to what looks like Charades or 20 Questions. I and others must observe her gestures and words and ask a series of questions to learn her intent. This can fail. My wife and I then become very frustrated; she becomes angry, and I think she believes that I am being obtuse intentionally.

One of the major consequences of these speech problems is a decline in the ways I involve my wife in making family decisions. She has always, and appropriately so, wanted to be involved in decisions ranging from social engagements to household expenditures. This has not changed one iota with her stroke. Nevertheless, out of my impatience and time constraints, I will slip and make a decision out of reluctance to engage in the sometimes lengthy process of learning her wishes. When this comes to her attention, she becomes very angry, and then I have to respond to that anger, which adds to the stressfulness of our situation.

Balancing My Personal and Caregiving Roles

The aforementioned list of caregiving activities takes up many hours of the day. They could consume more if I fulfilled all my wife's expectations. It is extremely important to me to continue my research and professional writing and participation in professional groups. This would have been true of me in retirement even if my wife had not suffered a stroke. I must now condense these activities into only part of the day. When I go to the university or to meetings, I leave my wife alone with a button that she can press that automatically dials for help. My greatest fear is that she will fall and injure herself. Because this has occurred several times, I worry about her when I am not with her. When I am working at home, my wife often calls me to help her, and this interrupts my work, so that it takes time for me to figure out where I was.

Obtaining Necessary Services

I have spent a lot of time on the phone arranging services for my wife. These calls include getting prescriptions refilled; setting up appointments with specialists in physical medicine, gynecology, and neurology, ophthalmology, and podiatry; searching for help in transporting my wife to appointments; and obtaining needed health supplies, such as support hose to prevent blood clots in her legs. Before her stroke, my wife could make her appointments and get to them. I must now be involved in all of this.

Anticipating Barriers

I must always anticipate barriers that make some situation difficult for a person with disabilities. Will there be stairs to climb at a home or at a business establishment? Is there an elevator to the balcony of a theater? Is there a wheelchair-accessible restroom? Does the distance from the car to the destination require the wheelchair? Is there disabled parking in the vicinity? If I don't think ahead and make inquiries, we encounter barriers that add to the stress of the trip. This means always making our needs known when calling for reservations or tickets. As a side note, one of the most frustrating experiences I've had is trying to push a wheelchair and open a door at the same time. I am grateful for businesses that install a button to open the door. I am most distressed at people who rapidly go through a door ahead of me without looking back, letting the door slam against the wheelchair as I try to dash through. I have become extremely aware of these things, and when I am alone, I am much more sensitive to the needs of disabled people around me than I ever was before.

Coping with Crises

There have been frequent crises with my wife, such as a new physical symptom or a fall resulting in injury. There have been the crises of everyday life such as breakdowns of household equipment or automobiles or problems in the lives of our adult children that require our attention. Previously I would have been able to take these in stride. Now, because they are stresses on top of other stresses, I have found myself feeling more overwhelmed by them.

Description of Theoretical and Service-Oriented Perspectives

I had the following perspectives that may have had some impact on how I responded to this situation:

- I have always believed that a major part of the way people cope with problems is through their ability to derive support from their social networks. I was part of several strong social networks composed of friends and family, and I was determined to make use of these.
- I also believed that people should draw on their strengths to cope with adversity. My strengths were my ability to organize my activities so as to be efficient in the use of my energy, my knowledge of the places to look for services, and my understanding that I needed to use my network to access services; this is known as a strengths-centered perspective (Saleebey 1997).
- My knowledge of the importance of selecting and carrying out tasks to reach one's goals, generally called a task-centered perspective (Tolson et al. 2003), served me well as I often thought in terms of tasks to be accomplished.
- I have always found role perspectives useful in understanding situations such as this one (Biddle and Thomas 1966). I particularly think of three role concepts as applicable to my caregiving situation: role conflict, role ambiguity, and role discontinuity.

Role conflict refers to situations in which a person is affected by incompatible expectations. In my case, these were my wife's expectations that I would give meeting her needs priority, whereas I expected that meeting some of my needs should be given priority. My method of coping with this conflict was by using the strategy of compromise.

Role ambiguity refers to situations in which the expectations are unclear. The lack of clarity involved my lack of knowledge of what health staff and my wife expected of me as a caregiver. Likewise, I was not sure what the health staff thought my wife would be able to do and how that compared with her expectations. My method of coping with this was to obtain information from rehabilitation specialists about these sets of expectations.

Role discontinuity refers to situations in which the role expectations for the current situation are in sharp contrast to those of the preceding situation. The expectations of spouses in which neither has a disability are in sharp contrast to those in which one has a severe disability. If this circumstance is predictable, one can pursue what is called anticipatory socialization. The abruptness of the stroke prevented this. The solution I used was to seek to anticipate future events and plan for them. An example of this is to anticipate the need for a companion to take my wife some of the places she wanted to go (e.g., shopping for clothes) and to locate a companion for half a day each week.

Factors Influencing Successes and Failures

The factors that I think most influenced my successes were as follows:

- My ability to solve problems and organize my time, and the rapidity with which I did this, helped me to be successful.
- Although I was not a medical social worker, I knew something about the organization of social and health services that saved me steps in searching for and using resources.
- I understood the importance of social networks for support and identification of resources and have sought to maintain and expand them.
- I have been trying to use my philosophy of life in coping with stresses. This philosophy includes a belief in the basic goodness of most people, a belief in the joy of life under even the most difficult circumstances, a belief that one's accomplishments will live on in the minds of others after one is gone, and a belief that we have an obligation to work for a better world and the end of injustice for the benefit of all humankind.

Factors Influencing Failures

- My impatience.
- My quickness to express anger and frustration.

- My tendency to obsess about problems and the way this tendency feeds the level of anxiety I experience as I even anticipate catastrophes that do not happen. I have always had these kinds of feelings, but I think they have been exacerbated by the fact that a catastrophe, the stroke, did occur. I have seen a therapist for help and been diagnosed as suffering from generalized anxiety disorder. I have an anxiety-reducing medication and a sleeping pill, but I choose to use these sparingly, perhaps once or twice a month.

IMPLICATIONS

My social work perspectives helped me a great deal in this situation. An important perspective related to my understanding of the interactions between one's personal experiences and the social and physical environment. This was basically a social-ecological approach. I was able to think about my own strengths and weaknesses in terms of how they were affected by external forces and also contributed to these forces. To make this clearer, I offer two examples.

When I became frustrated by insurance systems, I sought to change them. Thus, when our HMO refused to pay for speech therapy because the provider was out of the provider network, I appealed this decision. The reason we were out of the network is that the in-network provider referred us to the out-of-network provider as offering the kind of service my wife needed (i.e., more intensive speech therapy using equipment not available to the in-network provider). We have been engaged in a series of appeals to higher authorities for more than a year now. The last level decided in our favor, but the HMO went to the next level to appeal that decision. If we win this, it should benefit not only us but also others in similar circumstances.

The other example is my use of my network of personal friends. I am aware that no matter how well intentioned and caring they are, friends can burn out on us. They have their own stresses and can find those we provide, such as my wife's speech difficulties, too much for them at times. I have tried very hard not to ask too much of our friends. In turn, they have sometimes surprised me by making generous offers that I did not expect.

Another of my social work perspectives is my belief in resilience, the power of the human mind to create new solutions, and the ability of the individual to grow in the process. I have developed a new appreciation of my ability to cope, of my ability and my wife's ability to find joy in life, and of the generosity of most people.

For myself, I must continue to work on my tendency to catastrophize, to be impatient, and to fail to involve my wife in all of the decisions affecting her; I must also appreciate the goodwill of our friends, respect their need to take care of their own lives, and continue to fight systemic injustices, such as those in the health system.

For my wife, I must continue to patiently support her growing ability to take care of herself, appreciate her successes, and support her when she fails. Writing about other family members is difficult for me. I intellectually appreciate the desires of other family members, such as our adult children, to meet their own needs as well as ours, a kind of role conflict. They also experience a different kind of role discontinuity as they are required to be caregivers of their aging parents rather than being cared for as children by their parents. This issue could be the subject of an entire paper. Suffice it to say here that I expect them to empathize with what it is like to be in our situation; I must recognize that this will subject them to a variety of role problems as they reflect on the meaning of this situation and as they also seek to meet their own needs.

For families in similar situations, the caregiver must find ways to meet her or his own needs in addition to functioning as a caregiver. This means engaging in activities that fulfill one's own interests, maintaining relationships that do not necessarily serve the person being taken care of, searching out support systems and using them appropriately, and finding ways to extend the self-care abilities of the other person.

Professionals must be able to view the caregiving family as a system and to assess that system in terms of its strengths and limitations. The caregiver must be viewed as an important part of the system who has needs, fears, and aspirations. Recognition of this will benefit the entire family, including the care recipient. Professionals must learn about the environmental barriers and constraints, and they must study ways of coping with them that can be taught to caregivers. This particularly includes barriers in the healthcare system including health insurance, barriers in using public facilities, financial barriers to accessing services, and limitations in personal networks.

All of this has great implications for how we educate social workers. This chapter illustrates the importance of a social-ecological approach that portrays individual–environmental transactions because these affect people with every type of problem. It also illustrates the importance of the concept of empowerment, which must include helping people change the circumstances that oppress them.

The importance of a social-ecological approach is highly relevant to caregiving families. Caregiving families must be helped to view their opportunities and their stresses as an interaction between their own competencies and the resources of the environment. The difficulties in self-care of a person with a disability are a function of that person's views and feelings. That person's efforts to change and grow can be facilitated by the service environment and the resources supplied by that environment. Empowerment is important as caregivers challenge the healthcare system, the social service system, the insurance system, and the lack of assistance for people with disabilities in community institutions.

Policies must change so that necessary health and social services are made available to caregiving families. This includes abolishing severe limitations on the amount of rehabilitation services made available. This also includes the provision of more services to caregivers such as caregiver education and caregiver support groups.

For researchers, this volume attests to the importance now being given to the needs of caregivers. Research on the needs of caregivers exists, but there is little on the nature of effective programs to meet the needs of caregivers in all of their diversity. I summarize these suggestions for change in table 10.1.

REFLECTIONS AND CONCLUSIONS

Writing this chapter was difficult in many ways because it caused me to reflect on many events that were very painful at the time. As I have encountered new challenges and opportunities, these past events receded from my consciousness. On the other hand, writing this chapter has caused me to feel strengthened by the fact that my wife and I have met a series of challenges and overcome them; this may give us hope to face the new challenges and opportunities that lie ahead. The writing of this chapter was also a catharsis. It allowed me to express feelings that have always been present in my subconscious mind; perhaps I will feel less troubled by them and more at peace with myself. However, I never doubted that I would complete this chapter, and I never felt blocked from composing it.

My process in writing the chapter was first to describe my experiences and then find a way to analyze them. I did not first explore the literature to see whether what I have experienced has been the same for others in similar circumstances. I had not been interested previously in the topic of caregiving as

Table 10.1 Implications

	Issues and Problems	Strategies for Change
Individuals	Caregiver needs more resources to provide care. Caregiver needs more support.	Provide caregiver with more information on resources. Locate support groups in the community; help caregiver find appropriate ways of seeking support from her or his networks.
Families	Communication between family members is lacking.	Hold family meetings.
Communities	Support groups for caregivers of stroke victims are lacking or inadequate. Lists of potential companions who can provide transportation and other services for the care recipient are lacking or inadequate.	Promote awareness of need for such support in the community. Promote more awareness of the need for such companions.
Practitioners and educators	Training in the effects of strokes on patients and caregivers is lacking or inadequate. Discharge planners lack empathy.	Require training in hospitals and medical schools. Increase training in effective discharge planning. Incorporate family point of view into training program.
Institutions	Discharge plans are based on short-term perspectives.	Change discharge assessment procedures. Include postdischarge follow-up.
Researchers	The variables that affect the rate of recovery of stroke victims are not well understood.	Support better funding of research on recovery patterns of stroke victims.

social workers have involved themselves in it, and so I had almost no knowledge of the literature.

The easiest thing about writing the chapter was the description of actual events, even though many of these events were painful at the time. This may be because I had gone over these events many times in my mind, perhaps because they were so traumatic. Examples of these were when I first observed my wife having a stroke, the first hours at the hospital when I did not know what the outcome would be, the first efforts at rehabilitation, and the trip from Florida back home.

The most challenging things about the chapter were my efforts to be honest about my "negative feelings" such as anger, impatience, sadness, and frustration. The anger I felt was often toward my wife when she would do things (or refuse to do things) that made my caregiving role more difficult. The impatience occurred, for example, when I wanted her to be ready to go somewhere and she would tarry in the house straightening something or choosing to use the bathroom. I was sad when I thought of plans for some travel we had to relinquish or when I thought of friends who may have avoided us because of their discomfort with people with disabilities. I was frustrated mostly when my wife sought to communicate with me and I could not understand her. I also have been concerned about the confidentiality issues raised by this chapter. I do not believe my wife would want strangers to know about these experiences as she has always been a very private person. It would also prevent the publication of this chapter for a long time, perhaps forever, if I had to discuss its content with family members and deal with what they did or did not wish made public.

I find it hard to identify how writing this chapter influenced my perceptions of the caregiving experience or my perceptions of myself as a caregiver. In general, reviewing all the difficulties we faced makes them seem formidable. On a day-to-day basis, I coped as best as I could and met as many of my own needs as time allowed. I tried not to obsess about challenges that I might have to meet in the future even though I am somewhat of an obsessive type of person. I didn't always attach the term "caregiver" to myself as I have a lot of other roles (e.g., parent, writer, teacher, friend) that often seemed more important than being a caregiver. Perhaps this is an important part of my own sense of mental stability. If I had only the caregiver role to think about, I am sure I would have been much more depressed than was the case! I don't think that literature helped me to understand my experiences other than that I have read a great deal of professional literature and these readings by now are integrated into who I am and what I think.

I am very supportive of the narrative approach employed in this volume. I believe many of us can benefit from knowing about the experiences of others and how they cope. These narratives should have the following characteristics:

- Have sufficient descriptive detail so the reader can understand the situation and how the people in it coped.
- Describe the feelings of the writer.
- Portray events in which the writer had feelings that were problematic, had difficulties in coping—in other words some evidence of the writer's "dark side"
- Have events that many readers have experienced or will experience so that the narrative is not largely idiosyncratic.
- Show ways in which the writer sought to "make sense" of her or his experiences through relating them to readings, theories, or creative ways of thinking about life.

I hope that this narrative is of that caliber.

REFERENCES

Biddle, B. J. and Thomas, E. J. 1966. *Role Theory: Concepts and Research.* New York: Wiley.

Denman, A. 1998. Determining the needs of spouses caring for aphasic partners. *Disability and Rehabilitation: An International Multidisciplinary Journal* 20 (11): 411–423.

Grant, J. S., Elliott, T. R., Giger, J. N., and Bartolucci, A. A. 2001. Social problem solving abilities, social support, and adjustment among family caregivers of individuals with a stroke. *Rehabilitation Psychology* 46 (1): 44–57.

Han, B. and Haley, W. E. 1999. Family caregiving for patients with stroke. *Stroke* 30: 1478–1485.

Houde, S. C. 2002. Methodological issues in male caregiver research: An integrative review of the literature. *Journal of Advanced Nursing* 40 (6): 626–640.

Kerr, S. M. and Smith, L. M. 2001. Stroke: An exploration of the experience of informal caregiving. *Clinical Rehabilitation: Special Issue* 15 (4): 428–436.

Levine, C. (Ed.). 2004. *Always On Call: When Illness Turns Families into Caregivers.* Nashville: Vanderbilt University Press.

Saleebey, D. (Ed.). 1997. *The Strengths Perspective in Social Work Practice,* 2d ed. New York: Longman.

Tolson, E. E., Reid, W. J., and Garvin, C. D. 2003. *Generalist Practice: A Task-Centered Approach.* New York: Columbia University Press.

Van den Heuvel, E. T., DeWitte, L. P., Schure, L. M., Sanderman, R., and Meyboom-de Jong, B. 2001. Risk factors for burn-out in caregivers of stroke patients, and possibilities for intervention. *Clinical Rehabilitation* 15 (6): 669–677.

Wagner, D. L. 1997. Comparative analysis of caregiving data for caregivers to the elderly: 1987 and 1997. *National Alliance for Caregiving.* Retrieved April 12, 2007, from www.caregiving.org/content/reports/nacanalysis.pdf.

Zak, M. L. 1999. *The Impact of Post Stroke Aphasia and Accompanying Neuropsychological Deficits on Caregiving Spouses and Marriage.* Unpublished doctoral dissertation, University of Kentucky.

ELEVEN

What Goes Around Comes Around

Career Caregiving in the Caring Village

JOYCE O. BECKETT

I came roaring into my sixties with a weekend birthday party to celebrate a lifetime of blessings and wonderful relationships with my husband, family, and friends. The invitation read,

> I celebrate sixty years of life, family, friendship.
> I celebrate sixty years of blessings!
> I celebrate womanhood, service, growth.
> I celebrate wisdom born of questing, of waiting.
> I celebrate resilience born of suffering.
> I celebrate another day, another breath.
> I celebrate your beauty in my garden.
> It would bring me such joy to have you join in the circle of my celebration.
> Please, no presents except the gift of your presence!

What spurred the celebration of my sixtieth birthday was a 2004 accident. A tractor-trailer sideswiped my car while I was performing caregiving tasks. After a week of packing and readying my deceased aunt's home for sale and spending a night in my own bed, I was making the hour's drive to petition guardianship for my hospitalized and only sister. After the demolition of half my car and several days' hospitalization, miraculously, I was pronounced healthy. Tommie, a sister-friend since high school, said, "The accident was life altering." I moved quickly from being a person who carefully considered and executed actions to depending on the Supreme Being (God for me, the Universe, Allah, Buddha, and other titles for others) to unfold my life goals, paths, and actions. Thus I went from being primarily a left-brain person (logical, rational, analytic, objective, concentrating on parts) to incorporating more right-brain activities and views. My more right-brained approach to life (intuitive, synthesizing, subjective, holistic, seeing the whole) was similar to the peak experience or apex of the hierarchy of needs (Maslow 1970, 1999) and resolution of the integrity versus despair stage, ultimately resulting in appreciation and integration of life's complexities, aesthetic beauty, and wisdom (Erikson 1968).

DESCRIPTION OF CAREGIVER

I am a sixth-generation American Beckett, a surname meaning "demonstrated feats of valor" (*Eighth Annual Beckett Family Reunion* 1990). I, an African American, American Indian, and European American, was the younger, by thirteen months, of two daughters. A preacher's kid and teacher's kid, I was born in Norfolk, Virginia, to Bettye Bailey Beckett, a teacher, and William James Beckett Jr., a minister. My mother had thirteen siblings, six alive at my birth, and my father was one of eight. My grandfathers died before my birth. My paternal grandfather was a Methodist minister, and my grandmother was a teacher. A railroad worker, my maternal grandfather purchased a farm that the family ran. The Baileys and Becketts constituted a cohesive clan of biological kin, in-laws with their extended families, fictive kin, and neighbors.

After my grandfather's retirement and medical challenges, my paternal grandparents lived with my parents. Grandmother Beckett was my primary caregiver until she and Carlene, a sister-cousin, moved when I was around six. We visited Grandmother Bailey in North Carolina on holidays and during the summers. Mother's only living sister, Aunt Mary, and Uncle Bill, her husband, lived in North Carolina and visited us biweekly. My grandmothers were the central figures on each side of the clan. Their local children visited them weekly, and the distant ones visited annually.

A historical tradition, the boundaries to our household were ever-changing. Relatives and friends came and went; some became residents. For example, "Big Sis" Carlene, fifteen years my senior, lived with us while attending college.

My grandparents, parents, aunts, and uncles have all died. Mother died at age forty of a heart attack when I was nine. My father remarried a widow with three adult children when I was thirty. At eighty-three, my father died of pneumonia in 1999 after struggling with lifelong bipolar disorder, several physical illnesses, and vascular dementia during his later years. Mom Matron, my stepmother, died a few months later.

I attended segregated public schools in Norfolk, with intermediate stints in Portsmouth and Rocky Mount, North Carolina. In Virginia, European Americans padlocked schools rather than integrate. Whereas my family, teachers, and African American environment were usually positive and nurturing, the larger, sustaining environment (Chestang 1972, 1976; Norton 1976) was caustic, showing and telling African Americans of all ages that they had little value.

After graduating valedictorian of my high school class, I attended Temple University in Philadelphia, my first non–African American learning environment (Brown 2001). I quickly became engrossed in both my academic classes and my personal education on the foreign and often hostile worldviews of European Americans. The invitation to live with relatives in a three-generation, extended family household provided my nurturing environment. As my cousin Marilyn, the sage of the Bailey family, said at my birthday party, "The family just added more water to the soup pot." Each summer I worked and helped my Norfolk family. After college, I got an apartment, went directly to graduate school, and received my master's degree from Bryn Mawr College in 1969. I did not consider applying to Richmond Professional Institute, which became Virginia Commonwealth University, because Virginia dissuaded African Americans from attending its European American graduate schools by partially defraying the cost of out-of-state institutions.

I worked part time while in high school and college. My first professional position was at Eastern Pennsylvania Psychiatric Institute, an outpatient and inpatient psychiatric facility, supplemented by weekends at a nursing home. In 1971, I began my teaching at Bryn Mawr College School of Social Work and was the first clinical social worker in the Student Health Center. In 1975, I began a decade of teaching at the University of Michigan School of Social Work. The multidisciplinary learning opportunities, the academic and theoretic diversity of the faculty, and the school's commitment to diversity helped me cope with the weather, as did proximity to Aldene, my long-time sister-friend and her extended family in Detroit, and an attempt at marriage. In 1985, I completed a postdoctoral fellowship in gerontology at Duke University. Because of my father's physical and emotional challenges, I accepted a position near home, at the School of Social Work at Virginia Commonwealth University in Richmond,

Virginia. When I heard comments like "The South should secede from the Union," I knew I was back in my home state, former capital of the Confederacy. In 2005, I retired.

After a few months in Richmond, I met and later married John. We continue to live in metropolitan Richmond, which still has behavioral and attitudinal remnants of the Civil War era. We live in a rural area and share our property with various wild animals and fowl. It is a quiet and serene place where I grow flowers—including calla lilies, my favorite flowers—herbs, and plants. Because of my health challenges, John is the gardener, and I get to cut and arrange the flowers. John was trained as a clinical social worker and public administrator at Richmond Professional Institute when African American students could not eat on campus and, for more than thirty-seven years, has been the executive director at an agency that serves children and their families. John has two adult children who live in the area: a daughter, vice president at a local medical college and hospital, and a son, an attorney in a private practice. John's daughter has two daughters.

DESCRIPTION OF CAREGIVING EXPERIENCE

My caregiving was a family characteristic and expectation, my duty, an opportunity to demonstrate my love for important people to me, and, as *Five Smooth Stones* (Fairbairn 1966) suggests, payments for successes. There have been three components or areas in the continuum of my emotional and instrumental caregiving: observation and knowledge development, doing or actions, and being. Through observation and instruction I learned the importance my clan placed on the caregiving roles. My family and fictive kin, the immediate and larger communities, and my profession provided opportunities to execute these roles. I learned there were times when the only or best course was to be emotionally and physically present. A challenge in writing this chapter was deciding whom to exclude. I considered my primary or secondary roles in experiences such as those of John's parents, who died one year apart of pancreatic cancer in the early 2000s; Uncle Bill, who had lung cancer and died in the 1990s; Aunt Mary, who successfully fought leukemia for a decade, became critically ill in the summer of 2003, and died in December; and Miss Bernice, a co-tenant who "adopted" me and gallantly fought breast cancer in the late 1980s. Finally, I decided to include my grandmothers, father, mother, and sister. Although each caregiving experience was unique, there were commonalities that informed the implications I discuss later in the chapter.

Grandmother Beckett

Mother Beckett, the name the residents of our close-knit Liberty Park community used, was the most gentle, kind, patient, giving person I have known. With deep spiritual convictions yet without proselytizing, she provided my preschool caregiving training. Before Sunday dinner at a table set with neatly ironed linen tablecloths and napkins, my sister, Julie, and I donned our starched bib aprons. With my mother's help, Grandmother meticulously and lovingly placed food on the china. She added her tall, delicious homemade rolls and dessert and carefully placed all on a linen napkin–covered tray with another linen napkin atop. And so began the ritual of these two grandchildren delivering food to the neighborhood sick.

Grandmother's stroke and hospitalization, when I was eleven, was a shock even to her doctor. Julie and I lived in North Carolina during the school year but resided with Grandmother, my father, and other family members in Norfolk on holidays and during the summers. All grieved when the doctor said Grandmother Beckett would never walk again. Ms. Lucy, a middle-aged woman the family hired to help care for Grandmother, allowed me to wash Grandmother's face before and after meals. With deep pleasure and much gratitude, I helped prepare her meals and delivered the tray. Although I do not recall feelings, I imagine being frightened that I would lose my nurturing grandmother. What a blessing that the stroke did not affect Grandmother's cognitive skills! Using the African oral tradition, she shared many things about her life and diverse heritages—Cherokee, African, and European American—the Bible, and her views. This special time at her bedside was a continuation of my learning family history, her views about death and the afterlife, caregiving, and accepting diversity. For example, she suggested I could overcome my death fear if I touched a dead person and suggested that she be the one. We discussed my mother's death and its meanings. Her stroke also emphasized the importance of being there for Grandmother, just being.

When I was thirteen, Grandmother, with the secret help of my sister-cousin Loretta, made a full recovery and continued her usual routine of caring for others and the house, cooking, and going to Lodge meetings and church. Refusing to use a regular cane, she took Loretta's arm and proudly walked down to her church seat. We had our cheerful, nurturing Grandmother Beckett back for several years. Cheerfully, the clan again shared caregiving during her final decline, which progressed to her being bedridden for about a year. Uncle Ellis, a retired railroad chef who returned from New York, cooked the meals. Aunt Mary, her oldest daughter, bathed Grandmother and washed her clothes;

Carlene took care of her medical and financial concerns; and Julie provided care during the night. During summers and when home from college, I pitched in wherever needed. In July 1966, Grandmother was hospitalized with labored breathing. Over the next few days, she slept peacefully but was unresponsive, and family tasks shifted to being—just being there with her, holding her hand, whispering to and kissing her.

When the family visited, we were pleasantly surprised: Grandmother's eyes were open, and she was talking and she looked like her healthy self. A few hours later, Grandmother passed. She was ninety-three and died on Sunday, as my mother did. Obviously, in that last visit, when she said, "Reverend Beckett," Grandmother was talking to my Grandfather Beckett, not my father, and "the beautiful flowers on both sides of the walkway" were her view of Heaven. Grandmother Beckett taught me the art and science of caregiving and provided the opportunity to use the learning, doing, and being tasks with her, all the time providing unwavering and unconditional love.

Grandmother Bailey

Grandmother Bailey, a petite woman, lived about two hours away in a lovely old farmhouse that Grandpa, a tall, stately man with red hair and eyebrows, helped to build. When Julie and I visited on holidays and during the summers, Uncle Keither's six children, who lived next door, were like siblings, built-in playmates and later co-workers. A cousin usually stayed in the family home, providing overnight company for Grandmother. Everyone was especially happy with Mother's delicious rolls and homemade ice cream. For the Becketts this was a time to relax. Mother reminisced about her childhood, and Daddy enjoyed the quiet and shared his talents: molding clay articles for our playhouse, woodcarving, hunting, taxidermy, astrology, and botany. Julie and I played, helped with farm chores, learned about nature and the rural way, exposing us to a well, a night pot, an icebox, and a wood stove.

Like Grandmother Beckett, Grandmother Bailey allowed me to learn, do, and be in caregiving and to accept differences. Eventually, we learned, with Mother's help, to cope with Grandmother's excitability. I helped to feed the fowl and livestock and gather eggs. I was never proficient in milking the goats and cows, but Grandmother successfully taught me to churn butter and place it into beautiful round molds; make rich country cakes, plum wine and peach brandy, jellies, and jams; and harvest and cook fresh vegetables. It was a pleasure to hand and tie tobacco, especially when I was old enough to earn money.

I learned everything had a purpose. Dishwater and rotten fruit and vegetables became food for the hogs; grass sustained Betsy, the cow; lard from pigskins became lye soap for boiling clothes in the big black wash pot in the backyard; manure from the mule barn became crop fertilizer. Things were born and things died. Fruit trees bloomed, a unique color and aroma for each; the fruit ripened and fell or was picked. I saw piglets born and later enjoyed the delicious pork chops, ribs, and North Carolina barbecue. Sometimes the life transitions were painful, as when Betsy died and Henry, my pet rooster, was served for dinner. I learned that grieving was normal.

Grandmother Bailey's was also a place that I learned connections to our African heritage and rich family history. Her behaviors demonstrated links to African culture. For example, she used a tree branch from the yard to clean her teeth. Later, in Ghana, I witnessed this technique. The oral tradition gave significant snapshots of previous family life. While she was heating an iron in one of the fireplaces, Mother's dress caught fire, resulting in lifetime backside scars. We heard about Aunt Mary's childhood unauthorized visit to the loft where her brothers slept. Down the stairs she fell, sustaining a deep gash in one of her eyebrows. My family's intergenerational, extended family constellation was like that of many African Americans (Billingsley 1968, 1973; Hill 1971, 1999). These and other stories provided family themes that I would encounter repeatedly.

After our move to live with Aunt Mary and Uncle Bill after mother's death, Julie and I saw Grandmother Bailey twice a week, each time delivering home-cooked meals, enough for a few days. Ironically, we were repeating the caregiving Grandmother Beckett had taught. During the summers, Julie and I extended our visits, executing the caregiving of being.

As Grandmother Bailey aged, along with the Bailey clan, I increased the doing caregiving. A teen, I warmed her meals and helped with the house and yard cleaning and other tasks. In the summer of 1965, Grandmother's heart condition and hypertension worsened, and she needed a full-time nurse. The week after Aunt Mary returned from summer school, Grandmother passed, at age eighty-seven.

In some ways, the things I learned at Grandmother Bailey's were very different from those at Grandmother Beckett's. Yet from each grandmother I learned about caring—for people, plants, vegetables, animals, and nature—diverse ways of living, and how to respond to different personalities. Importantly, I quickly grasped that different did not mean better or worse, just different. By elementary school age, I knew several languages and the appropriate time to use each. In Virginia, *dairy* described the building complex where milk was processed; in North Carolina, it was the small blue wooden house with shelves under the huge oak tree next to the well where milk was stored. Learning the importance of voice inflection, I successfully communicated with the farm animals that responded by coming when I called. The education my grandmother provided in diversity, acceptance, and multiculturalism was essential in my profession and my ongoing, lifelong caregiving responsibilities.

Mother

Born in 1914, mother was a caring, patient, and supportive person and the first family member for whom I cared. As the oldest girl in a large family and having lost a number of siblings, my mother became a caregiver early and was familiar with grief. She was the primary caregiver to Aunt Mary, nine years her junior, establishing an enduring maternal bond. She was the oldest surviving girl, and my uncles were protective of and confided in her. Mother and her brother Clarence moved to Rocky Mount and lived with their oldest brother and his wife in order to complete high school, one I later attended. Their small town had no high school for African Americans. Mother and Uncle Clarence graduated together from both high school and college and became teachers. In the parlor at Grandmother Bailey's, my parents married in 1943. Mother joined Daddy in Norfolk and continued her teaching career and their home became the hub of the Beckett–Bailey clan. Each summer, Daddy's out-of-town siblings and their families visited, and the Baileys visited frequently.

I was quite attached to my mother. Family members would humorously tell the story of my nightly journey as a toddler from my bed to my parents', when I said, "I am going to see Mama." Mother spoke quietly and communicated with her large, beautiful eyes; they could tell Julie and me to be quiet, sit down, and other actions. Mother prepared Julie and me for life early. Before we reached age seven, she read us a book about menstruation. She taught us many household tasks, especially after Grandmother Beckett and Carlene moved, and she was generous with praise. Mother enjoyed teaching, and Julie and I looked forward to helping her grade papers.

Mother's Decline

When I was eight, my father, my mother, my sister, and I moved to the parsonage, next to Daddy's new church in Portsmouth. Before this move, I overheard adult discussions about Mother not feeling well and the possibility of having heart surgery in Philadelphia. She took vitamins and penicillin and visited the doctor regularly. In the fall of 1954, almost a year after our move, Mother changed; she had less energy, coughed often, could not walk far, and hired a housekeeper. Grandmother Beckett periodically spent several days helping, and church members and neighbors pitched in. When we had weekly summer guests Mother happily cooked, cleaned, planted flowers, combed the hair of my many visiting female cousins, did laundry, took us places for recreation, and was active in the church and organizations. Because no one talked about her health, sometimes I thought I was imagining changes, especially because Mother continued teaching.

By mid-September, I would awaken to Mother's coughing and movements. Daddy had gone to Chicago to visit a brother and was subsequently hospitalized for his bipolar disorder; therefore, Mother was sleeping alone. When Julie and I asked permission to sleep in the bed with her, Mother granted it. I wonder whether we wanted to be physically closer to Mother to comfort her and ourselves. In her bed, Julie and I observed firsthand when mother used a strange, red heat lamp aimed toward her chest. I imagine I was frightened, but I recall only missing Daddy and looking forward, with Julie and Mother, to our Sunday phone calls. Feeling that he would help Mother, weekly I asked him to come home soon. I doubt I told him that I was frightened or that Mother was ill, wanting to protect my strong but emotionally fragile father. Helping Mother meant Julie and I spent less time with friends, saddening us, but Mother was the priority.

The weekend of October 30, 1954, was to be a full one. Everything went like clockwork. Friday night, Mother had a rehearsal for her Sunday evening candlelight service. On Saturday, Julie and I visited Grandmother Beckett, Carlene, and Loretta, while Mother went to the cardiologist. Saturday evening Mother gave us a wonderful Halloween party in our new home. Sunday, October 31, we went to church and spoke with Daddy.

Mother's Death

October 31, 1954, is an evening I will always remember: Mother died after her beautiful candlelight service. Coughing and spitting up blood, Mother refused to leave until the program ended; deacons had to carry her next door to our home. Ann, a nurse and church member, accompanied us and called an ambulance. It never came, as often happened in African American neighborhoods in the 1950s. When carried to a waiting church member's car, Mother opened those huge, beautiful, powerful eyes, looked at us, and was unable to speak. Julie and I sat quietly as people whispered.

Carlene came, gathered up Julie and me, and took us to our old home, where we remained until December's move to Aunt Mary's. During the ride, I quietly prayed. After hearing our bedtime prayers, Grandmother Beckett said Mother died before reaching the hospital. I was in shock; Julie said, "I knew we would not see Mother again." Neither Julie nor I heard Grandmother's subsequent prayer. I lay awake wondering what would happen to Julie and me. At age nine and ten, we had no mother and a father hospitalized in a city we had visited but no longer visualized. We had the comfort of being with Grandmother, Carlene, and Loretta, each of whom loved us deeply, but the pain of Mother's death was overpowering.

Uncle Ernest and his family from Chicago drove Daddy home on a furlough from the hospital. Although he gave us huge hugs, many kisses, and prayers, he was in a daze. He almost compulsively stared at Mother's picture, sometimes with tears flowing down his face. We wondered how Daddy would make it without my mother. They had been an awesome team. I remembered little of the funeral, the largest I had attended. I realized the many lives Mother had touched. I cried continuously; Daddy, with tears in his eyes, and brave, tearless Julie consoled me. After the services, Daddy was transferred to a Virginia hospital, a couple of hours away.

Thanksgiving

Thanksgiving of 1954 was special. We were asked to take a can of food to school for the needy, and Grandmother gave Julie, Loretta, and me each a quarter in a white envelope. When I gave my contribution to my teacher, she said, "Oh, you do not have to do this." I replied, "Yes, I must because Grandmother told me to." My teacher reluctantly accepted my donation. Her hesitancy was because my gift was different, I decided: money instead of canned goods. That evening, someone knocked at our door and delivered a Thanksgiving basket. On top of the basket were the three unopened envelopes. For the first of many times, I heard Grandmother Beckett repeat the African proverb, "What goes around comes around," and she explained that God blesses the giver by multiplying the returned gifts. The basket was concrete evidence.

Daddy

Daddy, the youngest, was born in 1916 on the rural Virginia eastern shore in the parsonage, next to the Methodist church where Grandfather pastored. According to his older siblings who helped with his care, Grandmother and

Grandfather—in their forties and fifties, respectively, at Daddy's birth—were less strict with him. He was green eyed and red headed, and as a teen, while shooting rabbits with a friend, he sustained an eye injury, resulting in inability to read with that eye. Daddy moved often as the Methodist Conference transferred Grandpa to various churches (Butt 1908). The Methodist Conference moved Grandfather to Norfolk, and Daddy graduated from the same high school as I. Daddy completed a bachelor's degree in theology and graduate religion classes. He earned a doctor of divinity degree, an honorary recognition.

Daddy was lively, loving, caring, charming, and humorous, with an excellent solo voice. A family person, he enjoyed gardening and playing with Julie, neighborhood children, and me. He taught Julie and me to ride our bikes, skate, fly kites, sculpt with clay, and other skills. One day we found one of our kites wrapped around the electric pole: Daddy had been flying it solo. Daddy enjoyed walking, explaining nature, and participating in family and neighborhood joke-telling contests.

Minister

Daddy became a preacher in his early teens. His sermons, usually about twenty minutes, were packed with religious and secular information. He was proud that Julie and I joined church during a revival he conducted. Daddy pastored various churches in and near Tidewater. When I was in the first grade, the entire community was pleasantly surprised when a local television station selected Daddy as the first African American minister to preach on a daily religious program. Daddy was active in community and civic organizations to remove the poll tax and increase voting, among other goals. When I was a preschooler, Daddy supplemented his income by working in a woman's boutique and as a part-time holiday postal carrier. Many people knew Daddy and lovingly said, "Oh, you are Reverend Beckett's daughter." For example, during a social visit, the dean of social work at Norfolk State College introduced me to the president and faculty as "Reverend Beckett's daughter" before any other descriptions.

Symptoms of Mental Illness in Early Life

Daddy had a bipolar disorder, initially diagnosed as schizophrenia. Historically and currently, clinicians have given African Americans and other people of color more severe diagnoses, even when they display the same symptoms as European Americans (Chow et al. 2003; Franklin 1985; Howard 1997; McRae and

Noumair 1997; Rothenberg 1999; Smedley and Smedley 2005; Smedley et al. 2003; Williams et al. 1997). When psychiatrists began using lithium, they automatically changed Daddy's diagnosis, a requirement for the drug. I am unsure when Daddy had his first mental health crisis. Before Mother's death, Daddy's brothers from Chicago and New York helped arrange his hospitalizations, by either coming to Norfolk or arranging for Daddy to visit. I doubt I initially understood his brain disease, but I, like other family members, could quickly detect his symptoms: expensive purchases, changes in his sleep patterns, boundless energy, preoccupation with Masonic activities and symbols, rapid weight loss, sharp spikes in his blood sugar and hypertension, and changes in his eye color. Reflecting, I wonder whether Daddy's early trips to visit his brothers were his effort to spare our immediate family the pain of hospitalizing him, which required use of the criminal justice system.

Like those of many patients, Daddy's mental health symptoms changed as he aged; when younger, he had only manic episodes; in middle age he had only depressive symptoms; next, cycles of mania were quickly followed by depression; and finally, he had concurrent depression with mania and agitation. Initially Daddy became ill in the spring. After Mother's death, the episodes emerged between her September birthday and Halloween. His periods of mental illness were interspersed with long periods performing ministerial and family responsibilities. His longest period without hospitalization was about a decade. I give his psychiatrist the credit. The doctor, also diagnosed as bipolar, took the time to educate Daddy and our family about the disease, encouraged us to make an appointment at the onset of any symptoms, and was accessible. Our family grieved when this physician left the area. In his later life, Daddy's functioning was complicated by vascular dementia, heart problems, diabetes, hypertension, and the toll of years of various medications. His bipolar episodes increased in number, and his hospitalizations lengthened. With sadness, he decided to retire, a difficult event for his congregation because they were used to him returning from his hospitalizations as good as new. Soon after retirement, Daddy began his final and lengthy hospitalization.

Hospitalizations

My first of many visits to a state psychiatric hospital happened when I was in elementary school. I was sad when we had to leave, realizing Daddy could not. It was the first of many visits to various types of psychiatric facilities that ended in September 1999, when Daddy passed. The history of these visits chronicled not only Daddy's illness and final decline but also the movement from segregated to integrated mental health intervention. Physically, the state hospitals were different in almost every way from the African American hospital, which was smaller, with fewer amenities and a harsher physical environment. The hospital for European Americans had nicely appointed visiting rooms, some private, whereas visitors at the other facility often sat on wooden benches in the hallway.

What the African American hospital lacked was compensated for by the emotional environment. The staff saw Daddy as a biopsychosocial, spiritual, complete, individual person (Beckett and Johnson 1995) rather than only a mental patient. When speaking to and about him, the staff said "Reverend Beckett" or "Doctor Beckett," labels suggesting retention of personhood and all benefits accompanying a minister. The first time I heard the staff at the other hospital call him "Bill," I cringed when I realized it was my father. Using his first name was like calling him "boy" and displayed cultural insensitivity. Later the staff began to use "Mr." An improvement, this title did not recognize my father's profession. It was like my using "Mr." or "Mrs." instead of "Dr." for the psychiatrist. Interestingly, in this European American hospital, the African American staff always called Daddy "Reverend" or "Doctor." At the African American hospital, the chaplain, who became a family friend, allowed and encouraged Daddy to preach on a local radio program and help serve communion. This staff was willing to accept information Daddy gave, whereas staff at the European American hospital were prone to assume it was delusional. For example, they said that Daddy falsely claimed to have a doctorate and to have published books of poems. They were visibly surprised when I said all was true. I wondered whether the staff would believe these statements if the patient were European American, younger, or upper class.

Caregiving Tasks

I moved from primarily observing and learning to doing caregiving for Daddy after I permanently returned to Norfolk as an adolescent. Julie and I became responsible for arranging private court hearings to prevent jail detention. A wife, mother, and caregiver for her mother and Grandmother Beckett, Carlene was relieved to relinquish tasks. Julie and I continued our responsibilities after Daddy married. We detected symptoms, or Mom Matron called requesting that we do something, although she had known Daddy for many years and visited him in the hospitals. My roles included advocate, conduit of information to the medical staff and the family clan, and caring daughter. When Daddy was at home, Julie had daily contact, and when he was hospitalized she visited more frequently than I because she was unemployed because of her disability.

During Daddy's last hospitalization, Mom Matron and her family initially visited periodically, then slowed, and finally stopped. Mom spoke with Daddy almost daily on the phone while he was able to speak. I attempted not to analyze or discuss her actions because it would take energy that I needed to perform my tasks. Julie and I were tireless caregivers. She and I also brought him to our homes when we both could be present. During his last visit to my house in 1996, Julie and I realized that caring for him around the clock was too challenging. One night I awakened and saw that Daddy, now blind and dressed in my pajamas, was about to walk down the steps from the bedroom level. I reached him in time to prevent a disaster. Instead of reacting to his possible fall, I laughed hysterically that he had found and changed into my sleepwear. And we thought he could not dress himself! It was a funny sight: three family members standing in the hallway laughing at my prudish father dressed in ladies' pajamas. Humor and laughing relieved anxiety and fear. For the rest of Daddy's visit, Julie and I took turns sleeping and caring.

After this event, Julie and I spent many weekends and my spring breaks at a timeshare and took Daddy for day visits. It was homelike, with a fireplace that Daddy loved, a full kitchen for preparing his favorite meals, comfortable bedrooms to rest after tiring days, and a family celebration site for holidays and his birthdays. I was grateful for Julie's nursing experience, patience, and special bond with Daddy.

The importance of family and communication was apparent when Daddy was transferred to a Richmond hospital for a cardiac pacemaker. Julie, John, and I waited during the surgery. After several hours, I phoned the doctor, who, with a surprised tone, said that he was unaware that family was waiting. I wondered whether the doctor's expectation that an elderly mental patient would have no family present overrode the information I had provided both him and his resident in his 4 A.M. call to take a history. I visited daily, and once I heard Daddy screaming long before I reached his room. I took his hand and whispered, "Daddy, it's Joyce. You are okay. I am here. You are at a medical hospital and you are okay." He stopped screaming and said, "I did not know where I was. Everything is different. I don't recognize the voices." Leaving, I suggested that the nurses tell him who they were and where he was if he screamed again. It worked. I wondered why the nurses had not intervened effectively with a displaced, blind patient.

When Daddy no longer talked or recognized me, coupling visits with team meetings sometimes was the prod I needed. Julie's visits never slowed, even though she needed someone to drive her. Over time, I realized that my father's essence had already vacated this small, motionless body, with beautiful white hair, right before my eyes, and I had been unable to stop it. I grieved.

Daddy was kept clean, and I was grateful. When Daddy began frequently entering the medical building for various ailments, often pneumonia, the hospital complied with my request to transfer him permanently. An unanticipated consequence was that I could sit beside his bed rather than waiting for the staff to bring him from his ward to the visiting room. I increased my visits and their length, often incorporating schoolwork. I took a tape recorder and played gospel music, some with his voice. On previous occasions, cassette players and radios I left for Daddy disappeared before my next visit. About a year before his death, the medical staff installed a feeding tube, a decision I made reluctantly, because Daddy could no longer swallow. Both Mom and I had power of attorney, but Mom had transferred all decision making to me.

While I was at work, on Friday morning, September 10, 1999, Daddy's doctor called and said Daddy had died of pneumonia. The social worker asked me for the name of the funeral home. In a daze, I responded and quickly hung up the phone. Deep inside, I knew Daddy's body was tired, and yet I was shocked at his death. I was grateful his suffering was over and very sad to lose my wonderful father. Almost immediately, the social worker called again and performed her most helpful intervention. She invited me to visit with Daddy before the mortician came. I found him lying peacefully in a hospital bed with a rocking chair adjacent. I rocked and talked with him and the Lord as the sun shone brightly in the room.

I reminisced and remembered the worst thing that had happened while Daddy was a patient: an unexplained serious injury to his reading eye in 1996, resulting in total blindness and necessitating eye surgery. A meeting with the hospital administration and staff provided no further information. My review of the medical records at the local medical hospital indicated that another patient hit his eye. I was furious. My father, in a psychiatric hospital partly for his safety, had been irreparably injured in the facility. My anger and disappointment about Daddy's progressive and debilitating physical and mental illnesses and the need to spend his final years in a psychiatric hospital energized me. When I met Daddy at the ophthalmologist's office for his morning postsurgery visit, I became more determined to pursue legal avenues. Two hospital employees took Daddy to the doctor's office, left him, and returned in the late afternoon. The staff, unaware of my presence, left a weak, diabetic, postsurgical mental patient at the physician's office. After securing Daddy's needed snacks and meals, I called the hospital and asked when Daddy would be picked up. In the background someone said, "What is she doing there?" A couple of hours later, the two employees returned in a vehicle with several mall packages.

With the help of a friend, I finally found attorneys who successfully represented Daddy in legal action against the hospital. The monetary award funded the timeshare rental. The nonmonetary awards included quarterly external geriatric consultations by experts I selected. When I told him the outcome, Daddy's response was to say with a smile, "Gosh, I never thought I was worth that much." I immediately thought of the long struggles each Beckett generation had faced in Virginia. Then, I said to myself, "Not so bad."

At the end of my visit with my deceased father, the doctor said Daddy had had the last say. The hospital had planned to move Daddy to a nursing home the next week; now, their decision was moot.

Julie

At age fifteen, Julie first grieved for my mother, who died five years previously. In the middle of the night, she sobbed and awakened me, saying she saw mother at the end of the bed and wondered whether I saw her. As a clinician, I now realize Julie's experience was similar to that of many grieving people but quite delayed. At the time, however, I wondered whether her behavior was a symptom of an emotional problem. I held her close and cried with her, saying, "I do not see mother." Over the next year, Julie displayed other symptoms: sleeping problems, anorexia followed by weight gain, excessive talking, and sadness.

The doctor suggested that Aunt Mary take Julie for a psychological evaluation at the University of North Carolina. They had an early morning appointment but were seen in the afternoon after the European Americans. After the staff saw Julie, they interviewed Uncle Bill and Aunt Mary as if "we had the problems." Aunt Mary decided against the return appointment because "I do not have time to take off from work for such nonsense." I was hurt and angry: "Didn't they love Julie enough to see that she got the help she needed?" Aunt Mary, like many parents and the practitioners, probably saw Julie's illness as an indictment; therefore, any attention to it would mean Aunt Mary had to accept weaknesses in Julie and herself. This view, along with the stigma of having a "crazy" child, prevented Aunt Mary from getting the early, appropriate help Julie needed.

Born premature in 1944, Julie spent two months in a hospital incubator. As children, Julie and I were inseparable, wearing identical clothes and later the same style but different colors; our names, Julie and Joyce seemed like one because most people referred to both of us. People told me that Mother had said, "If something happens to me, I don't have to worry about Joyce, but I am concerned about how Julie would fare." This suggested that Mother had noticed some early vulnerability. Toward the end of her junior year, Julie attempted going out of the house in the middle of the night in her nightclothes; fortunately, I stopped her. The next day, her clothes were packed. Uncle Bill transported her to my father, who had Julie committed to the same African American state hospital where he had been a patient. At the end of a summer of working on the farm, I moved with my Daddy, Uncle Ellis, and Grandmother and became the "little lady" of the house. I blamed Aunt Mary and Uncle Bill for Julie's condition and was angry that they deserted her. I made and carried dresses to my hospitalized sister.

After her hospitalization, Julie returned to Norfolk as good as new. She graduated valedictorian, received a four-year scholarship to the local university, pursued her lifetime dream of becoming a nurse, and shared the household duties. Julie made friends, enjoyed her classes, and worked in New York in the summers. Two years later, she was hospitalized again. Afterwards, she attended a business school in Richmond and, with a few other young women from the hospital, lived with the family of a lovely woman, "Mom Maggie," who became a lifelong family friend. After completing the business course and returning to Norfolk, Julie completed a nursing aide course and did private duty for several years for the same family, followed by work in a nursing home for nearly fifteen years. She needed hospitalization. Like many siblings of emotionally and physically challenged people, I wondered whether my achievements were at her expense, and I felt guilty. Julie's behavior was diagnosed as bipolar, and when lithium became available, it was prescribed. The availability of the community mental health system and her long-term psychiatrist prevented several hospitalizations. Once, for example, the doctor asked me to remain in Norfolk for the week and bring Julie in daily. A week of intensive intervention prevented months of hospitalization. Something about entering the hospital system provoked deterioration and a longer intervention period. Unfortunately, community agencies did not provide this effective daily outpatient intervention.

Julie had a large network of friends, relatives, and coworkers who contacted me if I needed to help with her care. Paul, her friend and companion for more than thirty years, was a stabilizing force in her life and accepted her unconditionally. When hospitalized, she always knew that he, with some financial help from me, would have the apartment waiting. Like many people with bipolar disorder, Julie became more resistant to medication as she aged, and doctors tried new drugs. By the late 1990s, her episodes were more frequent, sometimes fueled by losses and toxic reactions to psychotropic medications. The year of 1999 was catastrophic, necessitating more active caregiving. Carlene died suddenly in April, Daddy in September, Paul in November, and our stepmother in November. While dealing with the losses, I had to muster enough energy to work, visit and support Julie, dismantle her apartment, and find an assisted living facility. I faced all or the rigors of long-distance caregiving yet wanted to honor Julie's wish to remain in Tidewater. Her large support system, especially her church and the mental health center staff, was a deciding factor.

Since 1999 I have been the primary caregiver for Julie, with family, friends, and her church family helping. We have faced many challenges, including Julie's 2000 knee replacement surgery. She remained hospitalized for more than a month battling psychotic behavior caused by the interaction of her fear, stress, anesthesia and psychotropic medications, and the search for a nursing home for postsurgical rehabilitation. I visited Julie each weekend and inspected and evaluated nursing homes as the hospital social worker requested. I was furious and frustrated when I discovered my efforts were irrelevant. For people with a psychiatric history and feisty personality, nursing homes evaluate and select the patient from the computer information the various hospitals send.

A lack of communication between the inpatient and outpatient psychiatrists prompted Julie's substantial decline. A psychiatrist in a private hospital developed a medical regime for Julie that drastically improved her functioning. On her first visit, the outpatient psychiatrist discontinued two medications. This resulted in her decompensation and rehospitalization at the same private inpatient facility, followed by transfer to the state hospital, where she remained for months. The hospital psychiatrist tried the previously successful prescription regime. It did not work and probably would never be effective again because of changes in her body chemistry. This was one of the most egregious occurrences in Julie's history because it robbed her of extraordinary progress and accelerated her decline. On several occasions, I have observed how the lack of communication between mental health staff leads to ineffective treatment, life-threatening situations, and hospitalizations. This is the revolving door of private and public mental health hospitals.

Julie faced many unacceptable events while residing in an assisted living facility operated by the state mental health department. These included lack of meals and of referrals to required programs, inadequate supervision, and falsification of her records. When I noted changes—weight loss, decreased alertness, increased argumentativeness, decreased interest in social activities, cessation of writing to me and other family members, and reduced attention to the cleanliness of the apartment—I expressed concern. Because neither the assisted living staff nor the mental health staff had noticed any changes in her behavior, they declined my request that Julie see the psychiatrist or at least get her lithium level checked. Subsequently, Julie was rushed to the medical center and diagnosed with lithium toxicity. When I reached the hospital, she was unable to walk or feed or bathe herself. I was furious and helpless. My years of observation and experience with Julie and my clinical skills counted for nothing compared with the staff, who knew Julie for less than a year. Now Julie had serious mental and physical illnesses that could have been prevented with an inexpensive laboratory test. The doctors told me that Julie could never use lithium again. Without lithium, her prognosis was guarded, at best. The physician arranged to have a sitter from the nursing staff with Julie around the clock for the several weeks she was hospitalized; this was the first time such a service had been provided. Initially, I stayed almost a week in the city, about one and one half hours from Richmond. After Julie began to walk with help, I returned home and visited her weekly. Julie was transferred to a psychiatric unit of a medical facility and finally was move to a state psychiatric hospital, where she remains on a Medicare-noncompliant gerontological ward. As the letter in the appendix shows, caregiving for Julie is active and ongoing.

ANALYSES

Several theoretical and conceptual approaches help explain my caregiving experiences. Life course theory describes how caregiving is related to my and the care recipients' life stages. My initial caregiving, in the initiative versus guilt stage (Erikson 1963, 1968), supported the related tasks—mastery of locomotion, language skills, and learning appropriate roles—and resulted in purpose and courage to define and pursue goals. Sometimes the interface matched well. Two examples are my learning family history while caring for my grandmothers, who faced generativity issues including the need to impart information to the next generation, and my father's sharing parental wisdom after I received my doctorate; he wanted me to applaud my achievements and enjoy life rather than constantly erecting additional goals. At other times, the interface was less smooth. For example, while in high school, I also cared for the house, my grandmother, my father, and my sister while I worked.

Role theory concepts (Aldwin 1994; Jacobson 2007; Shaw and Costanzo 1982)—acceptance, expectations, sharing conflict, transition, strain, overload, and mutuality—were helpful. Fortunately, sharing the caregiving roles prevented some role overload and strain. There were some role conflicts, however, as I faced competing role expectations—whether to attend a graduate class or travel home to help arrange the hospitalization of my father or sister. The role expectations of care recipients influenced their and my behaviors. For example, Julie often said, "I am the oldest; I should be taking care of you." Fortunately, reciprocity—recipients cared for each other and for me—was included in all my caregiving. The empowerment (Ackerson and Harrison 2000; Carter 1999, 2006; Cowger 1997; DuBois and Miley 2002; Gibbs and Fuery 1994; Gutierrez 1990; Gutierrez et al. 1995, 2000; Hill-Collins 2000; Lee 1996; Miley et al. 2001; Perkins 1995; Staples 1990), strengths (Blundo 2001; Burnett and Shadd 2006; Early 2001, Early and GlenMaye 2000; Graybeal 2001; Laursen 2000; Mortola et al. 2008; Munford and Sanders 2006; Saleebey 1996, 1997; Timberlake et al. 2008; Vakalahi et al. 2007), and resilience (Brendtro et al. 2006; Henderson et al. 2007; Hopkins et al. 2007; Mortola et al. 2008; Rapp and Goscha 2006) theories emphasized the skills, abilities, knowledge, insights, and caregiving behaviors the care recipients demonstrated while facing personal adversities and challenges (Robbins et al. 2006).

The timing of my socialization to caregiving, during development of my superego and moral code (Kohlberg 1969; Kohlberg and Kramer 1969; Piaget 1932), and the positive reinforcement resulted in my lifetime view of caregiving as a moral obligation and duty. Family history, behaviors, and expectations along with African American community norms, especially the importance of spirituality, facilitated my acceptance and performance of caregiving. Observation, modeling, and experiential learning, all social learning theory concepts, informed subsequent caregiving. For example, I learned that caregiving was a responsibility shared between clan, fictive kin, and community. Authors representing the early feminist discourse (Chodorow 1978, 1979; Gilligan 1982; Hill-Collins 2000; hooks 1984a, 1984b; Miller 1976) and the Africentric perspective (Chestang 1972, 1976; Hill 1971, 1998; hooks 2000a, 2000b; Norton 1978; Schiele 2000) who critique life span theories as being androcentric or male centered and ethnocentric, respectively, discuss the importance of interdependence, intimacy, nurturance, connectedness, and relatedness for women and African Americans. Like other African American women, I was trained to nurture and thrive on social connectedness. The care recipients' large and active social support systems provided physical and emotional aid, lessening my responsibilities and stress.

I also had direct, lifelong support from family members, teachers, friends, neighbors, colleagues, and others. During the stressful period of grading final assignments, for example, Carlene cooked complete meals, wrapped them in freezer-ready containers, and called me with the time they would arrive at the bus station. John, my husband, has been my live-in support system. As an early and continuing caregiver in his family, he had an intimate understanding of my responsibilities. He shared the household responsibilities equally, and his concrete help with my caregiving and reminding me of my limits were invaluable. Yoga, exercise, massage therapy, listening to peaceful music, frequent contact with friends, counseling, and flexible work environments constituted my arsenal of effective mechanisms. Medical diaries and journaling helped chronicle the multiple contacts with the formal resources and my reactions.

As a caregiver, I also faced many barriers at all societal levels. These barriers included the following:

- Practitioners who lacked knowledge of African American culture; viewed cultural differences as deficits rather than strengths; were unfamiliar with the strengths, empowerment, and resilience models; were hesitant to establish a working partnership with family caregivers; were burned out; and did not use a psychoeducation model.
- Insufficient cross-cultural communication, knowledge, and skills.
- Lack of communication and coordination between service organizations.
- Structural barriers erected by uninformed social policies and practices.
- The self-preservation goals of complex, bureaucratic organizations that undermine client needs.
- Deterioration in my health, the consequences of a fall on ice.

These stressors inspired creativity. For example, while in Michigan I taught a seminar in my home, ameliorating stress accompanying my uncertain health. In general, the barriers encouraged greater reliance on professional and formal caregivers, novel efforts to communicate effectively, and more monitoring of caregiving tasks.

Building on the ecological (Beckett and Coley 1987; Greif 1986) and Africentric (Schiele 2000) perspectives, the Beckett–Lee Ecological Africentric Model (Beckett and Lee 2004) in figure 11.1 emphasizes models—empowerment, resilience, and strengths—especially relevant to interventions with oppressed populations, groups the literature overlooks. The Beckett–Lee Model focuses on intervention with African Americans and can be adapted to any population. The model emphasizes understanding of and intervention with several

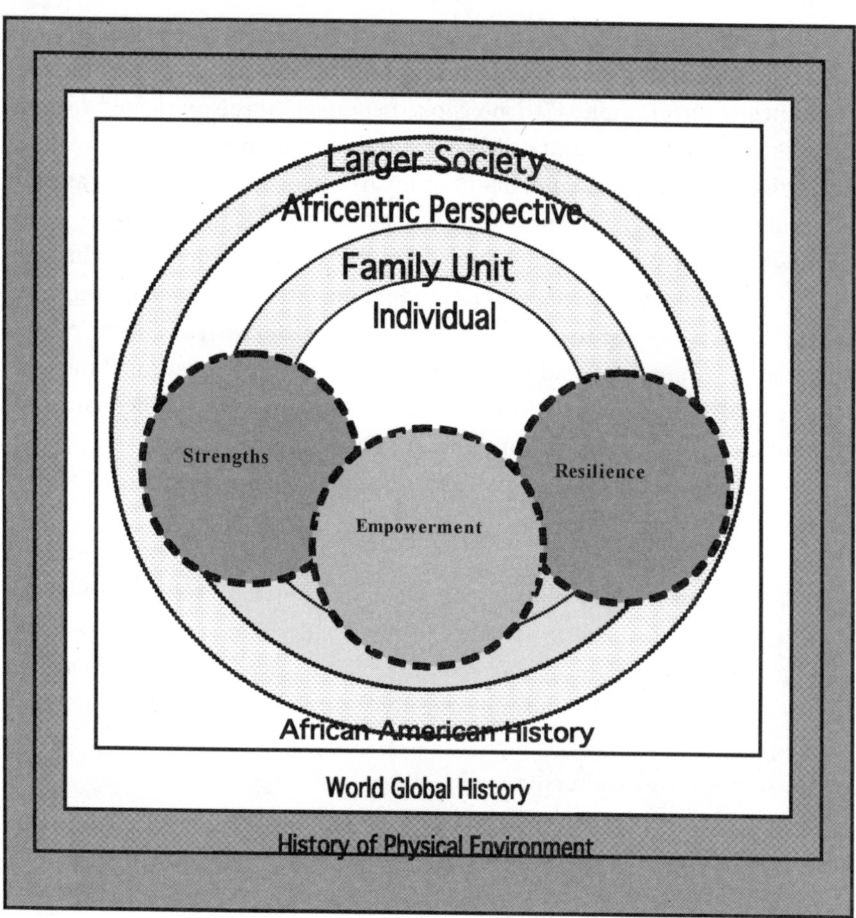

Figure 11.1 Beckett-Lee Ecological Africentric Model. (Adapted from Beckett, J. and Lee, N. 2004. Informing the future of child welfare practices with African American Families. In J. Everett, B. Leashore and S. Chipungu, Eds. Child Welfare Revisited: An Africentric perspective, (New Brunswick, N.J.: Rugters University Press, 93–123.)

social systems, from the individual to the larger environments; the importance of each system's history, culture, and physical environment; and the interactions between and within social systems. A practitioner can add pertinent institutions and models to the diagram; for example, she could place the mental health system in the larger society and a root doctor in the Africentric perspective, respectively. The model supports attention to any system characteristic. The influence of coercive and exploitative sociopolitical power, stripping or withholding resources, and inflicting injustice and suffering could become intervention targets. Appropriate interventions might include preventing insurance companies' redlining neighborhoods; changing practices and programs to reduce healthcare disparity, or establishing universal health and mental health coverage in the United States, the richest and only industrial country without it.

IMPLICATIONS

The implications discussed below are summarized in table 11.1.

Literature

The caregiving literature does not adequately address some of my caregiving experiences. Only recently has there been a discussion of caregiving by children, men, and grandmothers; the positives of caregiving; reciprocity in caregiving; and simultaneously and sequentially caring for several people. My story demonstrates the importance of multigenerational, extended, and fictive families, often observed in communities of color. For example, Tommie, my sister-friend, came to Richmond to care for me after medical procedures. Even though caregiving, especially when juggled with other tasks and roles, is stressful, it is rewarding. Giving to others is an excellent way to give to oneself. And caregiving provides a dimension of self-knowledge that is difficult to acquire from other activities.

Societal

The stigma of mental illness has many consequences, including clients' reluctance to seek services, insurance companies' refusal to cover services, and poor-quality and scarce services. Intervention for children whose parents are hesitant for fear of blaming, a factor for Julie, is possible through the "emancipated conditions" laws. One reason for stigma is the social construction of mental illness. Historically, society has labeled mental illness a sin, a moral failing, a character flaw, and a result of poor mothering. Few have conceptualized emotional illnesses as a societal problem or discussed the effect of the environment on emotional functioning. Augmenting the current individualistic approach with simultaneous interventions in ailing social systems and environments could reduce the stigma and improve mental health.

Although research and medical knowledge have demonstrated that many mental disorders are biological diseases, often related to physical disorders, society and the health and mental health system still separate intervention for physical and emotional concerns. For example, chronic pain can increase hypertension and change neurotransmitters, resulting in depression. Only when we view mental and physical health as complementary issues can society begin to remove the stigma and provide effective services. Until then, we must wonder whether the stigma is serving a societal purpose of withholding treatment from many who need it.

Research

What and how we study must change. Exploration of successful situations, environments, and people, not sole explorations of problems and challenges, provides methods that successfully overcome barriers, providing positive changes. For example, considering only his emotional challenges, one would not have predicted my father's successful pastoral career. Extending the attention from individuals and families to institutions and scarce resources underscores the need for macrosystems and structural changes. Studies to determine appropriate methods for specific situations and research questions are needed. Paying more research attention to African Americans and other people of color without a judging, ethnocentric perspective and allowing participants to give meaning to their experiences will provide increased understanding.

Social Work Education

In educating students and professionals through continuing education, social work needs to place greater emphasis on macrosystem interventions. Small organizational changes can have great returns. For example, the patients at two large medical complexes had very different experiences because of colored directional strips on one floor. It would be tragic if the poorly labeled environment resulted in prescribing medication rather than making changes to ensure navigation-friendly buildings. For example, social work schools in India have only macro practice curricula. Does this suggest that American social work education implicitly assumes problems exist in individuals and families rather than in communities, institutions, and social policies? Consider how many problems might be ameliorated if we had universal and effective physical and mental healthcare.

When preparing students for emerging areas such as gerontology, social work education must also teach topics that traverse the life span, such as loss and grief. Schools must prepare students for professional life as lifelong learners. Teaching critical analysis, self-awareness, and cross-cultural communication skills and promoting the integration of micro and macro practices and of research and practice will achieve this. An essential lifelong skill is self-care, and an excellent teaching method includes the professors' modeling and the school providing an environment that encourages such behaviors.

Social Work Practice

Social work intervention too often uses a deficit model rather than strengths and empowerment models. By shifting to include what is helpful, interventions can build on the strengths of practitioners, clients, and environments. Broadening the view from my nuclear family to the larger community of church members, teachers, friends, families of friends, and others showed a large pattern of mutual aid. Differences between Julie and me also pointed to the importance of genetic, constitutional, and environmental differences. For whatever reason, I had more "fight" than she. Although it could get me into trouble, it also helped me to be a survivor. This underscores that behavior that is adaptive in one situation may be needed less, or not at all, in another. When I was a child, watching for symptoms of my father's illness helped me develop keen observational skills. This began what my counselor calls "policing behavior," constantly looking for problematic behavior to report. While I continue to observe, the need to report has lessened.

Without adequate knowledge about clients, cultural sensitivity, and acceptance of difference, practitioners provide inappropriate and incorrect diagnoses and treatment. When the practitioner conceptualizes all interactions as cross-cultural—the practitioner and client differ in some way—additional communication emerges, providing important information (Beckett and Dungee-Anderson 1998; Beckett et al. 1998). Lacking information about the Beckett clan, practitioners often lost the opportunity to collaborate. Practitioners must also be prepared to help clients handle issues such as loss and grief that can occur over the life span. Some say that unresolved grief can lead to serious individual, family, and societal issues. I believe this was the case for Julie.

Greater emphasis on prevention and early intervention is needed. This probably will require several changes in our current service delivery systems. For example, on several occasions the practitioners who served Julie might have prevented her rehospitalization if they had been able to see the effects of some of their policies. The availability of a walk-in urgent care center for both physical and mental concerns, insurance coverage for prevention, and conceptualizing environments and social agencies as potential clients could benefit many. Diagnostic categories and specific intervention strategies for environments and institutions will ensure practitioners' attention to these important societal segments.

With the increasing number of social and structural problems and the scarcity of resources, social workers, who provide primarily clinical services, must give attention to larger systems and the sociopolitical environment. Maslow's (1970) hierarchy of needs suggests that clinical intervention may be a luxury for those whose basic needs are unmet. Practitioners must see that all populations receive their basic needs. Emerging technologies, such as conference calls and interventions using Web cameras, are useful additional strategies, especially for clients in rural and less accessible areas. The narrative approach can also be an effective information gathering, intervention, and teaching strategy (Paquin 2006, 2007). Instead of taking a history, one might ask the client to describe, in writing, her or his life story. This provides the practitioner with the client's view of what is important. Alternatively, the narrative can focus on certain issues; for example, my counselor asked me to write about the loss of Julie as a big sister. Because of the emotionally and physically challenging work environments (with forced overtime, burnout, staff turnover, ever-expanding knowledge base, and bureaucracy) and the personal, family, and professional stresses, social workers and other helping professionals must practice self-care. Vacations, hobbies, exercise, and other health and mental health enhancing mechanisms are essential. As this chapter shows, the practitioners we expect so much from may be also providing informal caregiving or managing their own health concerns.

The caregiver, who may also be a practitioner, researcher, or educator, must first care for herself or himself in order to give to others. The following list describes some self-care actions, especially for caregivers:

*R*est, relax, and re-energize. Obtain information to improve your self-care techniques.

*E*stablish a routine for yourself and the care recipient and plan for the inevitable deviation. This allows you to make better use of your time.

*S*ay "thank you" to yourself frequently. Speak to others in a manner that will be heard.

*I*nsist on good service. You and your care recipient deserve it, and the formal caregivers want to provide it. You may not receive it, but you will probably get more than you expected.

*L*augh often and deeply; it releases endorphins and increases your sense of well-being; listen to your body, your family, and your care receiver.

*I*nformation is crucial. Turn to resources, including the Internet, hospice, and respite care. Obtain second and third opinions in order to make informed decisions. Share age-appropriate information with children.

*E*stablish a helpful, sizable support system and use it often as you take respites.

*N*eeds. Ask others to help you identify what you, your family, and the care receiver might need and who might provide it.

*C*enter yourself. Find a place and position from which you work best and get as close to that as you can.

*E*ducate yourself and the care recipient about expected caregiving problems and challenges and proactively provide solutions.

Table 11.1 Implications

	Issues and Problems	**Strategies for Change**
Individuals and families	Self-care Lack of knowledge	Increase resilience.
Society	Stigma of mental illness	Include societal and environmental illnesses. View mental and physical health as complementary concerns.
Practitioners and educators	Burnout Use of deficit intervention models Focus on individuals and nuclear families Ethnocentrism Use narrative strategies. Present focus	Promote self-care and wholesome work environments. Use strengths and empowerment models. Extend focus to social, environmental, and community organizations and concerns.

	Issues and Problems	Strategies for Change
	Remedial intervention Preparation for emerging issues Use lifelong learning model.	Accept and appreciate differences. Pay attention to recurring life span themes (e.g., loss, grief). Use prevention and proactive interventions. Pay greater attention to critical analytic skills. Integrate courses. Collaborate with families.
Researchers and literature	Narrow focus	Include additional people (e.g., children, men, grandparents, fictive kin). Include additional types (e.g., career, sequential, reciprocal, simultaneous). Include positive and mutual benefits (e.g., increased self-awareness and positive rewards). Extend views of family (e.g., multigenerational, extended).

REFLECTIONS

A private person, I found that my greatest challenge was to share personal information about my family. I was concerned about the reactions of acquaintances and colleagues who had known me for long periods without my discussing some of the issues in the chapter, such as the emotional illnesses of my father and sister. Remarkably, I was less apprehensive about the reactions of the larger public.

Among the caregiving experiences, I was more ambivalent writing about my sister, who is still alive. However, she was eager for me to share our stories, thinking it might help others. She was particularly pleased that her accomplishments would be included because she thinks many have forgotten the person she was.

First, I wrote the beginning and end and then filled in the middle sections. I penned what could have been a book; I wrote about several experiences, such as long-distance caring for terminally ill Aunt Mary and Uncle Bill, which I later deleted to shorten the manuscript. Surprisingly, slashing the manuscript was less stressful than initially limiting the number of caregiving experiences. I consulted with others about facts, not wanting to rely only on my memory.

On several occasions, I wanted to terminate the project because it was emotionally intense—both painful and joyous. Fortunately, this was not an option because I had requested the participation of others I respected. Sometimes, I coped by moving to another topic in the chapter or putting the chapter aside for extended periods while I worked on other book tasks. Scheduling writing of the most emotionally laden sections for times I would be home alone or on weekend retreats worked well, allowing me to fully experience the emotions without concern about others. The intensity of the original accompanying emotions shocked me and helped me to view them differently, accepting them as an integral part of my being. The recalled comments of a clinical social worker friend often consoled me: "Grief is an ongoing process similar to peeling the multiple layers of an onion." I was triumphantly moving through new strata.

While I was caregiving, my professional training and the gravity of the situations helped me partialize and focus only on the immediate tasks. Like school assignments, the activities were just something I must do, no questions asked. However, while writing about them I faced the composite, which emphasized their complexity, enormity, and multiplicity. Facing the entirety of these vast multiple caregiving events for several people and my successful management of multiple and competing tasks and roles startled me. It also highlighted my strengths, multitasking capabilities, and resilience. I had been too busy caregiving to recognize these positive personal qualities caregiving had elicited.

I discussed my emotional reactions and increased self-knowledge with my husband, family, research assistants, and close friends. Their feedback, especially after they reviewed various chapter drafts, was invaluable. All were shocked to discover new things about my life as a caregiver. As book editor, I also had the advantage of reading all the chapter reflections and discussing them with the contributors. The discussions were especially beneficial because I realized we were all facing the same surprising flood of intense emotions. This sharing helped to normalize the experience, and I could then welcome it.

I prayed mightily for the guidance, simultaneously expressing gratitude for being carried over, around, and through numerous mountains.

If anything were easier, it was the integration of literature, especially in the "Analyses" section. This more objective and scholarly task I had done my entire academic career. I had some concerns, however, even with this familiar undertaking. The literature and theory somehow reduced the power and uniqueness of the caregiving experiences. Though probably unimportant to lay caregivers, the inclusion of the literature and analyses would resonate with academicians, students, and other professionals, I reasoned.

Describing the experiences allowed me to step into the shoes of care recipients and increased my respect for their courage, fortitude, resilience, and self-determination. I more clearly recognized the many times they cared for me or shared my caregiver roles. Until recently, I was never a solo caregiver. For example, I relied on Daddy and Julie to help care for each other and for Carlene to care for all of us. Junior, my cousin, moved in with Aunt Mary and Uncle Bill during their terminal illnesses, allowing them to remain in their home until death. Recalling and reflecting on the experiences expanded my personal and professional views of family caregiving to include more types (career or lifelong, sequential, reciprocal, dynamic, and multiple) and providers (children, teens, fictive kin, and neighbors). They emphasized the complexities of caregiving experiences (commonalities, uniqueness, joys, and challenges). These experiences increased my empathy for clients and improved my clinical effectiveness. My professional and personal caregiving experiences aided my understanding and interaction with the sometimes impenetrable bureaucratic organizational structures. Appalled at the behavior of some, I was sad and embarrassed that they were members of the helping professions.

These caregiving events highlighted the enormous need for both greater recognition of caregivers and more formal and informal supports for them. For example, the federal government should follow the lead of states such as Vermont and realize that funding for in-home caregiving is an essential and cost-containing intervention. More accessible, family- and client-centered services are also needed. Effective long-term residential community mental healthcare, for example, would be immensely helpful in my sister's situation, reducing my travel time, thus allowing more frequent visits.

Additional staff, more effective training, communication between formal and informal caregivers, greater appreciation for family input, more competitive salaries (especially for aides and other front-line professionals), and more pleasant working environments could reduce the horrendous problems I faced in most agencies serving my family. Available technological tools, such as videoconferencing and electronic data entry, would increase efficiency, allowing more time for client intervention. Streamlining bureaucracy could help fund needed changes. For example, I have contacted Medicare several times about payments for a hospital bed that my sister never had. The money spent on such overpayments could help to fund needed services.

Writing this chapter vividly demonstrated the power of the narrative process, renewing my respect for it as a teaching and intervention tool. Intuitively, I knew its benefits because of journaling and observing the struggles and tremendous growth of students and clients who used it. Finally, this project underscored that oppression, such as ageism, classism, racism, and sexism, still exists. If social workers, individually and collectively, do not address these injustices, who will?

CONCLUSIONS

My graduate assistant helped me pack my office after I decided to end my career early because of medical problems. When she asked who had been my caregiver during my recent illnesses, I was startled because I had not viewed myself as a care recipient. I slowly answered, "My husband, I guess." In my mind, I heard Grandmother Beckett: "What goes around comes around." In my caregiving, I have had many struggles; with the help of the village, I have successfully climbed many mountains. As the Negro spiritual says, "I would not take nothin' for my journey." My caregiving has been multiplied many times, as I have had many caregivers.

REFERENCES

Ackerson, B. and Harrison, W.D. 2000. Practitioners' perceptions of empowerment. *Families in Society: The Journal of Contemporary Human Services* 81: 238–245.

Aldwin, C. 1994. *Stress, Coping and Development.* New York: Guilford.

Beckett, J. and Coley, S. 1987. Ecological intervention with the elderly: A case example. *Journal of Gerontological Social Work* 11: 137–157.

Beckett, J. and Dungee-Anderson, D. 1998. Multicultural communication in human service organizations. In A. Daly (Ed.), *Diversity in the Workplace: Issues and Perspectives,* 191–214. Washington, D.C.: National Association of Social Workers.

Beckett, J., Dungee-Anderson, D., Cox, L., and Daly, A. 1998. African Americans and multicultural interventions. *Smith College Studies in Social Work* 67: 540–563. Special Issue on Social Work Intervention with African Americans.

Beckett, J. and Johnson, H. 1995. Human development: Biological, psychological and sociocultural perspectives. In R. Edwards (Ed.), *Encyclopedia of Social Work,* 1385–1405. Washington, D.C.: National Association of Social Workers.

Beckett, J. and Lee, N. 2004. Informing the future of child welfare practices with African American families. In J. Everett, B. Leashore, and S. Chipungu (Eds.), *Child Welfare Revisited: An Africentric Perspective,* 93–123. New Brunswick, N.J.: Rugters University Press.

Billingsley, A. 1968. *Black Families in White America.* Upper Saddle River, N.J.: Prentice Hall.

Billingsley, A. 1973. Black families and white social science. In J. Ladner (Ed.), *The Death of White Sociology,* 431–450. New York: Vintage.

Blundo, R. 2001. Learning strengths-based practice: Challenging our personal and professional frames. *Families in Society: The Journal of Contemporary Human Services* 82: 296–304.

Brendtro, L. K., Larson, S., and Calhoun, J. A. 2006. *The Resilience Revolution: Discovering Strengths in Challenging Kids.* Bloomington, Ind.: Solution Tree.

Brown, T. 2001. Exposure to all black context and psychological well-being: The benefits of racial concentration. *African American Research Perspectives* 7: 157–172.

Burnett, R. and Shadd, M. 2006. The kindness of prisoners: Strengths-based resettlement in theory and in action. *Criminology and Criminal Justice* 6 (1): 83–106.

Butt, I. 1908. *History of African Methodism in Virginia or Four Decades in the Old Dominion.* Hampton, Va.: Hampton Institute Press.

Carter, C. 1999. Church burning in African American communities: Implications for empowerment practice. *Social Work* 44: 62–69.

Carter, C. S. 2006. *Social Work and Women's Health Resources on Health Empowerment, Advocacy, and Literacy (HEAL).* Alexandria, Va.: Council on Social Work Education.

Chestang, L. 1972. *Character Development in a Hostile Environment.* Chicago: University of Chicago Press.

Chestang, L. 1976. Environmental influences on social functioning: The black experience. In P. Cafferty and L. Chestang (Eds.), *The Diverse Society,* 59–74. Washington, D.C.: National Association of Social Workers.

Chodorow, N. 1978. *The Reproduction of Mothering: Psychoanalysis and the Sociology of Gender.* Berkeley: University of California Press.

Chodorow, N. 1979. Feminism and difference: Gender, relation, and difference in psychoanalytic perspective. *Socialist Review* 46: 51–69.

Chow, J., Jaffee, K., and Snowden, L. 2003. Racial/ethnic disparities in the use of mental health services in poverty areas. *American Journal of Public Health* 93: 792–797.

Cowger, C. 1997. Assessing client strengths: Assessment for client empowerment. In D. Saleebey (Ed.), *The Strengths Perspective in Social Work Practice*, 2d ed., 59–73. New York: Longman.

DuBois, B. and Miley, K. 2002. *Social Work: An Empowering Profession.* Boston: Allyn & Bacon.

Early, T. 2001. Measures for practice with families from a strengths perspective. *Families in Society: The Journal of Contemporary Human Services* 82: 225–232.

Early, T. and GlenMaye, L. 2000. Valuing families: Social work practice with families from a strengths perspective. *Social Work* 45: 118–130.

Eighth Annual Beckett Family Reunion. 1990. Cheriton, Va.

Erikson, E. 1963. *Childhood and Society,* 2d rev. ed., enlarged. New York: Norton.

Erikson, E. 1968. *Identity: Youth and Crisis.* New York: Norton.

Fairbairn, A. 1966. *Five Smooth Stones: A Novel.* New York: Crown.

Franklin, D. 1985. Differential clinical assessments: The influence of class and race. *Social Service Review* 59: 44–61.

Gibbs, J. and Fuery, D. 1994. Mental health and well-being of black women: Toward strategies of empowerment. *American Journal of Community Psychology* 22: 559–578.

Gilligan, C. 1982. *In a Different Voice: Psychological Theory and Women's Development.* Cambridge, Mass.: Harvard University Press.

Graybeal, C. 2001. Strengths-based social work assessment: Transforming the dominant paradigm. *Families in Society: The Journal of Contemporary Human Services* 82: 233–242.

Greif, G. 1986. The ecosystems perspective "meets the press." *Social Work* 31: 225–226.

Gutierrez, L. 1990. Working with women of color: An empowerment perspective. *Social Work* 35: 149–154.

Gutierrez, L., GlenMaye, L., and DeLois, K. 1995. The organizational context of empowerment practice: Implications for social work administration. *Social Work* 40: 249–258.

Gutierrez, L., Oh, H., and Gillmore, R. 2000. Toward an understanding of empowerment for HIV/AIDS prevention with adolescent women. *Sex Roles: A Journal of Research* 2: 581–612.

Henderson, N., Benard, B., and Sharp-Light, N. 2007. *Resiliency in Action: Practical Ideas for Overcoming Risks and Building Strengths in Youth, Families & Communities.* Ojai, Cal.: Resiliency in Action.

Hill, R. 1971. *The Strengths of Black Families.* New York: Emerson Hall.

Hill, R. 1998. Enhancing the resiliency of African American families. *Journal of Human Behavior in the Social Environment* 1: 49–61.

Hill, R. 1999. *The Strengths of African American Families Twenty-Five Years Later.* Lanham, Md.: University Press of America.

Hill-Collins, P. 2000. *Black Feminist Thought: Knowledge, Consciousness, and the Politics of Empowerment.* New York: Routledge.

hooks, b. 1984a. *Ain't I a Woman?: Black Women and Feminism.* Boston, Mass.: South End Press.

hooks, b. 1984b. *Feminist Theory from Margin to Center.* Boston, Mass.: South End Press.

hooks, b. 2000a. *Feminism Is for Everybody: Passionate Politics.* Cambridge, Mass.: South End Press.

hooks, b. 2000b. *Where We Stand: Class Matters.* New York: Routledge.

Hopkins, G. L., McBride, D., Marshak, H. H., Freier, K., Stevens, J. V. Jr., Kannenberg, W., Weaver, J. B. III, Weaver, S. L. S., Landless, P. N., and Duffy, J. 2007. Developing healthy kids in healthy communities: Eight evidence-based strategies for preventing high-risk behaviour. *The Medical Journal of Australia* 186: S70–S73.

Howard, N. G. 1997. Race bias, social class bias, and gender bias in clinical judgment. *Clinical Psychology: Science and Practice* 4: 99–120.

Jacobsen, J. P. 2007. *The Economics of Gender.* Malden, Mass.: Blackwell.

Kohlberg, L. 1969. Stage and sequence: The cognitive developmental approach to socialization. In D. A. Goslin (Ed.), *Handbook of Socialization Theory and Research,* 347–480. Chicago: Rand McNally.

Kohlberg, L. and Kramer, R. 1969. Continuities and discontinuities in childhood and adult moral development. *Human Development* 12 (2): 93–120.

Laursen, E. 2000. Strengths based practice with children in trouble. *Reclaiming Children and Youth* 9: 70–75.

Lee, J. 1996. The empowerment approach to social work practice. In F. Turner (Ed.), *Social Work Treatment: Interlocking Theoretical Approaches,* 4th ed., 218–249. New York: The Free Press.

Maslow, A. 1970. *Motivation and Personality.* New York: Harper & Row.

Maslow, A. 1999. *Toward a Psychology of Being.* New York: Wiley.

McRae, M. and Noumair, D. 1997. Race and gender in group research. *African American Research Perspectives* 3: 68–74.

Miley, K., O'Melia, M., and DuBois, B. 2001. *Generalist Social Work Practice: An Empowering Approach,* 3d ed. Boston: Allyn & Bacon.

Miller, J. B. 1976. *Toward a New Psychology of Women.* Boston: Beacon.

Mortola, P., Hiton, H., and Grant, S. 2008. *BAM! Boys Advocacy and Mentoring a Leader's Guide to Facilitating Strengths-Based Groups for Boys, Helping Boys Make Better Contact by Making Better Contact with Them.* The Routledge Series on Counseling and Psychotherapy with Boys and Men, Vol. 2. New York: Routledge.

Munford, R. and Sanders, J. 2006. *Strengths-Based Social Work with Families.* South Melbourne, Victoria: Thomson.

Norton, D. 1976. Residential environment and black self-image. In P. Cafferty and L. Chestang (Eds.), *The Diverse Society,* 75–92. Washington, D.C.: National Association of Social Workers.

Norton, D. 1978. The dual perspective. In D. Norton (Ed.), *The Dual Perspective: Inclusion of Ethnic Minority Content in the Social Work Curriculum,* 3–18. New York: Council on Social Work Education.

Paquin, G. 2006. Including narrative concepts in social work practice classes: Teaching to client strengths. *Journal of Teaching in Social Work* 26 (1/2): 127–146.

Paquin, G. W. 2007. *Clinical Social Work a Narrative Approach.* Alexandria, Va.: Council on Social Work Education.

Perkins, D. 1995. Speaking truth to power: Empowerment ideology as social intervention and policy. *American Journal of Community Psychology* 23: 765–795.

Piaget, J. 1932. *The Moral Judgment of the Child.* New York: Free Press.

Rapp, C. A. and Goscha, R. J. 2006. *The Strengths Model: Case Management with People with Psychiatric Disabilities.* Oxford: Oxford University Press.

Robbins, S. P., Chatterjee, P., and Canda, E. R. 2006. *Contemporary Human Behavior Theory: A Critical Perspective for Social Work.* Boston: Pearson.

Rothenberg, P. 1999. *Race, Class, and Gender in the United States,* 4th ed. New York: Worth Publishers.

Saleebey, D. 1996. The strengths perspective in social work practice: Extensions and cautions. *Social Work* 41: 296–304.

Saleebey, D. 1997. Introduction: Power in the people. In D. Saleebey (Ed.), *The Strengths Perspective in Social Work Practice,* 2d ed., 3–18. New York: Longman.

Schiele, J. 2000. *Human Services and the Afrocentric Paradigm.* New York: Haworth.

Shaw, M. and Costanzo, P. 1982. *Theories of Social Psychology,* 2d ed. New York: McGraw-Hill.

Smedley, A. and Smedley, B. 2005. Race as biology is fiction, racism as a social problem is real. *American Psychologist* 60: 16–26.

Smedley, B., Stith, A., and Nelson, A. 2003. *Unequal Treatment: Confronting Racial and Ethnic Disparities in Health Care.* Washington, D.C.: National Academies Press.

Staples, L. 1990. Powerful ideas about empowerment. *Administration in Social Work* 14: 29–42.

Timberlake, E. M., Farber, M. Z., Sabatino, C. A., and Timberlake, E. M. 2008. *Generalist Social Work Practice: A Strengths-Based Problem-Solving Approach.* Boston: Pearson/Allyn and Bacon.

Vakalahi, H. F. O., Starks, S. H., and Hendricks, C. O. 2007. *Women of Color as Social Work Educators: Strengths and Survival.* Alexandria, Va.: Council on Social Work Education.

Williams, D., Yu, Y., Jackson, J., and Anderson, N. 1997. Racial differences in physical and mental health. *Journal of Health Psychology* 2: 335–351.

APPENDIX

Joyce Beckett, M.S.S., Ph.D.

January 5
Dr.
State Hospital
Box
City, VA

Re: Julie

Dear Dr.

I appreciate your changing the time of the December team meeting concerning Julie, my sister, so that I could attend. The meeting was very helpful, and we discussed several concerns I had about my sister. Thanks for taking my call today and for providing an update. As I mentioned in our phone conversation, I thought it might be helpful to the team if I mentioned the concerns in writing. There were several concerns that we discussed when met in December. Each is listed below with a description and possible solutions.

1. Julie's Missing Bottom Teeth. I was quite surprised that no one was aware that Julie's teeth were missing, and staff had no knowledge of what had happened. During the meeting, you asked Mrs. Smith, the nurse in attendance, to check with the nursing staff and said you would check with the dentist and advise me. Unfortunately, no one has given me an explanation. The week following the meeting, I called the nursing staff on the ward and asked about the teeth. They, also, had no explanation and suggested I talk with you after you returned from vacation. I left a message for you with the nursing station since I was told you do not have voice mail.

Solution: I would like a copy of the records that indicate what happened to Julie's teeth and to know when the teeth will be replaced. Proactive planning might include Julie's partials being placed in a container and secured at the nursing station between meals and at bedtime.

2. Julie's Missing Glasses. Julie did not have her glasses. When I asked about them, I was told they were being repaired, but no one knew when they would be ready. You indicated that someone would let me know when the glasses were returned. I do not know if Julie has received her glasses.

Solution: Please have someone let me know the status of Julie's glasses. My understanding is that she needs the glasses to see and to read.

3. Julie's Mammogram. I asked to get a copy of the results of Julie's mammogram. In November, Mrs. CSW told me that Julie had completed her mammogram and that Mrs. CSW would request that the medical records department send me the results. During our conference in December, Mrs. CSW called Medical Records and told us that Julie had never had the mammogram. In early fall, I had forwarded Mrs. CSW the notice of the need for the mammogram, sent to me by Community General Hospital. I shared with Mrs. CSW my concern that it be done because the results from the previous mammogram indicated that there was a breast lump.

Solution: If Julie has not had the mammogram, please give me the date of the upcoming mammogram. I would also appreciate the name and address of the physician who reviews(ed) the results of the mammogram.

4. Results of the Neuropsychological Testing. Mrs. CSW called me in early fall to tell me that Julie would be scheduled for neuropsychological testing. When I asked about the results in our meeting, no one could provide them, and you could not find a record of the request in Julie's medical record. Mrs. CSW had also indicated in October that she would have a copy of Julie's medical records sent to me because they were not available to her since they were not in her chart. I have not received a copy of these records.

Solution: For medical procedures Julie has had during this current hospitalization, please send me a list including the following information for each procedure: name of procedure, date of request, purpose of procedure, date treatment was provided, outcome of the treatment, and copy of the treatment notes. For all future medical procedures, please fax me a copy of your request for each medical and psychological procedure that is ordered for Julie and a copy of the results of those procedures, along with the medical notes.

5. Julie's Clothes. At the end of our meeting, I asked that Julie be allowed to change to cleaner and more appropriate clothes before I took her out. I was disappointed when staff brought her out with the same sweat pants that were dirty and torn and without a coat. The staff person said he could not find a coat. I am particularly disturbed that Julie did not have appropriate clothes because I send and take her new clothes on a monthly basis. I gave her a fall coat in October and a wool coat with her initials on the collar in early December and sent her two sweat suit sets in November.

Solution: Please give me an inventory and description of Julie's present belongings no later than *January* 20. This inventory will help me select the appropriate items for her and provide the requested information to the court about her belongings. As you know, I am Julie's guardian and must provide a record to the court of Julie's belongings. The next filing is the end of this month.

Because I am not sure who is responsible for the various concerns I mention, I am sending copies of this letter to other staff present at the meeting and other helpful persons. I appreciate your help in these matters and look forward to your written reply. I am so pleased that you and I are working toward the same goal of excellent treatment for my sister.

Sincerely,

Joyce Beckett
Guardian and Trustee for Julie

Cc: Ms ___________
Mr. ___________, Director
Dr. ___________, Psychologist
Mrs. ___________, RN
M. ___________, Dietitian
Mrs. ___________, CSW

Index